Contemporary Religion and Social Responsibility

Contemporary Religion and Social Responsibility

Edited by

Norbert Brockman, S.M.
University of Dayton

Nicholas Piediscalzi
Wright State University

ALBA · HOUSE   NEW · YORK

WITH ECCLESIASTICAL PERMISSION

Library of Congress Cataloging in Publication Data

Brockman, Norbert, comp.
    Contemporary religion and social responsibility.

    Includes bibliographical references.
    1.   Religion and sociology—Collections.
2.   Social ethics—Collections.   I.   Piediscalzi,
Nicholas, joint comp.   II.   Title.
BL60.B68   261.8'3   72-11982
ISBN   0-8189-0257-4

Designed, printed and bound in the U.S.A. by the
Fathers and Brothers of the Society of St. Paul
as part of their communications apostolate.

Current Printing (last digit):

9 8 7 6 5 4 3 2

FOR OUR PARENTS
Michael J. and Mary B. Piediscalzi
Norbert C. and Mary Elizabeth Brockman

Acknowledgments

Abingdon Press, for "The Abstractness of Concrete Advice," from Paul Ramsey, Who Speaks for the Church? Copyright © 1967 by Abingdon Press.

Andover Newton Quarterly, for "Ecological Responsibility and Economic Justice," by Norman Faramelli, which appeared in the November, 1970 issue.

Beacon Press, for "The Future as Threat and as Opportunity," by Jürgen Moltmann, from The Religious Situation: 1969, edited by Donald R. Cutler. Copyright © 1969 by Beacon Press.

B'nai B'rith, for "Torah and Society," by Morris Adler, from Great Jewish Ideas, edited by Abraham E. Millgram. Copyright © 1964 by B'nai B'rith Department of Adult Jewish Education.

Catholic World, for "A Very Personal Answer to My Critics," by William F. Buckley, Jr., which appeared in the March, 1961 issue.

Christian Century Foundation, "An Ecological Ethic," by Ian G. Barbour which appeared in the October 7, 1970 issue of The Christian Century.

Christianity and Crisis, for "A Critique of Paul Ramsey," by John C. Bennett, which appeared in the October 30, 1967 issue.

Daedalus, Journal of the American Academy of Arts and Sciences, for "The University Community in an Open Society," by Edgar Z. Friedenberg, which appeared in the Winter, 1970 issue.

Harper and Row, Publishers, Inc. for "An Ecological Ethic," as it appeared in Christian Century, October 7, 1970, from Science and Secularity by Ian G. Barbour. Copyright © 1970 by Ian G. Barbour. Reprinted by permission of Harper and Row, Publishers, Inc.

Logos, for "World Apartheid," by Tissa Balasuriya, O.M.I.

Rev. Dr. Johannes Metz, for his article "Creative Hope."

Perspective, for "The Christian, Violence, and Social Change," by Joseph Hough, which appeared in the Spring, 1969 issue.

Pontifical Institute of Medieval Studies (Toronto), for "Relationship of Church and World in the Light of a Political Theology," by Johannes Metz, from The Theology of Renewal, edited by L. K. Shook. Copyright © 1968 by the Pontifical Institute of Medieval Studies.

Dr. Rosemary Ruether, for her "Letter to Father Berrigan."

Scottish Journal of Theology, for "Ecumenical Theology of Revolution," by J. M. Lochman, which appeared in the June, 1968 issue.

Seabury Press, for "Man - In the Light of Social Sciences and Christian Faith," by James M. Gustafson, from Conflicting Images of Man, edited by William Nicholls. Copyright © 1966 by Seabury Press.

Society for Promoting Christian Knowledge, for "The Development of Ecumenical Social Thought and Action," by Paul Abrecht, from The Ecumenical Advance, Vol. 2, 1968.

Society for the Scientific Study of Religion, Inc. for "The Concept of Seculari-
zation in Empirical Research," by Larry Shiner, which appeared in the
Society's Fall, 1967 issue of the Journal of the Scientific Study of Religion.
Union of American Hebrew Congregations, for Chapter II of There Shall be
No Poor, and Chapter VI of Judaism and Cities in Crisis, both by Richard G.
Hirsch. Copyright © 1965 and 1964 respectively.
United States Catholic Conference, for translations from "The Church in the
Modern World," of Vatican Council II; from "The Development of Peoples"
and the "Apostolic Letter of May 14, 1971," both by Pope Paul VI. Also for
sections from the 1968 Pastoral Letter of the American Catholic Hierarchy.
The Village Voice, for "Letter to the Weathermen," by Daniel Berrigan, S. J.,
which appeared in the January 21, 1971 issue.
Westminster Press, for "The Three Heresies of Welfare," by Alan Keith-Lucas,
from his The Church and Social Welfare. Copyright © 1962 by Westminster
Press.
The World Council of Churches, for two articles from Christian Social Ethics
in a Changing World, edited by J. C. Bennett: "Church and Society in Greek
Orthodox Theology," by Nicos A. Nissiotis; and "Theology and Social Science,"
by Walter G. Muelder. Also for two articles from Man in Community, edited
by E. de Vries: "Secular Society or Pluralistic Community?" by Paul Verghese;
and "A Theology of Christian Community," by James M. Gustafson. The
W.C.C. also granted permission for "Christians and Economic Growth," from
Economic Growth in World Perspective, edited by D. Munby and written by
Ronald Preston; "The Christian in the Search from World Order and Peace,"
by Helmut Gollwitzer, from Responsible Government in a Revolutionary Age,
edited by Z. K. Matthews; "Sixteen Catholic Bishops Response to Pope
Paul VI," which appeared in Background Information, April, 1968.
A condensed version of "The Prophets and the Protesters," by Nicholas Piedi-
scalzi, appeared in the November, 1970 issue of the Yale Alumni Magazine.

The above-mentioned publishers and editors have been considerate and helpful
beyond the limits of their job descriptions; where we excerpted or edited, they
helped us obtain the approval of the authors; when we needed special permissions,
they usually hastened to work out any difficulties. Particular recognition must
go to Dr. Paul Abrecht of the World Council of Churches, whose suggestions
and help were invaluable.

Many times we have read through the lists of credits in a collection or
anthology, and found them meaningless. The names that follow may not bring
response in more than a few readers, but to us they are the names of those who
concerned themselves with this book, and offered time, talent, and hard work
to make our effort that much easier. Dr. William Baker of Wright State University was most helpful in providing editorial criticism and suggestions. Brother
John McGarty, S.M., at the initiation of this project, did prodigeous amounts of
background work

Mrs. Alice Martin, Mrs. Eddie Sims, and Mr. George Reed shared in the
tedious task of typing the manuscript, but special thanks must go to Mrs. Gertrude
Hazel and Mrs. Diane Johnson, who bore the brunt of the secretarial work,

always cheerfully.

Special thanks is due to the Wright State University Liberal Arts Research Fund for a grant which lightened our financial burden when we initiated this project.

N. B.

N. P.

TABLE OF CONTENTS

Part III: CRITICAL SOCIAL ISSUES

Contents)xiii(

Introduction

This book has evolved out of a continuing collaboration between the editors over the past several years. Both of us taught courses on Religion and Society. As we worked together we came to the conclusion that, on the one hand, the existing materials for our courses neglected some of the important theological questions of our times; and, on the other, the insights of the socio-behavioral sciences were being ignored. This collection is an attempt to include these two neglected areas.

The four main sections of this book parallel the chief aims of our own courses: (1) to point out the major Jewish and Christian theological positions on the social responsibility of religious communities; (2) to examine the relation between theologically-oriented social ethics and the social-behavioral sciences; (3) to present theologico-ethical analyses of some of the critical social problems confronting people today; and (4) to raise the question of the legitimacy of the authority by which religious communities address themselves to controversial social issues.

Behind our approach and selections lie certain presuppositions. First, we believe that the positions adopted by Jewish and Christian communities toward society and social problems partially stem from their basic theological commitments. It is imperative, therefore, to become acquainted with these positions. To adopt such a stance is not to ignore the fact that theological stances also are determined to a large extent by society. This observation leads to our second point.

We hold that no religious group today can examine social issues without understanding and utilizing modern social and behavioral sciences. These sciences provide the concrete knowledge which religionists need to use when they analyze contemporary society, religious communities, and the many proposed solutions for their ills. However, serious methodological and normative questions and problems arise when the religionist employs the social sciences in his work. These questions and problems must be studied, therefore, if there is to be a movement toward an effective synthesis between the two approaches.

Third, it is not necessary to justify, in a book such as this, studying the major social, political and economic problems that currently confront us. Most readers, however, may be surprised by one selection in Part III. Edgar Friedenberg's analysis of the role of the university in contemporary society will not seem to be theologizing in any traditional sense. It might be enough to point out that he is one of several "prophetic" scholars discussed by most serious students of social ethics. Beyond this, it also reveals something of our own notions of what the prophetic task of scholars and theologians is in our day.

This collection is not exhaustive. No one book could begin to contain a set of readings which would cover all the issues to which religious communities and the students of social ethics are addressing themselves. The editors have selected the articles as representative illustrations of how religious communities are addressing themselves to critical social issues.

The fourth focus—Who Speaks for the Religious Communities?—is included because it is being debated vigorously in both Catholic and Protestant circles. Whenever individual leaders, groups, or representative bodies speak out on social or political questions, controversy arises. Every religious community must deal with the type of response typified by the Catholic editor who replied to one of Pope John's encyclicals with the challenge: "Mater, Si! Magistra, No!" The reader will notice that the various authors speak from their own background and experience. None pretends to speak for all. The terminology used by them should, therefore, be interpreted with this in mind, e.g. "the Church" will be found to imply different things to different authors and positions claimed for "the Church" must be interpreted in this light.

It is hoped that this book of readings will be helpful to that growing number of professors and students who are concerned, as we are, with the dynamic interaction of American religious life and social and political problems.

NORBERT BROCKMAN, S.M.   NICHOLAS PIEDISCALZI
Department of Political Science   *Chairman, Department of Religion*
University of Dayton   *Wright State University*

Contemporary Religion and Social Responsibility

PART I

Theological Issues

Introduction

Two different sets of readings are found in Part I. The first is a series of position papers which illustrate the theological positions of some major Jewish and Christian theologians and/or communities which partially inform and determine their attitudes toward society and social problems. This set of readings reveals the range as well as the depth of the questions concerning religion and society which are being raised by some leading Jewish and Christian thinkers. These statements are not idle speculation; all of them have significant implications for the further development of both theology and social thought and action. However, the editors realize that the social witness of the religious communities is given not only in the theological questions which engage their intellectuals but also in the expressions of commitments and in the activities of their adherents. Yet the editors hold that even the commitments and activities of their adherents are partially informed and determined by their theological stance. Therefore, it is important to examine the theological stances of the religious communities in question.

After bringing together a series of statements which the editors regard as representative of contemporary, institutional positions concerning religion and social responsibility, readings from four key current theological problem areas are presented. These four discussions—on the theology of community, secularity, futurism and hope, and revolution—cover such topics as the editors feel are essential to understanding what the contribution of contemporary theological thinking is to social thought and action.

The religious response to the threat of personal alienation and communal disintegration has been multifaceted. The reading given here on community could not begin to exhaust the writing that has come out in recent years. James Gustafson's thorough discussion, however, represents an adequate summary and introduction to the major issues in this area.

Paul Verghese approaches the impact of secularity on the world and churches with an "orthodox" and reflective analysis of the implications of this phenomenon for the life of the churches. The consideration of this topic closes with Larry Shiner's excellent summary of the "state of the art" in current thinking on secularization.

The two most notable representatives of the Protestant and Catholic thinking in the area of futurism and hope— Jürgen Moltmann and Johannes Metz—offer some of the basic understandings of the issues. On reflection, it seems apparent that there is little that can be identified as exclusively proper to one or another denomination. The commonality of thinking is a striking example of the gradual merger of Protestant and Catholic thought on many fronts.

J. M. Lochman's perceptive analysis of different theological responses to the problem of revolution concludes this section.

TORAH AND SOCIETY

MORRIS ADLER

It would be fallacious and futile to seek in Judaism a ready and adequate answer to all the social problems by which our age is perplexed. To stretch classical texts to yield solutions for complex circumstances that the propounder of those texts could not have foreseen is to misuse the wisdom of the past. Reading into those venerated words our particular partisan views is in the last analysis an attempt to sanctify our opinion with an authority beyond our own. The study of the past may in some or many instances offer guidelines, suggest directions or goals; it can never yield a blueprint for the resolution of our present dilemmas. The intricacies of contemporary social and political conditions require a knowledge of facts which in many instances can be ascertained only by specialized and highly technical study. Policies for our times that are not based on such knowledge will not be relevant to modern problems and must in the long run prove ineffective if not mischievous in arriving at their solution.

Nor is there to be found in Jewish thought, teaching or literature a rubric "social doctrine," or "social views" or "the Jew's social gospel." The views about man's social life that may be distilled out of an examination of the Jewish tradition are integral to a larger context, and their validation and rationale are to be found in the totality from which they are abstracted. Judaism is neither a sociology nor a theology in the conventional sense. It is a living, developing and responding outlook vitalized by its experience and interacting with its environment. . . . It is a tradition that has not hardened into a dogmatic formulation; has not congealed into a structured philosophic system; has not remained imprisoned within the bound confines of its many volumes.

The social teachings of Judaism are . . . correlated with Judaism's belief in God and its concept of man and man's relation to God. They are conditioned by the historic experiences through which Israel has passed. They are informed with the vision of great masters who taught, interpreted and applied its laws. They are affected by the depressed status which it endured as a minority. (Thorstein Veblen related the Jew's passion for social justice to the marginal position which society forced upon him.) The Jew's outlook on society is compounded of doctrine, feeling, experience, faith and historic memory.

An example may suggest the difficulty, even the impossibility, of extricating from the total synthesis the single aspect of social attitude. The greatest figure of the rabbinic epoch and very likely the greatest of all post-Biblical figures, Rabbi Akiba, found the cardinal principle of the Torah in the verse "Thou shalt love thy neighbor as thyself" (Lv 19:18). Incomparable legalist that he was, he saw in the Golden Rule the heart and center of Jewish teaching. Who can estimate the impact upon the minds of unnumbered generations of an emphasis given authority by one of Israel's most venerated masters? Yet there was etched into the collective spirit of the Jew the memory of his people's experience as slaves in Egypt. "Ye shall love the stranger, for ye were strangers in the land of Egypt" (Dt 10:19) is a sentiment expressed many times in the Bible. At the Passover *Seder* the Jew annually re-enacts that experience by means of vivid symbols, relives the bitterness of bondage, the alienation of the rejected as well as the exhilaration of liberation. By what measures of judgment can we determine which predisposed the Jew more decisively to a humane attitude to others: the teaching of the great masters or the memory which tradition directed him to preserve in all vigor and freshness? Experience and doctrine, tradition and history united to inspire an alert and sensitive Jewish consciousness. The further fact that the religion of Israel grew out of the life of a community which believed itself to be covenanted to God and in which its members were linked one to another by intense bonds of mutuality allowed the Jew to carry over to his universal vision of human kinship an emotional intensity that gave it body and reality.

Doctrine and Experience

The term "theology," in the sense that it is understood in the Western world, is not present either in the Bible or the Talmud. Indeed, to this day the Hebrew language does not possess a term for this concept. For the Hebrew the belief in God was not the end of an intellectual examination and analysis; it was the great affirmation, the intense conviction with which he began. The God who was recognized as a result of the emotional and moral experience of Israel was a God of justice, love and righteousness. He was omnipotent and omniscient, but these attributes were secondary to His ethical nature. In a sense His power was the collateral for His justice and love. The Rabbis point out that wherever Scripture refers to God's power it also refers to His humility. The proof texts cited are "He doth execute justice for the fatherless and widow and loveth the stranger" (Dt 10:18), "With Him also that is of a contrite and humble spirit" (Is 51:15), and "a father of the fatherless and a judge of the widows" (Ps 68:6). The verses chosen indicate that the Rabbis were suggesting that God's power is always allied with His righteousness and compassion. God is celebrated in the Jewish tradition more often as the Father of all men and the Sovereign of human history than as the Creator of the universe and its galaxies. Judaism is a God-centered faith whose chief concern is man. God has stamped His divine image upon man and has thus endowed him with the capacity to fulfill his destiny, which is to love in accordance with His law.

The concept *imitatio dei,* emulation by man of God's qualities, represents the highest aspiration toward which man can strive. God is not only the King who commands but the Father whose example is to be lovingly followed. The Bible says, "Ye shall walk after the Lord your God" (Dt 13:4). The Rabbis ask how could man walk after God, who is described as a devouring fire (Dt 4:24)? The meaning, they explain, is to emulate His attributes. He clothes the naked (Gen 3:21); He visits the sick (Gen 18:1); He comforts the bereaved (Gen 25:11); He buries the dead (Dt 34:6). Man should similarly perform these benevolent acts.

The above was no mere mental image of the nature of the world which Israel had fashioned. These ideas took for the Jew the form of deeply-felt convictions, which burgeoned forth into commitments and immediate consequences for his behavior and attitudes. Since man was invested at creation with a cosmic dignity, he must bear himself in an appropriate manner. Secondly, he should accord to his neighbor the honor due one as royally born as himself. One profanes God when one dishonors the divine image with which His children are instinct. Man was created singly at the beginning to dramatize the unduplicated distinctiveness and uniqueness of each individual on the one hand, and the common ancestry of all men on the other. The tension between man's individuality and his inseparableness from mankind finds its resolution in his life in a community as a free and participating member.

The good society will not alone affirm and protect the individuality of each of its citizens but will also confer upon each a social dignity commensurate with his cosmic dignity.

The Deed Resides in the Thought

A whole family of principles or "value-concepts" (to use the term which Max Kadushin has so illuminatingly applied to what he terms the "organic" thinking of the Rabbis in contradistinction to philosophical thought) issues from this groundwork of conviction. As Dr. Kadushin points out, "organic thinking does not begin with preliminary definitions and end with the structured organization of the conclusions that flow from the assumptions. Rather the value-concept springs from a particular experience and is then transposed to a conceptual term. The concept, however, is never so completely severed from the experience as to achieve sovereign intellectual detachment. Therefore, it is not given to definition, since it never becomes purely reflection or generalization; and the impact of experience continues to persist within it. Such value-concepts are motored by an inner drive to concretion. Characteristic, therefore, of Jewish classic thought is its integration of both reason and an emotional power impelling its fulfillment. The concrete is generalized, but the generalization never becomes abstract.

The social ethic of Judaism, which is an integral part of the total outlook, partakes of this general character. Every "independent" statement or law has as its frame of reference the centrality of God's rule, the nature of man and his duty to God, and man's inseparable linkage with his fellow men. The immediate teaching or decision or admonition is organically related to the Jewish view of the ultimate reality. This is what gives coherence and consistency to Judaism, despite its lack of a systematic formulation of beliefs. The ethical teaching of the sage of the first century abides in the same universe of discourse as that of the teacher of the fifth or sixth century. The total view no less than the individual judgment goes beyond the intellectual and is apprehended emotionally as a felt experience.

In order not to impose upon Jewish social teaching a structure which is inherently alien to it, we shall not proceed with a systematic delineation of its principles. We shall attempt rather, by a series of quotations, to convey something of the quality of its sensitivity and the comprehensiveness of its concern. More than to marshal a compilation of Biblical verses or rabbinic dicta, the intent is to choose such texts as suggest and represent the larger context from which they are drawn. Only thus can one capture the passion, the religious fervor and power with which the content is inspirited, and glimpse the background of belief, aspiration, piety, experience and a will to achieve what one scholar has described as a non-ecstatic experience of the holy from which it sprang. Far from exhaustive, the selections here seek only to intimate the spirit of the whole.

Illustrative Selections

We start with the Five Books of Moses, replete with social teachings which in turn stimulated their further extension in all Biblical and rabbinic literature.

The fourth of the Ten Commandments unites the social with the religious motif.

> Remember the Sabbath day to keep it holy. Six days shalt thou labor and do all thy work. But the seventh day is a Sabbath unto the Lord thy God, in it thou shalt not do any manner of work, thou, nor thy son, nor thy daughter nor thy man-servant, nor thy maid-servant nor thy cattle, nor thy stranger that is within thy gates. For in six days the Lord made heaven and earth, the sea, and all that in them is, and rested on the seventh day, wherefore the Lord blessed the Sabbath day and hallowed it. (Ex 20:8-11)

The nineteenth chapter of Leviticus opens with an address that Moses is commanded by God to speak to the children of Israel. The prelude to the address is "Ye shall be holy; for I the Lord your God am holy." No definition of holiness is offered. The chapter, however, contains the following verses:

> And when ye reap the harvest of your land, thou shalt not wholly reap the corner of thy field, neither shalt thou gather the gleaning of thy harvest. And thou shalt not glean thy vineyard, neither shalt thou gather the fallen fruit of thy vineyard; thou shall leave them for the poor and for the stranger. I am the Lord your God. . . .
>
> Thou shalt not oppress thy neighbor nor rob him; the wages of a hired servant shall not abide with thee all night until the morning. . . .
>
> Ye shall do no unrighteousness in judgment; thou shalt not respect the person of the poor, nor favor the person of the mighty, but in righteousness shalt thou judge thy neighbor. . . .

Thou shalt not take vengeance, nor bear any grudge against the children of thy people, but thou shalt love thy neighbor as thyself. I am the Lord. . . .

And if a stranger sojourn with thee in your land, ye shall not do him wrong. The stranger that sojourneth with you shall be unto you as the home-born among you, and thou shalt love him as thyself; for ye were strangers in the land of Egypt; I am the Lord your God. Ye shall do no unrighteousness in judgment, in meteyard, in weight or in measure. Just balances, just weights, a just ephah and a just hin, shall ye have: I am the Lord your God who brought you out of the land of Egypt.

The insistence on impartial justice in the courts which stressed that the judge was to be moved neither by fear of the mighty litigant nor by sympathy for the poor man was summed up in the phrase so often cited in later literature, "Justice, justice shalt thou pursue" (Dt 16:20).

The Prophetic View

The prophets of Israel have been described as "tribunes of righteousness" and "spokesmen of God." Their God-centered, moral view of history led them to condemn with inspired fury the social evils and inequities of their own time. Their passion for righteousness and their lofty vision of the "end of days" imparted a deeper note of awareness and feeling to the entire tradition.

But they shall sit every man under his vine and under his fig-tree;
And none shall make them afraid,
For the mouth of the Lord of hosts hath spoken.   (Mi 4:1-4)

Morality for the prophets—individual and social—becomes the absolute and indispensable value in the religious life.

The anger of the prophet is especially enkindled by the oppressor of those who have no protector, namely, the orphan and widow.

Perhaps the most eloquent expression of the futility of ritual unaccompanied by virtue and moral behavior occurs in Isaiah. That these verses were chosen by the Rabbis to be read publicly on *Yom Kippur* is ample evidence that the entire tradition is pervaded by this prophetic idea.

Is such the fast that I have chosen?
    The day for a man to afflict his soul?
Is it to bow down his head as a bulrush,

> And to spread sackcloth and ashes under him?
> Wilt thou call this a fast,
> And an acceptable day to the Lord?
> Is not this the fast that I have chosen?
> To loose the fetters of wickedness,
> To undo the bands of the yoke,
> And to let the oppressed go free,
> And that ye break every yoke?
> It is not to deal thy bread to the hungry,
> And that thou bring the poor that are cast out to thy house?
> When thou seest the naked, that thou cover him,
> And that thou hide not thyself from thine own flesh?
> Then shall thy light break forth as the morning,
> And thy healing shall spring forth speedily;
> And thy righteousness shall go before thee,
> The glory of the Lord shall be thy reward.   (Is 58:5-8)

Unlike paganism and its ritual, shrines, priesthood, festivals and mysteries, the Torah relegates the cult to a secondary place as a means of expressing reverence for God and as an instrument for His worship. The Ten Commandments are preponderantly moral and social in character. Ritual is no longer the automatic guarantee of winning the favor of the deity. As Yehezkel Kaufmann points out, the prophets "did not unconditionally repudiate the cult or utterly deny its value." They gave such unquestioned primacy to morality as to make the cult valueless without it. Thus morality, individual and social, was placed at the very heart of the Jewish religion. This view recurs in many of the prophets.

With morality as the core and a universal God as the source, the Jewish Religion is expanded into a universalism that encompasses all mankind. The Book of Amos opens with prophecies concerning other nations: "The prophet moves around as in the swing of a scythe of destiny from Damascus to Gaza to Tyre, to Edom and Ammon and Moab before coming at length to his own people." The condemnation that is levied against these nations is based on a moral judgment. They are guilty of ethical and moral crimes which are an offense against the God of Israel, who is the God of righteousness. Israel remains at the center but is not the exclusive concern of God.

The finest summary of religion is offered by the prophet Micah.

> It hath been told thee, O man, what is good,
> And what the Lord doth require of thee:
> Only to do justly, and to love mercy, and to walk humbly with thy God.
> (Mi 6:8)

The Rabbinic Approach

In rabbinic law there is a fusion of the legal and the prophetic. As heirs of the tradition of the prophets, the Rabbis sought to transpose the great ideals and the passion for righteousness of the seers of Israel into the key of social legislation and stature. They attempted to incorporate in their enactments not only laws governing behavior and outlining relationships, but also the faith and principle with which Biblical law is instinct. The interweaving of spirit and statute, ethical ideal and practical need are characteristic of the rabbinic approach.

The tradition which the Rabbis espoused and interpreted was rooted in a community. A people rather than an ecclesiastical class was to be its bearer. The arena for the fulfillment of the Torah was the life of the Jewish people and beyond it—humanity. The Rabbis habitually thought in terms of community rather than of church. The individual was seen in the context of the group, for Judaism was not meant for isolation and monastic withdrawal. "Separate not thyself from the community" was an oft-repeated teaching of the saintly Hillel which was re-echoed by other teachers. The concept "worldly" with the specific connotation it received in Christianity was absent from the thought pattern of the Rabbis. The physical, economic and social were proper provinces of religious legislation. The Talmud recounts the Rabbi Huma once asked of his son Rabbah why he did not attend the lectures of Rabbi Hisda, who was noted for his wit. The son replied, "When I go to him he speaks of mundane matters; he tells about certain natural functions of the digestive organs and how one should behave with regard to them." His father rebuked him, saying, "He occupies himself with the life of God's creatures and you call that a mundane matter. All the more reason you should go to him" (*Shabbat* 8,2a).

The stress on social obligation was not a denial of the rightful and primary place the individual occupies in Jewish teaching. The dignity and welfare of the individual and indeed his inner development and fulfillment (to borrow modern terms) are fostered by a society in which men are responsive to their duty to one another and to God.

What Is Required of Man

The Rabbis said that *G'milut Hasadim*—the performance of deeds of loving-kindness—is superior in three respects to charity. Charity can be done only with one's money, while *G'milut Hasadim* can be done with one's person as well as with one's money. Charity can be given only to the poor, while *G'milut Hasadim* can be extended both to the rich and poor. Charity can be given to the living alone. *G'milut Hasadim* can be done both to the living and to the dead. But charity is not a substitute for justice, for the Talmud recognized that it is easier to be generous than just.

The Talmud considers it unworthy to give charity when one does not pay his debts or give his employees a proper wage. The giving of alms does not condone unjust practices, and one should not make charity a means for personal advantage.

But helping a man was not exhausted by providing him recurringly with the elementary necessities. The responsibility of the community was to raise him out of the condition of dependence to the status of a self-supporting individual.

The goals of both collective and individual striving are suggested by the rabbinic comment, "The world exists by reason of three things, truth, justice and peace. As it is written (Zc 8:16) 'Truth and judgment of truth and peace judge ye in your gates' " (Ethics of the Fathers 1:18). A further comment adds, "The three are in reality one, for when justice is done, truth prevails and peace is established" (Jerusalem Talmud *Ta'anit* 4:2). The Government is a means to these ends. When it sees itself as absolute and makes its power or aggrandizement the be-all and end-all of its effort, it blasphemes against God. . . .

It becomes the responsibility of each alert and high-minded individual to resist the encroachments upon justice, truth and peace which constitute the foundations of freedom. No man may stand aside and remain neutral in the ongoing struggle to achieve in human life a fuller approximation of virtue and righteousness. To abdicate such an obligation is to abet the forces of evil and to become an accomplice in the perpetuation of wrong. "Whoever is able to protest against the transgression of his household and fails to do so, will suffer the penalty of their sins; whoever is able to protest against the transgressions of his city or indeed the misdeeds of all mankind and fails to do so, becomes accountable for their sins" (*Shabbat* 54b). Apathy becomes a sin of commission, increasing the decadence that prevails.

Erich Fromm has indicated that religion, which has won such eminent respectability and wide acceptance in terms of its doctrines and values, meets defeat on the field of the daily practices, norms and mores which men habitually follow. The Rabbis read a man's theology not in his professions and creedal affirmations but in his customary actions. The faith in God which does not culminate in service to man is a mockery. . . .

THE CHURCH IN THE MODERN WORLD

VATICAN COUNCIL II

The joys and the hopes, the griefs and the anxieties of the men of this age, especially those who are poor or in any way afflicted, these are the joys and the hopes, the griefs and anxieties of the followers of Christ. Indeed, nothing genuinely human fails to raise an echo in their hearts. For theirs is a community composed of men. United in Christ, they are led by the Holy Spirit in their journey to the Kingdom of their Father and they have welcomed the news of salvation which is meant for every man. That is why this community realizes that it is truly linked with mankind and its history by the deepest of bonds.

A change of attitudes and in human structures frequently calls accepted values into question, especially among young people, who have grown impatient on more than one occasion, and indeed become rebels in their distress. Aware of their own influence in the life of society, they want a part in it sooner. This frequently causes parents and educators to experience greater difficulties day by day in discharging their tasks. The institutions, laws and modes of thinking and feeling as handed down from previous generations do not always seem to be well adapted to the contemporary state of affairs; hence arises an upheaval in the manner and even the norms of behavior.

People hounded by hunger call upon those better off. Where they have not yet won it, women claim for themselves an equity with men before the law and in fact. Laborers and farmers seek not only to provide for the necessities of life, but to develop the gifts of their personality by their labors and indeed to take part in regulating economic, social, political and cultural life. Now, for the first time in human history all people are convinced that the benefits of culture ought to be and actually can be extended to everyone.

Still, beneath all these demands lies a deeper and more widespread longing: persons and societies thirst for a full and free life worthy of man; one in which they can subject to their own welfare all that the modern world can offer them so abundantly. In addition, nations try harder every day to bring about a kind of universal community.

Since all these things are so, the modern world shows itself at once powerful and weak, capable of the noblest deeds or the foulest; before it lies the path of freedom or to slavery, to progress or retreat, to brotherhood or hatred. Moreover, man is becoming aware that it is his responsibility to guide aright the forces which he has unleashed and which can enslave him or minister to him. That is why he is putting questions to himself.

The Community of Mankind

One of the salient features of the modern world is the growing interdependence of men one on the other, a development promoted chiefly by modern technical advances. Nevertheless brotherly dialogue among men does not reach its perfection on the level of technical progress, but on the deeper level of interpersonal relationships.

Man's social nature makes it evident that the progress of the human person and the advance of society itself hinges on one another. For the beginning, the subject and the goal of all social institutions is and must be the human person, which for its part and by its very nature stands completely in need of social life.

Among those social ties which man needs for his development some, like the family and political community, relate with greater immediacy to his innermost nature; others originate rather from his free decision. In our era, for various reasons, reciprocal ties and mutual dependencies increase day by day and give rise to a variety of associations and organizations, both public and private. This development, which is called socialization, while certainly not without its dangers, brings with it many advantages with respect to consolidating and increasing the qualities of the human person, and safeguarding his rights.

Every day human interdependence grows more tightly drawn and spreads by degrees over the whole world. As a result the common good, that is, the sum of those conditions of social life which allow social groups and their individuals relatively thorough and ready access to their own fulfillment, today takes on an increasingly universal complexion and consequently involves rights and duties with respect to the whole human race. Every social group must take account of the needs and legitimate aspirations of other groups, and even of the general welfare of the entire human family.

At the same time, however, there is a growing awareness of the exalted dignity proper to the human person, since he stands above all things, and his rights and duties are universal and inviolable. Therefore, there must be made available to all men everything necessary for leading a life truly human, such as food, clothing, and shelter; the right to choose a state of life freely and to found a family, the right to education, to employment, to a good reputation, to respect, to appropriate information, to activity, in accord with the upright norm of one's own conscience, to protection of privacy and to rightful freedom, even in matters of religion.

Furthermore, whatever is opposed to life itself, such as any type of murder, genocide, abortion, euthanasia or wilful self-destruction, whatever violates the integrity of the human person, such as mutilation, torments inflicted on body or mind, attempts to coerce the will itself; whatever insults human dignity, such as subhuman living conditions, arbitrary imprisonment, deportation, slavery, prostitution, the selling of women and children, as well as disgraceful working conditions, where men are treated as mere tools for profit, rather than as free and responsible persons; all these things and others of their like are infamies indeed.

True, all men are not alike from the point of view of varying physical power and the diversity of intellectual and moral resources. Nevertheless, with respect to the fundamental rights of the person, every type of discrimination, whether social or cultural, whether based on sex, race, color, social condition, language or religion, is to be overcome and eradicated as contrary to God's intent. For in truth it must still be regretted that fundamental personal rights are still not being universally honored. Such is the case of a woman who is denied the right to choose a husband freely, to embrace a state of life or to acquire an education or cultural benefits equal to those recognized for men.

The Role of The Church in The Modern World

Everything we have said about the dignity of the human person, and about the human community and the profound meaning of human activity, lays the foundation for the relationship between the Church and the world and provides the basis for dialogue between them.

Christ, to be sure, gave His Church no proper mission in the political, economic or social order. The purpose which He set before her is a religious one. But out of this religious mission itself comes a function, a light and an energy which can serve to structure and consolidate the human community according to the divine law.

The Church recognizes that worthy elements are found in today's social movements, especially an evolution toward unity, a process of wholesome socialization and of association in civic and economic realms. The promotion of unity belongs to the innermost nature of the Church.

This council exhorts Christians, as citizens of two cities, to strive to discharge their earthly duties conscientiously and in response to the Gospel spirit. They are mistaken who, knowing that we have here no abiding city but seek one which is to come, think that they may therefore shirk their earthly responsibilities. For they are forgetting that by the faith itself they are more obliged than ever to measure up to these duties, each according to his proper vocation. Nor, on the contrary, are they any less wide of the mark who think that religion consists in acts of worship alone and in the discharge of certain moral obligations, and who imagine they can plunge themselves into earthly affairs in such a way as to imply that these are altogether divorced from the religious life. This split between the faith which many profess and their daily lives deserves to be counted among the more serious errors of our age. Long since, the Prophets of the Old Testament fought vehemently against this scandal and even more so did Jesus Christ Himself in the New Testament threaten it with grave punishments. Therefore, let there be no false opposition between professional and social activities on the one part, and religious life on the other. The Christian who neglects his temporal duties, neglects his duties toward his neighbor and even God, and jeopardizes his eternal salvation. Christians should rather rejoice that, following the example of Christ who worked as an artisan, they are free to give proper exercise to all their earthly activities and to their humane, domestic, professional, social and technical enterprises by gathering them into one vital synthesis with religious values, under whose supreme direction all things are harmonized unto God's glory.

Secular duties and activities belong properly although not exclusively to laymen. Therefore acting as citizens in the world, whether individually or socially, they will keep the laws proper to each discipline, and labor to equip themselves with a genuine expertise in their various fields. Laymen should also know that it is generally the function of their well-formed Christian conscience to see that the divine law is inscribed in the life of the earthly city; from priests they look for spiritual light and nourishment. Let the layman not imagine that his pastors are always such experts, that to every problem which arises, however complicated, they can readily give him a concrete solution, or even that such is their mission.

For God's Word, by whom all things were made, was Himself made flesh so that as perfect man He might save all men and sum up all things in Himself. The Lord is the goal of human history, the focal point of the longings of history and of civilization, the center of the human race, the joy of every heart and the answer to all its yearnings. He it is whom the Father raised from the dead, lifted on high and stationed at His right hand, making Him judge of the living and the dead. Enlivened and united in His Spirit, we journey toward the consummation of human history.

Some Problems of Special Urgency

This council has set forth the dignity of the human person, and work which men have been destined to undertake throughout the world both as individuals and as members of society. There are a number of particularly urgent needs characterizing the present age, needs which go to the roots of the human race.

Marriage and the Family

The well-being of the individual person and of human and Christian society is intimately linked with the healthy condition of that community produced by marriage and family.

Authentic married love is caught up into divine love and is governed and enriched by Christ's redeeming power and the saving activity of the Church, so that this love may lead the spouses to God with powerful effect and may aid and strengthen them in the sublime office of being a father or a mother.

This love is an eminently human one since it is directed from one person to another through an affection of the will; it involves the good of the whole person, and therefore can enrich the expressions of body and mind, with a unique dignity ennobling these expressions as special ingredients and signs of the friendship distinctive of marriage. This love God has judged worthy of special gifts, healing, perfecting and exalting gifts of grace and charity. Such love, merging the human with the divine, leads the spouses to a free and mutual gift of themselves, a gift providing itself by gentle affection and by deed; such love pervades the whole of their lives: indeed by its busy generosity it grows better and grows greater.

Thus the family, in which the various generations come together and help one another grow wiser and harmonize personal rights with the other requirements of social life, is the foundation of society. All those, therefore, who exercise influence over communities and social groups should work efficiently for the welfare of marriage and the family. Public authority should regard it as a sacred duty to recognize, protect and promote their authentic nature, to shield public morality and to favor the prosperity of home life. The right of parents to beget and educate their children in the bosom of the family must be safeguarded. Children, too, who unhappily lack the blessing of a family should be protected by prudent legislation and various undertakings and assisted by the help they need.

Those too who are skilled in other sciences, notably the medical, biological, social and psychological, can considerably advance the welfare of marriage and the family along with peace of conscience if by pooling their efforts they labor to explain more thoroughly the various conditions favoring a proper regulation of births.

Human culture has necessarily a historical and social aspect and the word "culture" also often assumes a sociological and ethnological sense. According to this sense we speak of a plurality of cultures. Different styles of life and multiple scales of values arise from the diverse manner of using things, of laboring, of expressing oneself, of practicing religion, of forming customs, of establishing laws and juridic institutions, of cultivating the sciences, the arts and beauty. Thus the customs handed down to it form the patrimony proper to each human community.

The circumstances of the life of modern man have been so profoundly changed in their social and cultural aspects, that we can speak of a new age of human history.

From day to day, in every group or nation, there is an increase in the number of men and women who are conscious that they themselves are the authors and the artisans of the culture of their community. Throughout the whole world there is a mounting increase in the sense of autonomy as well as of responsibility. This is of paramount importance for the spiritual and moral maturity of the human race. This becomes more clear if we consider the unification of the world and the duty which is imposed upon us, that we build a better world based upon truth and justice. Thus we are witnesses of the birth of a new humanism, one in which man is defined first of all by this responsibility to his brothers and to history.

For the above reasons, the Church recalls to the mind of all that culture is to be subordinated to the integral perfection of the human person, to the good of the community and of the whole society. Therefore it is necessary to develop the human faculties in such a way that there results a growth of the faculty of admiration, of intuition, of contemplation, of making personal judgment, of developing a religious, moral and social sense.

All this supposes that, within the limits of morality and the common utility, man can freely search for the truth, express his opinion and publish it; that he can practice any art he chooses; that finally, he can avail himself of true information concerning events of a public nature.

As for public authority, it is not its function to determine the character of the civilization, but rather to establish the conditions and to use the means which are capable of fostering the life of culture among all even within the minorities of a nation. It is necessary to do everything possible to prevent culture from being turned away from its proper end and made to serve as an instrument of political or economic power.

Economic and Social Life

In the economic and social realms, too, the dignity and complete vocation of the human person and the welfare of society as a whole are to be respected and promoted. For man is the source, the center, and the purpose of all economic and social life.

Reasons for anxiety, however, are not lacking. While an immense number of people still lack the absolute necessities of life, some, even in less advanced areas, live in luxury or squander wealth. Extravagances and wretchedness exist side by side. While a few enjoy very great power of choice, the majority are deprived of almost all possibility of acting on their own initiative and responsibility, and often subsist in living and working conditions unworthy of the human person.

Citizens, on the other hand, should remember that it is their right and duty to contribute to the true progress of their own community according to their ability. Especially in underdeveloped areas, where all resources must urgently be employed, those who hold back their unproductive resources or who deprive their community of the material or spiritual aid that it needs—saving the personal right of migration—gravely endanger the common good.

To satisfy the demands of justice and equity, strenuous efforts must be made, without disregarding the rights of persons or the natural qualities of each countryman, to remove as quickly as possible the immense economic inequalities, which now exist and in many cases are growing and which are connected with individual and social discrimination.

In economic affairs which today are subject to change, as in the new forms of industrial society in which automation, for example, is advancing, care must be taken that sufficient and suitable work and the possibility of the appropriate technical and professional formation are furnished. The livelihood and the human dignity especially of those who are in very difficult conditions because of illness or old age must be guaranteed.

Human labor which is expended in the production and exchange of goods or in the performance of economic services is superior to the other elements of economic life, for the latter have only the nature of tools.

In economic enterprises it is persons who are joined together, that is, free and independent human beings created to the image of God. Therefore, with attention to the functions of each—owners or employers, management or labor—and without doing harm to the necessary unity of management, the active sharing of all in the administration and profits of these enterprises in ways to be properly determined is to be promoted. Since more often, however, decisions concerning economic and social conditions, on which the future lot of the workers and of their children depends, are made not within the business itself but by institutions on a higher level, the workers themselves should have a share also in determining these conditions—in person or through freely elected delegates.

Among the basic rights of the human person is to be numbered the right of freely founding unions for working people. These should be able truly to represent them and to contribute to the organizing of economic life in the right way. Included is the right of freely taking part in the activity of these unions without risk of reprisal.

Although recourse must always be had first to a sincere dialogue between the parties, a strike, nevertheless, can remain even in present-day circumstances a necessary, though ultimate, aid for the defense of the workers' own rights and the fulfillment of their just desires. As soon as possible, however, ways should be sought to resume negotiations and the discussion of reconciliation.

The right of having a share of earthly goods sufficient for oneself and one's family belongs to everyone. The Fathers and Doctors of the Church held this opinion, teaching that men are obliged to come to the relief of the poor and to do so not merely out of their superfluous goods. If one is in extreme necessity, he has the right to procure for himself what he needs out of the riches of others. Since there are so many people prostrate with hunger in the world, this sacred council urges all to share and employ their earthly goods according to the ability of each, especially by supporting individuals or peoples with the aid by which they may be able to help and develop themselves.

Christians who take an active part in the present-day socio-economic development and fight for justice and charity should be convinced that they can make a great contribution to the prosperity of mankind and to the peace of the world. In these activities let them, either as individuals or as members of groups, give a shining example. Having acquired the absolutely necessary skill and experience, they should observe the right order in their earthly activities, in faithfulness to Christ and His Gospel. Thus their whole life, both individual and social, will be permeated with the spirit of the beatitudes, notably with a spirit of poverty.

The Life of the Political Community

In our day, profound changes are apparent also in the structure and institutions of peoples. Such changes have a great influence on the life of the political community, especially regarding the rights and duties of all in the exercise of civil freedom and in the attainment of the common good, and in organizing the relations of citizens among themselves and with respect to public authority.

Along with cultural, economic and social development, there is a growing desire among many people to play a greater part in organizing the life of the political community. In the conscience of many arises an increasing concern that the rights of minorities be recognized without any neglect for their duties toward the political community.

Yet the people who come together in the political community are many and diverse, and they have every right to prefer divergent solutions. If the political community is not to be torn apart while everyone follows his own opinion, there must be an authority to direct the energies of all citizens toward the common good, not in a mechanical or despotic fashion, but by acting above all as a moral force which appeals to each one's freedom and sense of responsibility.

It is in full conformity with human nature that there should be juridico-political structures providing all citizens in an ever better fashion and without discrimination the practical possibility of freely and actively taking part in the establishment of the juridical foundations of the political community and in the direction of public affairs, in fixing the terms of reference of the various public bodies and in the election of political leaders. All citizens, therefore, should be mindful of the right and also the duty to use their free vote to further the common good.

It is very important, especially where a pluralistic society prevails, that there be a correct notion of the relationship between the political community and the Church, and a clear distinction between the tasks which Christians undertake, individually or as a group, on their own responsibility as citizens guided by the dictates of a Christian conscience, and the activities which, in union with their pastors, they carry out in the name of the Church.

The Church, by reason of her role and competence, is not identified in any way with the political community nor bound to any political system. She is at once a sign and a safeguard of the transcendent character of the human person.

The Fostering of Peace and the
Promotion of a Community of Nations

In our generation when men continue to be afflicted by acute hardships and anxieties arising from the ravages of war or the threat of it, the whole human family faces an hour of supreme crisis in its advance toward maturity. Moving gradually together and everywhere more conscious already of its unity, this family cannot accomplish its task of constructing for all men everywhere a world more genuinely human unless each person devotes himself to the cause of peace, with renewed vigor.

Peace is not merely the absence of war; nor can it be reduced solely to the maintenance of a balance of power between enemies; nor is it brought about by dictatorship. Instead, it is rightly and appropriately called an enterprise of justice. Peace results from that order structured into human society by its divine Founder, and actualized by men as they thirst after ever greater justice. The common good of humanity finds its ultimate meaning in the eternal law. But since the concrete demands of this common good are constantly changing as time goes on, peace is never attained once and for all, but must be built up ceaselessly. Moreover, since the human will is unsteady and wounded by sin, the achievement of peace requires a constant mastering of passions and the vigilance of lawful authority.

But this is not enough. This peace on earth cannot be obtained unless personal well-being is safeguarded and men freely and trustingly share with one another the riches of their inner spirits and their talents. A firm determination to respect other men and peoples and their dignity, as well as the studied practice of brotherhood are absolutely necessary for the establishment of peace. Hence peace is likewise the fruit of love, which goes beyond what justice can provide.

Certainly, war has not been rooted out of human affairs. As long as the danger of war remains and there is no competent and sufficiently powerful authority at the international level, government cannot be denied the right to legitimate defense once every means of peaceful settlement has been exhausted.

But it is one thing to undertake military action for the just defense of the people, and something else again to seek the subjugation of other nations. Nor, by the same token, does the mere fact that war has unhappily begun mean that all is fair between the warring parties.

Any act of war aimed indiscriminately at the destruction of entire cities or extensive areas along with their population is a crime against God and man himself. It merits unequivocal and unhesitating condemnation.

The unique hazard of modern warfare consists in this: it provides those who possess modern scientific weapons with a kind of occasion for perpetrating just such abominations; moreover, through a certain inexorable chain of events, it can catapult men into the most atrocious decisions.

Men should be convinced that the arms race in which an already considerable number of countries are engaged is not a safe way to preserve a steady peace, nor is the so-called balance resulting from this race a sure and authentic peace. Rather than being eliminated thereby, the causes of war are in danger of being gradually aggravated. While extravagant sums are being spent for the furnishing of ever new weapons an adequate remedy cannot be provided for the multiple miseries afflicting the whole modern world. Disagreements between nations are not really and radically healed; on the contrary, they spread the infection to other parts of the earth. New approaches based on reformed attitudes must be taken to remove this trap and to emancipate the world from its crushing anxieties through the restoration of genuine peace.

It is our clear duty, therefore, to strain every muscle in working for the time when all war can be completely outlawed by international consent. This goal undoubtedly requires the establishment of some universal public authority acknowledged as such by all and endowed with the power to safeguard on the behalf of all, security, regard for justice, and respect for rights.

In order to build up peace above all the causes of discord among men, especially injustice, which foment wars must be rooted out. Not a few of these causes come from excessive economic inequalities and from putting off the steps needed to remedy them. Other causes of discord, however, have their source in the desire to dominate and in a contempt for persons.

If an authentic economic order is to be established on a world-wide basis, an end will have to be put to profiteering, to national ambitions, to the appetite for political supremacy, to militaristic calculations, and to machinations for the sake of spreading and imposing ideologies.

The following norms seem useful for such cooperation:

a) Developing nations should take great pains to seek as the object of progress to express and secure the total human fulfillment of their citizens. They should bear in mind that progress arises and grows above all out of the labor and genius of the nations themselves because it has to be based, not only on foreign aid, but especially on the full utilization of their own resources, and on the development of their own culture and traditions.

b) On the other hand, it is a very important duty of the advanced nations to help the developing nations in discharging their above-mentioned responsibilities. They should therefore gladly carry out on their own home front those spiritual and material readjustments that are required for the realization of this universal cooperation.

Consequently, in business dealings with weaker and poorer nations, they chould be careful to respect their profit, for these countries need the income they receive on the sale of their homemade products to support themselves.

c) It is the role of the international community to coordinate and promote development, but in such a way that the resources earmarked for this purpose will be allocated as effectively as possible, and with complete equity. It is likewise this community's duty, with due regard for the principle of subsidiarity, so to regulate economic relations throughout the world that these will be carried out in accordance with the norms of justice.

Not everyone who cries, "Lord, Lord," will enter into the kingdom of heaven, but those who do the Father's will by taking a strong grip on the work at hand. Now, the Father wills that in all men we recognize Christ our brother and love Him effectively, in word and in deed. By thus giving witness to the truth, we will share with others the mystery of the heavenly Father's love. As a consequence, men throughout the world will be aroused to a lively hope—the gift of the Holy Spirit— that some day at last they will be caught up in peace and utter happiness in that fatherland radiant with the glory of the Lord.

CHURCH AND SOCIETY IN GREEK ORTHODOX THEOLOGY

NICOS A. NISSIOTIS

Eastern theology has never crystallized its teachings in order to suggest a Christian sociology or to inspire a Christian social order. There are, therefore, many different Orthodox approaches to the relationship with society, and none can claim to express the genuine Orthodox attitude. The change in the political scene and the breakdown in the majority of Orthodox countries of the idea of Christendom make this task even more difficult, if not impossible. In this paper, therefore, we shall seek only to analyze some fundamental characteristics of Orthodox theology and tradition that might suggest a possible approach to the problem of relationships between church and society.

Appraisal of the Situation

It is no longer possible to regard eastern mystical theology as a deviation from authentic evangelical Christianity and as a negative spiritual power that has hindered developments on social ethics. To regard eastern mystical theology only as a negative spiritual power for social action is to ignore its main characteristic, which is to be found in the creative dynamism of the regenerating power of the Holy Spirit. True monasticism gives life to the people of God, pointing at the same time to the end of history and to the second coming of Jesus, when he will meet his own people. Monasticism is the missionary church going out into the world, possessing nothing, being a living witness to the second coming of the Lord.

Eastern theology sees in the monastic spirituality a legitimate and necessary maximalism; but the whole Orthodox Church is centered on the family principle of society, and lives according to principles that, rightly applied by a local church, help Orthodox Christians to relate themselves directly to all forms of social life. There is no doubt that

Orthodoxy seeks to express both the communal and the individual aspects of faith—"communal" in the sense of the group encouraging personal responsibility and not mere collectivism.

The contemplation and vision of the glory of God is another maximalism of Orthodox spirituality, but it would be totally wrong to identify this attitude with passivity in the social field. On the contrary, the eastern doxology is the continuous thanksgiving of Christians who receive, through the church, the gifts that God gives to the whole of his creation, recapitulated in Christ and regenerated by the Spirit. Doxology is not simply contemplation or a visionary illusion; it is dynamic participation in the glory of God, as revealed in Christ and in his Church, making possible continually renewed action in this world.

Criticism, if it is to be objective, must recognize a certain dualism in Orthodoxy's approach to the meaning of the world and its theological significance. On this point (which we shall discuss in more detail in the next section of this chapter), I would only say here that eastern theology has never adopted either of the theories that have been the basis of most western Christian social thinking: neither the Thomist understanding of order in creation preserved absolutely after the fall, which provided the framework for the ethics of natural law; nor the extreme Protestant understanding of the world after the fall as totally corrupt, and which provoked the response of liberalism. The debate about natural theology has remained quite foreign to eastern theology. This may be regarded as its weak point, but it gives it flexibility in all the situations in which Orthodoxy has to live and survive.

As a result of this equivocal theological attitude, Orthodoxy has been unable to shape a "social gospel": a definition of its relationship with the state, such as the doctrine of total separation, or the two-realms theory or even the system of the "Constantinian era" as it is understood by the West. All these forms of relationship are open but relative possibilities for the Eastern Church. But none of them can claim to express the Orthodox attitude to the problem of the relationship with state and society. Therefore, the Orthodox have no social systems and no fixed Christian theories regarding social relationships, no theological doctrine of work and profession or sexual ethics, no closed chapter on birth control, no guiding principles of industrialization, no theological appreciation of the modern secularization. The church is not here to suggest norms which would be applicable everywhere and which would give rise to a single form of technical civilization or culture.

Another reason is the fact that for the Orthodox, the Bible is not a code of guiding principles for social action. The wisdom of the Bible is relevant only for those who already live within the spiritual reality of the Christian community, the church. Therefore, one has to experience one's discipleship from within the church in the service of the world, and then the biblical message for regenerating society can be revealed and understood. Otherwise, social action will lead to a one-sided and limited interpretation of the world, because the biblical picture of the world and of society is a richly varied one, showing how the church can live in all kinds of situations, but without identifying any as authentically and absolutely Christian.

Eastern Orthodoxy is, of its essence, continually open to new developments in every situation, in the modern world.

The Theological Basis of the Relationship
Between Church and Society

This open Orthodox attitude to all forms of relationship between church and society is based upon some fundamental theological principles. In Orthodoxy, there is a dualistic concept of the world, embracing both positive and negative elements, which has deep roots in the biblical conception of cosmos. On the one hand, its positive and optimistic view of the world explains the Byzantine tendency to achieve harmony between church and state, and church and society, as well as the Orthodox understanding of man and its qualitative interpretation of the catholicity of the church. On the other hand, its recognition of the tragic element of history, of the disintegrating effect of the sin of man and the constant threat of secularism to the church, explains the Orthodox theology's hesitation to adopt a fixed form of Christian social ethics that would be valid for all situations.

The Orthodox Church ascribes primary importance to the triumphant Johannine presentation of the victory and Lordship of Jesus and his light over the darkness of the world. Its ecclesiology insists that in him who is the Head of the Body, the church everything in heaven and in earth is recapitulated (Col 1:19). It is also the church that tries to see the world within its martyrdom, the cruel historical reality through the event of the Resurrection.

Because it is centered on the risen and exalted Lord, Orthodoxy regards this world as a prelude to the final victory, which gives a glory to everything already in this world. The understanding of the world as exalted because of the Cross, and especially the Resurrection, enables us to see every human condition as potentially transfigured and regenerated by the certainty of the eschatological victory and the sure, triumphal return of the risen Lord to all. The Holy Spirit is at work in history, as another Creator after the Resurrection, giving new life, restoring the fallen creature in his Creator. On this theological basis, nature is not to be separated from grace. There is no opposition between the divine grace given in Christ Jesus and the world as an existence restored to him by the Paraclete. The Orthodox theology of the Holy Spirit overcomes the dualism between nature and grace by filling the gap between fallen nature and the risen Christ within nature. The Resurrection reveals the working of the Holy Spirit, who has always been present and active from the beginning of creation and is so now in an apocalyptic sense, as a power of the eschaton already present in time by anticipation, reflected and apprehended by man within history. All historical realities, even those that appear to be disastrous, are understood in Orthodox pneumatology as one more victory of the risen Lord in his Spirit, once they are experienced through the church community, of all ages, recapitulating in itself by faith the whole cosmic reality.

No one alone can have an optimistic view and evaluate correctly the historical situation of the world. Christian hope is not an individual experience any more than faith is. Everything depends on participation with the militant people of God in the Body of Christ. In this community, the whole world is reflected as transfigured, giving us a foretaste of the final fulfillment of the world in history. The church as the divine presence of the Paraclete, is the center and the axis of all history. The church cannot be separated from the world; it is its very heart. It is implanted precisely at the center of the historical reality, of which it is both the origin and the end. This is the qualitative sense of catholicity (sobornost in Russian), which produces the geographic reality of the church.

The optimistic view of man and of the world makes Eastern Orthodoxy aware of its historical responsibility and helps it to maintain a concern for all human conditions. But this is not the whole truth; if it were, then some of the accusations of Monophysitism would be justified. We risk, therefore, arriving at a superficial concern for human life, introducing an unbridgeable gap between the exalted Christ and the cruel historical situation in which we are inevitably involved.

The Orthodox View of History and the World

It is perhaps for this reason that Orthodox worship can become an end in itself, when it should be a springboard for social action. At three additional points, we can summarize the second dimension of Orthodoxy. Although they are separated here for the sake of a clear presentation, they are, in fact, inseparably bound together.

1. Eastern Orthodoxy has always emphasized the importance of history, against all kinds of radical existentialism, which see history simply as a sequence of successive moments without inner coherence. Orthodoxy sees in history a judgment of the living God. The acts of man as a historical being are inseparable from his faith in Christ Jesus as the center of history, not only in the church but particularly in daily life. History is not a narration about acts of God, nor is it an apocalyptic sign of things to come at the end of time, but it is the theater where God is in action.

The Orthodox fathers went so far as to speak of synergy with God in perfecting his creation, during the eighth day of creation that is human history. What they meant was that, in history, the Christian believer has to become a factor in the shaping of the new creation and the new world according to the victorious message of the gospel. The eastern tradition requires every member of the Body of Christ to play his part in the present historical situation, always dynamic and flexible, because it is acting in the image of Christ, that is to say, through the love of God, which takes the lead. In this way, the Christian can never remain a detached spectator of the given order or of God's action, simply affirming the presence of God. He must make out of his Parousia, his presence, a parresia, a bold action, a peaceful revolution in all situations.

2. In the eastern tradition, anthropology is expressed in terms of the sinner redeemed by Christ. Orthodox theology has insisted on the fact that our humanity assumed by Christ is the humanity of the Divine Logos, therefore the purified humanity, which (as the historical person, the Jesus of Nazareth) he presents sinless to God the Father. Orthodoxy never professed by analogy with the manhood of Jesus, any general idea of Christian humanism based on the goodness of man. Orthodoxy does not create by theosis the anthropology of an optimistic humanist,

disregarding sin or accepting it as a simple disorder. It is in Christ and through the work of the Holy Spirit in the church that one grasps the tremendous dimensions of sin, because there it is revealed to be a sin of relationships and never the abstract concept of a sinful nature. Sin is always a sin against my neighbor, revealing my apostasy from God, breaking communion with him and with man. This can be grasped only if one becomes a member of a Christian community where individualism is defeated. Orthodoxy has always maintained, in its effort to embrace the whole world and to sanctify it through the church, that sin is the element which the fall has brought into all human relationships and which tends to disintegrate the whole creation, whose motive power and purpose is *koinonia* in love. It is the deep sense of this reality that led the greatest spiritual leaders of Eastern Orthodoxy, though maintaining the principle of concord with the state and a positive attitude to the world, to retire from it and become monks, hermits and startsi, in order to rouse it from its self-complacency.

3. Eastern Orthodoxy sees the church as under a continual threat from its secular environment and directly affected by it. Political protection or persecution, as well as secularism in the form of theism or antitheism or indifferentism, always confront the church as something rooted in the world in which the church exists and whose existence is shaken when the church tries to proclaim the gospel of God's great victory in history.

We should never forget that this world is not yet fully under the direct rule of God, but is under the principalities and evil powers; and the church, as the Body of Christ, proclaiming his Lordship, cannot undertake evangelism and mission without immediately clashing with the powers of this world. The church's *diakonia* is inseparably united with martyrdom. Martyria and resurrection, in the sense of the Acts of the Apostles, is, for the eastern tradition, almost identical with martyrdom, when the good news of the gospel penetrates the world where this church exists. It is, therefore, a great error to regard the life of the Eastern Church, as western criticism has repeatedly done, as the place where mystics, as "aristocrats" among the chosen people of God, try to enjoy in peace and quiet the glory of the risen Lord by withdrawing from the historical scene and caring only for the salvation of their souls and the spiritual growth of the individual transfigured in the Holy Spirit apart from the world.

To be a Christian means becoming an active member of the new *koinonia* by the act of God. It means to pass from the state of *individuum* to that of a *persona,* or better, of a "personal being," a man in and for the others, for the wholeness. An *individuum* as *atomon,* believing in Christ but outside a church communion, cannot easily be called fully a Christian. The vertical individual confession of faith, God-man, which regards the church as secondary, as a necessary social organization, leads to a sectarian, individualistic view of society and introduces all kinds of separations between nature and grace, and grace and law. The vertical relationship with God in a living faith is to be found in its horizontal manifestation with others in the communion of the Holy Spirit, which cannot be separated from the institutional aspect of the church, its visible reality here and now.

In the Orthodox tradition, you may not use the term "person" in the humanitarian romantic or idealistic understanding of the word, as a subject having its own personality grounded in distinctiveness. "Person" in the Orthodox tradition must, I think, be understood as "personal being," which can be defined only on the basis of its relationship with the other members of the church community. "Personal being" means that its individuality springs only out of the reciprocal movement of love, which leads to the interdependence of men in Christ, brought together by the Paraclete. This togetherness is established by God in this world, in this history of ours, as one unshaken, unbroken community of men. It is a real visible community, with structure and institutions, which are not to be regarded as a necessary evil or an external instrument added by men to the invisible act of God. These structures cannot and should not be separated from the essence of God's revelation in time and the establishment of his community in the world. They are the outcome of the energy of the Spirit and they are quickened by his *charismata.*

It is therefore of basic importance that an individual or a group, facing a specific problem, should act together with the other members of the ecclesial community. An individual decision on any social problem can never fully express the will of Christ. Nor can the decision of a group isolated from the rest of the universal church fully express this will. All sectarian attitudes are excluded, especially when the church acts in society. The social witness of the church, apart from this solid ecclesiological basis, is going to produce new division in its own body. This kind of ecclesiology excludes every tendency of conformism with a given social structure.

Without separating church and world, and stressing the transcendent reality of the church in the world, as well as its holiness and sacramental nature, it allows the church to identify itself with the world, sharing all aspects of family, social and national life, yet on guard against every danger of conformism. The Orthodox ecclesiology can lead the church to a realistic solidarity with the suffering, the poor, a nation fighting for its freedom, in which laity and clergy are equally responsible; but not for a moment does the word that it preaches in this situation imply a passive acceptance of the given patterns of economic, social and national life.

We therefore arrive at the following conclusions about the Orthodox understanding of responsible society:

1. The Orthodox view of church and state is not a system that necessarily leads to either theocracy or caesaropapism. The so-called system of "friendly relationships" denotes only the good will of the church to the political authorities, an openness and a concern for their problems and a spirit of sacrifice for the spiritual upbuilding and the material welfare of the citizens of the nation. In no sense does this mean that the church must sacrifice the prophetic element of its ministry or its critical attitude to political leaders who are abusing their authority.

2. This ecclesiology does not look upon the world as a new creation in which the people inevitably pass from the state of individualistic existence to personal, conscious, responsible existence; rather, the new creation is the result of mission, evangelism and the active presence of the Church community and its members. It is something very basic for a man to live both as a member of the Christian community and as a responsible member of a secularized society. The meaning of such a situation does not come about automatically without the man's act of repentance and his perpetual nourishment by the sacraments and the experience of the reality of church life. An Orthodox would say that where this happens, he becomes in society a parresia, the presence in bold action of the church in the world.

3. What lies behind this attitude is a kind of acknowledgment of God and his Word. It means that everything we have and achieve and offer comes from God in Christ through the Spirit. Before the scientist begins his research or the sociologist his analysis, they have to realize that the divine activity of giving places us all in an attitude of reception. Hence, Christian action in society is to help man in all social situations, to see what is human and what is inhuman, what belongs in the gift

of God and what he has given for the sake of the whole body of his society. In discriminating this, the church must always preach the absolute priority of the divine, saving judgment over the human application of the possibilities of nature for development and progress.

The duty of the church is not simply to serve society or to acknowledge the automatic presence of Christ in society. The presence of Christ in society will clearly be seen only when the church calls everybody to be incorporated into the Body of Christ and to reinterpret in action—which distinguishes the human from the inhuman—his particular daily work as a service to the whole of society. We are in agreement with the evangelicals that the church is an extroverted movement, with the distinction that we maintain that the church is a solid building of God, has a center that is given in history by the Holy Spirit and is expressed through the prophetic teaching of his Word, radiating from his real presence in baptism and the eucharist. We agree with them that there is a "worldly spirituality," but it should always be the result of a rebirth through the baptismal waters and the eucharistic blood in the One Apostolic Church. Then, through the service of the Christian in society, these two flow out, and this should make all social action the fruit of the Spirit and the doings of the Word of God.

ON ECUMENICAL SOCIAL ETHICS

PAUL ABRECHT

A large part of the energy of the ecumenical movement has been directed to the search for a common Christian witness to the problems of modern society. Indeed, for laymen, most of the attraction of the ecumenical movement is in the creativity and vitality in facing social issues and in the challenge they have posed to Churches, too much identified with the political and social system of a particular region or country.

The discovery of the constantly changing interplay between Christian and secular thought has been fundamental to the development of ecumenical social thinking. It accounts for the double-sized character of that thought: on the one hand, the attempt to define the ends and purposes of social institutions and the criteria for judging these; on the other, the investigation of the way in which Christians or Churches in specific situations have met their responsibilities and the analysis they have made of their social problems.

It is almost fifty years since Archbishop Nathan Söderblom launched his idea of an Ecumenical Council of Churches. Despite the sense of urgency and the serious preliminary studies, the great hopes for a bold new Christian programme for world order and social reconstruction were disappointed. Indeed, it is often said that the first efforts (1919-25) to develop a new social teaching in the non-Roman Churches are interesting only because they provided the starting-point for what was later to become a theologically more profound and socially more perceptive movement.

Yet it would be wrong to overlook or underestimate some fundamental achievements of this first effort. Like Roman Catholic social movements in the latter half of the nineteenth century, Protestant, Anglican, and Orthodox leaders had committed themselves to a new involvement in the world in the interest of social justice. They perceived that the spirit of pious individualism which predominated at that time was no answer to the problems of industrial revolution and world conflict.

They sought to construct a new ecumenical concern based upon the inspiration of various Christian social movements of the day. These were prophetic movements, movements of outrage and protest against social evils, movements of reform and action.

The great work of Troeltsch on *The Social Teaching of the Christian Churches* (London 1911) had also opened world Christian thinking to a new concern for society by showing the ethical and sociological pattern of various forms of Christianity and their appeal to particular social classes and groups.

It would be instructive at this point to compare these developments with Roman Catholic social thinking as it developed in the great social encyclicals from *Rerum novarum* (1891) to *Quadragesimo anno* (1931). It might be argued that whereas in later years Roman Catholicism had to overcome an uncompromising rejection of socialism and Marxism, non-Roman social thinkers were obliged to rid themselves of some illusions about man and society which an idealist socialist reading of the Bible had fostered. The economic depression in the western capitalist countries and the rise of the totalitarian political systems in Europe showed the inadequacy of some of the theological and ethical ideas with which the Church was working. A deeper theological basis was needed.

The Oxford Conference of 1937

The Oxford Conference is noteworthy particularly for what it said about the economic situation and the problem of inequality in the distribution of wealth and income. It also brought into the open the debate about the theological and biblical basis of Christian social ethics which had been simmering since the 1925 Conference in Stockholm. J. H. Oldham, the chief architect of the Oxford Conference, summarized thus the three theological perspectives presented to the Conference:

1. A Christian ethics based on principles derived from New Testament teaching, especially the Sermon on the Mount, representing the position of Stockholm.
2. A personal ethic of salvation—suspicious of "Christian social programmes"—was held by several continental theologians who maintained that the Christian ethic could not be identified with

that of the Sermon on the Mount. Thus Emil Brunner of Zurich argued that "The Christian Church has no right to lay down a social programme, because it is not its business to establish any kind of system."

3. A Christian ethic of justice derived from the love commandment. In contrast to the first position, it stressed the reality of evil and the difficulty of direct applications of the love commandment.

The theological corrective which the Oxford Conference applied to the thinking of the 1925 Stockholm Conference is well illustrated in the report on economic life. It is argued that a Christian social ethic cannot be developed directly from the love commandment or the Kingdom of God, since these, because of human sinfulness, are in contradiction with the world. Therefore, "in so far as the Kingdom of God is in conflict with the world and is therefore still to come, the Christian finds himself under the necessity of discovering the best available means of checking human sinfulness and of increasing the possibilities and opportunities of love within a sinful world."

The Responsible Society

Ecumenical discussion of social questions was interrupted by the Second World War, but Churches in various regions struggled to prepare themselves for the post-war period by their discussions of the conditions of peace and post-war reconstruction. Their debates now focused on the issues of state planning and the welfare society, as alternatives to capitalism and communism, and this came to be the main social issue in the discussions of the First Assembly which constituted the World Council of Churches in Amsterdam in 1948.

In the Assembly report on "The Church and the Disorder of Society," the Churches refused to accept either complete state planning or unqualified freedom in economic affairs. "Coherent and purposeful ordering of society has now become a major necessity. Here governments have responsibilities which they must not shirk. But centers of initiative in economic life must be so encouraged as to avoid placing too great a burden upon centralized judgment and decision." The Assembly stressed that Christians should reject the extreme ideologies of both communism and *laissez-faire* capitalism, and "should seek to draw men away from the false assumption that these extremes are the only alternatives." It could not "resolve the debate between those who feel that the primary solution is to socialize the means of production, and those who fear that such a course will merely lead to new and inordinate combinations of political power, culminating finally in an omnicompetent state." The definition of the responsible society set forth at Amsterdam is as follows:

> Man is created and called to be a free being, responsible to God and his neighbor. Any tendencies in state and society depriving man of the possibility of acting responsibly are a denial of God's intention for man and his work of salvation. A responsible society is one where freedom is the freedom of men who acknowledge responsibility to justice and public order, and where those who hold political authority or economic power are responsible for its exercise to God and the people whose welfare is affected by it. . . . For a society to be responsible under modern conditions it is required that the people have freedom to control, criticize, and to change their governments, that power be made responsible by law and tradition, and be distributed as widely as possible through the whole community. It is required that economic justice and provision of equality of opportunity be established for all the members of society.

At the Second Assembly of the World Council of Churches in 1954 the term was broadened and its meaning as a guide for action clarified:

> Responsible society is not an alternative social political system, but a criterion by which we judge all existing social orders and at the same time a standard to guide us in the specific choices we have to make. Christians are called to live responsibly, to live in response to God's act of redemption in Christ, in any society, even within the most unfavorable social structures.

The Ecumenical Witness Against Racism

The Evanston Assembly of 1954 gave its attention primarily to social problems which had preoccupied the ecumenical discussion in the period after the Amsterdam Assembly.

Many of the Churches affiliated to the World Council of Churches had expressed their opposition to racial and ethnic segregation and discrimination, and the Oxford Conference had made a clear ecumenical critique of racism, but this was the first occasion when the issue was thoroughly debated within the Council. The report received by the Assembly and commended to the Churches for their study and action was unequivocal:

> Racial and ethnic fears, hates and prejudices are more than social problems with whose existence we must reckon; they are sins against God and His commandments that the Gospel alone can cure. To the Church has been committed the preaching of the Gospel. To proclaim the "healing of the nations". . . through Christ is verily her task. . . . As part of its task of challenging the conscience of society, it is the duty of the Church to protest against any law or arrangement that is unjust to any human being or which would make Christian fellowship impossible, or would prevent the Christian from practicing his vocation. Some of its members may feel bound to disobey such a law. The Church does not contemplate lightly the breaking of the law, but it recognizes the duty of a Christian to do so when he feels that he has reached that point where the honor and glory of God command him to obey God rather than man. In so doing, the Church must point out the possible consequent necessity for spiritual discipline according to the Gospel.

In 1960 the World Council established a Secretariat on Racial and Ethnic Relations within the Department of Church and Society to strengthen the ecumenical witness in situations of racial and ethnic tensions and to offer assistance to those churches which were seeking new and creative answers. A series of field visits and consultations was organized in many different regions of the world, perhaps the most remarkable being held in Kitwe, Zambia, in 1964. The finding that "the unjust patterns of race relations now prevailing in most of Southern Africa must be changed," provoked new intense discussion, especially in South Africa.

The Kitwe Conference emphasized that the problem of racial justice cannot be solved without great changes in economic and political structures, and this was reiterated in the 1966 Conference on Church and Society which pressed the Churches to become more deeply involved in the world-wide struggle against racism.

In the Fourth Assembly at Uppsala (1968) the ecumenical consideration of racism reached a new and sharper focus, reflecting no doubt the increasing violence of race conflict and the determination of the colored people, especially black Americans, to attain full equality of political and social rights with whites.

Rapid Social Change in the New Nations

It is a sobering thought that the ecumenical movement discovered the urgent problems of the nations of Africa, Asia, Latin America, and the Middle East only after the process of radical decolonization was well under way. There are institutional reasons which help to explain that fact. The World Council of Churches had very few member Churches from these countries in 1948 and most of the Christian concern for social and political welfare in these lands was expressed through western missionary societies, identified with the International Missionary Council until that body merged with the W.C.C. in 1961. Despite the real interest of western Christians, they could not be expected to see the need for revolutionary change as clearly as Christians in the emerging nations.

In 1952 the Study Department of the World Council, taking advantage of the first meeting of the Central Committee of the World Council to be held in Asia, organized in Lucknow an Ecumenical Study Conference for East Asia.

The positive programme proposed by the Lucknow Conference included radical reform of land tenure systems, planned economic development, support of the struggle for freedom and self-determination in East Asia, and new policies by western nations in support of political and economic change in Asia.

The Lucknow meeting had a great influence on the further consideration of Christian action in Asia and on the subsequent decision of the World Council to develop a comprehensive program in support of Churches facing issues of rapid social change in Africa, Asia, and Latin America. The decision to launch such a program was taken in July 1955 at the first meeting of the new working committee for the Department on Church and Society, in Davos, Switzerland.

The development of the World Council's concern for social change seemed at first to require no new theological-ethical categories. But inevitably it became necessary to think in terms of theological perspectives for radical change, and to find a Christian interpretation of the emancipation of the new nations and of their efforts at nation-building.

In contrast with the familiar ecumenical emphasis on gradual social change and reform, the inquiries in the new nations pointed to the rapid breakdown of old social change and reform, the inquiries in the nations pointed to the rapid breakdown of old social systems and traditions and the need for political and economic systems supporting rapid development. In contrast with western Christian thought which was based on assumptions of a society still greatly influenced by Christian values and institutions, Christian social thinking in the new nations tended to emphasize the human values in a national perspective. In contrast with the extremely critical attitude, manifested toward nationalism in many of the Western Churches, the "younger Churches" stressed the creative role of the new nation-states in the work of development and in creating a new sense of dignity and self-respect. In opposition to the Western Churches, which still placed great confidence in the traditional structures of world political and economic relations, Christians from the new nations pointed to their inherent biases, and challenged the assumption of an "international law" developed by the western powers and imposed on the rest of the world.

The Geneva Conference of 1966

With the formation of the World Council of Churches in 1948, it had been assumed that the Assemblies, meeting at regular intervals of six or seven years would provide the needed opportunity for official World Council action on social questions. Indeed the Assemblies of Amsterdam (1948) and Evanston (1954) had contributed significantly to ecumenical reflection. But New Delhi (1961) revealed that the amount of time which an Assembly could give to serious consideration of social questions was diminishing; and that the participation of laymen in the discussion of social questions was hampered by the predominantly ecclesiastical character and structure of an Assembly. Moreover, the "official" nature of an Assembly inhibited adventurous social thinking; it could only put the seal of World Council approval on ideas already accepted by the Churches, rather than risk new ideas which the Churches had yet to grasp. The search for a way around these obstacles led to the proposal of the staff in 1962 to convene a World Conference on Church and Society.

In structure and organization the World Conference on Church and Society held in Geneva in July 1966 differed from previous world Christian conferences in two fundamental respects: the majority of the participants were laymen rather than clergy or church officials, and of the 420 participants roughly equal numbers came from the countries of the "third world," from North America, and from western Europe, making it the first large ecumenical conference in which the participants from the western countries were not in a majority. The Geneva Conference was undoubtedly the most serious attempt on the part of the World Council of Churches to understand the revolutionary realities which shape the modern world. The Central Committee further agreed that the Conference should be empowered to speak *to* rather than *for* the Churches and the World Council, thus giving it freedom to explore issues and suggest new approaches.

Out of this process of ecumenical inquiry and debate have come many new insights and concerns, radically changing the scope of Christian social thought and action. The resulting debate in the Churches on three concerns of the Geneva Conference deserves special attention because they provide important clues to the future of the ecumenical social thinking.

1. *The Christian Responsibility for World Economic and Social Development*

The 1966 Conference made the issue of world economic development a major concern of the Churches. The conference report on this theme set before them a new comprehensive understanding of the hopes and concerns of the developing countries, the contributions needed from the "richer" nations, and the changes in world economic and political structures required if world economic growth was to be achieved. The report also recommended a number of practical steps which would involve new commitments on the part of the Churches to world economic and social justice.

The papal encyclical *Populorum progressio,* published early in 1967, supported similar goals of world development and opened the door to new common Christian action. As a result, a joint Roman Catholic-World Council Exploratory Committee on Society, Development, and Peace was formed. Also a conference on World Co-operation for Development, sponsored by the Pontifical Commission on Justice and Peace and the World Council of Churches, was held in Beirut in April 1968. This was the first major international Christian conference to be so jointly sponsored, organized, and financed.

Stimulated by the challenge of the Geneva Conference and the Beirut meeting, the Uppsala Assembly focused major attention on the issues of development. It is noteworthy that the Assembly's report urges the Churches to go beyond the charitable understanding of "rich" nations helping "poor" nations; it emphasizes the need for fundamental social changes based on a new urgent concern for social justice in a world perspective.

Thus, the Christian discussion of world development, formerly treated almost exclusively in terms of new and expanding forms of aid and trade, has tended more and more to merge with the discussion of revolutionary social change. This is due, no doubt, to the great disappointment with the results of previous efforts of world economic development and the recognition that the familiar patterns of world aid and technical assistance have often increased rather than diminished many of the social problems of the developing nations.

The Churches working within the ecumenical movement can make an important contribution in this area—especially in the search for new understanding and new ideas as the basis for new and effective action. It remains to be seen whether, having exposed themselves for a new understanding of human aspirations in the movement for world-wide development, they will discover the imagination, the resources, and the ingenuity to contribute to dynamic action in this field, and give practical expression to their concern for world economic justice.

2. *The Revolutionary Transformation of Society*

It is precisely because the call to development is a call to accept and even to initiate revolutionary change that many Christians have become suspicious or even hostile concerning the direction of ecumenical social thought today. Certainly, of all the issues raised by the 1966 Conference none has created more controversy and debate than that on the Church and revolution. Both the message and the report of the Conference reflect one fundamental point of agreement, that the Church must recognize the need for revolutionary change in social and political structures.

Around such declarations have arisen demands for a "theology of revolution," now being very widely debated by theologians in many countries. Some commentators have pointed to the ambiguity of the term "revolution," and the different meanings it has for Westerners, who refer to the profound and silent transformation of the structures of industrial society, and for the representatives of the Third World, who mean by it the violent transformations which characterize the post-colonial and pre-industrial period.

The post-conference discussion on this issue has sought to clarify the meaning of revolutionary change and to provide ethical guide-lines for Christians involved in contemporary revolutionary ferment. An ecumenical consultation of theologians and laymen convened by the Department on Church and Society and the Commission of Faith and Order, in 1968 (in Zagorsk, U.S.S.R.), offered its "Reflections on Theology and Revolution" which carry the debate a considerable step further. These may be summarized as follows:

Christian theology warns against sacralizing either the *status quo* or the revolution and should guard against the temptations of false messianism and the fury of self-righteousness. At the same time, theology should free Christians and the Churches for interpretations of creation, providence and law which have generally exaggerated the importance of order relative to justice, in order to make possible a more dynamic relation between order and justice.

Christians in a revolutionary situation have a moral duty to do all in their power to exercise a ministry of reconciliation to enable the revolutionary change to take place non-violently or, if this is not possible, with a minimum of violence.

Christian theology cannot remove the ambiguity of political ethics in a revolutionary situation. Nevertheless, it should relate the universality of the Church, which includes political opponents, to the Christian's special responsibility as a matter of vocation.

The ecumenical idea of a responsible society still has relevance to the new structures established after the revolutionary overthrow of old ones, when it becomes necessary to make power and technology responsible and to allow for a permanent renewal of structures without the disruption of order.

3. *Co-operation with the Roman Catholic Church*

One of the important discoveries made during the preparation for the World Conference on Church and Society was the convergence at certain points of Roman Catholic and World Council social thinking. The Second Vatican Council had begun its discussion of the Church and human needs at almost the same moment that the Central Committee of the World Council decided to convene the Church and Society Conference. The social encyclicals of Pope John XXIII showed a new trend in Roman Catholic social thinking which was carried further by the adoption by the Vatican Council of the *Pastoral Constitution on the Church in the Modern World* (1965). Two ecumenical consultations of Roman Catholic and World Council theologians and scholars, in 1965 and 1966, revealed wide areas of agreement and encouraged the making of plans for joint programs of study on theological and practical questions.

By June 1967 a joint R. C./W. C. C. Exploratory Committee was formed to search for ways relating the work of the Pontifical Commission and the World Council activities in this area of common concern. This has since become the Exploratory Committee on Society, Development, and Peace, with Monsignor Joseph Gremillion and Mr. Max Kohnstamm, a layman active in World Council studies, as co-chairman. In 1968, the two sides agreed to name as joint secretary to this Exploratory Committee, Father George Dunne, S. J., the first man to serve the Churches in such a large ecumenical enterprise. The Conference on Development in Beirut (1968) was the first project of the Exploratory Committee, and a major test of the reality of this new co-operative effort. Its success provided a strong indication that this joint work could expand substantially during the coming years. Such wider ecumenical collaboration is likely to influence greatly the shape and direction of ecumenical social thinking in the period ahead.

The Assembly at Uppsala welcomed this collaboration and emphasized "the importance of co-operating at every level with the Roman Catholic Church . . . and indeed with men of good will everywhere." The publication of the papal encyclical, *Humanae vitae* shows, however, that fundamental disagreements on certain social issues remain, and it would be wrong to expect that some of these will be quickly or easily overcome.

The Question of Theological Basis

Those who are sceptical about ecumenical social thinking ask:

How is it that theologians and laymen are able to come to a relatively large measure of agreement on practical Christian social action in spite of their inability to resolve certain fundamental theological issues of faith and order? This has raised the further question, debated repeatedly in ecumenical circles: How much of a common theological or ecclesiological rationale is necessary before an authentic ecumenical word on social questions can be spoken?

The failure to achieve prior agreement on basic theological or biblical perspectives appears as a serious weakness (and even deception) to those who believe that it is hazardous, if not impossible, to make common Christian declarations on social issues before the theological assumptions underlying them are made explicit. But opposed to that point of view is another which maintains that ecumenical agreement on social questions does not and cannot proceed always from basic theological principles to agreement on practical issues. This viewpoint recognizes that there will probably never be complete agreement on theological debate to be constantly enlivened by new questions. The fact that Churches with different theological outlooks have been able to agree on attitudes or actions in society can be a recognition of a common experience or even of some common theological assumptions which go deeper than the theological differences.

In recent years, the debate about inductive versus deductive social ethics or an ethics of principles versus a contextual ethic has shown how difficult it is to follow one line of reasoning. The World Council has constantly struggled to see the validity of these two perspectives, recognizing, on the one hand, the importance of exploratory work on fundamental theological issues relating to Church and society and at the same time launching inquiries on specific practical concerns. It can be demonstrated that ecumenical social thinking has been illuminated by both approaches. Thus, during the years 1948-52, the World Council Study on "The Bible and the Church's Message to the World," directed by the German biblical scholar, Dr. Wolfgang Schweitzer, helped to relate exegesis and interpretation to social ethics. And from 1951-4 a substantial study of the main theme of the Second Assembly, "Christ the Hope of the World," involving extensive discussions among thirty-five of the world's foremost theologians, gave much attention to the nature of the Church's witness in society. More recent studies on "The Lordship of Christ in an Age of Universal History" (1961-8) provided considerable theological background for the practical work of the World Council in the area of Church and Society.

It is true that there was, often, very little integration or cross-fertilization between these theological studies and the practical inquiries carried on simultaneously. It is also true that laymen have been looking for a more dynamic dialectical relation between the theological reflection and the concrete ethical problems facing them in society than was provided by the theological inquiries.

All these questions were examined at length in the Consultation of theologians and laymen meeting in Russia in 1968, called to make a theological evaluation of the 1966 Conference. The consultation reviewed the theological method as well as the ecclesiological rationale for ecumenical work on social questions. It observed that various denominations often proceed functionally along similar lines in thinking about the role of the Church in society. It acknowledged that this has made possible the formation of groups or movements within and between the Churches which can engage in social action and study and which in turn have led to the discovery of provisional agreements, bridging differences between Christians and showing the possibility of a larger corporate witness. It urged also that there be more systematic study of the ethical issues from the practical ecumenical work and welcomed the fact that this particular consulaion had been jointly sponsored by the Faith and Order Commission and the Department on Church and Society. Despite the achievements in recent years, ecumenical social thinking remains a precarious enterprise. A substantial number of Christians in our Churches are probably still very much opposed to the directions it takes or would criticize the World Council and other ecumenical bodies for giving too much attention to social issues. Moreover, as the pressures for rapid change in society increase, the polarization of opinion in our Churches on basic social questions will undoubtedly become greater rather than diminish. The continuing division of the Churches on basic issues of theology and ecclesiology also weakens the possibility of a more substantial Christian social witness.

Up to the present, the ecumenical consensus on Christian social responsibility has been limited, experimental, and provisional, and with relatively slight impact on the action of the Churches in society. And no doubt the ecumenical witness will become more difficult in the future. But wherever Christians struggle to maintain the transcendence of the faith to their fellow men, combining the desire for justice with the spirit of compassion, the search for the ecumenical community of ideas and witness will proceed. Possibly the most significant achievement of the ecumenical movement has been its ability to encourage and nourish that dialectic of obedience and unity even in situations where opposing points of view seemed to make real enocunter impossible. We can hope for no more and should aspire to no less in the future.

A THEOLOGY
OF CHRISTIAN COMMUNITY?

JAMES M. GUSTAFSON

One of the more overworked cliches about modern technological society and the Churches' participation in it runs something like this: In modern society there is a profound alienation of man from the structures of work, politics and other aspects of life. The large, powerful public world seems to be managed by a few persons in the seats of power or, in the view of analysts, appears to be running not only itself, but the persons who are supposed to manage it. The Church has no way of influencing these centers of real power in the world, for in an age of secularization its moral authority is no longer recognized, and it lacks the modes of exercise of social power to become a significant pressure group to countermand the tendencies that appear to be against its understanding of what life is meant to be. Alongside this powerful ordered public world is the private world of person-to-person relationships, of family life and of individual existence. It is in this sphere that some of the protests against the alienation from the structured world take place—the rebellions of youth or the efforts to achieve some compensating meaningful life by concentrating on family activities. The Church, we are told, has become functional with reference only to this private sphere. And even here its role has become supportive, therapeutic, pastoral and even idolatrous, for it functions to give religious sanctions to a culturally defined pattern of life that is itself not sufficiently subjected to theological and moral criticism.

The effect of much persuasive writing in this vein, by Marxists and existentialists, by theologians and some Christian sociologists, by world-renowned philosophers and street-corner culture critics, has been to create a mood of hostility toward the Church even on the part of many who continue to call themselves Christians. The Churches are seen to be part of the problem of alienation, for they have been attending to institutional demands for self-preservation, to cheap piety and to concern only for the private sphere, none of which rectifies in the least the moral impotence of institutional Christianity. They represent religion, and this, on testimony from antibourgeois theologians, is bad. The avant-garde Christians then call us to a radical secularity that, we are to assume, overcomes the embarrassment of Church life which seems to be merely pious and private in its morality, and institutional in its demands. Secularity also presumably overcomes the distance between Christian faith and the centers of power where things that really matter for the life of man are taking place.

Certain assumptions that inform this perspective need to be brought under serious question. They are both sociological-historical and theological in character. We may ask whether the division between the private and the public, the personal and the structural is not too sharply drawn, and whether significant relations do not exist between them. We may also, form a social-psychological perspective, where the person-forming communities are going to be in a program of action that looks with disdain upon the Church and other "private" spheres. What is to shape the mind and the spirit of the person who is told to be completely identified with the "world"? What is to provide a center of his own personal existence which informs his involvement in the secular order when religion, as a historical movement influencing persons and cultures, is apparently not to be cultivated? What kind of sociological assumptions lie behind the view that Christians can be socially more effective by involvement in secular institutions, since it is through these that history is being shaped, while at the same time the institutions and the religious culture that shape the Christians are judged to be increasingly useless? Where, also, is the positive place of custom and of cultural values, of *ethos,* in this critical material? In the antibourgeois stance, have critics failed to distinguish between false and suppressive moral customs and order, on the one hand, and the positive significance of cultural morality, on the other?

There appear to be theological assumptions lurking in this kind of social analysis as well. They are many, and they do not form a single consistent school. Insofar as the social analysis moves to the cultivation of an existentialist mood, one wonders if God is not seen primarily in terms of the accepter of persons, the lord who wills meaningful moments of self-realization in personal terms, rather than the sovereign ruler of depersonalized institutions as well. The mission of the Church becomes focused too exclusively on the personal and inter-

personal. . . . There is a stress on secularity without adequate delineation of how Christians judge the secular.

Debate over adequate social analysis and over theological assumptions has some significant effects on the actual life of the Christian community within the wider community. . . . Our institutional forms and activities are guided in part by the sociological perceptions and theological
interpretations. . . . The establishment of "coffee houses" as places of
ministry adjacent to college campuses in the United States, for example,
is informed often by crypto-sociological assumptions about what the
actual situation of society is—one in which students are alienated and
thus must be ministered to in terms of that alienation. . . . It is also informed by crypto-theologies, believing that God's grace is known in the
intimacies of coffee, poetry and jazz, and is not known in the course of
study or in the world of "establishment.". . . The founding of centers
for discussion of vocational and political problems may assume not only
that the Churches as they are now organized cannot effectively speak to
the world, but also that conversation about the world without embarras-
sing reference to theological conviction and to religious interest is the
way in which God (if there is a God) works in the modern world. . . . I
do not intend to be overly critical of the new forms of witness and mission, since for both sociological and theological reasons I affirm their
place in the life of the Church. . . . As many have noted, the traditional
routinized activities of institutional Churches in all parts of the world
also certainly rest upon sociological perceptions and theological interpretations that have to be brought under question.

It is my intention in the main body of this essay to suggest an interpretation of community, based upon sociological and theological perspectives, which I hope is more adequate to sources of truth and of insight than some perspectives that are currently in vogue or are historically influential in the life of the Christian community.

The Functions of Community in the Light of God's Purpose.

What purposes of God are being realized in the existence of men in
community? . . . We should have in mind all three aspects of human
community: cultural ethos, interpersonal relationship and institutions.
My answer to this question hinges on a number of verbs: God creates,
sustains, restrains and makes possible better qualities of life through the
existence of men in all three aspects of community.[1]

Common life in various segments of humanity is a means by which God's *creative purposes* bear fruit for men. What is new emerges out of the common life of old. Human creative achievement takes place within the patterns of life in which persons are related to each other, whether one is thinking of biological procreation, development of new forms of social organization, novel patterns of art and music or scientific and technological developments. Creative work is related to the past in dependence upon it, "as well as in rebellion against it. Creative persons are sustained by communities" as well as by defending themselves against them. . . . The continuities need to be stressed in an age that is preoccupied with finding discontinuities and celebrating the novel. Underlying these achievements of men is the potentiality and purpose of newness, or creativity, which is part of God's gracious gift to men in the giving of life. . . .

Even where the individual appears to "break through" with radical novelty, he is participating in an ongoing community. The rejection or transformation of a traditional pattern in one of the arts, for example, does not come into being as a creative act out of nothing.   It takes place as a creative virtuoso responds to the inadequacies of a tradition for the purpose of expressing what he perceives in the world, or what he feels about himself and his world. . . .

Common life is a means by which God sustains human existence in the world. . . . Human life is sustained by the continuities of custom and belief, of values and ideas, as well as by the creative perceptions which alter the traditions of men. The ethical importance of customs and of ethos is an area neglected by many Christian interpreters of society today, probably because a defense of a bourgeois outlook, and many Protestant theologians wish above all to be differentiated from that. . . . The rigid extrinsic code morality of nineteenth-century tradition is rejected in the hope that a more meaningful morality, intrinsic to man's deepest needs or to his Christian life, will come into being. Sustaining patterns of life deserve a dignity in a Christian interpretation of community that is sometimes overlooked, particularly in a time of revolutions and when individuals find custom and tradition to be so oppressive that authentic human existence is often defined in terms of radical freedom from them.[2]

A part of the sustaining function of community is the restraints that it places on individuals and on other communities. The organized interests of one nation act to restrain the aggressive interest of another.

The fighters for justice for those who are oppressed are limited in the means by which their struggle can be executed by the existence of a community that concerns itself for the preservation of civil order. . . .

Through communities the ordering (sustaining and restraining) work of God for the sake of men takes place. New patterns of this work come into being, and older patterns pass away. One of the mistakes of those who define "orders" of creation and preservation is that they often find a kind of revealed positive sociology in the fact that men exist within family and state, as if there were a clear pattern for these institutions ordained by God. This, as has often been seen, can lead to a false identification of an existing historical pattern with the divine order, and thus to an uncritical, conservative acceptance of a *status quo*. We have now properly learned to speak of ordering rather than orders, in the light of the errors of the past, or to use a different set of words, community can be interpreted functionally, as accomplishing purposes needed for human life. Its particular form or order is to be judged by its effectiveness in fulfilling its morally purposive functions. God sustains and restrains life through the functions of state and family and other institutions, as well as the historical occasions for them occur; through the development of mass public education, through the work of universities and their institutes, through political parties, through labor unions and through international organizations.

Through community, God also makes better qualities of life possible for men. Indeed, while sin is not redeemed by community, God's redemptive love can take particular historical force and form through the relations that persons have with and for each other. Even civil law, as an establishment of new patterns of justice and order in human society, functions to bring new possibilities or qualities of life into being in particular societies. The order of law and the order of society can be the means by which God's love makes possible better existence both for social groups and for individuals.

Community, then, through God's creative use of it, has a high order of theological dignity in a Christian interpretation; it is not merely something oppressive, hostile to authentic life, embodying sin and prejudice. The social mission of the Church, in turn, needs to be related to each of these aspects of God's purposes in view.

It would be very one-sided, however, to acknowledge that the corrupt, the demonic, the sinful did not also exist in human community. At least since the time of A. Ritschl and W. Rauschenbusch we have come to understand the existence of "kingdom [or perhaps better, realm] of sin." To cite the positive significance of custom and tradition for human community in the economy of God does not imply that custom cannot be perverse and run counter to God's purposes for man. The embedding of racial prejudice within social custom is one case in point. Tradition can also be oppressive, functioning as an idol that prohibits men from responding to the call of God in the openness of the present. . . . But we err if we see only their perversity, or if we fail to give them a high level of dignity in our understanding of God's work for men.

Community and Moral Action

These same patterns of God's care for man that are apparent in human community are also the patterns of mutual service, responsibility and obligation within which men are called to moral action. Christians together in the Church are particularly called to interpret their existence in community as the location in time and space of their responsibility to God for human society and for other persons. To participate in a cultural ethos, in a moral tradition, is to have responsibility for that ethos and tradition. To be personally related to another is joyfully to serve the other and to be obligated for his well-being. To function as a person within an institution is to see the power of the institution as the means for the upbuilding of humanity and to acknowledge the responsibility of the institution for the preservation of justice, liberty and order in the world. The patterns of common life are patterns of service, responsibility and obligation in a Christian interpretation of community, to God and to men. They are patterns in and through which moral activity takes place.

In response to God's goodness man freely and joyfully serves not only individual neighbors, but the common life that binds men together. This is most easily seen in the realm of interpersonal relations. . . . In response to the love of God and the love of theirs, freely given, faithfully given service is an expression of moral action. But service is not confined to the interpersonal.

Participation in a location of responsibility in an institution is also a call to service. Consciousness of the care of God for the human community through government and university, through voluntary associations and political parties, evokes a response of grateful service to others through these institutions. They are the spheres in which freedom, love and concern are expressed. Their own internal structures can be shaped in part by expressions of freely given love and care. They can be shaped in part to be consonant with purposes that express the Christians' response to God's goodness.

Life in community is also a life in common responsibility.[3] It is the acceptance of accountability for the shaping of the values and customs that inform much of the unconscious responses and actions of the members of the human community. Community is held together by custom and tradition; good and evil are embedded in custom and tradition; custom and tradition shape the character of persons and institutions so that loyalties and convictions drawn from them inform the responses and actions of persons, even when they are not aware of them. . . .

The Christian community has the responsibility to articulate and criticize this glue of custom that holds societies together. If tradition and custom regard Negroes or certain castes as inferior and dictate prejudiced attitudes and actions toward such groups, it is the responsibility of the Christian community to engage in the alteration of these forces. . . . Through instruction, prophetic writing, the nurturing of the minds and spirits of children and other means, the Christian community can exercise influence in shaping the forces that in turn invisibly shape the attitudes, responses and actions of men.

Interpersonal relations are relations of responsibility. They exist not merely as occasions of joyfully given service, and certainly not merely as occasions for self-realization. Faithfulness of one for the other is an aspect of the interpersonal. To be for the person is to be faithful to the other person, to accept responsibility for the well-being of the other. Through interpersonal relations, God cares for the well-being both of the self and of the other. As active persons in these relations, Christians interpret them as occasions of responsibility to God for the care of others. . . . Indeed, responsibility for each other is a structure of love, not merely the occasion for love. It is a pattern of service and responsibility. . . .

The formal and informal patterns of relationships established within institutions and between them are clearly patterns of responsibility. As active agents in institutions, Christians patricularly interpret them as centers of power and influence the conduct of which has moral consequences in the society, and therefore institutions are to be understood in terms of moral responsibility. This responsibility is not a thing, a substance, as it were, that institutions could have. It is rather to be articulated in detailed terms for particular institutions; for the political party, the management of a small business and so forth. Christian interpretation asks certain questions of institutions: For what is this institution responsible? How do its purposes cohere with an informed understanding of the manner and ends of life that Christians believe to be consonant with what God is seeking to say and to do? How can persons in institutions act to give direction to their activities so that the well-being of humanity is sustained and improved by the policies and activities of institutions? In the divine economy, institutions and their relations to each other are patterns of social life in and through which moral responsibility—to God, for the human community—are exercised.

Obligation—a stronger word than responsibility—also enters in. Life in community is life in a structure of moral obligations, of claims upon persons and of claims upon groups. To participate in the community of custom and tradition is to be obligated to God for its rectitude and its nurture, for its continuity insofar as its effects reflect an understanding of what God wills to do for men, and for its alteration insofar as it is a corruption of what God seeks to do and to say. To be sure, the Christian community is in a sense emancipated from cultural ethos; it certainly does not find its final righteousness and justification in its responsibility for the customs and traditions of the society of which it forms a part. Its loyalty to God gives it a position over against custom and tradition, its faith gives it a freedom from bondage to social custom and tradition. But this freedom ought not to imply that the Christian community has no obligation to God for the sustenance and cultivation of those customs and traditions which can be a means of God's governing and edifying work in the world. . . . The Christian community is obligated to God, who rules and upbuilds through culture for the moral quality of that culture.

Mutual obligation is an aspect of interpersonal relations as well. Personal relations, if they are significant, exist over long periods of time and across the boundaries of spatial separation. To be for the other person is to delight in his presence; it is also to be responsible for him, to be obligated to him. . . . In many forms of personal relationship there is a formal rite which not only confirms that two persons will be faithful to each other, but that they are obligated to each other. The marriage service is . . . an excellent example of this fact. There, a covenant is made between two persons, before God and a congregation of his people, which details some of the obligations that exist, by virtue not only of the freely given love of one for the other, but of the fact that this love is a faithful and responsible love. As such, it is fitting that there be an articulated, determined detailing of the structure of obligations that both express love and nourish love. Obligation in personal relations is not antithetical to love; it is a form or responsible and faithful love. Marriage is not the only interpersonal relationship in which this is the case.

"Steadfastness" or faithfulness as an aspect of interpersonal relations, with the implied duties and obligations toward each other, is a part of the Old Testament interpretation both of covenant and of love. It is not a nineteenth-century or post-Kantian imposition of extrinsic rules or duties upon persons. It is part of the Christian conviction, born of God's revelation of himself, that informs the Church's understanding of relations between persons. In the time of a "new morality" that comes into being under Christian auspices, a morality that smacks of a kind of shallow concern with self-realization, it is perhaps even more important to see the significance of the structure of personal relations as a structure of mutual obligations of persons to each other and for the consequences of their common life.[4]

In the institutional spheres of life, the aspect of obligation is more clearly seen. Institutions have rules and laws which articulate the obligations that persons have toward each other, and the duties that they have toward the institution. But a Christian interpretation is not mere support of obedience to institutional laws and rules; it is rather an understanding that institutions and those acting in and through them are obligated to God for the conduct of affairs, and thus obligated to the persons and society of which they are a part for the actions and effects of the state, the economy and so forth. Institutions are locations in which man's obligations to God and to other men have a concreteness, a virtually material quality, which expresses man's moral discernment and care. The Christian community is obligated first to God and then to and for the institutions in and through which duties toward God and the neighbors can be carried out.

Implications for the Mission of Church to Society

Some suggestions about the implications of this interpretation for the work of the Church seem to be in order. . . .

First, and most obvious, is the need to keep all three aspects of community in view. Those activities of the Churches and other agencies that view the Christian concern to be primarily personal obviously tend to neglect the institutional patterns of society. The concern for the personal often leads to a disengagement from the realm of the technical and the impersonal. . . . It becomes difficult to move from the existential and the personal to the technological and institutional if one's interpretation of modern communities, in the theological and sociological terms, places the weight of importance and dignity on the realm of subjectively meaningful existence. The kind of mutual involvement that develops between persons through the impersonal patterns of large-scale social organizations provides, in the light of my interpretation, both for significant, meaningful life, and for moral activity in giving some direction to the course of human events. God's purposes, as discerned in the Scripture and in tradition, relate to the historical course of events, and *ipso facto* to technology, bureaucracy and other aspects of industrial societies that are of crucial importance in our time.

Second, these activities on the part of Churches and other agencies that are institution—and "world"—orientated must not lose sight of the importance of the "private" and the personal as spheres that sustain persons in their institutions, and more particularly as places in which there is a formation of outlook and of values that in turn deeply affects the kind of judgments and actions that persons make in their "offices" or institutional responsibilities. The private sphere is not only a place of escape from the pressures of the institutional sphere; . . . it is a place in which are formed the attitudes, reflective moral commitments and motives that persons carry into the institutional and technical world. . . . If an understanding of community as a process of action within orderly patterns has validity, attention has to be paid to the spheres within which moral habits, character, decision, indeed, virtues and their opposites are shaped.

Third, the interpretation given in this essay calls for a far more extensive place for the virtues than popularly exists in Protestant ethics today. Basic selfhood is shaped in the "private" and interpersonal spheres, in the family, the congregation and other centers where the attitudes and values of persons are formed, criticized and in part re-formed. Protestant theology has for too long tended to assume that the language of the "virtues" necessarily implied an uncritical approval of bourgeois attitudes, or suggested that to take the task of shaping the conscience, or of shaping virtues seriously is to live by self-righteousness and law rather than by grace. Indeed, in societies which are undergoing rapid change, with traditional external standards in flux, it is all the more important that the basic loyalties and convictions of persons shall have a measure of stability and clarity, so that their participation in the world may receive direction and purpose.

Fourth, participation in institutions on the part of the members of the Christian community ought to be governed in part by their life of faith, and by purposes, objectives, means of action that reflect the Christian gospel and are informed by the ethical reflection of the community. Life in the Church is life revivified by fresh apprehension of God as the sovereign ruler of the world, by renewed dedication to his purposes that is engendered by worshipping him, by informed conscientiousness about the responsibilities and actions in the world that are coherent with the Church's understanding of what God seeks to have this world to be. It is in the common life of the Church that both intentions and dispositions on the internal, subjective side are to be engendered, fashioned, critically scrutinized and articulated. There is no doubt that the Churches as we know them have been remiss in fulfilling this moral function, but we have no other historical social unit within which these functions, in allegiance to Jesus Christ, are performed.

Fifth, culture, or ethos must not be left out of the purview of Christian interpretation and action in society. It is notoriously difficult to influence, since its values and styles are developed by so many different agencies. Protestant Churches, and others as well, when they have addressed the problems of culture, have often made sweeping critical attacks about "materialism" rather than finding ways in which to influence the goals and purposes that persons seem to absorb from their milieu. The place that is given to culture in the interpretation offered in this essay calls for a continuous dialogue between the Christian community and other groups, all of which are involved in the shaping of culture. . . . Rejection of culture is largely gone as a stance of the Christian community. But apart from persistent critique of it, accompanying our constant involvement in it, we are seriously faced with the temptation to become a new generation of culture Christians, and in our critique of it we often fail in two respects: the faith becomes too readily identified only with the movements of protest against mass culture, and it begins to look as if the Christians had their stakes exclusively in the causes of angry young men; and in our antibourgeois sentiments, some of which are in harmony with the claims of the gospel, we are prone to isolate the critical concerns for culture from the daily involvements in it of unexciting, hum-drum mothers, children, clerks, executives, laborers and professional people. Too often Christian critiques of culture are critiques of the Christian cultural *elite* who, by virtue of their own advanced tastes and training, have separated themselves from the masses whose daily involvement in ordinary affairs God uses and on whom the *elites* depend.

Finally, we need to find a way in which to reintroduce the idea of obligations and responsibilities without falling into the traps of legalism and heteronomy. These are the traps that ethics is most conscious of today, sometimes at the expense of the right sense of duties and obligations. Indeed, it becomes easy to slip from an antilegalism into an ethic of self-realization in which immediate fulfillment of desires, rather than deepest human needs, is the goal of life. Grace and love drive us from within to become involved in the needs of the neighbor and in the suffering of the world, but under God's sovereign rule we are obligated to take on the burdens of the world as his responsible deputies, even when inner disposition is weak. Life is to find fulfillment in the relations between persons of each sex, but the fulfillment is also one of the duties and obligations that we have toward each other by virtue of these relationships in the divine economy. Faith and love bring us a new sense of freedom, but a pattern of responsibilities and obligations exists to keep that freedom directed toward those things which are helpful and which build up. Neither we nor the world is as "mature" as we are often told, and in the absence of such maturity the necessity of rule and authority under God in determining conduct and activity is indispensable. God's concern for the ordering of human society so that freedom and fulfillment can abound is as much a part of his purposes as is his emancipating men from the bondage of false orders and outdated rules. The interpretation given in this essay calls for more detailed understanding of the Church's activity in society in terms of the ordering of institutions and of the duties and obligations of persons at each place of Christian life in the world.

1. This section has clear echoes of the thought of my late colleague and teacher, H. Richard Niebuhr, which I readily and gratefully acknowledge, although he would not necessarily approve of precisely what I have done here.

2. A question is implicit here that deserves long and serious study. One gets the impression that much of the Christian social leadership and experimentation is now directed toward those who are alienated from the past and from present communities, and some of it makes for an attitude not just of criticism of "establishment," but of sheer rebellion against establishment as a prime virtue. I do not wish to suggest that particular attention to the depressed and the "outsiders" is not important, but some of it is being given to the neglect of meaningful interpretation of the significance of pattern and order for human beings, and of the ways in which old orders can be reformed to fulfill better the necessary functions of human social life. We seem to be much clearer about the oppressions of custom and institutions that sustain us than we are about their positive functions in the sustaining of human life, and thus about how these patterns themselves can be altered better to fulfill their essential moral purposes.

3. For a succinct account of the nature of responsibility, see **H. R. Niebuhr: The Responsible Self,** New York, Harper & Row, 1963.

4. One looks in vain for any serious discussion of obligations in the books that often are covered by the appellation "new morality," such as J. A. T. Robinson's chapter, "The New Morality" in **Honest to God,** and Paul Lehmann's **Ethics in a Christian Context,** New York, Harper & Row, 1963. One suspects this is so because obligation suggests law, and law seems to be antithetical to an ethics of grace in which the "divine indicative" has such clear centrality of attention.

SECULAR SOCIETY OR PLURALISTIC COMMUNITY?

PAUL VERGHESE

The secularization of society in which many Christian thinkers have shown an approving interest should be clearly distinguished from the ideology of *secularism*. Christian advocates of the former roundly repudiate the latter, although the two have this in common: they are both concerned only with this world and not with any other. Ideological secularism confers on the *seculum* an absolute meaning and value, which can be discovered by rational means. For the Christian advocate of secularization, *seculum* must be understood in reference to a reality which is not human; for the secularist, "man is the measure of all things."

Secularization is a process, continuing and dynamic, which has been described as "the withdrawal of areas of life and thought from religious—and finally also from metaphysical—control, and the attempt to understand and live in these areas in the terms which they alone offer." But here is its dilemma: the secularist and the Christian may agree on both the definition and the positive response to secularization, and yet differ in their basic assumptions, and in their evaluation and expectations of man, nature and history.

The secularist is basically optimistic about man, his reason, his destiny and his nature. The Christian advocate of secularization cannot be described as a pessimist: he would rather call himself a realist. He has no illusions about the perfectibility of man, no preconceived notions of what is or what to expect. He is agile and plastic, willing to adjust to new circumstances, never surprised by the turn of events, ready to reconsider earlier judgments in the light of subsequent experience. All but crushed by the realization of the complexity of the relationships within which he lives, he yet seeks valiantly to retain his freedom as a person and not to be crushed by the leveling forces on mass society. He seeks with great skill and some success to identify the new gods of the secularist—whether they be an idolized technology, an absolutized scientism, the worship of power, a frantic nationalism or even a secular-cultural religion—and to expose them as vain idols. Even cynicism, which recognizes no absolutes and is in this sense dangerously close to this type of Christian position, is exposed as making self-interest the ultimate view. The Christian secularists do not belong to any of the philosophical schools, though they learn from them all.

The current definitions of secular society all seem to agree that it is a state of human relations in which no religion or world view (ideology) dominates. But this is not a practical possibility. We do not know of the existence of any such society at any time, including the present. Even modern science and technology have their origin in a "religion" or "world view," as Edwin A. Burtt demonstrates in *The Metaphysical Foundations of Modern Science* or C. F. von Weizsacker in *Zum Weltbild der Physik.* Man can refuse to formulate his "metaphysical" world view, but he cannot live, think or act without consciously or unconsciously holding such presuppositions. All he can hope for, within the limits of the human mind and its time-existence, is that he will be aware of the tentative and hypothetical character of his world view, and be constantly on the alert to revise it in the light of experience and experiment.

Even if "religion" were to be banished by the concerted efforts of the secularizers, some world views would still dominate. Not only the Marxists, but even Christian secularizers have a world view. It may not be articulately or consciously held, but it is there. They may not hold their world view as a final absolute, but they would like to see it dominate.

Some theologians also tend to argue that the concept of the secular implies the absence of a common understanding of the timeless order of reality. But what is the "timeless order of reality"? Those religious schools, like Vedanta or Zen Buddhism, which seem to know, insist that it be beyond human conception, without quality or extension. Christians can think only of the creator God as belonging to the timeless order, since time belongs to creation and God is not part of it. We ought not to speak of the "reality of God" as a secular reality since god is not simply a reality within the *seculum,* though our knowledge of that reality is secular, or acquired in time-existence. And if that is so, then it is impossible for Christians to "believe in one God the Father Almighty, maker of heaven and earth, and of all things visible and invisible" and not to have faith in some order of reality that transcends time and space.

The problem of adequately defining "secular" has led the present writer to be skeptical of the efforts not only of his Christian friends in the West, but even of his own country's non-Christian government. The anomalies of Indian "secular" society have been adequately lampooned by critics both within and without the country. Yet it remains true that we are all groping toward a certain type of society for which we have yet neither an adequate name nor an articulate theoretical conception. If we were to speak of an "authentic" rather than a "secular" society, we would soon discover that Greek *authentia* means *absolute sway* or *absolute authority* (from *autoentes*—one who does something with his own hand), which may mean that the "authentic" society, recognized no norms outside itself. This cannot be what the secularizationist seeks, for he wants "to understand and live in these areas in the terms which they alone offer," but does not want to invest those terms with any degree of finality. Is it possible for a Christian to conceive of a society which has no norms outside itself? Would not the "declaration of human rights" of the UN come into the category of something which transcends the terms which society normally offers? On what secular basis do we assert the dignity of man or the principle of equity— on the basis of social experience?

We need, at least for our own use among Christians, a slightly different voocabulary. It is not easy to find a surrogate term for the "Kingdom of God manifesting itself in history," which is what we are groping for. This kingdom could not be "secular" in any "authentic" sense. Its very roots would be in the transcendent *eschaton,* in that "timeless order of reality" whence it has entered into the order of time-space. A happier term may be "pluralistic human community," provided "pluralistic" and "human" are precisely defined. Pluralism means more than mere variety. Without some unity within the diversity, we should simply have a chaotic or anarchic rather than a pluralistic society. That element of unity should be spelled out as the definition of the term "human."

But this society cannot constantly be working out its own terms from within itself. It will need the presence within it of a transcendent unit which will constantly challenge its attempts to become "authonormic." This unit will normally be a small prophetic group within the Christian church of the country, though they may be joined by men of good will who are not Christians. They will not make this challenge on the grounds of any temporal authority vested in them. They may use all the normal channels provided within the structure of "law and order." But it will be for them to decide in conscience when the challenge must assume extralegal forms. This will mean the acceptance of suffering and of opposition from the majority in society, and, if necessary, of death. But this cannot be undertaken by a group of people who have no transcendent loyalty, though radicalism often goes with professed atheism. It would be strange indeed if a constitution were to provide for the "right of conscience" to violate the constitution. That right in the final analysis will have to remain something which transcends the constitution itself—the right of appeal to the deepest elements of freedom in the human person.

The yearning for a purely "secular" society among some western thinkers seems to be a reaction to the history of ecclesiastical ideological domination in the western past. As a "reaction ideology" it may be creative in challenging the entrenched positions of the old order. It may even be aware of the danger of becoming itself an "ideology." However, it can never claim to become an adequate substitute for the traditional Christian pattern of social thinking.

The Elements of a Pluralistic Community

What then are the elements of a "pluralistic human community" as a Christian conceives it? The concept of "pluralism" comes, for the Christian, not from social experience, but rather from the doctrine on the Holy Spirit. Similarly, the concept of "human" has its roots, not in the tradition of secular western or eastern humanism, but in the fact of the Incarnation itself. It is methodologically important to start our Christian social thinking from these two fundamental realities of the Christian faith, rather than from the Old Testament doctrines of the call of Abraham, or the "history of salvation." Underlying these twin doctrines of the Incarnation[1] and the Holy Spirit is the fundamental concept of "freedom in love."

Freedom is by definition not open to definition, since what is defined is no longer free. Yet certain statements can be made about freedom, including that already made in the previous sentence. "Freedom" is both a relational or functional concept and an "ontological" or "being" concept. The being of God is a "free" being, and therefore does not lend itself to exhaustive definition or even exhaustive revelation. The revealed God is also a *deus absconditus*. He is Yahweh, God who will be what he is or is what he will be (*"ehyeh asher" ehveh*). This is an ontological and not a functional or relational statement about the being of God; but not about a static being, who can be defined even by this statement. When we say that God is "free," we do not mean to define God. We mean primarily that God's being is not determined by anything outside it, but by his own will. And that will is free—free not only *from* external constraint or bondage, but free *to* fulfill that which it wills. That is the twin meaning of freedom—the absence of heteronomy and the presence of infinite power to accomplish what is willed.

"God is love" is also a biblical statement, though the converse, "Love is God" is not.[2] Love exists only in a context of freedom in a community of persons. Love also defies definition. But some statements could be made about it. It is nothing less than beneficent intersubjectivity in freedom, the principle of interpersonal relationship within the Holy Trinity and therefore of human relationships within society. This twin principle has, as far as we can see, an enduring validity for all societies. And therefore we need to consider it in connection with the Incarnation of our Lord Jesus Christ.

Man is made in the image of God, and Jesus Christ is the image or *eikon* of God. An icon is not a representation of someone who is absent (as is often the case of a photograph or a statue) but the mark of a presence. The presence of man in the creation is thus a concrete presence of God within it. Jesus Christ is the *presence par excellence* of God, not only within history, but in physical nature. "God became flesh" is not simply a historical statement, but is related equally to physical reality or nature. "Became" refers to history, "flesh" relates to matter or nature. Any separation of history and "nature" seems therefore contrary to the Incarnation. The Incarnation is both "ontic" and historical. It is by *fiat,* since he is free and his will is unbounded. But precisely because he is free, and man is made to be his *eikon* in love and freedom, he chose the means of incarnate involvement rather than imperious *fiat.*

The tragedy of the Corpus Christianum lies in its forgetting of this fundamental principle. The "two-edged sword" of the medieval papacy and the *cuis regio eius religio* principle of the Lutheran Reformation both militated against this principle of the incarnation. In a genuinely pluralistic human society there can be no imposition of religious or political views by *fiat,* instead of loving persuasion. But this immediately raises the related question of the role of authority, law and punishment in such a society.

Incarnation does not effect a radical break with the past. Automatic righteousness which needed no law was often associated with the hopes of a messianic age. But in practice the tension between the external authority of the law and the loving and wise actions of freedom continued to manifest itself even in the apostolic community. The "royal law"—"Love thy neighbor as thyself"—comprehends statutory law but, until society achieves maturity, statutory law will be the form in which most of the negative and some of the positive requirements of the royal law will be met. For example, statutory law can regulate murder but not hatred; it can give structure to the needy (through social security or other forms of taxation) but not to compassion as a free expression of intersubjectivity. In the pluralistic human society authority and law have to be constituted as frameworks which can be finally dispensed with, when voluntary love, or beneficient intersubjectivity in freedom, can progressively grow to fruition. This is why neither law nor authority can be ultimate in society. Education, through family, school or "mass media," should be seen as a tool in the progressive elimination of authoritarian legal structures and the introduction of higher degrees of voluntary beneficence. Punishment yields to correctional education, no longer seen as a deterrent based on fear, but as a means of redeeming the culprit himself.

Law and order thus become relative to the ultimate objective—the production of creative intersubjectivity in freedom. Revolution becomes a necessary corrective to outmoded structures of law and order rather than a threat to security and well-being. The transition from a law-and-order state to a welfare state can thus be seen as a progressive step toward the kingdom; yet the welfare state itself stands under the judgment of the principle of creative and beneficent intersubjectivity in freedom. Insofar as it stifles freedom and promotes lazy parasitism, it must itself be resructured and remodeled.

The Place of the Church in a Pluralistic Human Society

The destruction of the Temple (A.D. 70) is often adduced as an argument for desacralization and secularization. Nothing could be more misleading. The cleansing of the Temple at the beginning of Christ's ministry was symbolic of the destruction of the temple that was to follow the establishment of the church. To conceive of the Temple as a symbol of the "ontocratic" pattern is to misunderstand it completely. For the Jews it was the *eikon* of the "presence" of Yahweh in the midst of his covenant people. The *shekinah*-presence in the temple and in the person of Christ[3] are serially related to each other. Equally important is the Old Testament figure of the ladder which reaches up to heaven in Jacob's dream, which van Leeuven would too easily interpret in terms of the "ontocratic pattern" rather than in terms of the more biblical scheme of antetype and fulfillment. In the Fourth Gospel, Christ is the true ladder (John 1:51); and the true temple (John 2). He boldly calls the temple "my father's house" (*ho oikos tou patros mou*), and goes on to identify it with the "temple of his body" (*ho naos tou so matos mou*).[4] The first phrase is repeated in Chapter 14, with reference to the place which he is going to prepare for his disciples.

The destruction of the temple is thus to be seen as the result of its replacement by a living temple. "We (plural) are the temple of the living God."[5] The temple is the new community. God is now to be encountered by Jews and Gentiles, not at Jerusalem, but wherever the community is. There is no "desacralization" or "secularization," but the fulfillment of the antetype of the temple by its archtype, Christ, and his body the Church. The new temple, not made with hands, remains in the midst of the world as the organism of the new community, Jesus Christ himself being the chief cornerstone. This is a recurring theme in the New Testament,[6] which we overlook at great peril to the very core of our faith.

The Church can be called a secular reality only insofar as it manifests itself in time. But the church certainly transcends the *seculum*. If it is truly the risen and ascended Body of Christ, then its limits are not set by the curvature of the time-space cosmos. Its foundation is in Jesus Christ, who is seated at the right hand of the Father. He was present in the time-space world at a certain point—Palestine in the first century. But that is not where we encounter him today.

The Ascension is an integral part of the Incarnation. Jesus told his disciples that it was necessary for him to ascend to the Father. Only so could he prepare for an abiding place for them. The very existence of the Church was a consequence of Ascension and Pentecost, both of which events link time with the transtemporal.

The presence of this transtemporal "secular" society within human society alone gives the latter meaning and purpose. The Church serves the society in which it is placed in a threefold sense: (a) as the Temple of God in the midst of time-space existence; (b) as the royal priesthood within that temple; (c) as the model and pattern for the human commonwealth. The idea that the Church is placed in time-space only to preach the gospel constitutes a major misconception of Reformed ecclesiology. The Church does exist to proclaim the gospel and to speak the prophetic word about the will of God for the world, but the very performance of that function depends on the fulfillment of its threefold vocation in the Holy Spirit:

a. *The temple of God.* The theologian claims that modern secular man is so desacralized that he no longer has any use for temples. On the contrary, he needs and desperately longs for a temple—a place where he can encounter the living God. Modern literature is full of veiled or explicit references to this deep hunger in the secular man's consciousness. Both those who proclaim that "God is dead" and those who are either seeking to be "honest to God" or "waiting for Godot" express this need.

The Church exists in the midst of secular society as something that does not easily fit in. That is its vocation. It cannot be the temple of God, if it becomes merely a lecture room or a "gospel hall." If God is totally other, and has to be encountered, the time and place of that theophany have to be distinct from the timespace of ordinary existence. The Church need not set out to be archaic, obscure, irrelevant and peculiar, but if it is the community of the Holy Spirit, it will express itself in forms that do not fit in to the "secularized" world. We shall discuss below how the community is to become such a temple.

b. *The royal priesthood.* . . . No secular society can be authentic without the presence within it of the Christian community as temple of God and royal priesthood. But to be the royal priesthood also means to exercise a perpetual ministry of self-offering and intercession. The Church's continuous worship and prayer in the midst of the secular community preserves, transforms and sanctifies that community, often without its knowledge, sometimes against its will.

Worship is an act of freedom and love, not subsidiarity to anything else; and yet worship and prayer become instrumental in the transformation of society itself. Christ was a man of action. So were the apostles—or at least some of them. But Christ and his apostles spent much more time in prayer than in action. Our perennial temptation is to put our trust mainly in our words and actions. Claiming to be prophets, we can miss the secret of the prophets and the true mark of the royal priesthood—sustained and disciplined prayer. The secular society for which we are struggling is then in peril of becoming anything but authentic.

c. *The model and pattern for the human commonwealth.* It is perhaps only an idle dream or a pious wish. But the Church is called to be the manifestation of the kingdom of God in history. And that kingdom has three fundamental interrelated principles: love, freedom and wisdom.

The Church does its work in the world, not through ecclesiastical domination, but by identifying with the world in such a way that it continues to be a true agent and is not reduced to a passive listener or recipient. It is in this sense that the Church becomes a model for the human commonwealth.

The Three Principles

The three principles of a "pluralistic human community"—love, freedom and wisdom—have their origin in the very being of God and, as the Church manifests these, it becomes a theophany or the temple of God.

a. *Freedom.* There is no definition for freedom—nor for love nor wisdom: all three have their origin in God. One of the few things we can say about God is that he is free, loving and wise. In fact he *is* freedom, love and wisdom. We should be careful about making "is-statements" about God. He is. But to put a "subjective complement" to the verb can be dangerous, for that is to try to define God. And yet neither freedom nor love nor wisdom is a definitive concept. They derive their meaning from the "being" or "is-ness" of God, which is itself beyond definition and constantly free.

Freedom is more than the liberty of choice, or the absence of external constraint. Freedom means the possibility of achieving what one wills, unhindered by external constraint or lack of power. Power in this sense is synonymous with freedom: lack of power is lack of freedom. God alone is free. He wills, and it is done. Nothing "outside" him limits his freedom, except that which he has willed to create. But even the creation does not exist "outside" God. It is always in him and therefore under his power. Man is made "in the image" of God and therefore made for freedom. In Christ, man is adopted as the Son of God. "The sons are free," says our Lord in Matthew 17:26. We have been called "into the freedom of the glory of the children of God" (Romans 8:21).

Stemming from St. Augustine, there exists, especially in the western tradition, what Eric Fromm calls "the fear of freedom."

The fear of freedom, which denies freedom to err, too easily assumes the possession of articulate truth. The Church thus sought to guard the truth both by temporal power and by exact formulation. Ever since the Reformation we have been witnessing the effective revolt against both the false claim and the human attempt to defend the truth. That very revolt, however, has led to new errors which made individual judgment the arbiter of truth and developed a new corpus of pseudo-biblical truth. The present secular revolt asserts the freedom of man over against the dogmatic formulations on both sides of the sixteenth-century controversy. It has its roots in the freedom of man rather than in Christianity as van Leeuwen claims. Confronted by the apparently contradictory authority of "church" and "Bible," modern man slowly discovered the experimental or pragmatic notion of truth which bases itself neither on dogmatic authority nor on individual judgment, but on repeatable, demonstrable, public experiments and eventually on the laws of mathematics.

Technology also has its roots in the freedom of man. Man belongs to the biological continuum of evolution and has been carried along by it. The evolution of his consciousness has also resulted in his emancipation from the blind movement of evolution. He has become aware of himself and of his environment. Instead of being transmuted by the forces of the cosmos, he seeks to understand them and to transmute them and himself. Even primitive man's patterns of social organization and methods of forming tools are part of this evolution of human freedom. The Greeks held that *techne* and *politike* were the gifts of the gods to men. Modern science and technology belong to this continuum which has its origin in pre-Christian and extra-Hebraic society. Whenever men learned through experience and devised tools, there were science and technology. They belonged to the freedom of man to emancipate himself from the cosmic forces and to gain control of them.

Christians in the past have always tended to look upon power as neutral, if not evil. This springs from a basic misunderstanding. The ability to transcend the evolutionary process through self-awareness and through understanding of the environment, and then to redirect the evolutionary process itself by changes in the self and in the environment is an integral part of human freedom. Insofar as they help to create that ability, science and technology—and the power derived from them—are good, not evil or neutral.

One must welcome freedom, even when its emergence is accompanied by acute suffering. For example, the liberation of the Congolese people from the Belgian yoke may not seem to be an unmitigated good. It is accompanied by savage and brutal acts of inhuman cruelty. Is it not destroying the dignity of man? Would it not have been better if Belgium had kept the Congolese under tutelage for another thirty or sixty years as they had originally intended? The answer is an unequivocal No. Freedom could not have emerged in western Europe if the primary concern had been for nonviolence, law and order. Some lessons have to be learned by experience. If Europe, after centuries of "civilization," has not yet learned to avoid war and to respect the dignity of men, we should give the Congolese at least half a generation in which to come to terms with their own situation. Freedom should be welcomed by the Christian, even when it is freedom from forces favorable to Christianity and the Church. Freedom should also be granted to err, since the truth cannot fear error. Every advancement in the knowledge and power for mankind should be heartily welcomed by the Church.

There are areas, however, where freedom does not so easily emerge. The New Testament speaks of freedom as being free from sin, law and death (Romans 5:8). Man's bondage to evil and guilt, to dependence on heteronomous structures and to fear of death, as well as to the disintegration of personality and society, must also be broken, if a genuinely human society is to emerge.

The greatest problem of freedom, however, is the possibility of its dissociation from love and wisdom.

b. *Love and justice.* To say that "justice" is an approximation of love can be misleading. Both justice and love are social realities. But justice, understood in the traditional Roman sense, seems to be opposed to love rather than to approximate it. Underlying the concept of justice is the notion of rights and duties, which do not properly belong to love. This is the crisis of western society. It has proceeded on the assumption that "social justice" is the highest attainable value and has often failed to see the great gap between it and love. The end result is that while western societies are incomparably more "just" than societies in eastern Europe or in Asia, Africa and Latin America, genuine intersubjectivity is becoming increasingly problematic in the West.

Here we come to the delicate question of structures and persons. Can "love" be built into structures? Justice certainly can. But justice operates primarily in the areas of external actions and cannot deal directly with the "inner" man.[7] However, even the maintenance of justice cannot be assured by the structures. Where men are willing to sacrifice their freedom for the sake of some lesser good, justice always succumbs despite all structures. To think therefore of the "principalities and powers" as resident primarily in the power structures is a gross oversimplification. The demonic cannot be kept out by structures of any kind. Only the vigilance of human freedom and love combined with divine wisdom can struggle successfully against the principalities and powers. Social injustice is indeed demonic, and the demons must be unseated from the control-chambers of society. Yet even within the most just social structures the most demonic of all forces—the denial of freedom and love—can persist.

But what is this love that we oppose to justice? It is the greatest gift of the Spirit, greater than the power of miracles or of speaking in tongues. It is the one gift that is bestowed on all and without which all other gifts of the Spirit are of no avail (I Corinthians 13:1-3). All social action and all acts of sacrifice are without value if they are not accompanied by love. Even faith, without love, is nothing.

Although love should never be identified with the merely sentimental and emotional, it does involve sentiments and emotions as well as the will and the mind. Paul begins his famous exhortation on love by describing it in the concepts of generosity . . . and kindness. . . . Our own traditional understanding of love includes two characteristics which are contradictory to the Pauline understanding—*limitation* and *possession*. We love someone more *than* we love others. We have to exclude others, in order to love one. We choose the person whom we love. Family love is limited to those who are related to us by blood or marriage. The objective of romantic love is the possession of the beloved.

The range of Christian love is as wide as humanity. Whoever the man is whom I confront, I am to love him. Samaritan, Jew and Gentile are alike: humanity is the limit. And *com-passion* rather than possession is the motivation. We enter into the other's being, feel, think and act with him and in his best interests. We allow him to enter into ours as well. This is true *com-passion,* true Kindness, true intersubjectivity. It is not simply dialogue or communication, but rather communion, or *koinonia,* the word we often translate as "fellowship." This ability to enter into all men, and openness to all men that they may enter into us, is the precondition of love and its primary expression. It can hardly be built into structures of social justice, though these structures are necessary for its expression. A truly pluralistic human community is one where love exists. A just society does not guarantee love. Love can exist even where there is social injustice. But without love even the just society perishes.

c. *Wisdom.* Knowledge is not wisdom. Knowledge can assist wisdom, but the two can exist apart from each other. The foundation of wisdom is truth itself, not the knowledge of truth.

The Spirit is always the spirit of truth. Our Lord promised the "spirit of truth" (Jn 14:17) who leads us into truth itself (John 16:13), not merely to a knowledge of it. Wisdom is a "being" rather than a functional category. One has to be in the truth in order to be wise (Jn 8:44). To "know the truth" (Jn 8:32) is to participate in it, to stand in it (Jn 8:44). True freedom and true love require this being in the truth. The movement from falsehood to truth is faith (the fear of the Lord) and the beginning of wisdom.

Time-space existence can be false existence. To be *ek tou kosmou* is to have a false existence. If the ground of our existence is the time-space world, that existence is founded on that which is not true is that which abides: the world passes away. The *seculum* is a flow, a passing away. We find true existence in the evanescent course of time-existence only if our foundations are in something that transcends that course and abides "forever."

The only absolute truth within the *seculum* is the presence of God within it. The Incarnation is not so much a "revelation" as a presence. Christ can therefore say that he is the truth, and the Johannine prologue can say, "We beheld his glory, full of grace and truth." The precondition of wisdom is less "knowledge" (in the sense of cognition) of this truth, than "knowledge" (in the Hebrew sense) by participation in him.

Unless our objectives and foundation of our life go beyond the *seculum,* we continue in the folly of human wisdom. Our decisions, our purposes, our science and technology cannot provide an adequate and abiding foundation for our life. These can be properly utilized only when this foundation is in the truth. Wisdom comes by the hearing of the gospel, by faith in Christ and by baptism into his Body, which alone abides. When we are in the Body of Christ, and not in our own bodies, the Spirit helps us to grow in wisdom.

Can there, then, be wisdom outside the Church, in a "pluralistic human community"? This question is wrongly formulated, for the Church and the world cannot be seen as two mutually exclusive spheres. The Church penetrates the world, as the "soul" does the body, to borrow a rather archaic analogy. The Church, though not of the world, exists in a symbiotic relationship to it. This is not to claim that whatever good there is in the world belongs to the Church by right. The spirit of truth operates in the whole of creation. Even where there is no conscious faith in Christ, no sacramental baptism into the Body of Christ, "the Spirit bloweth where it listeth."

Nor is this a question of the Church appropriating the wisdom in the world and offering it to God. As Etienne Gilson once said, it would be too easy if the scientists and technicians were to do all the work and the lazy Christians to pick it up and offer it to God. Pluralism is a true precondition of wisdom: the Church has no monopoly on it.

It seems to be God's purpose that the pursuit of knowledge should take place largely outside the Church. But this does not mean that the Church can too lightly appropriate this knowledge and transmute it into wisdom. It appears to be God's will that the Church will depend on the experience of the whole world for its own wisdom, which gives us a good reason for our "dialogue" not only with "secular" man but also with "religious" men of all faiths. But neither is the Church selfishly to seek wisdom for itself, profiting from the experience of the whole world.

The wisdom of history teaches us that the Church needs opposition and external criticism in order to be faithful to its calling; and God seems, therefore, to have decreed that the Church can find true wisdom only in a pluralistic society. The tragedy of western theology is precisely its development in an essentially homogenous society. It is to be hoped that as pluralism develops in the West and the western Church is thrown into a pluralistic world community, it will clarify its wisdom thus to the benefit of the whole world. Only thus can it have a more balanced understanding of its own contribution to wisdom, which though great, is often exaggerated.

Conclusion

Man finds himself in a pluralistic society; it is his task to make it more human and more free. The Church's role in history has been ambiguous. In large measure, it has been used of God to humanize and liberate society. But in no small measure has it strode in the way of freedom.

The growth of freedom by itself does not assure that society will be more human. The dynamic interaction and growth of power, love, and wisdom alone can make a pluralistic community more human and therefore more divine.

1. The Incarnation as a theological term in eastern Christian thought denotes the whole **oikonomia**, which begins with the Annunciation and ends with the Pentecost and the coming into being of the Christian Church. The doctrine of the Holy Spirit is thus integral to the doctrine of the Incarnation.

2. See **Bishop Robinson's Honest to God**, SCM Press, 1963, pp. 52ff.

3. John 1:14.

4. Jn 2:16-21.

5. II Cor 6:16; cf. I Cor 3:16ff., 6:19.

6. See I Cor 3:9-16, 17; 6:19, II Cor 5:1; 6:16; Eph 2:19ff.; I Pet 2:4ff.; Heb 5:6.

7. Bonhoeffer denies the existence of any distinction between inner and outer man in the Bible: **Letters and Papers from Prison**, Fontana, ed., 1963, p. 118. This is surprising in a man who knew his Bible rather well and must often have read Rom 7:22, II Cor 4:16 and Eph 3:16.

TOWARD A "POLITICAL THEOLOGY"

JOHANNES B. METZ

The subject of this paper requires development under two considerations: one, reflecting on the meaning and the task of "political theology" the other, investigating the relations between Church and world
in the light of this "political theology."

I.

The notion of political theology is ambiguous, hence exposed to
misunderstanding because it has been burdened with specific historical
connotations. I understand political theology, first of all, to be a critical
correction of present-day theology inasmuch as this theology shows an
extreme privatizing tendency (a tendency, that is, to center upon the
private person rather than "public," "political" society). At the same
time, I understand this political theology to be a positive attempt to
formulate the eschatological message under the conditions of our
present society. 1. Let me first explain the function of political theology
as a critical corrective of modern theology. I shall begin with a few
historical reflections.

The unity and coordination of religion and society, of religious
and societal existence, in former times acknowledged as an unquestion-
able reality, shattered as early as the beginning of the Enlightenment
in France. This was the first time that the Christian religion appeared
to be a particular phenomenon within a pluralistic milieu. Thus its
absolute claim to universality seemed to be historically conditioned.
This problematic situation is also the immediate foundation of the
critique developed by the Enlightenment and, later, by Marxism. From
the beginning this critique took on the shape in which it still appears
today. It approaches religion as an ideology, seeking to unmask it as
a function, as the ideological superstructure of definite societal usages
and power structures. The religious subject is being denounced as a

false consciousness, that is, it is viewed as an element of society which has not yet become aware of itself. If a theology seeks to meet such a critique, it must uncover the socio-political implications of its ideas and notions. Classic metaphysical theology failed to discharge its responsibilities in this quarrel. The reason is that its notions and categories were all founded upon the supposition that there is no problem between religion and society, between faith and societal practice. As long as this supposition was true, it was indeed possible for a purely metaphysical interpretation of religion to be societally relevant, such as was the case, for instance, in the Middle Ages with its great theologians. However, when this unity was broken, this metaphysical theology got itself into a radical crisis as the theoretical attorney in the pending case between the Christian message of salvation and socio-political reality.

The prevailing theology of recent years, a theology of transcendental, existential personalist orientation is well aware of the problematic situation created by the Enlightenment. We might even say that, in a certain sense, it originated as a reaction against this situation. Still this reaction was not direct and sustained: the societal dimension of the Christian message was not given its proper importance but, implicitly or explicitly, treated as a secondary matter. In short, the message was "privatized" and the practice of faith reduced to the timeless decision of the person. This theology sought to solve its problem, a problem born of the Enlightenment, by eliminating it. It did not pass through the Enlightenment, but jumped over it and thought thus to be done with it. The religious consciousness formed by this theology attributes but a shadowy existence to the socio-political reality. The categories most prominent in this theology are the categories of the intimate, the private, and apolitical sphere. It is true that these theologians strongly emphasize charity and all that belongs to the field of interpersonal relations; yet, from the beginning, and as though there were no questions, they regard charity only as a private virtue with no political relevance; it is a virtue of the I-Thou relation, extending to the field of interpersonal encounter, or at best to charity on the scale of the neighborhood. The category of encounter is predominant; the proper religious way of speaking is the interpersonal address; the dimensions of proper religious experience is the apex of the free subjectivity of the individual or the indisposable, the silent center of the I-Thou relation. It seems clear then that the forms of transcendental existential and personalist theology, currently predominant, have one thing in common: a trend towards the private.

The deprivatizing of theology is the primary critical task of political theology. This deprivatizing, it seems to me, is in a way as important as the program of demythologizing. At least it should have a place with a legitimate demythologizing. Otherwise, there is a danger of relating God and salvation to the existential problem of the person, of reducing them to the scale of the person, and so of downgrading the eschatological kerygma to a symbolic paraphrase of the metaphysical questionableness of man and his personal private decisions.

No doubt there is an emphasis on the individual in the message of the New Testament. We might even say that it is the gist of this message—especially in its Pauline expression—to place the individual before God. When we insist on deprivatizing, we do not in the least object to this orientation. On the contrary, for it is our contention that theology, precisely because of its privatizing tendency, is apt to miss the individual in his real existence. Today this existence is to a very great extent entangled in societal vicissitudes; so any existential and personal theology that does not understand existence as a political problem in the widest sense of the word, must inevitably restrict its considerations to an abstraction. A further danger of such a theology is that, failing to exercise its critical controlling function, it delivers faith up to modern ideologies in the area of societal and political theory. Finally, an ecclesiastical religion, formed in the light of such a privatizing theology, will tend more and more to be a "rule without ruling power, a decision without deciding power." 2. With this, the positive task of political theology comes to light. It is, to determine anew the relation between religion and society, between Church and societal "publicness," between eschatological faith and societal life; and, it should be added, "determine" is not used here in a "pre-critical" sense—that is, with the intention of a priori identifying these two realities—but "post-critically" in the sense of a "second reflection." "Theology, insofar as it is political theology, is obliged to establish this second degree reflection," when it comes to formulate the eschatological message under the conditions of the present situation of society. Hence let me briefly describe the characteristics both of this situation, that is, how it should be understood, and of the biblical message, which is the determining factor of this theological political reflection.

(a) I shall explain the situation from which today's theological reflection takes its starting point, by referring to a problem which, at least since Marx, has become unavoidable. According to Kant, a man is enlightened only when he has the freedom to make public use of his reason in all affairs. Hence the realization of this enlightenment is never a merely theoretical problem, but essentially a political one, a problem of societal conduct. In other words, it is linked with such socio-political suppositions as render enlightenment possible. Only he is enlightened who, at the same time, fights to realize those socio-political presuppositions that offer the possibility of publicly using reason. When, therefore, reason aims at political freedom and, consequently, theoretical transcendental reason appears within practical reason, rather than the reverse, a deprivatization of reason is absolutely necessary. Properly speaking, the so-called fundamental hermeneutic problem of theology is not the problem of how systematic theology stands in relation to historical theology, how dogma stands in relation to history, but what is the relation between theory and practice, between understanding the faith and social practice.

(b) Biblical tradition, in its turn, obliges us to undertake this "second reflection" on the relation between eschatological faith and societal action. Why? Because salvation, the object of the Christian faith in hope, is not private salvation. Its proclamation forced Jesus into a moral conflict with the public powers of his time. His cross is not found in the intimacy of the individual, personal heart, nor in the sanctuary of a purely religious devotion. It is erected beyond these protected and separated precincts, "outside," as the theology of the Epistle to the Hebrews tells us. The curtain of the temple is torn forever. The scandal and the promise of this salvation are public matters. This "publicness" cannot be retracted nor dissolved, nor can it be attenuated. It is a recognizable fact attending the message of salvation as it moves through history. In the service of this message, Christian religion has been charged with a public responsibility to criticize and to liberate.

Political theology seeks to make contemporary theologians aware that a trial is pending between the eschatological message of Jesus and the socio-political reality. It insists on the permanent relation to the world inherent in the salvation merited by Jesus, a relation not to be understood in a natural-cosmological but in a socio-political sense; that is, as a critical, liberating force in regard to the social world and its historical process.

It is impossible to privatize the eschatological promises of biblical tradition: liberty, peace, justice, reconciliation. Again and again they force us to assume our responsibilities toward society. No doubt, these promises cannot simply be identified with any condition of society, however we may determine and describe it from our point of view. The history of Christianity has had enough experience of such direct identification and direct "politifications" of the Christian promises. In such cases, however, the "eschatological proviso," which makes every historically real status of society appear to be provisional, was being abandoned. Note that I say "provisional," not "arbitrary." This eschatological proviso does not mean that the present condition of society is not valid. It is valid, but in the "eschatological meanwhile." It does not bring about a negative but a critical attitude to the societal present. Its promises are not an empty horizon of religious expectations; neither are they only a regulative idea. They are, rather, a critical liberating imperative for our present times. These promises stimulate and appeal to us to make them a reality in the present historical condition and, in this way, to verify them. The New Testament community knew at once that it was called to live out the coming promise under the conditions of what was their "now," and so to overcome the world. Living in accord with the promise of peace and justice implies an ever-renewed, ever-changing work in the "now" of our historical existence. This brings us, forces us, to an ever-renewed, critical, liberating position in face of the extant conditions of the society in which we live. Jesus' parables—to mention another biblical detail in this context—are parables of the kingdom of God but, at the same time, they instruct us in a renewed critical relationship to our world. Every eschatological theology, therefore, must become a political theology, that is, a (socio)-critical theology.

II.

Let us consider the concrete relation between the Church and the world in the light of political theology. The scope of this theology does not allow "world" to be understood in the sense of cosmos, in opposition to existence and person, nor as a merely existential or personal reality. It requires it to be understood as a societal reality, viewed in its historical becoming. In this context, "Church" is not a reality beside or over this societal reality; rather, it is an institution within it, criticizing it, having a critical liberating task in regard to it.

1. If formed by the eschatological promises, faith again and again takes on a critical task with regard to the society in which the faithful live. This was the conclusion of our considerations on political theology. The question now is: Can this task be left to the individual believer? Will he be able to perform it authoritatively and effectively? Is it not, therefore, precisely this critical task of faith which, in a new way, raises the problem of institutionalizing faith? It is easy to admit ideas, even to propagate them, when they agree with the needs of the time, or a certain order of culture and society. But what if they are critically contradicting these needs and, at the same time, left to the judgment of the individual? It should be noted that the institution and the institutionalization considered here are in no way repressive; on the contrary, they are assisting the formation of a new critical consciousness. It is to be asked whether it is not necessary for faith to be institutionalized so that the faithful take on their responsibility of critical liberty in the face of today's society. If this is necessary, are we not obliged to work out a new understanding of the ecclesiastical institution? Would the Church not then be necessary as the institution of the critical liberty of faith?

2. If the Church is tentatively so defined, then two objections come immediately to the fore.

(a) There is, first, the question of principle. Can an institution as such have the task of criticism? After all, would not "institutionalized criticism" be like squaring the circle? Is not institution by its nature something anticritical? Hence it is not going to utopian limits to postulate this "second order institution," which is not only the object but also the subject of critical liberty and which, therefore, has to make possible and to secure this criticism? In this context, I can only answer briefly by posing a question in reply. Is it not, on the contrary, the specific note of the religious institution of the Church to be, and even to have to be, the subject of this critical liberty? As institution the Church herself lives under the eschatological proviso. She is not for herself; she does not serve her own self-affirmation, but the historical affirmation of the salvation of all men. The hope she announces is not a hope for herself but for the kingdom of God. As institution, the Church truly lives on the proclamation of her own proviso. And she must realize this eschatological stipulation in that she establishes herself as the institution of critical liberty, in the face of society and its absolute and self-sufficient claims.

(b) But, granted that in this way our first objection is answered, there is still one additional critical question addressed to the Church: What is the historical and and social basis of her critical task? When was the Church truly an institution of critical liberty? When was she in fact critically revolutionary? When was she not simply counterrevolutionary, resentful, and nagging in her relation to the societal world? Did not the Church often neglect to speak her critical word, or come out with it too late? Did she not again and again appear to others as the ideological superstructure of societal relations and power constellation, and has she, indeed, always been able, with her own strength, to confound such accusation? Take recent centuries: is it not true that, more and more, religious institution and critical reflection have become incompatible things, so much so that, today, there is a theological reflection that ignores institution and an institution that ignores reflection? Where, then, is the historical and social basis of the claim made when defining the Church as a critical institution in the face of society? This objection is valid. There is hardly one idea of critical societal importance in our history—take Revolution, Enlightenment, Reason, or again—Love, Liberty—which was not at least once disavowed by historical Christianity and its institutions. No theory, no retrospective reinterpretation is of any help. If anything is to help here, it will be new ways of thinking and acting in the Church. May we hope for this? I think we may. All that follows is supported by this confidence.

3. In what does the critical liberating function of the Church, in view of our society and its historical process, now consist? Which are the elements of that creative negation which make the progress of society to be progress at all? I should like, without pretending to either a systematic or a complete presentation, to specify a few of these critical tasks of the Church.

(a) In virtue of its eschatological proviso in the face of every abstract idea of progress and of humanity, the Church protects the individual man, living here and now, from being considered exclusively as matter and means for the building of a completely rationalized technological future. The Church contradicts the practice that would see individuality only as the function of society's progress technically directed. It is true that even our societal utopias may contain a positive notion of the individual; still he is of value only inasmuch as he is the first to inaugurate new societal possibilities, in other words, inasmuch as he in himself anticipates the revolutionary social change that is to come, and inasmuch as he now is what everybody will have to be later. But then, what about the poor and the oppressed? Are they not poor because they are unable to be first in the sense just explained? In this case, it is the Church's task, in virtue of the eschatological proviso and with all her institutionalized, socio-critical power, to protect the individual against being taken as a number on a human-progress-computer-card.

(b) Today more than ever, when the Church is faced with the modern political systems, she must emphasize her critical liberating function again and again, to make it clear that man's history as a whole can never be a political notion in the strict sense of the word, that for this reason, it can never be made the object of a particular political action. There is no subject of universal history one can point to in this world, and whenever a party, a group, a nation, or a class sought to see itself as such a subject, thereby making the whole of history to be the scope of its political action, it inevitably grew into a totalitarian ideology.

(c) Lastly, the Church must mobilize that critical potency that lies in her central tradition of Christian love. Indeed it is not permissible to restrict love to the inter-personal sphere of the I-Thou. Nor is it enough to understand love as charitable work within a neighborhood. We must interpret love, and make it effective, in its societal dimension. This means that love should be the unconditional determination to bring justice, liberty, and peace to the others. Thus understood, love contains a socio-critical dynamism that can be viewed in two ways.

First: Love postulates a determined criticism of pure power. It does not allow us to think in the categories of "friend or enemy," for it obliges us to love our enemies and even to include them within the universal orbit of hope. Of course the Church, which calls herself the Church of love, will be able to express a credible and efficient criticism of pure power only if, and to the extent that, she herself does not appear in the accoutrements of power. The Church cannot and must not desire to press her point by means of political power. After all, she does not work for the affirmation of herself, but for the historical affirmation of salvation for all. She has no power prior to the power of her promises; this is an eminently critical proposition! It urges the Church on, again and again, to a passionate criticism of pure power; it points an accusing finger at her when—and how often has this been the case in history—her criticism of the powerful of this world was too weak, or came too late, or when she was hesitant in protecting all those, without distinction of persons, who were persecuted or threatened, and when she did not passionately stand up and fight whenever and wherever man was being treated contemptuously by man. This criticism of power would not oblige Christians to withdraw from the exercise of political power in every case. Such a withdrawal, if it were a matter of principle, could be a sin against love, for Christians possess in their very faith and its tradition, a principle of criticism of power.

Second: The socio-political dynamism of love points in yet another direction. If love is actualized as the unconditional determination to freedom and justice for the others, there might be circumstances where love itself could demand actions of a revolutionary character. If the status quo of a society contains as much injustice as would probably be caused by a revolutionary upheaval, a revolution in favor of freedom and justice for the sake of "the least of our brothers" would be permissible even in the name of love. Therefore, we should not underestimate the seriousness of Merleau-Ponty's remark that no Church has ever been seen supporting a revolution for the sole reason that it appeared to be just. At this point it becomes clear once more, that the socio-critical task of the Church becomes the task of criticizing religion and Church as well. The two go together like the two faces of a coin.

4. The socio-critical function brings about a change in the Church herself. Ultimately, indeed, its objective is a new self-understanding of the Church and a transformation of her institutional attitudes toward modern society. Let me say a few words about this point of political theology. We started by considering that, not only the individual, but the Church as institution is the subject of a critical attitude with regard to society. There are several reasons for this. One of these springs from the general philosophy and sociology of modern critical consciousness. Criticism, therefore, must be institutionalized and a "second order institution," which can be bearer and guardian of critical freedom, is necessary. But there is a question: Is the Church such a "second order institution"? In her present form she is not; but I dare say, she is not yet. How, then, and under what conditions will she be such an institution? Are there signs that she will be such? I shall add a few remarks on this point.

(a) What happens—this is our first question—when the Church today makes a concrete socio-critical assertion? What exactly did happen when these assertions were made? At this point the Church was obliged to take into account and to elaborate data which did not simply result from inner ecclesiastical theological reflection. Hence these socio-political pronouncements bring to life new, non-theological resources. The Church must receive such data in order to fulfill her mission to the world, which is not merely, not simply, to reproduce herself. All this will not fail to dissolve an uncritical, monolithic consciousness within the ecclesiastical institution. Moreover, the novelty of these data, which indeed are the foundation of new ecclesiastical pronouncements, require a new mode of speaking in the Church. Assertions founded on such data cannot be expressed simply as a doctrine. The courage is needed to formulate hypotheses suitable to contingent situations. Directives have to be issued which are neither weak and vague suggestions nor doctrinal-dogmatic teachings. This necessity of today's Church to speak out concretely and critically brings about, at the same time, a sort of demythologizing and deritualizing in her speech and conduct. For it is evident that the ecclesiastical institution is now undergoing a new experience; it must bear contradiction. Its decisions cannot avoid taking one side and therefore being provisional and risky. If this institution learns the new language, it will no longer encumber the societal initiative of individual Christians with doctrinal rigidity; although, on the other hand, it will also remove arbitrariness from their initiative.

(b) A further point comes to mind immediately. Ecclesiastical criticism of society can ultimately be credible and efficient only if it is supported more and more by a critical public opinion within the Church herself. If not this public opinion, what else is to be on guard, lest the Church, as institution, become an illustration of the very conditions which she criticizes in others? It should be noted, however, that, because of lack of data, it is difficult today to give a detailed account of this critical public opinion. I shall at least enumerate some of its tasks. One of them is to interpose a veto, whenever the ecclesiastical institution oversteps the boundaries of its competence. Here I have in mind the case where the authorities attempt by institutional measures to carry through their own decisions in a matter of socio-political or economic relevance.

Another of these tasks is the criticism of the inner ecclesiastical milieu: I am thinking of the fact that, within the Church, certain mentalities prevail—usually, middle class mentality—while others are thought to be irrelevant and, as it were, pushed to the background, out of the glare of the spotlight. A criticism of these uncontrolled yet powerful prejudices should be the object of public opinion. A further critical task is to show the historical conditioning and the change of the societal notions in the Church itself; the change of ideas is not always synchronous with the facts, it is less easy to see but, nonetheless real. It is also important—this is still another example of public criticism —to denounce the Church's struggle on wrong battle fronts, if necessary. The skill sometimes spent in the defense of certain social positions would, indeed, be sufficient for radical and courageous change. And again, why is it that Christianity seems to have relatively little to say in matters of reconciliation and toleration? Finally, why is it that the Church does not appear unmistakably and effectively as the one institution in which certain sociological prejudices are not admitted; for instance, racism, nationalism, and whatever ways there are to express contempt for other men? These indications may suffice here. The courage to build up such a critical public opinion can, no doubt, be drawn only from the confident hope that there will be a certain change of the institutional customs of the Church. But this confidence is perhaps one of the most important concrete features of membership in the Church today.

(c) In the pluralistic society it cannot be the socio-critical attitude of the Church to proclaim one positive societal order as an absolute norm. It can only consist in effecting within this society a critical, liberating freedom. The Church's task here is not the elaboration of a system of social doctrine, but of social criticism. The Church is a particular institution in society, yet presents a universal claim; if this claim is not to be an ideology, it can only be formulated and urged as criticism. Two important aspects may be pointed out on this basis. In the first place, it is clear now why the Church, being a socio-critical institution, will not, in the end, come out with a political ideology. No political party can take as its object of political action that which is the scope of the ecclesiastical criticism of society, namely, the whole of history standing under God's eschatological proviso. And in the second place, one can see now, again on the basis of the Church's critical function with regard to society, how cooperation with other non-Christian institutions and groups is possible in principle. The basis of such a cooperation between Christians and non-Christians, between men and groups of even the widest ideological differences, cannot primarily be a positive determination of the societal progress or a defiinite objective opinion of what the future free society of men will be. In the realm of these positive ideas there will always be differences and pluralism.

This pluralism in the positive design of society cannot be abolished within the conditions of our history if complete manipulation is not to replace its free realization. In view, therefore, of the afore-mentioned cooperation, there is a negative, critical attitude and experience to which we should pay our chief attention: the experience of the threat to humanity, that is, the experience of freedom, justice, and peace being threatened. We should not underestimate this negative experience. There is to it an elementary positive power of mediation. Even if we cannot directly and immediately agree as to the positive content of freedom, peace and justice, yet we have a long and common experience with their contraries, lack of freedom, justice and peace. This negative experience offers us a chance for consensus, less in regard to the positive aspect of the freedom and justice we are seeking, than in regard to our critical resistance against the dread and terror of no freedom and no justice. The solidarity which grows out of this experience offers the possibility of a common front of protest. This must be grasped; this must be exploited. The danger of new wars is too close. The irrationalities of our actions in the social and political field are too manifest. There is still with us the possiblity that "collective darkness" will descend upon us. The danger of losing freedom, justice and peace is, indeed so great that indifference in these matters would be a crime.

THE CONCEPT OF SECULARIZATION IN EMPIRICAL RESEARCH

LARRY SHINER

Secularization, once branded the enemy, has suddenly become the darling of Protestant theology, and . . . some Roman Catholic theologians. . . . [However,] in both the empirical and interpretive work on secularization today, the lack of agreement on what secularization is and how to measure it stands out above everything else.

The following analysis is an attempt to bring the concept of secularization at least partially into focus by considering (1) its current definitions, (2) its use in empirical research, and (3) its weakness as an analytical tool and some possible alternatives.

Types of Secularization Concept

Six types of secularization concept [appear] in use today. Since what we are about to delineate are types, most of the actual definitions or usages one encounters in the literature will deviate to some degree or else represent combinations. Each is presented in terms of a brief definition which describes the kind of process involved and its theoretical culmination. Then . . . a critical assessment is attempted.

1. *Decline of religion.*
The previously accepted symbols, doctrines and institutions lose their prestige and influence. The culmination of secularization would be a religionless society. J. Milton Yinger, for example, terms secularization the process "in which traditional religious symbols and forms have lost force and appeal."[1]

There are two major difficulties with the decline thesis. One is the problem of determining when and where we are to find the supposedly "religious" age from which decline has commenced. David Martin has noted that even secularists tend to take a utopian view of medieval religious life.[2]

... Gabriel Le Bras ... argues that in "dechristianized" France today there are among practicing Catholics probably more who participate voluntarily, faithfully and with an understanding of what they are doing than there were before 1789.[3] [This] suggestion regarding the seriousness of contemporary religious practice points to the other problem with the decline thesis: The ambiguity of most measures which are used. The easily measurable variables—church attendance, replies to belief questionnaires, proportion of contributions—are notoriously difficult to assess. . . .

2. Conformity with "this world"

The religious group or the religiously informed society turns its attention from the supernatural and becomes more and more interested in "this world." In ethics there is a corresponding tendency away from an ethic motivated by the desire to prepare for the future life or to conform to the group's ethical tradition toward an ethic adapted to the present exigencies of the surrounding society. *The culmination of secularization would be a society totally absorbed with the pragmatic tasks of the present and a religious group indistinguishable from the rest of society.* Harold W. Pfautz has defined secularization as "the tendency of sectarian religious movements to become both part of and like 'the world.' "[4]

As in the case of the decline thesis, the main difficulty with the idea of secularization as conformity to the world is the ambiguity of the measures applied. Moreover, simply by employing the Church/world or "this world/other world" dichotomy, the social scientist has taken over a particular theological framework as his own. In any given case we must ask whether something integral to a religious tradition is being surrendered in favor of "this world" or whether the change which is taking place may not be quite compatible with the main stream of the tradition. . . .

These observations are not meant to depreciate the usefulness of Pfautz's typology, but rather to question the value of terming the process one of "increasing secularization" when this implies a deviation or subversion from a more genuinely religious position. . . .

3. Disengagement of society from religion

Society separates itself from the religious understanding which has previously informed it in order to constitute itself an autonomous reality and consequently to limit religion to the sphere of private life. The culmination of this kind of secularization would be a religion of a purely inward character, influencing neither institutions nor corporate action, and a society in which religion made no appearance outside the sphere of the religious group. Hannah Arendt defines secularization in one place as . . . "Simply the separation of religion and politics. . . ."[5] Roger Mehl describe[s] secularization as the "historical process which tends to contest the public role of religion, to substitute other forms of authority for religious authority, and finally to relegate religion to the private sector of human existence."[6]

Although more specific than the thesis of decline or conformity with the world, the concept of secularization as disengagement suffers from parallel handicaps. [Donald] Smith's argument that the Indian state is secularized because it is neutral on religious beliefs and practices has been criticized as overlooking the fact that the Hindu and Islamic faiths have been a matter of purely private beliefs and practices.[7] Smith's critics suggest that Indian secularism, involves a strong dose of secularism, by which they mean a commitment to an ideology which seeks to embrace the whole of life and to replace the role once held by the religious communities.[8] A number of Christian thinkers have made a similar distinction between "secularization" or "secularity," which they take as signifying the rejection of religious or ecclesiastical tutelage of society, and "secularism" as signifying an all-embracing ideology which seeks to deny religious institutions or viewpoints any formative role in society. In reply, Smith acknowledges that the same sort of distinction is actually accepted by many Hindus and Moslems who find the relative restriction of their religious life to the private sphere fully consonant with the integrity of the faith.[9]

By its careful attention to the conceptual problem, Smith's work illustrates the pitfalls of defining secularization as disengagement. His work has also clearly raised the important question of how one decides when secularization in this sense has taken place and when we should speak rather of an internal adjustment within the religious tradition, or even of the triumph of one religion or religiously colored ideology over another.

4. Transposition of religious belief and institutions

Knowledge, patterns of behavior, and institutional arrangements which were once understood as grounded in divine power are trans-

formed into phenomena of purely human creation and responsibility. In the case of disengagement, the institutions or social arrangements which are secularized are seen as something which did not necessarily belong to the sphere of religion, whereas in the case of transposition it is aspects of religious belief or experience themselves which are shifted from their sacral context to a purely human context. *The culmination of this kind of secularization process would be a totally anthropologized religion and a society which had taken over all the functions previously accruing to the religious institutions.*

The difficulty with the transposition thesis ... is the problem of identifying survivals or transmigrations. Is a supposed transposition really a Jewish or Christian belief or practice now appearing under the guise of a more generalized rationale, or is it something of separate origin and conception which has taken over some of the functions of the former religious phenomenon?

The German philosopher Hans Blumenberg has offered what is perhaps the most complete and also the most perceptive critique of the concept of secularization as transposition. Using as his test case the theory that the idea of progress is a secularization of Christian eschatology, he points out that neither is there proof of causal dependence, nor are the two ideas really the same in content; the parallel, rather, is one of function.[10]

5. Desacralization of the world

The world is gradually deprived of its sacral character as man and nature become the object of rational-causal explanation and manipulation. The culmination of secularization would be a completely "rational" world society in which the phenomenon of the supernatural or even of "mystery" would play no part. Historian Eric Kahler writes that secularization means "that man became independent of religion and lived by reason, face to face with objectified, physical nature."[11]

The inherent problem with the desacralization view is its assumption that religion is inextricably bound up with an understanding of the world as permeated by sacred powers. There is in the Hebraic faith, however, a definite desacralization of the world through the radical transcendence of the Creator, who alone is eminently holy and who has, moreover, given the world over to the dominion of man (Gen 1:24). In Christianity the process is carried further through the separation of religion and politics and the notion of sonship through Christ in which man is free from the elemental spirits of the universe (Mk 12:17 and Gal 4:1ff.). This phenomenon of a religious tradition which itself desacralizes the world suggests that the desacralization view of secularization is not applicable to at least the Western tradition without qualification.

6. *Movement from a "sacred" to a "secular" society*

This is a general concept of social change, emphasizing multiple variables through several stages. According to Howard Becker, its chief developer, the main variable is resistance or openness to change. Accordingly, *the culmination of secularization would be a society in which all decisions are based on rational and utilitarian considerations and there is complete acceptance of change.*[12] A theological version of this type of secularization concept has been developed by Bernard Meland, who defines secularization as "the movement away from traditionally accepted norms and sensibilities in the life interests and habits of a people."[13] Since Meland means by sensibilities a capacity to "respond appreciatively and with restraint to accepted ways of feeling or behavior," secularization does not refer merely to religious phenomena but to any traditional norms and perceptions.[14]

Conclusion

During its long development the term "secularization" has often served the partisans of controversy and has constantly taken on new meanings without completely losing old ones. As a result it is swollen with overtones and implications, especially those associated with indifference or hostility to whatever is considered "religious."

On one hand, Martin has gone so far as to suggest that it has been a "tool of counter-religious ideologies," which define the "real" basis of religion and claim that religion so defined is in a process of irreversible decline. Martin believes the motives behind this are partly "the aesthetic satisfactions found in such notions and partly as a psychological boost to the movements with which they are associated."[15]

At the other end of the spectrum are the all too familiar clerical lamentations over the increase of "secularism." Blumenberg . . . even suggests that the concept of secularization has been a tool of . . . theologians and clerics who want to impugn the legitimacy of the modern world.

As if the conceptual situation were not confusing enough, the current enthusiasm in theology for styling one's version of Christianity "secular" muddies the conceptual waters almost to the point of hopelessness. . . . Behind the present secular theology fad lies the work of several more sober theologians (Bonhoeffer, Gogarten, Michalson) who have worked out a sophisticated defense of secularization conceived in terms of man's coming into responsibility for his own destiny. . . . Although Bonhoeffer and Gogarten do not style themselves "secular" theologians, the recent rash of books proclaiming "the secular meaning of the Gospel" or a "secular Christianity," or praising the "secular city" as the solely authentic place of Christian existence have made "secularization" once again an ecclesiastical battle slogan by stinging traditionalists and conservatives into a counter attack on this "secularization of Christianity."

This accumulation of contradictory connotations would be enough of a handicap, but there is an even more serious one in the fact that so many different processes and phenomena are designated by the term "secularization." Often the same writer will use it in two or more senses without acknowledging the shift of meaning. Thus Weber could employ it not only for "disenchantment" but also for transpositions (spirit of capitalism), and at times even in the sense of becoming "worldly," as when he speaks of the "secularizing influence of wealth" on monasticism.[16]

The appropriate conclusion to draw from the confusing connotations and the multiple of phenomena covered by the term secularization would seem to be that we drop the word entirely and employ instead terms such as "transposition" or "differentiation" which are both more descriptive and neutral.

Since a moratorium on any widely used term is unlikely to be effected, however, there are two ways of salvaging "secularization" as a useful concept in empirical research. One, of course, if for everyone who employs it to state carefully his intended meaning and to stick to it.

The other is for researchers to agree on the term as a general designation or large scale concept converging certain subsumed aspects of religious change.

1. J. Milton Yinger, **Religion, Society and the Individual**, New York: Macmillan, 1957, p. 119.
2. David A. Martin, "Utopian Aspects of the Concept of Secularization," **International Yearbook for the Sociology of Religion**, Vol. II, Koln and Opladen:

Westdeutscher Verlag, 1966, p. 92.

3. Gabriel Le Bras, "Deschristianisation: mot fallacieux," **Social Compass**, X, 1963, pp. 448 and 451.

4. Harold Pfautz, "Christian Science: A Case Study of the Social Psychological Aspect of Secularization," Social Forces, 34, 1956, p. 246.

5. Hannah Arendt, **Between Past and Future**, Cleveland: Meridan Books, 1963, p. 69.

6. Roger Mehl, "De la secularisation à l'atheism," **Foi et Vie**, 65, 1966, p. 70.

7. Donald E. Smith, **India as a Secular State**, Princeton: University Press, 1963.

8. Marc Galanter, "Secularism, East and West," **Comparative Studies in Society and History**, 7, 1965, pp. 148-53.

9. Donald E. Smith, "Secularism in India," **Comparative Studies in Society and History**, 7, 1965, pp. 169-70.

10. Hans Blumenberg, "Sakularisation: Kritik einer Kategorie Historischer Illegitimitat," in **Die Philosophie und die Fragenach dem Fortschritt**, ed. by Helmut Kuhn and Franz Wiedmann, Muchen: Anton Pustet, 1964, pp. 249-50.

11. Eric Kahler, **Man the Measure**, New York: Pantheon Books, 1943, p. 333.

12. Howard Becker, "Current Secular-Sacred Theory and its Development," in **Modern Sociological Theory in Continuity and Change**, ed. by Howard Becker and Alvin Boskoff, New York: Dryden Press, 1957, pp. 133-86.

13. Bernard E. Meland, **The Secularization of Modern Cultures**, New York: Oxford University Press, 1966, p. 3.

14. **Ibid.**, p. 9.

15. David Martin, **op. cit.**, p. 176.

16. Max Weber, **The Protestant Ethic and the Spirit of Capitalism**, New York: Charles Scribner's Sons, 1958, p. 174.

THE FUTURE AS THREAT
AND AS OPPORTUNITY

JURGEN MOLTMANN

A sudden and amazing upgrading of the "future" is taking place in almost every area of contemporary life. Future-oriented thought, planning, prognosis, hope, and mobility are becoming accepted everywhere and fascinate us as never before. Books with such titles as "Getting Hold of the Future," "Race for the Year 2000," and "Models of the World of Tomorrow," and cultural discussions with such themes as "Fear and Hope in Our Time," "Man and His Future," and "The Future as Threat and as Opportunity" are on the increase. Christians and atheists, scientists and scholars in the humanities, politicians and technicians are trying to work out new forms of cooperation in the future of our world, for we can get hold of the future only through communal effort. It is obvious that separately our efforts will come to naught.

The future has not always been the theme of the present; this development seems to be characteristic of the sixties. . . . The reasons for this are numerous. There is the general uneasiness with the politics of the status quo behind which "security" is sought while others are making plans and changing it. There is growing awareness that the utopia of the status quo is the worst of all possible utopias, even though and precisely because it presents itself in so "realistic" and "sober a fashion" as Hegel put it in a play on words, clear-headed (nüchtern) thinking is hungry thinking (nüchtern means having an empty stomach), not the satiated and saturated thinking that takes things as they are. There is also the reorientation of the economy away from demand backlog to long range investment. Only when a meaningful and necessary conception of the future has penetrated the general consciousness can the necessary factors of material and human investment be made accessible and entrepreneurial initiative (not only among professionals) be developed.

Futurological extrapolations from existing conditions have made us, at the least, aware of the future. On the one hand, predictions of a crisis in education (Georg Picht) have prompted both long term planning in education and extensive investments in new universities and schools. On the other hand, forewarnings of over-population and the resulting food crisis in the next thirty years have certainly made insightful persons aware of the necessity of taking appropriate measures, but in fact they have not brought about any genuinely effective help. The supra-national institutions that would be capable of remedial action do not exist, or, where they do, as with UNESCO, they lack the means and the personnel. National egos and political divisions are the greatest obstacles here.

Considering German cultural developments during the last twenty years insofar as they have been influenced by theology, we find a similar picture. In 1945 we had a "theology of ruins and rubble." In a time of world war, people called upon God in response to the dark future promised by history; they called upon Him as the absolute in the relative, as an eternal home in an estranged world, as the only permanent thing in transitoriness. The Christian Churches had come out of the guilt, suffering, disappointment, and degradation of those years relatively intact. Many people, deserted by other institutions (the state, the university, the courts, medicine, and others), had found an atmosphere of freedom, openness, and truth in circles of believing Christians.

The Lord of The Church

But then came the reorganization of the Church and its installation in a "Christian" society, which involved the presence of its representatives in almost all public institutions. The "God in the abyss of the world" now became the "Lord of the Church," and indeed, of a Church that occupied and enjoyed a position of undisputed preeminence in society. The certainty, devotion, and community that appeared during the time of persecution became something taken for granted, something institutionalized and slightly clerical, now that the hour of need was past, and its necessity became ever more difficult to understand for those who thought about it. A theology of ecclesiastical organization, of the distribution of jurisdiction between the Church and the world, of the distinction (difficult for the Church to make) between Church and world, aroused dissatisfaction and protest. People tried to break away from the dilemma of the Church into "gen-

uine worldliness" with Bonhoeffer; with Tillich they attempted to cor-
relate worldly questions and theological answers; with many others
they sought "God in fellowship" and a theology as anthropology. Many
took part in these movements out of protest against Church-centered
theology, clericalism, and other-worldly belief, but they remained caught
in polar thinking: clericalism vs. laicism, annunciatory theology vs.
genuine worldliness, dogmatic vs. undogmatic Christianity, the manifest
and organized state Church vs. the latent Church with its peripheral
members in solidarity with their unbelieving contemporaries, and so
on: These are controversies that probably had to arise, but they recall
the saying: "Parliament discusses while revolution is breaking out in
the streets." In our case and in our time this means that the revolution
of the future and our obligations to it relativize the contradictions
of the present and demand new cooperation.

This is apparent in the changing conception of God. Is the God
of the Bible only something to hold on to in the instability of history?
Is belief no more than comfort in despair? Is the Bible only a religious
book? Is it not also a subversive book (Bloch) and a revolutionary
book (C. F. von Weizsacker)? If the God of the Bible is the God of
Israel's exodus from the captivity and the fleshpots of Egypt, if he is
the God of the raising of Christ from degradation and desecration and
from death on the cross, then we must understand him as the God
of the kingdom to come, of a kingdom in which the high will be made
low and the lowly will be exalted, and peace and righteousness will
renew the face of the earth. But if he is the God of a future in which
the world will be transformed, then he is not a God dwelling above us,
nor is he a God in the depths of our existence—not a "Lord of the
Church" and not a name for fellowship, but a "God in front of us."

But in that case belief means not only calling on God because
of fear of the future of the world, but invoking God in hope for the
future of the world. And if belief means confident hope for the world,
then belief is, prior to any doctrine, an initiative toward a loving and
unselfish transformation of the world so that it may be recognizable
as the world of God in the kingdom of God. Out of the "theology of
ruins and rubble" arose a theology of the Church. Out of it arose the
familiar oppositions of Church and world. We can overcome these
oppositions, theoretically and practically, only by a theology which is
an eschatology, i.e., a belief that takes the initiative toward transforming
the world by means of the possibilities of the present.

Future or Advent?

Futurological studies necessarily begin with tendencies existing in the present and the past in order to make calculations about the future. But if faith looks forward to the coming of God and the future of His kingdom, the coming of the Son of Man and a future of the humanity of men, it must in actuality do the opposite, that is proceed from the future in order to define and transform the present. God, after all, dwells not in the future as an actual development, but rather in the advent of the future. Faith cannot conceive the future it awaits and hopes for by extending the lines of the present; it must grasp the present in terms of the future to which it is present. For the Christian faith, the future is not a dimension in the process of historical becoming; rather, history is the means by which the future is anticipated or, possibly, hindered. The future of faith is not contained in the process of the development of things, nor in the process of its own or the Church's development; rather, the process of history revolves around something contained in the future.

This distinction can be made clearer. Futurology extrapolates the future from the present; this future is calculated. Christian faith, however, anticipates a future that is hoped for and mediates in practice between it and the possibilities of the present; this future is, of course, the advent of a truly fulfilling world. It is not the future of western Christianity, of Christian society, or the future of the Church as it is, or the future of the faith of the faithful. All that would be nothing more than an extrapolation from what presently exists into an eternal future.

If this Christian faith orients itself toward the advent of a free, pacified, and redeemed world, moreover, it does not look with fear from the present into the future, full of concern for itself, but rather looks from the bright future which has been disclosed into the torn present. Hope, the mode in which Christian faith relates to the future, cannot therefore be realized in disregard to the world and its future. Hope must attest to and answer for the promised future and, by the same token, the future of the world. Faith hopes not for itself but for things other than itself. What it realizes in itself and what believers realize in themselves is, where this is successful, a making-present of the future of the world, as sign, promise, and sacrament of the salvation to come: peace, freedom, identity, and the nearness of God.

The One Future of The One God

We must therefore take as our starting point the thesis that the future both of a disunited mankind and of its experience of oppression is a united future. The reason for this is, on the one hand, theological. Just as in the Old and New Testaments God Himself is believed in as the One God, so too all His concrete historical promises have as their goal His one kingdom. This kingdom is not simply the future of Israel, not only the future of Christians; it is a united future, one which will pass judgment on the nations and their people and on the earth where they live, work, suffer, and die. If, as the apostles and the prophets put it, God glorifies himself in a kingdom that renews heaven and earth, then, because of God's Oneness, the future of the world in his kingdom is one future only.

On the other hand, the reason is a soteriological one. If God's future brings judgment and crisis upon everything that wants to live and has to die, if it brings salvation and peace to everything, then there cannot be several futures; rather, the future of peace and salvation must be the future of the whole—a future in which the crooked will be made straight, the torn and divided be made whole. Christian faith, therefore, cannot hope for only a fragment of the whole, the future of only a particular group of men, the future of only the soul as a part of the human being in his wholeness.

We must radically renounce the peaceable distinctions that are easily made when we as Christians speak of the future, the distinction made, for instance, when we say that politics is concerned with the worldly future and the Church with the transcendent future; that reason produces the relative future, the one within man's capabilities, while faith awaits the absolute future, which is simply not at our disposal; that technology and the economy plan the future of things and affairs, but faith watches over the personal future; that in practice one knows what will come but not who will come, while faith knows full well who will come but does not know what will come.

We are all familiar with these distinctions and we imagine ourselves able to say something about the future through them. But all these neat, detached formulations about the future are as empty of content as they are pregnant with meaning. They fit every period in history and therefore say nothing about any particular period. In making use of such distinctions Christians betray the unity of God's future and the totality both of the crisis to come and of the salvation to come. Such thought is thought about the future under the conditions imposed by the fragmentariness of the present. It can neither bear witness to salvation, nor can it save anything. It is thought about the future based on the self-assertion of temptation and impotence. And it is therefore incapable of mobilizing an initiative by Christians for the problems of the present. We should realize that the belief in "God, without hope" always produces a "hope without God."

It is belief in an unreal God that opens the way to a godless reality. Hence we should not be surprised to find atheists making the same distinctions. Heinrich Heine wrote, "Sweetpeas for everyone as soon as the pods break open—we can leave heaven to the angels and the sparrows." And after him, Friedrich Engels said: "Both Christianity and workers' socialism preach imminent deliverance from servitude and misery; Christianity locates this salvation in an other worldly life in heaven after death, whereas socialism locates it in this world, in a reorganization of society." In making such separations Christians and atheists made a pact, a pact for the death of God in the world. Just as things are reversed in a mirror image, so these two antagonistic brothers have come to resemble each other.

But that which perceives the future in terms of distinctions and divisions is at bottom the divisions in which we live at present. We have to become conscious of our present misery if we are to find footholds for work in the present based on hope for the whole.

The Sorcerer's Apprentice

Many in modern society feel that they possess numerous characters; many are conscious of being torn between publicity and privateness, between the firm and the family, between business and pleasure, thing and soul, concerns and concerts. They lose their personal and social identity and often their integrity as well. The feeling of being helpless in the world grows.

Resignation and the retreat into the better world of private life are imminent. The world outside, where we work and are governed, appears as a world of anonymity, as a drama in which each is given a role, as an environment that alienates, frustrates, and baffles us with a variety of refined but incomprehensible means. "You see manual laborers but no men. Thinkers, but no men. Masters and servants, young and mature people, but no men. There are no men left in Germany, only people with occupations." This is Holderlin's complaint in *Hyperion*. Would he have written otherwise today? But what use to us is his ironic complaint? It gives expression to his schizophrenic consciousness but cannot heal it.

Why does modern self-consciousness retreat from reality along this path? It does so because it submits to the world of occupations and of publicity without a meaningful future which might be achieved through that world, because it finds itself crossed in its expectations and will no longer accept this frustration, the suffering and pain of alienation. In such a world there is no hope, and one hides his "bleeding heart in ice and scorn" (Nietzsche). If we could provide the modern world of public life and of occupations with a meaningful future, we would be able to accept the pain of finitude and of alienation, and we would be able to accept present conditions as an occasion for the investment of human forces to gain a more human world. We would find strength to identify with work in the public sphere, work which is becoming continually more constraining and more oppressive, and thus overcome alienation through the strength of exertion for a better future. To the extent to which we approached our occupation as an occasion to work toward a more human world, we would be able—in the face of mocking criticism—to be absorbed in our work and nevertheless remain men.

The Frozen Christian

In "The Capitulation, or German Catholicism Today" (1963), Carl Amery assets the provocative thesis that, after the war, Christianity, whose influence was in constant demand in the public world, gave itself up to captivity in a strangely Christian-achristian milieu, and that this milieu effectively overpowered it. "Milieu-Catholicism has become absolute." For this reason Amery demands that Christians desert this Christian milieu: *"Sentire cum ecclesia* can demand that we break with existing Catholicism. ... In the name of the Church, of the one pure indivisible truth, we must begin to oppose a dictatorship that makes Christian existence, i.e., credible, existential witness to the kingdom of God, increasingly more difficult and less effective." Frequently affected by the "Christianity" as defined by Catholicism, Protestant Christians and Churches in Germany got themselves into the same dilemma.

It is becoming more and more difficult to become a Christian when one already is a Christian—through milieu and social pressure. A symbiotic realm, which is the Christian world, has made its appearance between the Church and the world, between belief and action. This realm makes many things vague so that neither Christians nor atheists can find their true identity. Should that not be a sign that Christians and churches have also lost sight of the future of the world to which they bear witness?

Two things are therefore necessary to abandon the milieu of adaptation to given conditions and to the approval of the masses; this means self-criticism of our own public image and workings. Not all of the possibilities Christians have for influencing the shape of the public world are possibilities for cooperation. For the most part they are also possibilities for the public world to influence Christians in order to be able to use their name to other ends. Christians and Churches can regain their freedom of action only through repentance and self-criticism, not through criticizing others and counseling repentance.

It is also necessary for Christians to abandon the confines to which they have been exiled. Christians must escape not only from worldliness but also from the hinterlands where they have been sent. They must use their freedom of action in readiness to invest their strength for the future of the world, for salvation and peace, for the freedom and justice of the whole. And so part of the exodus from captivity is an investment in the Promised Land.

Consequences of an Expanding Horizon

Let us try to assess the practical consequences of expanding the horizon of God's future in our historical world, of our beginning to live with hope.

We still tend to conceive the relationship between Church and world in spatial terms. We begin with two distinct spatial groups and then attempt to find something that will mediate between them. But is the Church anything other than the world; are Christians anything other than men? What are we turning to when we turn to the "world"? In reality we cannot begin with such a separation, for the Church is not not-world, and Christians are contemporaries. The Church is that world that tries here and now to live, believe, love, and hope in terms of God's promised future. And Christians are only men converted to God's future. Seen this way, the relationship between Church and world should be defined not spatially but temporally. The Church is the world open to the future. This is what is meant when the Church is called an eschatological community. Its sacraments, which remember Christ's death and make it present, are a promise of his future. The Church is not the goal of its own movement; the goal is the Kingdom of God, the world redeemed.

And so they themselves, the Church with its sacraments and Christians with their callings in the world, are signs of hope for the healing of the world as a whole. The more aware of this Church and Christianity become, the more they are forced to question every present that is interested in understanding itself only in terms of itself and its own possibilities and is positivistically absorbed in itself. Questioning in this way, however, they become the forward-driving forces of a revolutionary crisis in every existing world. It is precisely this crisis with which the apostles' warnings are concerned: "Do not be conformed to this world, but be transformed by the renewal of your mind . . ." (Rom 12:2), and "do not love this world" but love the future appearance of Christ.

Nonconformism and flight from the world, then, represent not flights into an imaginary beyond of the absolute but a necessary side of hope's battle for the future of the world. It is only as citizens of the future world that Christians are strangers of the future of the world, and alienation can be meaningful only when it takes place for the sake of that future. Simple and straightforward talk about "a Church for the world" becomes meaningless when the Church no longer wants to be a Church. The much-touted "being for others" becomes meaningless when one is no different from the others. Only one who has the courage to be different from others can be for others; otherwise he is there only for those who are the same.

For Christian hope, God's new world does not simply wait ready-made in the future so that hope can be content with waiting. Christian hope is not a quietistic expectation for which time and the world are a kind of waiting room in which one sits around disinterested and bored until God opens the door of his office (J. B. Metz). Only those who seek find, and the door is opened only for those who knock. To speak without biblical references: we are not only on the future's waiting list; we are also the builders of the future, whose power, in hope as well as in fulfillment, is God. For us hope is not only something to drink but also something to boil (Ernst Bloch). As the old Church preached, the blood of the martyrs is the seed of the Church, and in the New Testament we find that God builds his kingdom out of the sacrifices of love, just as life and resurrection were awakened from the blood of Him who was crucified. In actuality, the Christian initiative at this time anticipates the renewal of the world, as the new Vatican ecclesiastical constitution says. The Christian is a fellow worker participating in the building of the kingdom. But how can he anticipate the future as salvation here and now?

Acts of Hope

The "first act of hope" is without doubt the preaching of the gospel of the kingdom to the poor. In this world of nations, of Jews and heathens, of Greeks and barbarians, and of all the other divisions which prevent man from being a man among men, the world's one future in God is anticipated in the spreading of the gospel "to all." The gospel announces the reconciliation of the world with the coming God and thus effects transformation and renewal. It is directed to all men; not to all men in their status as humans—for all men differ in the allegedly positive sphere—but to all men in their common misery of guilt and suffering and mortality, in order to provide them with certainty about the salvation to come. In positive things we are separate, in the negative ones we form a community. The unity of salvation is anticipated by the gospel in the conflicts of history. We can call this infecting the world with hope (A. Loisy, Hoekendijk). Only the "universal priesthood of all believers" can realize this. It is up to Christians in their professions, not to professional Christians, to spread these bacilli.

The "second act of hope" can be identified as the founding of the Christian community. This community is constituted not of people who are the same but of people who are different. It is always constituted at the borders that men have instituted in order to distinguish themselves from others through positive characteristics.

The Christian community becomes "God's people" and coincides with the future it preaches only when it is composed and constituted, as Paul says, of Jew and heathens, of Greeks and barbarians, of masters and slaves, of men and women. State churches, national churches, regional and milieu churches impede de facto the oneness and the universality of God's future. Only by trespassing these boundary lines can the Christian community abolish them on its way from reconciliation to transformation. Then it will become the *tertium genus,* the third race of man. Then it will become a sign of hope for a fraternal world.

It is not difficult to indicate the boundaries that prevent the Christian community from functioning as such a sign of hope today. They are the boundaries of race, which have not only led to clashes in America but will in the future also lead to an uprising against the "Christian West." They are the boundaries of rich and poor, which also will lead to murderous conflicts. They are the boundaries of ideology. The Christian community can trespass these boundaries if it realizes that it itself is an anticipation of God's unified and unifying future.

The "third act of hope" is creative, entrepreneurial, and fighting obedience in the everyday life of the present world. This obedience, too, is enjoined by the New Testament as part of beginning to live now through the promised future and to transform life here accordingly. As bodily obedience it anticipates the resurrection of the body, and as social obedience the renewal of the earth.

From "Social Service" to "Social Action"

Today the range of possibilities for the Christian ethic in modern society is greater than the courage of the Christians who take advantage of these possibilities. Up until now we knew of the possibility of private help in alleviating want, liberating bondsmen, and providing justice to those deprived of it. The systems of charity and social service function, free and adapted to existing conditions. They make use, however, only of the powers of free men in their free time, outside of social organizations and professions.

Both devotion to one's calling and communal charity aim at preserving the established order and at alleviating the distresses that this order unfortunately produces. But meanwhile these institutions have been established. Men are no longer responsible to the social order, they are responsible for it. The institutions lose their authenticity and become functional structures of the social process. In the meantime, too, people have become conscious that there are social institutions that produce injustice and misery with a certain inevitability. In such social orders social service by Christians, performed with the aim of alleviating distress and out of devotion to one's calling, tends despite all good intentions to stabilize the very thing that produces the trouble. In such societies Christian charitable action is transformed in effect into the opposite of love. Christians must therefore manage a transition from social service to social action. They must hear from religion, as Marx once did, a protest against the real misery of men; it is not only a critique of religion but also the realization of religion when God's protest against man's increasing misery rings out in the form of a categorical imperative "to reverse all relationships in which man is a degraded, enslaved, deserted, contemptible creature" (Marx). For such an evolutionary—and perhaps revolutionary—ethic, we need a new context to give action its meaning. Only the eschatological horizon is broad enough to mediate between faith and the historical world. In other words, in its public activity Christendom must create an audience the world over for the warning of the prophet Isaiah: "To relieve the weary of their burdens and set the oppressed free."

An Ethic for the Technical World

Modern man . . . gained his freedom vis-a-vis through science and technology and in the same instant lost this freedom to the power and autonomy of his works. His rationality produced the "irrationality of the dynamic of civilization" (Fr. von Weizacker). It will be a task to develop an "ethic of the technical world," though such an ethic for dealing with scientific and technical power cannot be deduced from science itself. Nevertheless, such an ethic is necessary, for at present we are not the masters of technology but its victims. For this reason the old separation of theory and practice can no longer be maintained. Medicine, the science whose subject is man, has the Hippocratic oath, which enjoins responsibility for life. Other sciences do not have such an oath, although today they are capable of furthering or destroying life in an equally grave way.

A general professional oath for the natural science would not, of course, prevent the results of research from being misused, for mankind with its divisions is still far from ethical solidarity. Increasing consciousness of the threat of mankind's self-destructions, however, makes it possible for the naive competition of the two world powers to be brought under control. Practical reason can catch up with theoretical reason only in a relationship of increasing mutual control and the mutual trust that would develop out of it. In itself technical reason offers no moral criteria for the uses to which it is put. But moral reason in itself is powerless. A human future can be achieved only through constant mediation between means and ends.

A first stage of Christian solidarity might involve simply a heightened consciousness of the pervasive threat of self-destruction, a consciousness that would enable groups, institutions, and nations to become unified in negativity, that is, via an attempt to avert the coming evils, even if common goals for the future have not been specified.

A Division and A Categorical Imperative

With the beginning of the modern era, western Christianity divided into two movements. A radical, messianic, chiliastic movement arose bent on transforming the world. It was immediately affected by secularization and helped to produce the spirit of enlightenment, science, and revolution. The secularization of these radical tendencies left behind a conservative, ecclesiastical Christianity.

From this separation arose the division of our world into religion and revolution, faith in God and earthly hope, belief and knowledge, grace and human freedom. Church Christianity allowed revolution to absorb the strength of its hope and the natural sciences to absorb the strength of its faith in creation (Fr. von Weizsacker). The revolutionaries inherited the prophetic protest against man's real misery. What was left over was something religious that laboriously tried to assert its validity in a constantly changing world. In the schism of the modern world Christian hopes left the Church in order to transform the misery of the world and in this transformation they also took on heretical and atheist forms. But on the other hand it must also be admitted that, measured against the prophets and the apostles, what was left behind in the Church, the religious and conservative spirit, has also taken on heretical forms. But how can the two be reconciled and made to bear witness to the whole truth? Certainly not by turning to the earthly Messianism of militant hope and forgetting all the truth preserved in the Church's tradition of Christian history. I would like to make the nature of this integration clear by discussing what seems to me to be the crucial point.

To describe the Christian faith as an initiative toward the task of overcoming man's real misery, not in consolation but in effective protest—this can be meaningful only if we presuppose that God's future meets us halfway. "As I set off on my way to You, I found You coming toward me," wrote Jehuda Hallevie, a Jewish poet quoted by Max Brod, of the divine mystery.

The certainty of Christian hope is based on the belief that God's future has approached man through and in Jesus: in his resurrection from death on the cross, that future of God's kingdom entered into history. As Mary sings (according to Luke): "He thrusts the mighty from their seats and raises up the humble, the hungry he provides with goods, the rich he sends away empty-handed." When the future comes to meet us this way, there is reason for us similarly to go out to meet it.

Still more profound is Paul's explanation of the way in which the future comes to meet us, the end to which all historical action and progressive impulses should be directed: absolution. There is no other way of emerging from the well-known dilemma—it is impossible to anticipate the end of history from within history, impossible to overcome the alienation of man from man from within that alienation, impossible (as the Bible says) as sinners to overcome sin without producing new sin. In attempting to do the impossible, man creates new misery in overcoming his misery.

All revolutions which have as their goal a better future are blind in this one respect. The final result of the English revolution was not the rule of God but representative democracy. The end result of the industrial revolution was not the age of reason but the irrational dynamic of civilization. Communism produced not a classless society but a very effective hierarchy and bureaucracy of officials and specialists. "In the *citoyen* of the French Revolution lay the future bourgeois; God preserves us from what lies in the comrade," wrote the Marxist Ernst Bloch in 1930. The way in which a bad situation is overcome, once understood, is always partly determined by the enemy. And so the overcoming of misery produces new misery. Given this discrepancy, one cannot act with certainty and wisdom without being aware that the future will not only be built by our hands but that it will also be full of consideration, support, and kindness. Brecht composed as an emigrant what may be his most profound poem:

> We who prepared the ground for friendliness,
> could not be friendly ourselves.
> But you, when things have come so far that
> man helps his fellow man—make allowances for us.

Those lines were certainly not meant as a justification of Stalinist violence but rather as an insight into the way the human future can be ruined through precisely the same people who try to build it, and also as an insight into the way one yearns for deliverance from the conditions of strangeness in which one lives. Only the awareness that the future will "make allowances" for us—in Christian terms, that the kingdom of justice makes itself present in the forgiveness of sin—can liberate from compulsive illusions our work toward the future. On the other hand, awareness of mercy and of the forgiveness of sins can never lead us to make peace with bad conditions here, for the forgiveness of sins, mercy toward the other, and friendliness are anticipations of the future and the beginning of a free and fraternal world. Thus no one can have such awareness without heeding the categorical imperative to transform inhuman conditions.

CREATIVE HOPE

JOHANNES B. METZ

Christian faith has to answer for its hope to contemporary man where sensibility is characterized by being directed to the future; he is more concerned with effective action than with contemplation.

A feature of the contemporary world is its concern for what is "new." This drive to the "new" has its effect in the contemporary revolution in the social, political and technical fields. Modern humanity knows only one fascinosum: the future as the what-has-not-yet-been.

This new sensibility is, in other words, determined by what Kierkegaard called the "passion for the possible." Meanwhile, the force of tradition grows weak; the old quickly becomes out-of-date; the "golden age" is not behind us, but ahead of us; it is not remembered in dreams but rather creatively awaited from the future. The relationship to the past takes on more and more a purely aesthetic, romantic or archaic character or it depends on a purely historical interest which simply has a confirmation that the past is over and done with. This modern consciousness has a purely historical relationship to the past, but an existential relation to the future. It frees man from the tyranny of a history concerned only with origins, and turns him towards a history conceived with ends.

The future is essentially a reality which does not yet exist, which has never been: the "new" in the proper sense of this word. The relationship to such a future cannot be purely contemplative and cannot remain in the order of representations, since representations and pure contemplation both refer to what has already come into existence or what still is. Rather, the relationship to the future is an operative one and the theory of this relationship is directed to effective action. In this approach to the future, man no longer experiences his world as a destiny imposed on him, as inviolable nature surrounding him, but as a "stone-quarry" out of which he must build his own "new world." He transforms the world and fashions it into the setting of his own historical activity. The world depends on man and his technical activity and so it is a secularized world. The process called "secularization" and the contemporary primacy of the future are intimately connected with each other.

All effective world views and humanists in the East and the West are today directed to the future: We only have to think of Marxism and its theory of the classless society in a future which is to be brought about by the activity of man.

The salvation sought—the successful and fulfilled humanity is to be found not "above us" but "ahead of us." The modern critiques of religion, and especially that of the Marxists, can be reduced to one common factor: Christianity as well as religion in general is powerless when faced by the primacy of the future in modern sensibility. That is why this new sensibility often claims to be an instrument for the elimination of religious consciousness altogether and the inauguration of a post-religious age in which any concern for transcendence is dismissed as purely speculative and replaced by a practical attitude to the future.

What account does Christian faith give of itself in this situation? How does it answer for its hope (cf. I Peter 3:15)? Can it understand this situation in a way which does not exclude completely theological consciousness or reduce it to empty and formal paradoxes? Yes, it can—but under one condition: if faith is appalled at the unimportance of eschatology in its theology, if it is disturbed by the way the future has been forgotten in theology, which in the end goes so far that all modern theological discourse on the historicity of faith stresses only the relationship of the past to the present.

Contemporary man's orientation to the future and his understanding of the world as history are themselves grounded in the biblical faith is God's promises.

On this position we can give here only a few hints. This direct reference to statements of Scripture is not arbitrarily made: it is based on the findings of recent exegesis. This, in its post-Bultmann phase, has brought out the inner unity and relationship between the Old and the New Testaments, and has likewise stressed the fact that the Old Testament provides the background and the setting for the thought and expression of the New Testament.

Most recent research has shown that the word of revelation in the Old Testament is not primarily a word of information or even a word of address, nor is it a word expressing the personal self-communication of God, but is rather a word of promise. Its statements are announcements, its preaching is the proclamation of what is to come and therefore an abrogation of what is. The principal word of promise points to the future; it founds the covenant as the solidarity of those who look forward in hope, those for whom the world for the first time has a history ordained to the future—in contrast to the Greeks for whom the world appears as a consistent and closed cosmos.

Central passages of the Old Testament reveal this touching sense of the "now," of the "not yet"—again in contrast to the Greeks for whom the "not-yet" is the impossible since there is for them "nothing new under the sun"; all that is to come is simply a variation of what has been, a renewal and consolidation of memories. History is for the Greeks only the indifferent return of the same thing within the fixed frame of the cosmos. The sequence of history is the cycle, and history can be said in a sense to devour again and again its own children; nothing really new happens and the essence of history is basically nihilistic.

I stress this contrast between biblical and Greek ways of thinking, so as to bring out sharply the specific quality of the biblical understanding of the world and existence: as an historical process directed to God's promise, for whose fulfillment those who look forward to it in hope are responsible. Even the creation stories of the Old Testament are originally stories of promise, a faith in creation is faith in the promise. This eschatological horizon appears most clearly as the central point of God's self-revelation in Exodus 3:14, which a modern exegete has taught us to translate: "I will be who I will be." The divinity of God reveals itself here as the dynamism of our future and not primarily as a being "above us" in the sense of an unhistorical transcendence. God is a "God before us." His transcendence is revealed as the power of our future.

He is revealed as a future which is grounded in itself and belongs to itself. As a future which does not come into being out of the possibilities of our human freedom, but who calls our freedom to its historical possibilities. For only a future which is more than a correlative and a projection of our possibilities can free us for something truly "new," for new possibilities, for that which has never been. Insofar as it relates human existence to the "new," biblical faith contains a revolutionary dimension.

It would be a mistake to think that after the Christ-event our future already is over and done with, as if after the birth of Christ there is no future to be realized but only one to be unfolded. On the contrary, the Christ-event gives added stimulus to attempts to shape the future. The preaching of the resurrection which can never be separated from the preaching of the cross, is essentially a missionary preaching of promise. In obedience to it the Christian attempts to transform the world in the direction of that new world which is promised to him once for all in Christ Jesus. Creative expectation is the secret essence of Christian existence in the New Testament.

All this demands the development of theology as eschatology. Paul defines Christians simply as "those who have hope" (cf. Eph 2:22; I Thess 4:13). Christians must therefore develop eschatology in all parts of their understanding of faith. It must not be reduced to a part of Christian theology but must be understood radically: as the determining factor in all theological statements. The attempt to understand theology as anthropology is an important achievement of contemporary theology. Yet this anthropological theology, so long as it is not understood as eschatology, runs the risk of becoming nonhistorical and out of this world. For it is only in the eschatological horizon that the world appears as a becoming reality whose development is entrusted to the freedom of men. Christology and ecclesiology must also be developed in the context of eschatology or they run the risk of being reduced to a purely existential or purely cosmological system.

It would be tempting and important to show that the development of the so-called "secularization of the world" was only possible because the world was experienced and interpreted in the eschatological and inviolable pre-established harmony, but rather as a becoming reality, which can be transformed through the free historical activity of men into a yet greater future. The universal transformation of the world through an offensive of human freedom upon it characterizes that process which we call secularization. But we must leave this question here and move on to our next thesis. The responsibility of Christian hope towards the world of history can be theologically determined through the idea of "creative eschatology." This implies intrinsically a kind of "political theology."

The discussion and founding of this position can best begin with a reference to a thought-provoking opinion of St. Thomas Aquinas. He says in his scholastic language: Man has not an ultimate natural end and an ultimate supernatural end, he has only one single ultimate end, namely, the future promised by God. In relation therefore to mankind's future one distinction disappears, which theology uses, and all

too readily uses: the distinction between the natural and the supernatural.
In relation to the future and the end to which history is moving, theology
cannot be content with this distinction and cannot separate the natural
future of the world and the supernatural future of faith and of the
Church. The two dimensions converge in relation to the future. The
hope which relates Christians to the future cannot ignore the world
and its future.

The Church is not the goal of her own movement; this goal is the
Kingdom of God. "The Church, if we rightly understand it, lives always
from the proclamation of her own provisional character and her progressive historical surrender to the coming Kingdom of God towards
which she moves like a pilgrim." The hope to which the Church bears
witness is not a hope which bears upon the Church herself, but upon
the Kingdom of God as the future of the world. *Ecclesia est universale
sacramentum spei pro totius mundi salute.* This the relationship of the
Church to the world is not chiefly one of place but of time. The Church
is not simply the not-world, she is that world of men who draw their
stimulus and inspiration from the future promised by God and who
call into question the world which is emerging from the present and
human possibilities. She offers to the Self-confident world with its hopes
and dreams a liberation and a positive critique. For the Church looks
towards that "new world," whose "newness" is not simply the planned
product of our own potentialities which in the end would only lead
to the "melancholy of fulfillment." The "Newness" here rather corresponds to a promise which originally set in motion our search and our
creative and active drive to the future.

How does the Church realize this mission for the future of the
world? It cannot be achieved through pure contemplation, since contemplation by definition is related to what has become and what is now.
The future for which the Church hopes for the world is rather something which is being formed and to be formed. And so the hope to which
the Church commits herself for herself and for the world must be
essentially creative and militant, and must be realized in a creative-
militant eschatology. The goal of our eschatological hope, the heavenly-
earthly Jerusalem, the promised city of God, is not simply ready-made
ahead of us like a distant goal which would be already there, and
simply hidden for the time being and for which we yearn in imagination.
The echatological city of God is still coming into being. And as we
move forward to it in hope, we build it up, as collaborators in and not

simply interpreters of a future whose driving force is God himself.

The Constitution on the Church says: "The renovation of the world . . . is in a sense really anticipated in this world." The Christian is a collaborator in this promised Kingdom of universal peace and justice. The orthodoxy of his practice, his activity ordered to the last end; for the promised truth is a truth which must be "done" as St. John makes clear (cf. 3:21). Christian eschatology is not simply an eschatology of the present, in which all passion for the future would be set aside in the making present of eternity in the individual moment, however much this eschatology may have been developed in the theology of today and however right it is in understanding the present as the permanent starting-point of eternity.

But neither is Christian eschatology an eschatology of passive expectation, for which the world and the present age would be like a kind of waiting room, in which man would have to sit around bored and uncommitted—the more bored, the more hopeful—until the door of God's audience room is opened. Christian eschatology must be seen rather as a productive and militant eschatology. Christian hope is a home in which we—as Ernst Bloch has already remarked—"have not only something to drink but also something to cook." Eschatological faith and temporal commitment do not exclude each other, but rather imply each other.

The theology of the world which is guided by this creative militant eschatology cannot be developed in the style and with the categories of the older theological cosmology. Nor can the task be done in the style and with the categories of a purely transcendental personalistic or existentialist theology, which as far as this task goes remains too private.

The theology of the world is neither a purely objective theology of the cosmos nor a purely transcendental theology of personal existence, but rather and above all political theology—I grant that this expression could be misunderstood. The creative militant here which command such theology is essentially related to the world as society and to the forces in society which transform it. Such a theology must be concerned with the great political, social and technical utopias, with the modern promises of universal peace, universal justice and the universal liberation of man for which our society longs. For the salvation to which Christian hope is related is not simply primarily the salvation of the individual— whether this is understood as the salvation of one's soul or as individual resurrection of the body—but as salvation of the covenant, of the people, or the many: in a word salvation as "resurrection of the flesh," where "flesh" in contradistinction to "body" indicates, according to biblical usage, interpersonal and social existence and characterizes the existence of man in the covenant. This "salvation of all flesh" is found originally and not subsequently in the concrete social dimension of human existence, and it aims at a universal peace and final justice (cf. II Pet 3:13) so that "tears are dried and there shall be an end to death and to mourning and crying and pain" (Rev 21:4). This dimension of the creative hope of salvation in Christianity seems to have been overlooked in recent times. The importance and the insistent emphasis of modern theology on the subjectivity of the believer, on his need to say a personal "yes" to salvation, brought with it at the same time a dangerous tendency to turn salvation into a private reality, and this affected the understanding of salvation in general. This transformation of salvation into a private matter though transcendental, personalistic or existential factors, must be overcome through the working out of a theology which we have characterized with the phrase "political theology." The creative militant eschatology is not an ideology of the future.

This creative eschatology is essentially distinct from any militant optimism. It does not canonize the progress we are bringing about. It is and remains the expression of a hope—against all hope—which we set among the self-erected idols of our secularized society. Three remarks on this point:

1. Christian hope is not the attempt of reason to pierce through the future and so to rob it of mystery. The man who hopes is not making the irritating claim to know more about the future than others. Christian eschatology therefore is not an ideology of the future. It values precisely the poverty of its knowledge about the future. What distinguishes it from the ideas of the future both in East and West is not that it knows more but rather that it knows less about the hoped-for future of mankind, and that it stands by the poverty of this knowledge. "By faith Abraham obeyed the call to go out to a land destined for himself and his heirs and left home without knowing where he was to go." (Hebrew 11:8).

2. The creative hope of the Christian does not seek to outbid by its optimism all forms of human alienation or the "pain of finiteness," not to unmask them as provisional. It concentrates rather on those forms of human alienation which can in no way be removed through any

economic and social transformation of situations and destiny, however perfect they may be. For example: the experience of guilt and of evil, or the experience which theology describes with the word "concupiscence."

Here we have an experience of self-alienation which plainly cannot be overcome simply by social and economic means. For man always feels the discrepancy between the level on which he projects to live and that on which he in fact lives, between idea and existence. He constantly falls below the great experiences of his life and does not allow himself to be changed by them, but rather transforms them and levels them down to every day banalities. As Camus put it: "It seems that great men are less disturbed by pain than by the thought that it does not last." It does not last because we are not equal to its claims and do not remain equal to its claims. In such and similar experiences we become aware of a situation of human self-alienation which cannot be removed or nullified by social, economic and social or technical progress. Christian hope strives to remain faithful to such experiences and precisely through them to realize all the painful breadth and depth of its hope against hope.

3. Finally, Christian hope is aware of the greatest risk of all: It is aware of death, before which all glittering promises are threatened and grow dim. Christian hope has been called an anticipated practice for death, practice, that is, in a hope against all hope.

But even this movement of hope should not be narrowed down to an individualistic hope which forgets the world; it has lost its private character or should lose it. This too must take place with a glance on the world, on the world of our brothers, in the self-forgetting oblation of love for others, for the "least of the brethren," in selfless commitment for their hope.

For through our love of the community, we overcome death in anticipation: "we know that we have passed over from death to life because we love the brethren." (I Jn 3:14). Only one who loses his soul in this way will gain it. Christian hope draws itself and overcomes the passion of death, which threatens our promises, as it accepts the adventure of brotherly love of the least—in imitation of Christ, whose being is not originally self-perfection, not a *reditio subjecti se ipsum* but a being for others (Bonhoeffer).

Christian hope is creative imitation of this being for others; and so it is at the service of creative responsibility for the world.

ECUMENICAL THEOLOGY OF REVOLUTION

J. M. LOCHMAN

One of the most stirring moments of the World Conference on Church and Society held in Geneva in 1966 was . . . [the session on] "The Challenge and Relevance of Theology to the Social Revolutions of Our Time. . . ." There were three main speakers on the theme.[1]

"The great revolutions of modern history . . . have created the world in which we live." These were the opening words . . . by Professor *Heinz-Dietrich Wendland.* "The question then arises: what is the connexion between the revolutionary element in the Christian message and revolution in history?" (p. 12). It is answered dialectically by referring to the thinking of Paul Tillich and Arthur Rich, who maintain that there is an affinity with the biblical thinking about revolution, but that the Bible also places limits on revolution. The affinity (say Tillich and Rich) lies mainly in the eschatology of the Bible, in the message of the coming Kingdom of God, whose dynamic force confronts Christians (also in society) with the basic principle *societas semper reformanda.* . . ."Man is the administrator who organizes and reforms the state, the economy, society" (p. 15). Moreover it is never a "Christian revolution." Christians "do not set up any 'Christian' orders, systems, states and societies; for their task is to *humanize* the secular orders and the slightest real progress that can be attained there is more important than the most perfect Christian Utopia, because it guarantees real help to definite people or social groups" (pp. 16-17).

What is said above already indicates the distinction between the "revolutionary element" in the Bible and secular-revolutionary absolutism or fanatical Utopianism. No historical revolution "opens the door to the reign of freedom, which at the same time offers the inexhaustible satisfaction of all human needs" (p. 6). The Kingdom of God will never be directly established within this aeon.

In Wendland's view the effect of the revolutionary element in the Bible is to be understood differently: "The rule of God *indirectly* has social and political repercussions, not by stirring up rebellion, not by the use of political and military force, but solely through the 'quiet,' unarmed, loving action and service of Christian groups scattered all over the world, and yet united in Christ" (p. 13). "Thus the Church itself becomes the source of constant revolutionary changes in state and society" (p. 18).

The carefully weighed statements of Professor Wendland were immediately followed by a real thunderbolt—the revolutionary theology of *Richard Shaull's* address . . . [Before the conference convened Professor Shaull wrote that] in the present world situation, which is characterised by an unprecedented gulf between the different societies (especially between the "rich" and the "poor" nations), the social revolution is the first question which must be honestly faced by our generation. The crucial questions of the humanization or de-humanization of human life in the contemporary world are decided "on the frontiers of revolution."[2] "As a political form of change, revolution represents the cutting edge of humanization."[3]

In his address to the Conference, Shaull expressed the same view of the world situation and drew the same consequences for Christian ethics and Christian action. . . . [He declared that in] certain situations it might be incumbent upon Christians to take part in revolutionary action which involved the use of force. His arguments were directed especially against those who, in regard to the highly developed technical structure of the industrial countries, exclude the possibility of a revolutionary change there. In face of this, Shaull did not proclaim the "end of revolution" but "a new strategy of revolution." This consists in "developing those bases from which a system unwilling to initiate major changes when they are most urgently needed, can be constantly bombarded by strong pressures for small changes at many different points" (p. 3).

What then is the relevance of theology for such revolutionary thought and action? Not mainly to issue warnings against turning revolutionary ideologies into absolutes (although that is also one of theology's tasks), and certainly not to draft "abstract principles or ideas" (like that of the responsible society). It is much more important for Christians to bear witness to all those perspectives "which free him to break the bonds of the secular, empirical ethos, dream new dreams about the future of man, and cultivate the creative imagination so as to be capable of thinking about new problems in new ways, and defining new goals and models for a new society" (p. 5). What is required of the theologian is "not a new language, but a new involvement, in those places in the world where God is most dynamically at work"; an effort "to keep going the difficult but not impossible running conversation between the full biblical and theological tradition and the contemporary human situation" (p. 7).

As a sort of counterpoint to the above addresses, the third speaker was Archpriest *Vitalij Borovoy* of the Russian Orthodox Church— a Church "which has lived for almost half a century in the conditions of the social revolution which lies at the root of almost all the social revolutions of our time" (p. 1). He spoke about these actual experiences —without concealing the difficulties of the theme nor the reality of the revolution. Particularly for Orthodox Christians it was difficult to find an open-minded attitude towards revolution, owing to their tradition: "Of all Christian cultures, Byzantium is the one which contributed most of all to the mere sanctification of social evil" (p. 3).

However, a conflict between the Church and revolution . . . is not inevitable. On the contrary, biblical thinking in its original form is "social and revolutionary. . . ." "Christian life begins in crisis; it also continues in crisis" (p. 3). This insight is true not only of the individual soul but also of man's social existence. One may therefore sum up by saying: "Christianity is by its very nature revolutionary; and new life required by Christian social ethics is more radical, more profoundly revolutionary, more novel than any other social system or doctrine which has grown up outside Christianity" (p. 4).

Ecumenical Divergences

If one tries to compare the addresses given at Geneva, in order to discover signs of an ecumenical consensus on the question of revolution, . . . one soon encounters difficulties. It is not easy to reduce the three "revolutionary speakers" to one common denominator.

To begin with, each of them has a different concept of revolution. Borovoy appeals for Christian understanding for the social revolution, by drawing an analogy between the concept of revolution and the starting-point of the spiritual life—"conversion," "change of heart" and "new life." Wendland's concept of "total revolution" goes far in another direction (and corresponds to some extent to the central theme of the Conference, which speaks not only of the social revolution but also of the technological revolution). To Wendland "total revolution" means the all-embracing revolutionary process of our technological-scientific civilization with its upheavals not only in the social sphere, but also in the realms of culture and religion. Shaull does not ignore the general background of this "total revolution," but he deliberately concentrates on the most crucial aspects of the revolution of our time, namely the social aspects; his main concern is to bring about a radical change (which is long overdue) in the unjust national and international "order."

The sharpest difference, however, is in relation to the concrete ethical problem: the problem of force. In the theological reflections about revolution this question has always played an important role. It was also the crucial point (explicitly or implicitly) of the discussions at the Conference. Already in the addresses this question gave rise to open dispute. Despite all the insistence on the possibility and the need for a Christian-revolutionary commitment, in Wendland's view the use of force (especially of military force) is excluded as a legitimate instrument which Christians could use for "transforming the world" (p. 16). On the other hand, Shaull takes the view that "there may be some situations in which only the threat or use of violence can set the process of change in motion" (p. 4). In the discussions some supported one of these views, some the other—with different nuances.

Sometimes the division cut right across the geographical and confessional fronts. But sometimes a certain "rule" was apparent. Most of the delegates from the developing countries (especially from Africa and Latin America) approved the use of revolutionary force in order to effect changes in the unjust social structures; they did not take this view lightly, but they were quite definite about it.

On the other hand, the delegates from the highly industrialized countries on the whole showed a more reserved attitude to the problem of force; not only the pacifists (who were of course represented at the Conference) but also "realistic politicians."

If one compares these two concepts and places them in the context of the social situations involved, the question arises: is not the problem of force in the ecumenical movement today "ideological" rather than "theological"? Do not the different answers simply reflect the different social positions in the "world-wide struggle" of our time between the rich and the poor nations? The "poor" nations want revolution, even if it involves the use of force. The "rich" nations regard the use of force as a problem—apparently a theological one, but in reality an ideological one. This aspect of our ecumenical discussions should not be swept aside in a self-righteous manner. The "ideological" aspects and the non-theological factors certainly do play a role and we ought to take sober account of them (especially in our own minds). And yet the problem of revolutionary force cannot be solved ideologically. It is certainly not only those who defend a privileged "status quo" who express serious misgivings about the use of force; sometimes it is quite the contrary. Many of them support the need for a radical change in the social structures.

The tensions and divergences in the ecumenical theology of revolution are strong. In spite of this, can one speak of a certain convergence, or even of a consensus? I should like to answer in the affirmative. In support of doing so, three points may be made.

1. *Revolution in ecumenical social ethics*

I understand this ambiguous slogan simply as a definition of an incomparably greater role which the phenomenon of revolution should play in Christian thinking on social ethics today. For centuries revolution was the "step-child" of Christian social ethics. Usually it came up only on the periphery of ethical considerations, and was overshadowed by other problems. "Hitherto theological ethics have paid inadequate attention to the problem or revolution."[4] To put it more bluntly: "There is no authoritative theological literature in this field at all."[5]

In this connection the Conference on Church and Society, and the years of work on social ethics which preceded it, reveal a very definite change.

2. *From the ethic of the "established Orders" to the ethic of "Change"*

The phrase about "revolution in ecumenical social ethics" cannot, of course, be understood only as an indication of the increasing importance of the theme of "revolution" in the ecumenical movement. It also denotes the change which is taking place in the social ethic itself. Ecumenical thinking on social ethics is moving on from an "ethic of the established Orders" to an "ethic of change. . . ." Since the Middle Ages the ethics of the Church had increasingly developed into an ethic of the established Orders; the first and last concern of Christian ethics was to arrange natural and supernatural life in accordance with a *lex naturae* or *lex divinum*. In society this ethic aims at protecting the Christian (i.e., the traditional) order. This explains the conservative trend of traditional Christian ethics—not only in the Roman Catholic Church.

This form of traditional ethic is being challenged in the ecumenical movement today. In the world of very ambiguous orders the first concern of Christian obedience cannot be to sanctify this ambiguous world by giving it religious approval. The concern of Christian obedience is rather to change this world, to "humanize" it—not theoretically but in actual fact, in the light of Christian humanity. This perception was another important aspect of an ecumenical consensus·

3. *Dynamism of the biblical perspective*

Among the voices which determine the ecumenical theology of revolution that we have so far described, the intention and the claim to represent a program based on theology cannot be ignored. The theological basis varies, of course: from the Orthodox theology of the resurrection and of rebirth (Borovoy), via the concept of the Kingdom of God and social action (Wendland), to the radically secularizing and humanizing motives of Shaull.

However, a surprising convergence is taking place amid all these divergences; this theology is impelled by the dynamism of the biblical approach. Especially it is biblical eschatology which plays the guiding role here. Our world is not a self-constituted quiescent world. We are living "between the aeons" and are therefore caught up in the eschatological movement of God's Kingdom. The future is therefore opening up to the transforming action of the Christian. Consequently we are no longer bound to the existing orders of a "status quo." "The eschatology of the Christian faith (releases) a 'revolutionary humanity.' "[6]

If the ecumenical theology of revolution takes this "revolution of God's" as its guide, then it cannot be considered "a clearance-sale of the spiritual substance of the Church." If, amid all the divergences (to which the ecumenical movement must devote a great deal of further thought) the theology of revolution can maintain that promising "convergence," it may open up new roads of Christian social ethics for Church and society in our revolutionary world.

SOME THOUGHTS ON VIOLENCE*

1. Ecumenical thinking and commitment in the social sphere, as a result of current social tensions, have two major charteristics. On the one hand, there is a growing understanding of the Christian's radical witness to the cause of peace, pacifism. On the other, there is a growing understanding of the necessity for radical, revolutionary changes in the structures of society. Put in the form of a paradox, at the very moment when the traditional teaching of the "just war" is called into question as an option for the Christian, the theme of the "just revolution" seems to be increasing in urgency. It is the current responsibility of the ecumenical movement and of social ethics to master this tension.

2. Many people in our churches are diagnosing in this state of tension the signs of a fatal "schizophrenia." More than anything else, the heated discussions on the ecumenical Program to Combat Racism led many critics to this conclusion. The theme of violence played a central role in these discussions. The decision of the World Council of Churches was (mis)interpreted as a blank check for the use of violence. In these circumstances it is time attention was given to the problem of violence. The study of violence as a possible method of achieving social change is, in this context, a priority for the ecumenical study program. I include some fragmentary remarks on this.

3. The controversy over the ecumenical anti-racism program had, among other things, one very astonishing aspect: it was by no means the pacifist groups which made an issue of the problem of violence in this context, but, on the contrary, it was representatives of the traditionally non-pacifist churches who took exception to it. This paradox gives food for reflection. The question of violence is not an abstract-general problem. It is always situated in a specific and concrete context and should be seen, not only in its theological, but also in its historical and social setting.

4. The theological context signifies that Jesus' non-violent attitude is not an isolated principle; it is connected with the main purpose of His life and Passion in solidarity with those who are in trouble or oppressed. The historical-social context implies that the problem of violence does not just emerge when the oppressed and deprived begin

*This section, which was not in the original article, has been added by Prof. Lochmann, and is here published for the first time.

to offer resistance. Violence is present in all degrading and inhuman conditions. Objectively, the primary concern of Christian social ethics relates to changing inhuman conditions; subjectively, it implies the practice of our solidarity with the oppressed.

5. Jesus' command in the Gospel, Matthew 25, that we should show our solidarity with "the least of (His) brethren" is the prime mover of Christian social ethics. Even the ecumenical anti-racism program should primarily be understood and criticized from this point of view, and in this perspective the question of the means is not an irrelevant one. From the story of Jesus Christ it is obvious that a non-violent solution is preferable and should be sought with imagination. However, this clear preference—in the light of the original command—should not be made into an abstract law and generally forced on those to whom we owe solidarity. This is why the argument of the non-pacifists on the question of the use of violence in connection with the discussions on the anti-racism program did not carry conviction. Christians from the rich and privileged countries can only make their witness of non-violent love creditable today by showing their ecumenical solidarity with the hungry and the victims of discrimination in the developing countries, and by supporting their justified revolutionary demands.

6. The ecumenical discussion on the question of violence, at least since the Geneva Conference of 1966, seems to have three dialectically linked accents: (i) the primacy of non-violence as the most likely course for the Christian; (ii) the dilemma of violence as a factor of our world; (iii) the use of violence in this violence-ridden world is only justified for the Christian as the ultimate reason. This threefold ecumenical consideration of the problem offers no solution, but sharply defines the field of tension within which one should grapple for further theological and socio-ethical clarifications.

7. In the search for such clarifications, certain models from church history may prove helpful. I am thinking, for example, of the struggle with the question of violence within the Czech Reformation. This struggle was marked by the unprecedented tension between the theological advocates of revolutionary violence and the supporters of a non-violent religious struggle (Peter Chelcicky). What was significant in this was that each side emphasized obedience to the coming kingdom of God. The revolutionary Hussites endeavored to change the way of life of the entire society and were, therefore, concerned with the problem

of the responsible use of violence. The Bohemian Brethren endeavored to apply the full binding force of the authority of Jesus Christ through non-violent means to the Christian minority. It is essential in my opinion to consider both points of view: their common motive, and its different expressions. Each is important for the current ecumenical study of the question of violence.

8. If the question of violence is understood within its context, then the above-mentioned tension between rejecting the traditional theme of the 'just war' and accepting the theme of the 'just revolution' no longer leads to schizophrenia, but is a legitimate dialectic, although one which still urgently needs clarification. I agree with Helmut Gollwitzer that "the use of military violence justified in a specific and limited way by theological tradition is more problematical than the use of revolutionary violence rejected by theological tradition. In the latter case, and with the same criteria, the distinction between the 'just revolution' and the 'unjust revolution' can be made. A 'just revolution' is concerned with gaining a better, more humane order (Lenin's conception of the 'just war'), whereas a 'just war' is only concerned with maintaining the existing order. In the 'just war' the subject obeys the command of his government, relying upon its decision. In the 'just revolution' he must rely on his own decision and take a joint share in the responsibility of changing the existing state of affairs." (*Diskussion zur Theologie der Revolution,* München 1969, p. 63)

9. It never can be the task of theology to provide justification for revolutionary violence. Violence can never be justified theologically by the Cross of Jesus Christ. The *proprium christianum* in the sphere of social ethics will always be to endeavor to stress non-violent possibilities and strategies. The dialectic is animated from here. However, in this animation it will always try to distinguish, in a concrete fashion, in a given social context, between enslaving, contrarevolutionary violence, and that of the revolutionaries aimed at liberating the oppressed.

1. The three addresses were as follows: H. D. Wendland: "The Church and Revolution" [Germany]; Richard Shaull: "The Revolutionary Challenge to Church and Theology" [U. S. A.]; Archpriest Borovoy: "The Challenge and Relevance of Theology to the Social Revolution of Our Time." [Russia] I quote from the mimeographed versions of the addresses given at the Conference on Church and Society, to which the page-numbers refer.

2. **Christian Social Ethics in a Changing World**, edited by John C. Bennett, Association Press, New York, 1966, p. 250.

3. **Ibid.**, p. 33.

4. See E. Fahlbusch, **Evangelisches Kirchenlexikon,** III, Sp. 646. Fahlbusch's article is one of the best things written on the subject by a Protestant.

5. See Wendland's paper at the Conference on Church and Society, footnote 6

6. A. Rich, **Glaube in politischer Entscheidung,** Zürich, 1962, p. 96.

PART II

SOCIAL ETHICS
AND BEHAVIORAL SCIENCE

Major Jewish and Christian theologians and social ethicists contend that it is impossible for contemporary religious communities to address themselves responsibly to the problems of society without utilizing the methods, theories, insights and studies of the socio-behavioral sciences. There are sound reasons to support this contention.

First, it is impossible to address oneself theologically and/or ethically to the problems of contemporary society without a thorough, concrete knowledge of the structure, operations and functions of contemporary society. The socio-behavioral sciences provide such concrete knowledge and thereby prevent the theologian, social ethicist and religious communities from addressing themselves to abstract, irrelevant or unreal issues and problems.

Second, as Walter G. Muelder in the first article below points out, the socio-behavioral sciences, when utilized properly, make several significant contributions to theology, ethics and social ethics. These contributions include supplementing the knowledge, theories and work of theology, ethics and social ethics; helping these disciplines raise theological and ethical questions in new and more relevant ways; and, finally, examining the capacity the socio-behavioral sciences have to force theology, ethics and social ethics to re-examine their basic assumptions and presuppositions about nature, human beings and society.

Serious conflicts and problems occur when religionists utilize the socio-behavioral sciences in their work. The basic presuppositions, methods, norms, values and goals of all these disciplines frequently come into conflict. As Gibson Winters points out, while theology, ethics and social ethics share a common ground, *viz.,* the shaping of social action, there is a sharp division between the realms of theology, ethics and social ethics and the socio-behavioral sciences. This conflict is due to the fact that the theological and ethical disciplines are concerned with the universal and ultimate factors which shape social action while the socio-behavioral sciences address themselves to the immediate societal structures which determine social actions. Furthermore, both groups tend to claim superiority over the other. Therefore, it is important to single out the areas of conflict and to seek ways of ameliorating them in order that both may be of greater service to the religious communities and society.[1]

The two essays in this section seek to define the problem areas confronting theology, ethics and social ethics and the socio-behavioral sciences and to suggest ways in which these conflicts may be resolved.

1. "Theology and Social Science," in **The Scope of Theology,** Cleveland, Ohio: World Publishing Co., 1965, pp. 174-175.

THEOLOGY AND SOCIAL SCIENCE

WALTER G. MUELDER

The problem of values and value judgments in the social sciences is rarely looked at from the perspective of Christian Theology. Yet the social sciences are inescapably involved in questions of value, not only interpreting data but as an inherent element in their basic presuppositions and methodology. Theologians must inevitably be concerned with the values that emerge in the work of social scientists and the role and function of social science within the domain of truth. It lies beyond the purpose of this chapter to elaborate a theological analysis of the presuppositions of the behavioral sciences. On the other hand, it is evident that theologians must develop greater competence in the social sciences in order to understand their contribution to theology. Some of these contributions supplement theology; others raise theological questions in a fresh way; still others drive theology into a re-examination of assumed facts about man, nature and society. One of the main contributions of the functional method in social science may be to assist theology to clarify its statements and to make them more relevant to ethics and social policy. Since Christian theology involves not only ultimate perspectives and concerns, but also existential decision, it must traverse the domain of behavioral science.

Problems of value inevitably arise in the social sciences, because they deal with persons, groups and their interaction. Moreover, different scientists bring different assumptions of value and fact to their work. There is a sociology of knowledge, but, at present, no over-all theory of value (axiology) of the social science. Various societies and nations put their social scientists to work on distinctive problems. There are change-goals to be achieved and pressing problems—such as crime, mental health, population control, legal medicine, and racial and industrial relations—to be studied. The responses of science are of significance for theology.

Many years ago, because of church-state relations, theologians were consciously concerned with political science. But in recent times, economic theory, psychology and sociology have pressed for attention. As rapid social change has engulfed whole societies, a concern to understand cultural anthropology and to relate it to the Christian understanding of man and society has emerged. As the community has challenged the social scientist to investigate many problems, the scientist has striven for the integrity and autonomy that are required for his discipline. At times, he has attempted to eschew all normative elements in the quest for defensible empirical generalizations. At the same time, the policy makers' use of social science has raised normative questions which can be properly handled only within the context of ethics. In any event, behavioral science assumes the worth of persons and is caught up in the investigator's own evaluative situation.

The meaning of these assertions and the purpose of this chapter will become clearer if we illustrate briefly from specific situations. Before doing so, we must remind the Christian theologian and the scientist of a contextual relationship which governs the discussion as a whole. A Christian view of the relation of theology and the social sciences must recognize at least the following: (a) that man has a social setting; (b) that this social setting is cultural and historical; (c) that both society and history are lockstitched into nature through man's biophysical constitution; (d) that personality must be explored in terms of depth, decision and rational wholeness; (e) that selfhood involves self-transcending freedom and (f) that ultimate "I-Thou" relationships mean facing God personally as creator and redeemer as well as through society, history and nature.

Representative Instances of Value Problems in Social Science

The social sciences raise value problems the solution of which involves more than the selection and recording of meaningful data: it is inseparably bound up with interpretation and analysis. Thus, even in making a map the scientist does not include everything, but makes his selection according to some established criterion.

Determinism as a scientific idea is reinforced in the psychiatric field by the humanitarian idea that the patient is sick and that his displeasing behavior is to be accepted with equanimity as an expression of his illness. In dealing with the patient, however, the physician cannot maintain the completely deterministic belief about himself, because he must choose wisely how to behave in order to help the patient. Faith in freedom is a value which somehow enters into the behavioral aspects of the psychiatrist-patient working relationship.

A final illustration is taken from the scientific study of race relations. When Gunnar Myrdal wrote *An American Dilemma,* he spelled out in an important appendix entitled "A Methodological Note on Facts and Valuations in Social Change"[1] some of the methodological problems which are encountered in dealing with facts and values. His major finding deserves special notice: "The social scientist is part of the culture in which he lives and he never succeeds in freeing himself entirely from dependence on the dominant preconceptions and biases of his environment." Such biases touch the center of scientific method and procedure in terms of (a) the objects chosen for research; (b) the selection of relevant data; (c) the recording of observations; (d) the theoretical and practical inferences drawn and (e) the manner of presenting results. Of special significance for this essay are value attitudes in the social sciences and their dependence, at least in part, on the central values of the society within which the scientist works.

A Critique of Theological Perspectives on Science

As theology confronts issues of value like those above, it does so properly from its own perspective. Theology operates from a different level or in a different dimension from that of science. One formulation says that science works with the tools of discovery, and that theology works from the vantage point of disclosure. Discovery and disclosure have a wider bearing than questions of value, but belong in a coherent unity of truth about value. We shall examine these ideas more fully, to show that the disjunction between discovery and disclosure (man discovers, God discloses), though useful up to a point, may be less tenable than is often proposed, for the disjunction does violence to the unity of man, whether approached scientifically or theologically.

By viewing man's experience as a whole, theology acknowledges that his spiritual life is a unity. There are, conceptually conceived, distinct elements in man's spirit. Yet, as Paul Tillich rightly observes in *Dynamics of Faith,* "all spiritual elements in man are within each other."[2] Thus, for example, faith and reason properly understood do not structurally conflict: they "lie within each other." If reason is used in the sense of scientific method, logical strictness and technical calculation, it "provides tools for recognizing and controlling reality, and faith gives the direction in which this control may be recognized."[3]

If reason is used to designate the source of meaning, of structure, of norms and principles, as it has been in western culture, it points to the humanity of man which distinguishes him from all other beings. And it is important that this designation shall not be lost amid the merely analytical, intellectualistic, formalistic and rationalizing emphases concerning reason in society in our day. Properly understood, it is reason that makes possible an integrated personal life and participation in community. Faith could not possibly be opposed to reason, for then, as both Tillich and the personalists have insisted, faith would rob man of his humanity. Faith which destroys reason or regard for reason dehumanizes man. As Albert C. Knudson has said, a theological faith based on radical skepticism will perish thereby.

Somewhat different from Tillich's position is that of John Dillenberger, who affirms that "revelation has to do with the mystery of *disclosure,* while science deals with the mystery that is associated with *discovery.*"[4] This approach regards the unity of knowledge as at best an ideal which cannot at any moment in history be made a reality; it thus retreats into the uniqueness of the disciplines.[5] On this basis the unity of the mystery in God and the unity of spirit in man are lost.

Another approach is to adopt a kind of existential posture. The thrust of some existentialism has been against positivism in science and against making man an object, an "it." Similar protests have come on scientific, methodological grounds from many fronts: from Marx in economics (his doctrines of value and alienation), from many democratic and personalistic philosophers and even from anthropologists. Some theologians have seen the emergence of existentialism in theology as a recovery of the concept of the nature of man more congenial to classical theology than that which saw him as the embodiment of value or as moral personality, claiming that the latter makes of him only an idea or ideal object. But theology has no twentieth century monopoly on man as a real person, a real subject. It would be arbitrary to say that the choice lies between science and existentialism (as theology).

The values and dilemmas of existentialism must be faced in terms of the social sciences. Dillenberger properly points out that in Heidegger, Kierkegaard and Nietzsche science stands for unauthentic existence:

Science is a matter of indifference, of concern with selected objects or items, whether of nature or history. It conceals, man in his totality, in his mystery, by a concern with the multiplication of knowledge essentially indifferent to himself as an existing subject. Although thrown into being, man is a mysterious being whose wholeness must be affirmed. Such affirmation constitutes history, not nature. ... His being or his freedom is affirmed as he "stands out" from any objective thing which is "over against" him.[6]

In such a statement, theology expresses a thoroughly historical and personalistic concern for man and protects against any program in social science or society which dehumanizes him. Yet, the sources of the existentialism which some theology seems to adopt may be less a biblical disclosure than an accommodation to some strains in European culture—for example, in Heidegger. At this point, anthropology and cultural history may assist the critical work of theologians.

Theological existentialism stresses man as sinner, of course, and notes that apart from sin he is not at the level of humanity; and in opposition to some forms of existentialism and naturalism insists that the loss of the risk to be and therefore of being at all."[7] Yet sin is a category that falls outside the social sciences (though some find it useful in psychotherapy) and that, being so universal in its relevance, tends not to be operationally or functionally relevant at all. But discriminate judgments are necessary both in social science and in ethics.

It is in the area of ethics that the problems are often most clearly seen. The tendency in much theology is to reject all biblical legalism in favor of a *kerygma* which affirms minimal cultural content and maximum insistence on *disclosure* by and *about* Jesus Christ, preferably about him as an act of faith. Absolute insistence on authority of revelation is sometimes linked with maximum relativity in concrete ethical judgments. When principles are rejected, the basis of discriminate judgment is highly relative, even relativistic. What is often left ambiguous is the relationship between man's sin and the idea that there are no universal moral answers because there are no common moral questions and no common verifiable theory of human nature.

There are both social scientists and theologians whose relativism rests in an ultimate indeterminism. Such relativism sees descriptive variety, uniqueness in value situations, conflicts of values and subjectivity as all in some sense ultimate, irreducible and irreconcilable. It affirms or assumes that there is no pattern or generalization of which the varied or the unique are but different expressions. Hence neither the conflicts nor the individual's isolation can ever be resolved. Indeterminacy, Abraham Edel claims, is at the heart of the relativist position.[8] A radical, irrationalist type of existentialism, whether Christian or other, would seem to leave indeterminacy in social science eventuating in ultimate skepticism, and to leave dread, anguish and loneliness unresolved.

Theological relativism often seeks to overcome the indeterminacy through an appeal to revelation. But revelation alone only postpones the problem, for it is then simply transferred to the diversity of God's interpreters. The indeterminacy here roots in the fact, not simply of actual disagreement, but of there being no mode of decision by which, in principle at least, the issues can be settled.[9] Much of the crisis in hermeneutics today is traceable to the irrationalism and subjectivism that underlie some of these theories.

The behavioral sciences do not, however, necessarily imply the indeterminacy and relativism that are suggested above. Theology and science can meet each other halfway at least in ethics through what is scientifically known about man. Edel[10] is probably correct in stating that ethical absolutism and ethical relativism in their extreme forms have tried short cuts to avoid the necessity of empirical investigation and because they have enshrined as common sense assumptions the results of earlier chapters of the history of science. The preliminary and provisional character of the work of science, on the one hand, and of all hermeneutics, on the other, does not necessarily imply indeterminate relativism. When, for example, guilt-feelings are appealed to in the area of ethics, it is well to explore one's assumptions about human nature, the origin and development of guilt-feelings in interpersonal processes, and the like. There are many tools in the behavioral sciences for dealing with such problems.

Rationality in science and in theology meet in the appeal to the person as a whole. Reason has, when properly approached, the authority of the whole in ethics where so many valuation issues deriving from these fields meet. Edel notes:

From today's psychological perspective it is established theory that there is a system of forces in the internal economy of the biological individual, even where consciousness shows the extreme of a split personality. In that sense it is a lesson of science that rationality involves the whole person. This serves to incorporate at least the whole-

person perspective in ethical judgment. The history of the moral mandate of unity and system is itself one of the most striking cases of the tremendous scope of scientific knowledge that is really required to justify what on the face of it looks like an obvious injunction of reason.[11]

Any theory of ethics, theology or psychotherapy—and all existential decision making—must assume that man (as person and subject) has a degree of mastery over himself and some insight into himself and his goals. But, if this is granted, then man also has some control in relating means to ends and in reflecting about alternate ends. In principle, then, science can offer a great deal. Stated ideally, the contributions would include at least these:

It is elementary that a person's whims are to be distinguished from his stable and enduring goals, and that a rational man who is to be regarded as master of himself must have some insight into himself and his aims. But once this door is opened, the passageway leads on and on. Ideally, full advice to the person who asked for a cost estimate of the envisaged goals would include their scope and function in his life, their mode of development, intensity points, termination points, possible transformations, relation to common ends, possible interaction with others and their mutual alternation, and so forth—in short all the lessons that a psychological, social and historical perspective could offer in application to the particular case.[12]

Ideology, Sociology and Theology

The social sciences and theology as developed in any particular historical era tend to reflect the ideologies of the day. In a world of competing ideologies, axiological issues influence both scientists and theologians. Christian faith and ethics do not constitute an ideology; yet one of the tendencies of culture is to reduce religion to an ideology. When Christianity is used to serve the interests of some social group and thus is robbed of its transcendent majesty of revelation and comprehensive reason, or when it is presented as if the kingdom of God could be identified with any particular economic, political or ecclesiastical order, it is reduced to the ideological level.

Karl Marx and Karl Mannheim have done much to develop the category of ideology. Marx insisted that in historical and political matters there could be no "pure theory." Behind every social theory lie collective points of view; class interests are involved. Political theories reflect social situations and limited-interest goals. Plausibility of argument in seeking to establish ideology is readily discernible in the thought of an opponent; it is not so easily noted in one's own. Marx thought of ideology as a taint, but the more careful study of Mannheim and his successors attributed to it a less sinister meaning.

Karl Mannheim, whose work has had wide influence, defined ideologies as "more or less conscious disguises of the nature of the situation."[13] This conception of ideology implies skepticism about the ideas advanced by our opponent and, even more, that if our opponent did recognize the truth, it would not be in accord with his interests. Mannheim also used ideology in another sense, that is, when "we are concerned with the characteristics and composition of the total structure of the mind of this epoch or this group."[14] In either case "the ideas expressed by the subject are . . . regarded as functions of his existence. This means that opinions, statements, propositions and systems of ideas are not taken at their face value but are interpreted in the light of the life situation of the one who expresses them."[15] Today ideologies are part of the cold war, of racial and national conflict, of the struggles of the developing nations. They belong to the arsenal of offensive and defensive weapons.

In Europe, the period of great change from the seventeenth to the nineteenth century has been called the "age of ideology," in that it saw an extraordinary outpouring of theories about the nature of man in relation to the present and future state of society. Today in the period of worldwide rapid social change—the revolutionary shift from colonialism to modern nationhood—we have another ideological surge. Despite great differences regarding the appropriate methods by which to reach their goals, the leaders of many of these new nations are united by a group of beliefs that express common feelings about the past, present and future. Paul E. Sigmund, Jr., has pointed out that these beliefs are ideologies in that they "elicit an emotional commitment by the leadership and their followers and are directed toward action—the development of a new society in a certain direction, in conformity with certain goals."[16]

Sigmund notes[17] that these ideologies cluster around the goals of modernizing nationalism: "national independence; rapid economic development; the creation of a nation-state governed by a regime based on a populist identification of leader, party and people; regional federation; and non-alignment in international affairs." It is instructive that in many of these countries there is no mention in their ideologies of the values of liberal pluralistic democracy which many social scientists in the West take for granted. This does not mean that these countries are all deeply infiltrated by communist ideologies. Quite the contrary. It may mean that the single party, democratic centralism and the emphasis on elites should be understood from a deeper dynamic perspective than is customary. Ideology has a function. It draws on various traditions to carry people through "the period of modernization of traditional society and to justify the ensuing sacrifices and dislocations."[18] The need of a developing country to establish its own sense of identity is frequently expressed in its disinterest in the ideological struggles of the great powers.

Theological self-awareness made perceptive by the critical methods of the sociology of knowledge should assist Christian social ethics in understanding such dynamic processes. These combined disciplines should also help scholars to understand how the religious beliefs of the developing nations inevitably become involved in their national ideologies. Religion (including theology) is so entwined in the integrating myth-structures of peoples that we should expect modern man to unite social criticism with the criticism of religion and to unite theological criticism with the criticism of social systems whose myth structures rival the Christian faith at all levels of expression.

Christian social ethics is itself not an ideology, because it recognizes the provisional character of all historical embodiments of great ideas and purposes. Even when the heritage of values acknowledges the great norms of traditional Christian ethics, the political, economic and educational embodiments of these norms are all provisional. Hence the Christian social ethic is able to interact with and respond to the ideologies of the time. It may do this through an enlightened Church which has an ecumenical mission of evangelism; through a community of faith which is in, but also transcends, nations and cultures; through a decision not to exploit the new powers released in the revolutions, but rather to serve; and through the training of persons who make decisions in specific localities and institutions, but who as servants of Christ humbly seek to transcend ideological perspectives.

There are a number of elements in the theoretical issues involved in the sociology of knowledge as developed by Mannheim which theology should note. Do "facts" and "values" have a common ontological source, or do they arise from completely different sources? Both seem to arise out of the unitary life process in which the individual evolves a knowledge of the world—that is, life in a community of persons with a complex of values. Cognitive and valuational processes are complexly entwined, and valuation ultimately offers a basis of interpretation. Since facts and values are both integral aspects of knowing, the problem of validity in one area is affected by that in the other. Mannheim observes: "The position of the observer influences the results of thought." Some sociologists would add that *position means role* and *role* means one's status in action.

The relativity in the relationships of "facts" and "values" does not justify either moral or epistemological skepticism. Sociology of knowledge should provide a refinement in our understanding of human perception and an illumination of the conditions qualifying that perception. Despite Mannheim's constant emphasis upon the *social* conditioning of cognitive and valuational processes, there is in his work a pervasive stress upon uniqueness, individuality, spontaneity and self-determining conscience, and a genuine affirmation of the ultimacy of the *person*.

In "The Role of Value in Karl Mannheim's Sociology of Knowledge,"[19] Warren Rempel has shown that Mannheim never fully came to terms *at the theoretical level* with the *normative* aspects of the science of human behavior. Mannheim's work shows the potential role of philosophy and theology because of the necessity of integrating, through interdisciplinary study, the sociological and the normative, or ethical dimensions of the study of man, as complementary disciplines. Social science cannot finally disavow or eliminate metaphysical issues. If, as in Mannheim, they are pushed into the bacground, this only confirms the notion that social scientists must at some point become self-conscious in regard to the metaphysical and axiological assumptions that they hold and that pervade and guide their thoughts. The dialogue with theology must go on.

Theology's Use of the Social Sciences

Many theologians today express the Church's involvement in the secular order and a concern for responsible social change. A great deal of work is at present going on in the field of the sociology of religion which draws on the assumptions and methods of both theology and social science. Christian thought today amply stresses various elements of doctrine as imperatives and motives in social actions. There is, finally, in existentialism and various types of Christian ethics, an emphasis on decision in social situations. In all these ways theologians are being led to make empirical claims and to relate values to social science.

Because of this, some social scientists, like D. L. Munby, lift up "the importance of technical competence."[20] He expresses legitimate concern when he notes that theologians often do not employ empirical analysis precisely; or when they make a too simple distinction between means and ends, allocating means to science and ends to theology and in addition, overlooking their complex interpenetration; or when they are poorly informed in economics and in their ignorance are unaware of its limitations; or when they indulge in false searches for "Christian" answers, giving a misplaced Christian concreteness to certain schemes and programs; or when they lack relevant expertise. To emphasize this latter point he says: "It is exceedingly rare that one can find sound theological insight unadulterated with economic nonsense."[21] Munby summarizes the two foundations of effective Christian social analysis and action as the theological/metasociological assertions about the nature of man and the willingness to accept wholeheartedly the facts as they are found to be. There are no shortcuts to responsibility.

If we are to understand critically theology's use of the social sciences, we must distinguish clearly between the intellectual processes of moving from theology to science and those of going from science to theology. Although the earlier portions of this paper voiced a warning against a too easy disjunction between *disclosure* and *discovery,* the methodological steps from disclosure to discovery are different from those involved in going from discovery to disclosure. Some thinkers wish to set up a continuum between theology and the unity of truth support the idea of an ultimate unity between faith as response to disclosure and knowledge as verified discovery. Yet no easy scheme of continuity should blur the autonomy, the different methods, the contrasting modes of verification and the distinct functions, of science and theology. This is one side of the problem. The other side is that empirical inquiry is able to clarify the operational meaning of theological concepts and claims. Theology needs to develop functional definitions of religion and of the way in which religious believing and behaving take place in different settings and cultures. The behavioral sciences have *discovered* many things about man and human nature which biblical revelation did not *disclose,* and these findings are often important for personal and intergroup relationships. Theology, like science, should be open to some kind of truth test if it is to make some truth claim. As Frederick Ferré says: "Any proposition responsibly asserted or assented to must offer some means of 'verification,' in the broad sense that some good reason or reasons for maintaining that proposition's truth rather than its falsity must be able to be provided."[22]

It is evident, as a consequence of all that we have noted above, that man's understanding of the secular forces of society is part of his obligation to obey God, and that technical competence is also part of that obedience. Patient cooperation is required between the theologian and the social scientist, to build up understanding and develop technical competence. Empirical work requires careful scientific operation in the most diverse situations on earth. For example, there is a great deal of qualitative as well as quantitative social research in selected favorable areas of the world, but we lack a hard core of data on some of the greatest conflict areas of interpersonal and intergroup relations. There are few verified scientific models for conflict resolution. The facts are so diverse, and society is so complex, that only the bare outlines of a synthesis of Christian social thought—or of its middle axioms—are at present conceivable. But since we believe as Christians that a responsible social order will be one where men and women live as their creator intended them to live, all that can be learned about fact, value and interpretation in theology and social science will become part of responsible living in the secular order.

1. Appendix 2, p. 1035. New York and London: Harper & Bros., 1944, 1947.

2. New York: Harper Torchbooks, pp. 74-75.

3. **Ibid.,** p. 75.

4. **Protestant Thought and Natural Science,** Garden City, N. Y.: Doubleday & Co., Inc., 1960, p. 283.

5. **Ibid.,** p. 256.

6. **Ibid.,** pp. 264-265.

7. **Ibid.,** p. 265.

8. **Ethical Judgment, The Use of Science in Ethics,** Glencoe, Ill.: The Free Press, 1955, p. 30.

9. **Ibid.,** p. 32.

10. **Ibid.,** p. 36.

11. **Edel,** op. cit., p. 59.

12. **Edel,** op. cit., p. 54.

13. **Ideology and Utopia.** New York: Harcourt, Brace, 1936, p. 49.

14. **Ibid.**, p. 49-50.

15. **Ibid.**, p. 50.

16. Paul E. Sigmund, Jr., ed., **The Ideologies of the Developing Nations,** New York: F. A. Praeger, 1963, p. 4.

17. **Ibid.**, p. 40.

18. **Ibid.**, p. 37.

19. An unpublished doctoral dissertation, Boston University, 1962.

20. See D. L. Munby: "The Importance of Technical Competence," in **Anglican Self-Criticism,** D. M. Paton, ed. London: SCM Press, 19 pp. 45-58.

21. **Ibid**.

22. Frederick Ferré, "Verification, Faith and Credulity," in **Religion in Life,** Winter, 1962-1963, p. 52.

MAN–IN LIGHT OF SOCIAL SCIENCE AND CHRISTIAN FAITH

JAMES M. GUSTAFSON

What one understands about man depends upon the particular light in which he is ˙ seen, or more precisely, upon what vocabulary and relationships one chooses as the framework for interpretation. In theology man is interpreted in his relationship to God the Creator and Sustainer, to Jesus Christ the Son, and to the presence of the Spirit in the Church and the world. The fact that man is seen in this relationship . . . predisposes the writer to use language appropriate to it. Man is seen as creature of God; he is seen as fallen from a state of faith and trust in God; he is seen as sinner in relation to God and to other men; he is seen as responsible to God in all his words and deeds; he is seen as participating in new life in Christ; he is seen in Christian freedom. All of these things that can be said about man in relationship to God, however, obviously do not exhaust what can be said about man in other relationships.

The secular philosopher of ethics has another light to turn upon man, different from the theologian's. He asks about man's moral action: Is it determined by his sentiments and his emotions? Or is it determined by a fundamental moral law that is grounded in human nature? Does he decide what his conduct ought to be in relation to the prevailing moral consensus of his community? Or is his behavior basically determined by some fundamental drives for self-preservation that reside in his psycho-physical being? Can he perceive values in things? Or does he act according to some rules of conduct set up by society?

Theological language and the vocabulary of ethics by no means exhaust the ways we have to describe and interpret man. There is political language, psychological language, aesthetic language, and many other forms. In this chapter, with an opening confession of necessary oversimplification, we are concerned to see what man looks like in the light of social science. The task is appallingly broad, and justice cannot be done to refinements in viewpoints, and to competing forces at debate within the sciences that deal with social behavior. To make it manageable, three themes have been selected as fairly pervasive in the social sciences: (a) man is viewed genetically—that is, in terms of the causal processes, and thus there is an emphasis on the determination of his present state by past events; (b) man is viewed functionally—that is, in terms of a creature with needs that seek fulfillment in various ways in order to survive; (c) man is viewed as researchable—that is, he can be defined in terms measurable by contemporary social research procedures.

Throughout the exposition of these themes, certain contrasts will be drawn with theological and moral interpretations of man. This is done not to demonstrate the superiority of theology and ethics to give the picture of "real" man, but to indicate the differences in frame of reference, and thus in the characteristics that are accentuated in the portrait of man. Nor is the procedure of contrast used to demonstrate the greater adequacy of social science themes about man; they will always be inadequate taken in themselves for those who think of man in relation to God, and who think of man in relation to moral responsibility. Actually, however, most Christians have absorbed much of the fundamental vision of man that is embedded in studies of his social behavior without consciousness of discrepancies between that view and those provided in the Christian tradition. Most of us act as if social determination is the whole story of man. Finally, however, both our action and the views of social sciences need to be questioned in the light of our Christian confession.

Behavior Is Determined

One of the oldest arguments among Western views of man deals with the extent of man's freedom versus the extent of his determination by forces outside himself. This has been an issue in philosophy: at one extreme Spinoza seems to say that the only freedom man has is his acquiescence to necessity; in his acceptance of the fact that he is determined by other forces, he finds the measure of freedom that he has. In contrast, Kant, who was interested in preserving a strong sense of moral responsibility, asserted that the essential character of the human self was outside the realm of the effects of causal factors, and could exercise reason and free will to determine behavior. The issue of freedom and determinism also has a long history of theological debate. Finally is each man predestined? Or does he determine his own destiny? If he is predestined, are all the detailed decisions of life governed by God's power? Or is there a realm of responsibility for the exercise of free choice? This debate continues in theological discourse: Christian existentialists stress the capacity for a free response of faith and obedience to God, and thus the ability to shape life and events. Theologians who still desire to interpret the providence of the almighty God are forced to find qualified ways to deal with freedom.

The social scientists have not taken part in this debate in philosophical and theological terms. Indeed, they tend to eschew such language, and aver that they are concerned only with such generalizations about human behavior as can be developed from observation and from refined empirical evidence. But social scientists do belong to a community of scholars who seek to understand what now exists in the light of cause-and-effect analysis; they look at the self in an effort to find out what conditions, causal factors, relationships, and occasions are most important in shaping behavior. Thus there is in the social sciences a predisposition to think in "behavioristic" terms, that is, in terms of the determination of human selfhood and action by turning to the antecedents of the present experience. There is a tendency to view the present self particularly in relation to its past experiences, and in relation to other selves, cultures, and institutions that presently exert decisive influence on behavior.

The theologian might find the analysis of human behavior given from the viewpoint of social science to be interesting, and even helpful, in understanding the characteristic continuities of behavior. But his questions relate to another object, the divine Being. He might, however, wonder what patterns of Providence can be interpreted as present in the ordering of life that the student of social life describes. Or he might question whether both the continuing patterns and the particular actions of a person are in accord with what God has meant man to be in the world. The theologian's questions are governed by his concern— man in relation to God. The social scientist's questions are governed by his concern—man in relation to factors that condition or determine his behavior.

The response of some theologians to the social scientist's interpretation of man has been one of critical dismissal. The grounds for this seem to be the excessive confidence that many scientists have had, particularly in their assumptions that what they have known provides grounds for predictability of behavior. Certainly most social scientists are now cautious about predictions, though they would affirm that their studies enable one to project certain probabilities with reference to future behavior, both of persons and of groups. Theologians also believe that the most important questions about man cannot be answered by science, namely, those that pertain to man's status before God and to man's moral obligations to his neighbor. This is no doubt the case, but within their limited sphere of concern, the scientists of behavior offer illuminating evidences.

Indeed, for the religious person, one of the functions of genetic interpretations of man is to unmask illusions and pretensions to which our faith tempts us. Christians are often likely to assume that their behavior is governed by their trust and loyalty to Jesus Christ, when the larger part of it is actually determined by their relationships to parents and to social groups. They are likely to assume that in faith they are freed from bondage to their personal histories, to ideologies and groups, when in actual behavior they are not. Indeed, the amount of light that social science can shed on behavior, including the behavior of Christians, ought to chasten believers; it might lead them to self-examination and repentance. As Hannah Arendt, no friend of behaviorism as a general philosophy, has observed, one reason the social scientists are so effective and popular in North America is that so much of what they say about American behavior is true. We do "behave" as conditioned, rather than "act" in the light of reason or faith.

Man, the Creature of Needs and Desires

A basic model for the interpretation of human behavior in a number of the social sciences has been taken from the field of the biological sciences. It is the language of "organism," and if this word is rejected, part of its meaning is carried over into a "functional" theory. These terms point to a view of both individual selves and societies as entities that live for the sake of surviving with the least possible strain within and between persons and groups. Persons find ways of "adjusting" to what is happening to them, just as animals adapt to a changing physical environment. Societies seek to approximate a status of "equilibrium" in which the elements of conflict and dissent are reduced to a tolerable point, and something approaching harmony exists, just as in nature the various forces relate to each other in such a way that most beings and plants can survive. There are needs that have to be met, and human beings find ways to meet these needs. Indeed, for many sociologists, psychologists, and anthropologists man is finally an organism in an environment, seeking to establish those patterns of life that make for survival under the most harmonious conditions possible.

This view has been particularly offensive to many Christian interpreters of humanity, for it posits man and his survival as the final reality to which all things refer. Behavior has reference to God who created man, who requires man to meet certain conditions if life is to be sustained, who demands a faithfulness that might well bring the denial of harmony and equilibrium. Behavior is finally explainable with reference to need-fulfillment.

Functionalism readily becomes itself a pseudo-theological doctrine insofar as it provides a fundamental principle in the light of which almost everything is interpreted and understood. Religion itself, not to mention other phases of life and culture, is often explained on functional grounds. Religion, like all other aspects of culture, is a human invention by which people manage to meet needs, and come to grips with the strains and tensions of life.[1]

Some critical moralists would acquiesce to the assertion that human needs form the fundamental basis of human morality, but would quarrel with particular determinations of what these needs are. A Roman Catholic might agree that what is right and good is what fulfills the deepest human needs, but he would hardly take a poll, or rely only on his observations of current behavior to determine what these needs are. He has a conviction that determines his definition of need, and in turn the ordering of life: namely, that man finally seeks the good and avoids evil; but the good is not simply the fulfillment of every desire, or the realization of impulses. To think about it properly one must introduce terms like justice, the virtues of prudence, temperance, and courage, and other things that are not derived from assessments based on analysis of behavioral evidence in some simple way.

The Roman Catholic, like other Christians, also would see the realm of human needs within a framework of God's creation, and of purposes that exist because God has so ordered human life. The point of stumbling is that most functional interpretations of man believe that there is no point of reference beyond the self or beyond nature, to which life refers. This becomes clear when a functional interpretation of religion comes into view. Religion has no point of reference that is objective to the needs of self and society. To speak of God is to speak of something that is incapable of empirical verification, whereas to speak of human needs is to define something which, men can agree, does exist. There is a "positivism" that informs functional views of man: only the observable, measurable man exists; he is not related to anything beyond himself. Man, in functionalism, is viewed only with reference to nature, and to nature defined in a particular way. Societies, like individual persons, seek an adjustment not to the will of God but to a state of equilibrium in which strains and tensions are reduced to the point of toleration.

The Christian might be most offended when he sees religion reduced to a human need, but he also ought to wonder whether economic and political life do not have some purpose with reference to the kind of order through which God can sustain human societies. Where the functionalist stops is but a station in the Christian interpretation of man: God's work is done through the orders of preservation, the establishment of justice, the fulfillment of human potentialities.

Functionalism, however, cannot be lightly dismissed. Human needs are a kind of prism through which all light goes; for this reason functionalism can become an inclusive principle of explanation for human existence. Faith, Christians affirm, relates men to God, but faith in God also fulfills human longings and needs. Thus even faith goes through the prism of human need, man's need for God, and this provides the temptation to explain all that is involved in faith by that through which it is refracted. Further, when functionalism is applied to the interpretation of behavior, religious included, it has an unpleasant effect on the pretensions of Christians and other moral men. It enables men to see how much of action reputed to be engaged in for lofty purposes is really a matter of adjustment to the world. The functionalists provide a point of view for a critique of much religious life: We like to believe that men worship to praise God, but many of us worship to get a psychic serenity we need to adjust to the ambiguities of daily life. We like to believe that confirmation is a rite in which a child's reception into the Body of Christ by baptism is really confirmed, but for both parents and children it is often a puberty rite in which a new stage of physical and social maturity is celebrated. So much of behavior can be accounted for on functional grounds that it is no wonder the point of view has a persuasive power in contemporary culture.

Behavior Is Researchable

It is obvious that for many centuries scholars and poets, as well as businessmen and farmers, have been making observations of human behavior in which they have confidence, and from which they make certain generalizations. Aristotle made many shrewd remarks that seem to penetrate human behavior, such as "man is a political animal," and so have most philosophers. The fact that man can be "researched" is not novel. But some of the procedures used to research human behavior are increasingly refined in character. Among social scientists— sociologists, psychologists, political scientists, and others—the current effort is to find ways in which human behavior can be converted into numerical terms, can be recorded on IBM cards, and can be delineated in highly precise generalizations as a result of these refinements. One symptom of this is the way in which a course in statistics is required for most graduate students of society, persons, and politics. It is as if the way to reality was by the quantification of things, and unfortunately in some instances the assumption is that if something is not reducible to number it is not researchable, and therefore (almost) it is not real.

These refined measurements of behavior are not without significant value, although they are probably overvalued by some of the researchers. Certainly they are a rigorous check upon impressions; persons who assume that they can perceive and generalize on human behavior have often merely projected what they wish to see onto the world around them. No longer need this be the case; the perceptions and imaginative generalizations can become the hypotheses for more careful assessment of what is and is not the case. For example, for generations there have been assumptions about the political behavior of various social groups in the United States, based on impressions from election returns. If a particular ward was heavily Democratic, and there was a large Roman Catholic Church in the ward, men felt rather secure in saying that Roman Catholics vote Democratic. And they were probably correct. But with various sampling techniques, refined schedules of inquiry, etc., one can find out not only how many Roman Catholics vote Democratic, but whether other factors are not more important than the religious one, e.g., the income status, the ethnic group identification, the family system, and the like. General impressions are corrected and refined by research into political behavior.

The measurement research into behavior professes to be interested only in accurate description of what exists. Description includes not only an account of what is at any particular time and place, but also an analysis of the correlation of factors that enable one to begin to understand some reasons why "what is" is. Thus, there is an easy movement from description to causal analysis, and at this point other questions sometimes need to be raised. First, if the methods of measurement begin to dictate what can be researched, can one be sure he is finding out the most important things that need to be known about behavior? This question might be answered by various social scientists in different ways. The more modest and self-critical might suggest that all one gets at are certain indices of behavior, and that these are limited to some extent by the number of variables the researcher seeks to ferret out in his research design. Even when one can make significant correlations between aspects of human life, one has not yet proved a causal sequence. Less self-critical practitioners of the measurement procedures often claim more for what they find out; crudely stated, they assume that if something is not quantifiable it is not real, and in effect rather than conforming method to the human behavior to be studied, they rule out the significance of all behavior that cannot be reduced to their methods. At its worst, this kind of work is mechanical, presumptuous, and "genius-proof."

Second, there is a great deal of dubiety in assuming that correlations declare unambiguously clear assertions of causation. Robert Merton, in refining the procedures for the sociology of knowledge, suggests some of the words that need to be carefully selected in determining the character of the relationship of things that are correlated: they "correspond" to each other; or one is the "condition" of the other, or there is a "functional interdependence" between them, or one "determines" the other.[2] In the selection of appropriate words, there is a heavy weight of philosophical decision, of predisposition, that is not necessarily verifiable, or requires even more refined studies to validate accurately. For example, juvenile delinquents in one area are Negroes, Protestants, come from lower-income families, have a high incidence of broken families, live in slums, and are poorly educated. In another area they are white, Roman Catholic, of Italian extraction, from families with lower income, have traditional Italian family systems, etc. How does one assess which factors are "causally" most significant in delinquency? There are refined ways to proceed with such analysis and, without doubt, through social analysis one can be surer about which factors are more important than one can be without social analysis. But judgments have to be made, even of the data, and these obviously require more than measurement—a fact social scientists would agree to. But social analysis of behavior is not prejudice-proof; one can be disposed to look at Protestant religious behavior, for example, as the result of large segments being members of the middle class; but a case is also made for the fact that Protestant religious faith and life tends to push people toward middle-class goals and behavior. I merely wish to indicate the complexity that is involved in making judgments of causality between factors of behavior that are significantly correlated statistically.

The Christian interpreter can be informed about what is actually taking place by the work of social research. He often wonders if what he finds out is worth all the time, effort, and money that went into such study, but that query is not so much the result of his Christian viewpoint as it is of other bases of judgment. But the Christian interpreter generally wonders whether the most significant dimensions of human behavior can be reduced to the measurement procedures. Some things that formerly seemed out of the range of research now are coming into it, for example, research on the "values" that people hold, and the extent to which behavior is governed them. But can something like loving the neighbor be measured? If one could get consensus on which acts are "loving" acts, which attitudes are "loving" attitudes, etc., something might be done. But insofar as love of neighbor is a spontaneous act, stemming from God's gracious love, and freely given to the other, perhaps the task is more difficult if not impossible.

Future, Christians have believed that man is related to God (a "non-empirical factor" for social research). There are dimensions of the meaning of human behavior that are governed by faith in God. It is at this level of the framework for interpreting the *meaning* of human existence that Christians part company with the social researcher. This parting of the ways does not mean a rejection of what research has found out, but a critical approach to it, seeking to make clear the assumptions of such research. It also requires that the Christian interpreters carefully develop the significance of what is known about man through research, for the moral and theological purposes that are given in the Christian community. The data are interpreted with reference to the knowledge of God and his will and work.

Similarly, the secular ethicist might be grateful for information on voting behavior, but he necessarily incorporates other bases for judgment and interpretation into his efforts to define what political and social policies are "good" for a given society. The research may help him at the level of tactics for achievement of moral ends, if he wills to put policy into action, but he has other purposes in view and thus reinterprets what is known. Max Millikan, in an essay "Inquiry and Policy," suggests that what the researcher comes out with in his conclusions is not so important for the policymaker as are his arguments. "The purpose of social science research should be to deepen, broaden, and extend the policymaker's capacity for judgment—not to provide him with answers."[3] Obviously, then, the measurement research into behavior is worthwhile if the problems to which it is addressed are important, and if it needs to be used by Christian and secular interpreters of man. But the moral judgments that go into policy judgments cannot be derived from research.

What is the Christian's response to the general views of man in the social sciences? Properly, first it is gratitude for the kinds of knowledge and understanding of human behavior that can be derived from the perspectives and procedures that inform the social scientist. He sees things because he has a particular view; he depicts behavior because he has refined procedures to use. But the Christian's response is also critical—though certainly not rejection. He is critical of claims made indiscreetly that all there is to know of man can be known from the scientific perspective and method. But such a critique must be discriminatingly applied only to those social scientists who assume the posture of omniscience. The Christian claims the right to interpret man from the Christian perspective as well, and he sees things in this light that the lights from social science do not expose. Finally, the Christian carefully interprets and uses the knowledge from the social sciences in his own particular interpretations of men, and in his ethical considerations. For the Christian is interested in the quality of human life and in the moral character of human action.

1. Bronislaw Malinowski, **A Scientific Theory of Culture.**

2. Robert Merton, **Social Theory and Social Structure,** (Glencoe, Ill.: The Free Press, 1949), pp. 221-222.

3. Max Millikan, "Inquiry and Policy," in **The Human Meaning of the Social Sciences,** ed. by Daniel Lerner (New York: Meridan Books, 1959), p. 167.

PART III
Critical Social Issues

This section will comprise the most important part of the book for many of our readers. It contains a set of statements by religious bodies and individuals addressed to some of our major social problems. In collecting these representative articles we have attempted to illustrate the wide range of views that can be found among the religious communities concerning social problems. It would be impossible to have represented every issue of importance, or to have given a representative article on every position held within the religious bodies. What has survived our pruning is, we hope, a collection of topics and views that will be stimulating and as much "on target" as a collection of this size can be. Also, it is our hope that this selection illustrates how the major religious communities approach and address themselves to social issues in various and sundry ways.

The majority of believers in America today probably still are convinced of the efficacy of evolutionary change. Most Jews and Christians adhere to a faith in measured progress which, while increasingly challenged, continues to have vitality. A striking example of this has been the growing awareness of the importance of "development," particularly in Roman Catholic thought. "Development is the new name for peace!" Paul VI has said. The four articles in this section set forth the state of thinking in this emerging area, along with some of the hard questions that the churches must face in dealing with the developing countries.

The range of views expressed in the section on war and peace illustrate the conflicting values to be found even among those who proceed from a religious background. Helmut Gollwitzer speaks from the perspective of viewing war as a moral problem which can be dealt with through the institutions of contempoary society. The American Catholic Bishops, however, question a number of these institutions, especially compulsory military service without selective conscientious objection.

The next two issues are in many ways interconnected. The articles under "Revolution and Violence" confront, in various ways, this central problem. The leadership in the rising spirit of revolution has been the youth, and their aspirations and concerns, deeply felt, are explored in the next collection. Nicholas Piediscalzi offers theological insights into the meaning and challenge of the revolutionary youth movements. Edgar Friedenberg's analysis of the role of the university in contemporary society and the need for its reform in our revolutionary situation concludes this section.

Identifying the key issues in the relation of religion and the urban-technological crisis proves itself more complex than at first it would seem. We finally limited ourselves to three: race and poverty, the nature of the urban life-style, and environmental pollution and destruction. Arguments could have been made for the inclusion of other questions but we felt that these three bring together the most critical problems. All the policy questions, law and order, unemployment, education, pollution and so on through the litany of social ills that beset the cities, seem to us to flow from these basic issues. It is our judgment that these are the seminal questions.

CHRISTIANS AND ECONOMIC GROWTH

RONALD H. PRESTON

Anyone who studies the history of Christian social thought will realize that for centuries it has suffered from the grave defect of irrelevance. There was a time in the high Middle Ages when Christian thought had more or less come to terms with the current social order, understood it and spoke relevantly to it. But soon the empirical situation shifted, and Catholic thought became increasingly out of touch with it by working within a priori categories. It intended to deal with particular situations, but it did not allow sufficiently for autonomy of "secular" studies and in consequence misunderstood much of the secular world. Protestant thought has been little more relevant, chiefly because it has been particularly prone to an individualistic pietism which has simply bypassed the problem of social ethics. In practice this has resulted in an uncritical acceptance of the status quo. Now, however, we have through the Ecumenical Movement a theological basis for Christian social ethics which pays attention to the facts of economic and social and industrial life, and has gone a long way to securing them.

Meanwhile, the fact remains that for the first time for centuries Christians have up-to-date knowledge of what is happening and a diagnosis of significant changes.

Christ the Transformer of Culture

There is underlying this whole ecumenical development of Christian social thinking a stress on the necessity of paying attention to facts. The stress is a corrective to all theologies which proceed in a deductive a priori way. Beyond that, there are various possible theological frameworks which could serve as the pattern for Christian thinking in social ethics; and it would be idle to pretend that there is unanimity about them in ecumenical circles. But, if one takes, for example, the late Richard Niebuhr's well-known analysis, in his book *Christ and Culture,* of five different theological positions which have persisted in Christian history (an important corrective to Troeltsch's classical delimitation of only three positions), it is clear that there is something of value in the five or they would not have persisted through the centuries. It is also clear that Niebuhr thinks that the fifth (Christ the transformer of culture) is more adequate than the others.[1]

It is within this fifth position that the theological basis for dealing with the dynamic problems of economic growth will be found. The reason is that it is the only one which is specifically geared to a dynamic and changing society. This is what all the world is now living in. For most of recorded history social change has been very slow. But now rapid and continuous social change is the great new fact of our time. The theology associated in Niebuhr's fifth position is best fitted to deal with endemic rapid social change, and it is a true interpretation for such a situation. Traditional Catholic theology will need to have a more empirical concern, and traditional Lutheran theology will need a more dynamic outlook (and we can see in someone like Bonhoeffer the struggle to arrive at one). Neither Catholic natural law theology nor Lutheran order of creation theology is precluded, but they need developing in a new way.

The Evanston Assembly adopted a flexible and pragmatic attitude to the social order within the broad criterion of the responsible society. A study conference at Arnoldsheim in Germany in 1956 took up the theme in more detail, but it is the Thessaloniki Conference of 1959 which is the most significant one for us. The conference analyzed the problem of rapid social and cultural change, and then discussed the Christian responsibility for political action, for economic development, and for the promotion of community life in both rural and urban areas. Recognizing the social dislocation and moral confusion caused by rapid social change and the danger which affluence can bring, it elaborated the Christian attitude toward the development of the world's resources. It said that "providentially it provides opportunities for the development of each person, for the enrichment of the equality of human living, and for the subduing of the earth and exercising dominion over it of which the Bible speaks." It affirmed that "it is right and Christian, however, to insist on the need for a reasonable level" (standard of living), and that "in discovering and making use of the wealth of the earth and of the human mind we have some of our greatest opportunities to give God the worship due to him," calling in the parable of the talents to support it. But it emphasized that these resources must be used for the benefit of all men, "for God looks on the whole human family as one." No man, or country, therefore, has the absolute right to enjoy by themselves, either the fruits of material riches they happen to inherit, or the fruits of ability or effort. God does not draw boundaries of responsibility at national frontiers, nor can we."

The report discussed some of the ethical issues involved in the methods of economic growth. The report is realistic about the inescapable problems involved in developing a competent and socially responsible industrial leadership, and what this means in terms of both management training and the development of trade unions. It urged Christians to help with both these tasks and with the achievement of the increased productivity that is the urgent need of most countries. It remarked how few examples there are of Christians doing this, and indeed how isolated the Church is from the life and needs of the industrial workers. It faced the problem of strikes. All this is far removed from the ethical outlook that is customary in the churches of the underdeveloped countries. The report stressed the need for the churches to understand both the real costs of economic development in terms of human values and at the same time the human cost of inaction. Within this general awareness "Christian responsibility involves decisions as to whether a particular economic choice is really a moral or merely a technical choice. In the former case responsible Christian action is required. In the latter, Christians should help to divert the choice of moral and theological overtones."

On the question of the spiritual dangers of economic development the report mentioned five points:

1. Men do not necessarily know how to consume responsibly.
2. Men become absorbed in the means and techniques that make for an affluent society.
3. When men get richer they worship riches and forget God.
4. Society may become marked by new forms of social stratification, conspicuous consumption, and status seeking, as people look for marks and symbols of personal prestige and success.
5. Men may become slaves of the production machine and victims of the vast and elaborate apparatus upon which they have come to depend for material abundance.

In addition to ecumenical thought in Christian social ethics, there has been a good deal of miscellaneous material covering similar ground from various church sources.

In this discussion there has been a notable change in the theological mood in the past few years. This is something that grows out of what has gone before but that would have been difficult to foresee. It has taken the form of a new theological humanism. It is not that the Christian faith has been abandoned for a secular humanist one, but that the concern in the Christian gospel for the truly human in life has been emphasized, and with it a sense of the solidarity of the Christian with all men. Jacques Maritain's book, *True Humanism,* in a sense foreshadows this development, and is one indication among many to the extent to which Roman Catholic thought and that of the Ecumenical Movement are arriving by different routes at similar positions. John XXIII's encyclical *Mater et magistra* is another.

Ethical Problems of Economic Growth

In the more-developed countries we have a very high production of goods and services; the pressure is to consume more as luxuries come to be considered necessities. The basic question for Christians to consider is how far we can baptize economic growth and affluence in the name of Christ. The question is acute because of the warnings in the Gospels about the danger of riches and of covetousness. Indeed, Jesus explicitly reversed the current belief, shared by his disciples, that riches were a sign of God's favor. He clearly regarded them as a main cause of anxiety, and anxiety as a key symptom of lack of trust in God. It would be true to say that the Church has never found it easy to come to terms with this note in the Gospels. Its radical note has sometimes been held to apply to the few who are called to the "religious" life, following the counsels of perfection as distinct from the precepts binding on all. But the voluntary poverty of those who answered this call has nearly always been accompanied by the enormous wealth of the order to which they belonged. The more usual position has been to urge on the rich the duty of being charitable to the poor without challenging the basic distribution of riches. An obvious position would have been to stress the need for greater common ownership of wealth, but on the whole it has been left to secular socialist critics to develop this criticism. Certainly any Christian justification of private property that has been worked out would presuppose the widest possible diffusion, though this has seldom been remembered by Christian teachers and preachers. It would perhaps be ironical if Christians began to take exception to economic growth only when for the first time in the world's history it appeared that there might be the possibility of removing the crippling poverty, squalor and disease from the backs of the majority of humanity who have hitherto always suffered them.

Poverty and riches are terms relevant to their situation. The task of Christians would appear to be, first of all, to admit that the Church has far too easily accepted worldly standards of wealth, and to regard this a challenge to deal more effectively with the new problems of economic growth and affluence. This means being suitably wary of the pressures of the affluent society to ever greater consumption, and translating the Gospel warnings on riches from their *Sitz im Leben* in first-century Palestine to the entirely different economical circumstances of today. This will involve a right use of individual and corporate wealth within one country and between richer and poorer countries; it will also mean thinking out afresh the relation of work and leisure. We shall then see that economic growth may well be accepted as one of the most signal examples of man's mastery over nature which he is given by divine command in the Genesis parable of creation. We shall realize that although economic growth, properly controlled, can remove terrible privations from the majority of the human race, this may not in itself make them any happier. Human life will always present human beings with pain, loss, disappointment and frustrations, no matter what level of economic growth we may achieve. The Christian challenge comes in the way these inevitable deprivations are met and in the quality of our relationships with others in the bundle of life in which we are tied up with others. Here the Gospel warnings against the deceitfulness of riches and the call to a responsibly corporate use of wealth will always have their place.

The question may still arise as to whether the Christian can sanction indefinite social accumulation. Do we look to an economic system which requires an even greater proliferation of wants in order to keep going? Does it mean that we must establish a deliberate system of built-in obsolescence, scrapping things long before they are worn out in order to keep the system going with new production? In that case the whole economy would be run on the principle on which women's fashions are already run. Would it be possible to give a Christian sanction to such a system? Clearly it would not. There are various factors which may make this prospect less immediate than might appear. One is the growth in population. Another is the vast amount of resources that are needed if anything like a satisfactory urban environment and town development is to be secured. A third is the scope there is for helping consumers to be much more exacting in their requirements, much less satisfied with the careless and the shoddy.

Need for New Social and Human Attitudes

Perhaps the underlying Christian concern is to insist that "economic growth is made for man and not man for economic growth," a conviction that springs directly from the Christian belief in the status of man made in God's image, remade in Jesus Christ, and destined for eternal fellowship with God and with his fellowmen in God.

One would expect, for instance, for the Church to be sensitive to the underdog, to those who get a raw deal in life. It was the scandal of the first industrial revolution that it was so callous to those who suffered in the process. There will always be the old, the lonely, the neurotic, the mentally handicapped, the unskilled, those burdened with large families, for whom "ambulance work" is needed and for whom the Christian conscience should be alert.

Rapid and continuous social change, however, brings strains which affect much of the population. Pursuit of productivity regardless of its social effects may have serious effects on the power of adjustment of individuals and families. A skill learned at age twenty may be valueless at age forty. It is hard then to learn a new skill. Yet the shock of becoming unskilled is great. How many times in a working life can a man stand the strain of becoming redundant and having to adapt himself to a new occupation? Anxieties of this kind arise in white-collar as well as manual jobs.

A further point one has to query is whether in the pursuit of productivity enough thought is given to the using up of nonrenewable resources like fossil fuels. There are limits to the extent to which it is a moral duty to consider an unknown future, but Christians ought to help society to look beyond the end of its nose.

We need to look further at the problem of directing the ever-increasing productivity to socially desirable ends. Here the influence of advertising has to be critically examined. It is easy to exaggerate the scale of the problem and to succumb to the exaggerations with which the industry surrounds itself. Disquiet arises because much of it does not respect the dignity of the human person. It is designed to produce impulse buying rather than considered behavior, it is inclined to appeal to social status and snobbery; or to profit by human weakness, fears and anxieties; or to exploit fundamental human traits like the concern for one's children or the need for security, status, and love. That is why the consumers' movement in many countries is a welcome counterbalance to aspects of modern advertising and salesmanship techniques.

Equally important is the question of collective expenditure. There is the wanton ugliness of much industrial environment, the mean housing, the out-of-date hospitals, schools and prisons. What is lacking is sufficient concern for the common good and awareness of the corporate nature of society.

In most industrialized countries it is still the stage where the mass of wage earners find their relative affluence so new that when statutory hours of work are reduced, they are eager for more overtime in order to accumulate more goods and enjoy more services. In the U. S. there are said to be four million people doing two jobs. In fact the prospect of leisure presents a challenge. Before the century is out, a three-or-four-day working week should be possible in many economically developed countries, but most people at the moment do not know what to do with such resulting leisure and are frightened of it.

There seems an undeniable loss of vision in the West compared with a few years ago. The underdeveloped countries need aid, but they need trade as well. They need a more certain income through more stable prices for primary products, and they also need free entry for their manufactured goods in the markets of the "West." This in turn means a willingness of the West to modify its internal economics to this end, and the willingness to make the social adjustments necessary. A larger vision and a vigorous public policy are called for. Neither is as yet readily secured because people in the relatively affluent West do not want to be disturbed in their ways.

Help for developing countries needs increasing if the growing disparity in standards of living is to be checked. The West should consider whether some of the money it is spending on military and space research and development could not be better spent. It should also consider whether it does not need a higher annual rate of economic growth to fulfill these obligations to others. This would be in order to discharge responsibilities to the less wealthy rather than to get rich still more quickly at home. Merely to state this is to realize how far the West is from grasping it. Yet can the moral responsibility of those who have riches such as the West possesses be any less? Has any western government ever begun to plan how to lead its citizens in this direction? One of the most striking features of the economic affairs of states is that their domestic decisions affect other states far beyond their frontiers. The less strong countries economically are particularly vulnerable to those with developed economies. Here again the sense of the common good is only rudimentarily developed, and the moral responsibility of the wealthy countries correspondingly great.

The Moral Dynamics of Change

It is evident from this inquiry into economic growth that much depends on the actions and attitudes of the underdeveloped countries themselves, including the development of what are sometimes called the "Protestant virtues" of thought, efficiency and the avoidance of waste. These are not traditional attitudes in such countries, but have become established in industrial societies. The precise role of Protestantism in this is an issue much discussed. But without going into this question it is clear that any religious motivation suitable to a country beginning to develop must have a dynamic element and not merely provide a sanction of the status quo, as religion has so often done in human history.

This discussion has presupposed that there is a real struggle to achieve the economic growth which both the West and the rest now presuppose. There are some who so emphasize the productive power of technology, with the new achievements of automation and cybernetics as to suggest that this whole discussion is beside the point. Automation takes over labor, memory and logical choice. The machine has only to be fed with the right program. Repetitive jobs for human beings will go. The distinction between work and leisure will go. There is no prospect of providing jobs for most of the inhabitants of the developing countries. The problem will be boredom not fatigue. They should be encouraged to retain the old tribal virtues to cultivate the more passive and contemplative ones. Men should be issued with a basic income by right without working for it. It would be foolish to rule this out as a possibility in the future, but it is unlikely to be within the future that we have to adjust ourselves to now. Future generations must deal with it if and when it comes. But it could well be that by the turn of the century a twenty-hour working week would be the usual stint in the West, and this would give rise to the beginnings of many problems of work and leisure to which we have already referred. In the immediate future, however, there is no doubt that big efforts must be made by the underdeveloped countries.

How best to help the poor countries to achieve a "take off" is in fact a difficult question. W. W. Rostow, the economist, in his book *Stages of Economic Growth,* distinguished five stages: (1) a traditional society, (2) when ten per cent of national income is invested, and there is the beginning of an elite, (3) the "take off," (4) an economically mature society after sixty years, (5) when a level of high consumption is reached. It is not necessary to accept every detail of this analysis to see that the problem is how to get from the first to the third stage. There are many technical problems here, and it is a hard fact that much of the effort can come only from within the country concerned. Nevertheless, imaginative trade, aid, cultural, educational and administrative policies pursued by developed countries can immensely help or hinder. In all countries the control and use of power is a major matter of concern to the Christian conscience. Too many have been brought up in pietist forms of a Christianity that is politically irresponsible and regards participation in political activities as worldly and wrong. Power centered in private hands can easily become anonymous in giant corporations, and it becomes very hard to ensure that the private power is responsibly used, and indeed is not more powerful than the government. Similarly the development of power in trade unions can have a tyrannous effect. In some cases a member can find little redress against abuse of power by officials of his own union, which can in effect keep him out of employment.

We can imagine a society that has pruned away artificial inequalities and that has achieved a career open to the talents and promotion by merit only. In fact, the pressure for economic growth may work toward this. We should then have what has been called a meritocracy. It could merely mean an opportunity to get on, with the gap between the classes widening, leaving a lumpenproletariat at the bottom with no way of escape from the knowledge of its own lack of talent. Where would human solidarity be then? Indeed, one of the problems of advanced economies in the future will be to find jobs for those of low intelligence and mental handicap. And there is nothing worse than the feeling that one has no status and is not wanted.

Somewhere in this realm of a crusade for the human, with all that this means in terms of the criteria of justice, freedom and equality, may lie the springs of social enthusiasm, which is badly needed, now that the furious ideologies of the earlier years of the century are no longer what they were. In the more economically developed countries there is a certain disillusionment with past causes, a vacuum of enthusiasm. The poor countries are at the moment fired by "the revolution of rising expectations," which is associated with a heady nationalism and finds a convenient bogey in neo-colonialism. It is not easy for those who have had their share of nationalist fervor, and are only slowly growing out of it into supranational (for example, regional) conceptions, to be believed if they point to the dangers of nationalism. And it is of course a necessary advance in building new nations from tribalism. A crusade for the human, for making economic growth the servant of man is needed. Christians have the strongest reasons for wanting this, but it is something that they can share with those who lack the profound Christian grounds for wanting it. Christians should be able to demonstrate a distinctive style of life and an obedience to the call of Christ in the world that can have profound, if indirect, results in the struggle to work with God to make and to keep human life human under the stresses and opportunities of economic growth.

1. The others are (1) Christ against culture, (2) The Christ of culture (i.e. the accommodations of Christianity to culture, (3) Christ above culture, (4) Christ and culture in paradox. They are not of course found in Christian history in distinct separation from one another, but in varying proportions in different theologians. But in a very broad way it could be said that the first is particularly characteristic of pietist Protestantism, the second of liberal protestantism, the third of Thomism, the fourth of Lutheranism, and the fifth of St. Augustine and Calvinism.

2. Cambridge University Press, 1960.

THE DEVELOPMENT OF PEOPLES

POPE PAUL VI

Freedom from misery; the greater assurance of finding subsistence, health and fixed employment; an increased share of responsibility without oppression of any kind and in security from situations that do violence to their dignity as men; better education—in brief, to seek to do more, know more and have more in order to be more; that is what men aspire to now when a greater number of them are condemned to live in conditions that make this lawful desire illusory. Besides, people who have recently gained national independence experience the need to add to this political freedom a fitting autonomous growth, social as well as economic, in order to assure their citizens a full human enhancement and to take their rightful place with other nations.

Though insufficient for the immensity and urgency of the task, the means inherited from the past are not lacking. It must certainly be recognized that colonizing powers have often furthered their own interests, power or glory, and that their departure has sometimes left a precarious economy, bound up for instance with the production of one kind of crop whose market prices are subject to sudden and considerable variation. Yet while recognizing the damage done by a certain type of colonialism and its consequences, one must at the same time acknowledge the qualities and achievements of colonizers who brought their science and technical knowledge and left beneficial results of their presence in so many underprivileged regions. The structures established by them persist, however incomplete they may be; they diminished ignorance and sickness, brought the benefits of communications and improved living conditions.

Yet once this is admitted, it remains only too true that the resultant situation is manifestly inadequate for facing the hard reality of modern economics. Left to itself it works rather to widen the differences in the world's levels of life, not to diminish them: rich peoples enjoy rapid growth whereas the poor develop slowly. The imbalance is on the increase; some produce a surplus of foodstuffs, others cruelly lack them and see their exports made uncertain.

At the same time, social conflicts have taken on world dimensions. The acute disquiet which has taken hold of the poor classes in countries that are becoming industrialized, is now embracing those whose economy is almost exclusively agrarian. There is also the scandal of glaring inequalities not merely in the enjoyment of possessions but even more in the exercise of power.

Furthermore, the conflict between traditional civilizations and the new elements of industrial civilization break down structures which do not adapt themselves to new conditions. Their framework, some-times rigid, was the indispensable prop to personal and family life; older people remain attached to it, the young escape from it, as from a useless barrier, to turn eagerly to new forms of life in society. The conflict of the generations is made more serious by a tragic dilemma: whether to retain ancestral institutions and convictions and renounce progress, or to admit techniques and civilizations from outside and reject along with the traditions of the past all their human richness. In effect, the moral, spiritual and religious supports of the past too often give way without securing in return any guarantee of a place in the new world.

The Church has never failed to foster the human progress of the nations to which she brings faith in Christ. Her missionaries have built not only churches, but also hostels and hospitals, schools and universities. Without doubt their work, inasmuch as it was human, was not perfect, and sometimes the announcement of the authentic Gospel message was infiltrated by many ways of thinking and acting that were characteristic of their home country. But the missionaries were also able to develop, and foster local institutions. In many a region they were among the pioneers in material progress as well as in cultural advancement.

However, local and individual undertakings are no longer enough. The present situation of the world demands concerted action based on a clear vision of all economic, social, cultural, and spiritual aspects.

The Vocation of Self-Fulfilment

In the design of God, every man is called upon to develop and fulfill himself, for every life is a vocation. Coming to maturity, which will be the result of education received from the environment and personal efforts, will allow each man to direct himself toward the destiny intended for him by his Creator. Endowed with intelligence and freedom, he is responsible for his fulfilment as he is for his salvation. He is aided, or sometimes impeded, by those who educate him and those with whom he lives, but each one remains, whatever be these influences affecting him, the principal agent of his own success or failure.

By reason of his union with Christ, the source of life, man attains a new fulfilment of himself, to a transcendent humanism which gives him his greatest possible perfection: that is the highest goal of personal development.

But each man is a member of society. He is part of the whole of mankind. It is not just certain individuals, but all men, who are called to this fullness of development. Civilizations are born, develop and die. But humanity is advancing along the path of history like the waves of a rising tide encroaching gradually on the shore. The reality of human solidarity, which is a benefit for us, also imposes a duty.

This personal and communal development would be threatened if the true scale of values were undermined. The desire for necessities is legitimate, and work undertaken to obtain them is a duty. But the acquiring of temporal goods can lead to greed, to the insatiable desire for more, and can make increased power a tempting objective. Individuals, families and nations can be overcome by avarice, be they rich or poor, and all can fall victim to a stifling materialism.

Increased possession is not the ultimate goal of nations nor of individuals. All growth is ambivalent. It is essential if man is to develop as a man, but in a way it imprisons man if he considers it the supreme good, and it restricts his vision. Then we see hearts harden and minds close, and men no longer gather together in friendship but out of self-interest, which soon leads to oppositions and disunity. The exclusive pursuit of possessions thus become an obstacle to individual fulfilment and to man's true greatness. Both for nations and for individual men, avarice is the most evident form of moral underdevelopment.

If further development calls for the work of more and more technicians, even more necessary is the deep thought and reflection of wise men in search of a new humanism which will enable modern man to find himself anew by embracing the higher values of love and friendship, of prayer and contemplation. This is what will permit the fullness of authentic development, a development that is for each and all the transition from less human conditions to those which are more human.

A Call to Action

The Bible, from the first page on, teaches us that the whole of creation is for man, that it is his responsibility to develop it by intelligent effort and by means of his labor to perfect it, so to speak, for his use. If the world is made to furnish each individual with the means of livelihood and the instruments for his growth and progress, each man has therefore the right to find in the world what is necessary for himself. All other rights whatsoever, including those of property and of free commerce, are to be subordinated to this principle. They should not hinder but on the contrary favor its application. It is a grave and urgent social duty to redirect them to their primary finality.

It is well known how strong were the words used by the Fathers of the Church to describe the proper attitude of persons who possess anything towards persons in need. To quote Saint Ambrose: "You are not making a gift of your possessions to the poor person. You are handing over to him what is his. For what has been given in common for the use of all, you have arrogated to yourself. The world is given to all, and not only to the rich."[1] That is, private property does not constitute for anyone an absolute and unconditioned right. No one is justified in keeping for his exclusive use what he does not need, when others lack necessities. In a word, "according to the traditional doctrine as found in the Fathers of the Church and the great theologians, the right to property must never be exercised to the detriment of the common good." If there should arise a conflict "between acquired private rights and primary community exigencies," it is the responsibility of public authorities "to look for a solution, with the active participation of individuals and social groups."[2]

If certain landed estates impede the general prosperity because they are extensive, unused or poorly used, or because they bring hardship to peoples or are detrimental to the interests of the country, the common good sometimes demands their expropriation. The available revenue is not to be used in accordance with mere whim, and no place must be given to selfish speculation. Consequently, it is unacceptable that citizens with abundant incomes from the resources and activity of their country should transfer a considerable part of this income abroad purely for their own advantage, without care for the manifest wrong they inflict on their country by doing this.

Liberal Capitalism

But out of these new conditions some opinions have arisen in human society—we do not know how—that considered profit as the most important incentive to encourage economic progress, free competition as the supreme norm of economics, and private ownership of the means of production as an absolute right which would not accept limits or a corresponding social obligation. One cannot condemn such abuses too strongly by solemnly recalling once again that the economy is at the service of man.

However, if one must admit that one form of capitalism, as it is called, has been the source of so much suffering, injustices and fratricidal conflicts whose effects still persist, it would nevertheless be wrong to attribute to industrialization itself those evils that more truthfully must be blamed on the disastrous opinions about economics which were connected with this growth.

We must make haste: too many are suffering, and the distance is growing that separates the progress of some and the stagnation, not to say the regression of others. Yet the work required should advance smoothly if there is not to be the risk of losing indispensable equilibrium. A hasty agrarian reform can fail. Industrialization if introduced suddenly can displace structures still necessary, and produce hardships in society which would be a setback in terms of human values.

There are certainly situations whose injustice cries to heaven. When whole populations, destitute of necessities, live in a state of dependence barring them from all initiative and responsibility, and all opportunity to advance culturally and share in social and political life, recourse to violence, as a means to right these wrongs to human dignity, is a grave temptation.

We know, however, that a revolutionary uprising—save where there is manifest, longstanding tyranny which would do great damage to fundamental rights and dangerous harm to the common good of the country—produces new injustices, throws more elements out of balance and brings on new disasters. A real evil should not be fought against at the cost of greater misery.

Individual initiative alone and the mere free play of competition could never assure successful development. One must avoid the risk of increasing still more the wealth of the rich and the dominion of the strong, while leaving the poor in their misery and adding to the servitude of the oppressed. It pertains to the public authorities to choose, even to lay down the objectives to be pursued, the ends to be achieved, and the means for attaining these, and it is for them to stimulate all the forces engaged in this common activity. But let them take care to associate private initiative and intermediary bodies with this work. They will thus avoid the danger of complete collectivization or of arbitrary planning, which, by denying liberty, would prevent the exercise of the fundamental rights of the human person.

This is true since every program, made to increase production, has, in the last analysis, no other raison d'etre than the service of man. Such programs should reduce inequalities, fight discrimination, free man from various types of servitude and enable him to be the instrument of his own material betterment, of his moral progress and of his spiritual growth. To speak of development, is in effect to show as much concern for social progress as for economic growth. It is not sufficient to increase overall wealth for it to be distributed equitably. It is not sufficient to promote technology to render the world a more human place in which to live. The mistakes of their predecessors should warn those on the road to development of the dangers to be avoided in this field. Tomorrow's technocracy can beget evils no less redoubtable than those due to the liberalism of yesterday. Economics and technology have no meaning except from man whom they should serve. And man is only truly man in as far as, master of his own acts and judge of their worth, he is author of his own advancement, in keeping with the nature which was given to him by his Creator and whose possibilities and exigencies he himself freely assumes.

It can even be affirmed that economic growth depends in the very first place upon social progress: thus basic education is the primary object of any plan of development. Indeed hunger for education is no less debasing than hunger for food: an illiterate is a person with an undernourished mind. To be able to read and write, to acquire a professional formation, means to recover confidence in oneself and to discover that one can progress along with the others.

It is true that too frequently an accelerated demographic increase adds its own difficulties to the problems of development: the size of the population increases more rapidly than available resources, and things are found to have reached apparently an impasse. From that moment the temptation is great to check the demographic increase by means of radical measures. It is certain that public authorities can intervene, within the limit of their competence, by favoring the availability of appropriate information and by adopting suitable measures, provided that these be in conformity with the moral law and that they respect the rightful freedom of married couples. Where the inalienable right of marriage and procreation is lacking, human dignity has ceased to exist. Finally, it is for the parents to decide, with full knowledge of the matter, on the number of their children taking into account their responsibilities towards God, themselves, the children they have already brought into the world, and the community to which they belong. In all this they must follow the demands of their own conscience enlightened by God's law authentically interpreted, and sustained by confidence in Him.

What must be aimed at is complete humanism. And what is that if not the fully-rounded development of the whole man and of all men? A humanism closed in on itself, and not open to the values of the spirit and to God Who is their source, could achieve apparent success. There is no true humanism but that which is open to the Absolute and is conscious of a vocation which gives human life its true meaning. Far from being the ultimate measure of all things, man can only realize himself by reaching beyond himself.

The Spirit of Solidarity

"If a brother or a sister be naked," says Saint James; "if they lack their daily nourishment, and one of you says to them: 'Go in peace, be warmed and be filled,' without giving them what is necessary for the body, what good does it do?"[3] Today no one can be ignorant any longer of the fact that in whole continents countless men and women are ravished by hunger, countless numbers of children are undernourished, so that many of them die in infancy, while the physical growth and mental development of many others are retarded and, as a result, whole regions are condemned to the most depressing despondency.

But neither the private and public funds that have been invested, nor the gifts and loans that have been made, can suffice. It is not just a matter of eliminating hunger, nor even of reducing poverty. The struggle against destitution, though urgent and necessary, is not enough. It is a question, rather, of building a world where every man, no matter what his race, religion or nationality, can live a fully human life, freed from servitude imposed on him by other men or by natural forces over which he does not have sufficient control; a world where freedom is not an empty word and where the poor man Lazarus can sit down at the same table with the rich man. This demands great generosity, much sacrifice and unceasing effort on the part of the rich man. Let each one examine his conscience that conveys a new message for our times. Is he prepared to support out of his own pocket works and undertakings organized in favor of the most destitute? Is he ready to pay higher taxes so that the public authorities can intensify their efforts in favor of development? Is he ready to pay a higher price for imported goods so that the producer may be more justly rewarded? Or to leave his country if necessary and if he is young, in order to assist in this development of the young nations?

The same duty of solidarity that rests on individuals exists also for nations. Although it is normal that a nation should be the first to benefit from the gifts that Providence has bestowed on it as the fruit of the labors of its people, still no country can claim on that account to keep its wealth for itself alone. Every nation must produce more and better quality goods to give to all its inhabitants a truly human standard of living, and also to contribute to the common development of the human race. Given the increasing needs of the under-developed countries, it should be considered quite normal for an advanced country to devote a part of its production to meet their needs, and to train teachers, engineers, technicians and scholars prepared to put their knowledge and their skill at the disposal of less fortunate people.

In order to be fully effective, these efforts ought not remain scattered or isolated, much less be in competition for reason of power or prestige: the present situation calls for concerted planning. A planned program is of course better and more effective than occasional aid left to individual good will. It presupposes, as We said above, careful study, the selection of ends and the choice of means, as well as a reorganization of efforts to meet the needs of the present and the demands of the foreseeable future.

But it is necessary to go still further. At Bombay We called for the establishment of a great World Fund, to be made up of part of the money spent on arms, to relieve the most destitute of the world.[4] What is true of the immediate struggle against want, holds good also when there is a question of development. Only world-wide collaboration, of which a common fund would be both means and symbol, will succeed in overcoming vain rivalries and in establishing a fruitful and peaceful exchange between peoples.

Besides, who does not see that such a fund would make it easier to take measures to prevent certain wasteful expenditures, the result of fear or pride? When so many people are hungry, when so many families suffer from destitution, when so many remain steeped in ignorance, when so many schools, hospitals and homes worthy of the name remain to be built, all public or private squandering of wealth, all expenditures prompted by motives of national or personal ostentation, every exhausting armaments race, becomes an intolerable scandal.

Contractual Justice Between Nations

If the positions of the contracting parties are too unequal, the consent of the parties does not suffice to guarantee the justice of their contract, and the rule of free agreement remains subservient to the demands of the natural law. What was true of the just wage for the individual is also true of international contracts; an economy of exchange can no longer be based solely on the law of free competition, a law which, in its turn, too often creates an economic dictatorship. Freedom of trade is fair only if it is subject to the demands of social justice.

Moreover, this has been understood by the developed nations themselves, who are striving by means of appropriate measures, to re-establish within their own economics a balance that competition, if left to itself, tends to compromise. Thus it happens that these nations often support their agriculture at the price of sacrifices imposed on economically more favored sectors. Similarly, to maintain the commercial relations that are developing among themselves, especially within a common market, the financial, fiscal, and social policy of these nations tries to restore comparable opportunities to competing industries which are not equally prospering.

What holds for a national economy or among developed countries is valid also in commercial relations between rich nations and poor nations. Without abolishing the competitive market, it should be kept within the limits that make it just and moral, and therefore human. In trade between developed and under-developed economies, conditions are too disparate and the degrees of genuine freedom available too unequal. In order that international trade be human and moral, social justice requires that it restore to the participants a certain equality of opportunity. This equality is a long-term objective, but to reach it, we must begin now to create true equality in discussions and negotiations. Here again international agreements on a rather wide scale would be helpful: they would establish general norms for regulating certain prices, for guaranteeing certain types of production, for supporting certain new industries.

Obstacles to Overcome

Among still other obstacles to the formation of a world that is more just and better organized toward a universal solidarity, We wish to speak of nationalism and racism. It is only natural that communities which have recently reached their political independence should be jealous of a national unity which is still fragile, and that they should strive to protect it. Likewise, it is to be expected that nations endowed with an ancient culture should be proud of the patrimony which their history has bequeathed to them. But these legitimate feelings should be ennobled by that universal charity which embraces the entire human family. Nationalism isolates people from their true good. It would be especially harmful where the weakness of national economies demands rather the pooling of efforts, of knowledge and of funds, in order to implement programs of development and to increase commercial and cultural exchange.

Racism is not the exclusive lot of young nations, where sometimes it hides beneath the rivalries of clans and political parties, with heavy losses for justice and at the risk of civil war. During the colonial period it often flared up between the colonists and the indigenous population, and stood in the way of mutually profitable understanding, often giving rise to bitterness in the wake of genuine injustices. It is still an obstacle to collaboration among disadvantaged nations and a cause of division and hatred within countries whenever individuals and families see the inviolable rights of the human person held in scorn, as they themselves are unjustly subjected to a regime of discrimination because of their race or their color.

Hospitality to Foreigners

The world is sick. Its illness consists less in the unproductive monopolization of resources by a small number of men than in the lack of brotherhood among individuals and peoples.

It is painful to think of the numerous young people who come to more advanced countries to receive the science, the competence, and the culture that will make them more qualified to serve their homeland, and who certainly acquire a formation of high quality but who too often lose the esteem for the spiritual values that often were to be found, as a precious patrimony, in the civilization where they had grown up.

The same welcome is due to emigrant workers, who live in conditions that are often inhuman, and who economize on what they earn in order to send a little relief to their family living in misery in their native land.

Our second recommendation is for those whose business calls them to countries recently opened to industrialization: industrialists, merchants, leaders or representatives of larger enterprises. It happens that they are not lacking in social sensitivity in their own country; why then do they return to the inhuman principles of individualism when they operate in less developed countries? Their advantageous position should on the contrary move them to become the initiators of social progress and of human advancement in the area where their business calls them. Their very sense of organization should suggest to them the means for making intelligent use of the labor of the indigenous population, of forming qualified workers, of training engineers and staffs, of giving scope to their initiative, of introducing them progressively into higher positions, thus preparing them to share, in the near future, in the responsibilities of management. Let no one, whatever his status, be subjected unjustly to the arbitrariness of others.

Hence, necessary technical competence must be accompanied by authentic signs of disinterested love. Freed of all nationalistic pride and of every appearance of racism, experts should learn how to work in close collaboration with all. They realize that their competence does not confer on them a superiority in every field. The civilization which formed them contains, without doubt, elements of universal humanism, but it is not the only civilization nor does it enjoy a monopoly of valuable elements. Moreover, it cannot be imported without undergoing adaptations. The men of these missions will be intent on discovering, along with its history, the component elements of the cultural riches of the country receiving them. Mutual understanding will be established that will enrich both cultures.

Between civilizations, as between persons, sincere dialogue indeed creates brotherhood. The work of development will draw nations together in the attainment of goals pursued with a common effort if all, from governments and their representatives to the last expert, are inspired by brotherly love and moved by the sincere desire to build a civilization founded on world solidarity. A dialogue based on man, and not on commodities or technical skills, will then begin.

Prayer and Action

The prayer of all ought to rise with fervor to the Almighty. This prayer should be matched by the resolute commitment of each individual —according to the measure of his strength and possibilities—to the struggle against underdevelopment. Many individuals, social groups, and nations join hands in brotherly fashion, the strong aiding the weak to grow, exerting all their competence, enthusiasm and disinterested love. More than any other, the individual who is animated by true charity labors skillfully to discover the causes of misery, to find the means to combat it, to overcome it resolutely.

Development is the New Name for Peace

Excessive economic, social and cultural inequalities among peoples arouse tensions and conflicts, and are a danger to peace. To wage war on misery and to struggle against injustice is to promote, along with improved conditions, the human and spiritual progress of all men, and therefore the common good of humanity. Peace cannot be limited to a mere absence of war, the result of an ever precarious balance of forces. No, peace is something that is built up day after day, in the pursuit of an order intended by God, which implies a more perfect form of justice among men.

The peoples themselves have the prime responsibility to work for their own development. But they will not bring this about in isolation. Regional agreements among weak nations for mutual support, understandings of wider scope entered into for their help, more far-reaching agreements to establish programs for closer cooperation among groups of nations—these are the milestones on the road to development that leads to peace.

Towards an Effective World Authority

Instrumental collaboration on a world-wide scale requires institutions that will prepare, coordinate and direct it, until finally there is established an order of justice which is universally recognized.

Some would consider such hopes utopian. It may be that these persons are not realistic enough, and that they have not perceived the dynamism of a world which desires to live more fraternally—a world which, in spite of its ignorance, its mistakes and even its sin, its relapses into barbarism and its wanderings far from the road of salvation, is, even unawares, taking slow but sure steps toward its Creator. This road towards a greater humanity requires effort and sacrifice; but suffering itself, accepted for the love of our brethren, favors the progress of the entire human family.

1. De Nabuthe, c. 12, n. 53; (P. L. 14, 747).
2. Letter to the 52nd Session of the French Social Weeks (Brest, 1965). Documentation catholique, t. 62, Paris; 1965, col. 1365.
3. Jas. 2: 15-16.
4. Message to the World, Dec. 4, 1964. AAS 57 (1965), p. 135.

A RESPONSE TO POPE PAUL FROM THE THIRD WORLD

SIXTEEN CATHOLIC BISHOPS

As bishops of some of the peoples who are striving and struggling for their development, we unite our voices with the anguished appeal of Pope Paul VI in his letter *Populorum Progressio*. We wish to clarify the responsibilities of our priests and faithful and to address some words of encouragement to all our brothers of the Third World.

Our churches, in this Third World situation, find themselves embroiled in a conflict which is no longer just a confrontation between East and West. There are now three major groups of people: The Western powers which grew wealthy in the last century, the two large Communist countries, which have become great powers, and finally the Third World which is still seeking to escape the hold of the great powers and to develop freely. Even within the developed countries certain social classes, races or peoples have not yet obtained the right to a truly human life. An irresistible pressure moves these poor peoples toward their advancement by liberating them from all forces of oppression. While most nations have succeeded in obtaining political freedom, peoples with economic freedom are still rare. Just as rare are those with social equality, which is an indispensable condition of true brotherhood—there can be no peace without justice. The peoples of the Third World form the proletariat of mankind today. They are exploited by the great and threatened in their very existence by those who, because they are more powerful, assume the right to be the judges and policemen of the less fortunate. Our people are neither less wise nor less just than the great of this world.

Freedom in Political, Economic and Social Systems

Revolutions have happened or are happening in the present evolution of the world. All the powers which are now established were born in an era more or less far removed from revolution—and by "revolution" we mean a rupture with a system which did not secure the common good and the inauguration of a new order better able to obtain it. Not all revolutions are necessarily good. Some are only palace coups which do nothing but change the people's oppressors. Atheism and collectivism, with which certain social movements think they must be bound, are grave dangers for humanity. History shows, however, that some revolutions were necessary, and rose above their temporary anti-religion, producing good fruit.

Doctrinally, the Church knows that the Gospel requires the primary and radical revolution which is called conversion—the complete about-face from sin to grace, from selfishness to love, it concerns the whole man, corporeal and social as well as spiritual and personal. It has a communal aspect of immense consequences for the whole society, not only for men's life here below but especially for the eternal life in Christ who, raised from the earth, draws all humanity to himself. In the eyes of the Christian, this is man's complete fulfillment. Thus for twenty centuries the Gospel has been the most powerful ferment for profound changes in mankind, whether visibly or invisibly, whether within or apart from the Church.

Nevertheless, in its historical pilgrimage the Church is in the practice always linked with a political, social and economic system which, for that moment of history, assures the common good or at least a certain social order. Sometimes the churches even find themselves so bound to a certain system that the two seem to be identical, unified in a single flesh as in marriage. But the Church has only one spouse; Christ. It is never married to any system, whatever it be, and especially not to "the international imperialism of money," nor will it be married to-morrow to this or that socialism. In the face of the present develop-ment of the imperialism of money, we address to our faithful and restate for ourselves the advice given to the Christians of Rome by the seer of Patmos before the imminent fall of this great city, prostituted in luxury based on the oppression of the people and on the slave trade: "Come out, my people, away from her, so that you do not share in her crimes and have the same plagues to bear" (Rev 18:4).

We bishops and priests have an obligation to remain at our place. For we are the vicars of the Good Shepherd who does not desert like a hired servant in time of danger, but remains with his flock, ready to give his life for theirs (Jn 10:11-18). When Jesus told his disciples to flee from one town to another (Mt 10:23), it was only in the case of personal persecution for the faith. This is quite different from war or revolution involving a whole people when the pastor must remain in solidarity with them. It is his duty to stay with his people. If all the people decide to go into exile, the pastor can follow his flock. But he cannot save only himself or a minority of profiteers or cowards.

Taking account of some necessities for a certain material progress, the Church for a century has tolerated capitalism with lending at legal interest and its other practices which scarcely conform to the morality of the prophets and the Gospel. But it cannot but rejoice to see the appearance among men of another social system which is less distant from this morality. The Christians of tomorrow should, following the initiative of Paul VI, return the moral values of solidarity and fraternity to their true Christian source. Far from remaining cool to socialism, we can adhere to it with joy as a form of social life better adapted to our time and conforming more to the spirit of the Gospel. Thus we can avoid the confusion some make between God and religion and the oppressors of the poor and the workers—feudalism, capitalism, imperialism. These inhuman systems have begotten others which, in the attempt to liberate the people, oppress individuals when they fall into totalitarian collectivism and religious persecution.

With pride and joy, the Church greets a new humanity in which honor no longer goes to money accumulated in a few hands, but to laborers, workers, and peasants. The Church is nothing without him who ceaselessly gives it its being and action, Jesus of Nazareth, who worked with his hands for many years to show the important dignity of workers. This is to say that the Church rejoices to see within humanity the development of forms of social life in which work finds its true primary place. As Archpriest Borovoy of the World Council of Churches recognized, we were wrong to accommodate ourselves to the pagan legal principles inherited from ancient Rome. Unfortunately, the West has sinned no less in this respect than the East.

Fidelity to the Word of God

No one should look for any political inspiration in our words. Our only source is the Word of him who spoke by his prophets and apostles. The Bible and the Gospel denounce as sin against God any violation of the dignity of man created in his image. In this necessity of respect for the human person, atheists of good faith today join believers for common service to mankind in the search for justice and peace. We therefore address these words of encouragement to all of these. For all need much courage and strength to succeed at the immense and urgent task which alone can save the Third World from misery and hunger and deliver humanity from the catastrophe of a nuclear war: "No more war, down with arms!" (Paul VI at the U.N.)

The people hunger primarily for truth and justice, and all those charged with their instruction and education should work enthusiastically for it. Certain errors must be dispelled quickly: No, God does not want there to be poor people who are always miserable. Religion is not an opiate for the people. Religion is a force that raises the humble and humbles the proud, which gives bread to the hungry and makes the satisfied hunger. Certainly, Jesus warned us that there will always be poor among us (John 12:8), but that is because there will always be the rich to monopolize this world's goods and also always certain inequalities due to differences of capacities and other inevitable factors. But Jesus taught us that the second commandment is equal to the first because one cannot love God without loving his fellowman. He warns us that we and all men will be judged by a single word: "I was hungry and you gave me food ... I was the one who was hungry ..." (Mt 25:31-46). All the great religious and sages of mankind echo this statement. Thus the Koran announces the final trial at which men are submitted to God's judgment: "What is this trial? It is the ransom of the captives, the feeding of the orphan in time of famine ... or of the poor man sleeping on the cold hard ground ... and effecting a law of mercy" (Sour. 90:11-18).

We have the obligation to share our bread and all our goods. If some hoard for themselves that which is necessary for others, public powers must impose the sharing which was not done in good will. What is true of individuals is also true of nations. Unfortunately, there is today no truly world government which can impose justice among the peoples and distribute goods equally. The economic system now operating permits the rich nations to increase their wealth, while giving bits of aid to the poor nations who are becoming proportionately poorer. The poor must therefore demand, with all the legitimate means at their disposal, the establishment of a world government in which all peoples, without exception, would be represented. This government would be able to demand, indeed even impose, a just distribution of goods, the indispensable condition of peace. Within each nation, workers have the right and obligation to join in real unions in order to demand and defend their rights: a fair wage, paid vacations, social security, family allocations, participation in the management of the business. It is not enough that these rights be recognized legally on paper. The laws must be applied, and it behooves governments to exercise their powers in this area in the service of workers and the poor. Governments must work to bring an end to the class conflict which, contrary to popular opinion, the rich too often have set in motion and continued to conduct against the workers by exploiting them with insufficient salaries and inhuman working conditions. We exhort you to remain firm and fearless, as evangelical ferment in the world of labor, confident in Christ's words, "Stand erect, hold your heads high, because your liberation is near at hand" (Lk 21:28).

The signatories were sixteen Catholic bishops from dioceses in Brazil, Algeria, South Pacific, UAR, Colombia, Yugoslavia, Lebanon, China and Laos.

WORLD APARTHEID

TISSA BALASURIYA, O.M.I.

The world as a whole has today the means of offering its population a decent standard of life—something that for a host of reasons is simply unavailable for much of mankind. This fact alone makes it necessary that a way be found which, within a reasonable period of time, say twenty-five to thirty years, will bring about a sufficient redistribution of wealth among nations, adequate development within the poor countries, and, at the same time, remove the humiliation-paternalism syndrome of the present receiver-donor relationship between the poor and rich countries. For this we should first develop principles of world justice in economic relations and endeavor to establish the political structures which would make the exigencies of justice a reality.

The current social thinking on these problems seems to be hamstrung by too great a respect for the concept of national sovereignty and too little regard for the rights of human beings. The problem is similar to the one facing individual states which have to cope with internal poverty without humiliating their citizens. The theory of social justice and the welfare state has grown around the idea that the poor should receive as a right the minimum required for a decent human existence. Our theory of international social justice must develop along similar lines.

A first principle: Every man has a right to life, and the world is given to all mankind to "increase and multiply and fill the earth. . . ." There is a primary right of all mankind to obtain the means for a decent existence from the resources of the world. The rights of nations and other subdivisions of mankind are secondary. The principle of subsidiarity is still effective, but not to the point where human rights are made unrealizable.

Property within national frontiers has a function for the world common good. No nation may use its property to the detriment of the common good of the human race. Indeed, before luxuries are provided, the basic needs of food, clothing and shelter must be met. There should be institutions at a world level that could bring about, as a matter of right, the redistribution of property to establish these priorities. If this basic (Christian) principle was accepted, one could think of a solution, that over a period of time could meet, in terms of justice, the problems of poverty in the midst of plenty. It might be called a principle of ecnomic democracy, which demands economic rights for all men and the end of a regime of monopolistic privileges in the economic field, especially when they are founded on and defended by force.

In this perspective, possible solutions might be discussed within two frameworks: (1) presupposing present national frontiers, with the redistribution of money and movable resources; (2) adding the further possibility of redistribution of land and manpower.

Under the first hypothesis, the basic principle of redistribution should provide for each nation obtaining from the world society sufficiency of means to ensure a decent life for its citizens; in return receiver nations would give according to their means to the human society. The terms of trade would not be the result of respective bargaining powers; rather, like the wage contract within a nation, the trade contract would be subject to international regulations. The purely atomistic, capitalistic principle that regulates world trade today is basically unjust, and more equitable and effective solutions must be found based on the principle of human solidarity. This is not a demand for alms, but an exigency of international social justice. Otherwise, it is at present difficult to reverse the process by which poor nations become relatively poorer and rich nations richer.

The social obligations of property must be thought of on an international level. If within nations the principle of income tax is accepted, why should not the principle of human solidarity in this "one world" lead to the acceptance of a principle of national income tax for the benefit of nations in need. This can be a method by which a peaceful redistribution of wealth can be brought about in the world. No country would probably be worse off because the expenditure on defense could be generally reduced if there were a world authority to enforce a tax on national incomes.

One further possibility would be national indirect taxes on the production of luxury goods or armaments, at least as they enter the international market. Many present structures, including the United Nations and the World Bank, could serve here if the nations were willing.

The teaching about the use of surplus wealth is found in Christian thinkers including St. Thomas Aquinas and the social encyclicals of modern Popes from Leo XIII onwards, as well as in the *Pastoral Constitution on the Church in the World.* This doctrine must be extended to cover international society. Surplus wealth must be used by the countries for the common good of humanity.

Foreign Investments

Also in need of development is the question of the property rights of former colonial rulers, or simply wealthy foreign powers, in poor countries. Many international problems arise from this issue, e.g., French holdings in Algeria, the Suez seizure, Cuba's nationalization of U. S. property. What, for example, are the rights of colonizers to earn income from property often taken more or less by force? To what extent is nationalization of foreign property without compensation justifiable in cases where the country deems that the investor has already earned the original investment several times over?

These questions are not easily resolved, yet they must be confronted by our moral theology if it is to be relevant and adequate to some of the central problems of our day. The theory of "macro-justice" needs further elaboration; at present, by omission, it seems to operate in favor of the possessors.

A Redistribution of Land and Population

The second hypothesis, envisaging a redistribution of land and population, is strongly handicapped by race, prejudice and deep cultural cleavages. Although I am aware of the complex and debatable aspects of these problems, I would like to touch on some points, particularly the demographic revolution occuring in Asia and the land-grab of uninhabited areas begun in the sixteenth century by the developed Western races and virtually completed today. At present nonwhites are being systematically kept out of these regions. This brief space is not the place to examine the anti-Asian immigration laws of countries like Australia, Canada, the U. S. and Brazil, which along with the eastern portions of the U.S.S.R. contain some of the great uninhabited land masses of the world. But everybody is aware of the underpopulated western parts of the U.S. and Canada. They are in a sense undeveloped lands.

Comparisons of the average holding of a Canadian farmer and those of the Indian, Chinese or Japanese peasant are quite as stark as those commonly made between the rich and poor in underdeveloped countries. China today increases yearly at a rate roughly equivalent to Canada's entire population. Yet Canada consistently excludes nonwhites, as does Australia, placed at the tip of Asia. Indeed Australia pays whites to emigrate to her sparsely populated shores. If I were born of white parents, almost the entire underinhabited world would be open to me to settle down and reproduce my kind. Australia, Canada, South Africa, Southern Rhodesia, etc., would not speak of unemployment and other difficulties. Yet these same countries generously give non-whites arms to fight the Communists to make the world safe for political democracy and "Christian civilization." And they blame us when we are not enthusiastic.

There is nothing sacrosanct about the present distribution of the earth's surface. The present distribution of land in the world among the races is the result of means far worse than those used by some capitalists to amass personal fortunes. The mere fact of occupation over a period of time does not constitute an inalienable right. If a starving man can jusifiably encroach on food in private property, what would we say of the empty fertile lands from which hungry men are excluded?

International Authority Needed

We need a theory of international social justice that faces this problem squarely, and practical remedies that will have effects at least over a few generations. World peace depends on it. The present policy of "increase and multiply and stay where you are, for we have filled the earth," cannot, humanly speaking, last. The need for an international authority in this matter is crucial today, yet when one proposes this part of the question, all kinds of alibis are offered for not discussing it seriously. Catholic authors are no different in this respect from others. Only Marxists seem to take it seriously. We must face this issue as one of the macrojustice, that is, concerned with giving each one his due in the macroevolution of world society.

Imaginative and bold thinking is essential for a peaceful solution of the redistribution of the earth's surface among the different peoples. We must provide adequate, peaceful, long-term readjustments in a world where the population complexus is fast changing in character, or less peaceful means are likely to be resorted to by countries which feel the pressure of population and the temptation of the underdeveloped lands. Why is it that in the discussion of this entire problem, the aspect of the availability of land is hardly even seriously considered. Surely vast areas like Western Canada, the West of the United States, Brazil and the East of the U.S.S.R. are unused factors among the resources of the world.

There is no doubt that the problems of international migration are enormous and varied; involving politics, race, culture, ideology, climate, etc. Yet are not the problems of hunger, side-by-side with plenty and empty lands even a greater challenge to humanity? We need solutions of a global nature. In any case the map of the world is being gradually redrawn. Could this not be done rationally and with international planning? I might mention a few suggestions for the sake of indicating the scope of the changes that seem necessary and would be feasible—if man were not so inhuman to man.

Thus, if at worst, it is true that the white race cannot really cohabit with others, then, is it unfair to ask it not to appropriate so much of the earth's surface for itself? If Australians and New Zealanders desire to preserve their racial, cultural, religious and linguistic identities, why could not the New Zealanders migrate to Australia and leave the islands to the Japanese? Or the United Nations could transport over a period of thirty years the twelve million Australians to the U. S. leaving Australia to the Indians? Or, again, the three to four million Western Canadians could descend to the U. S., freeing the vast plains of the west for Chinese as they gradually come over from Mongolia and Siberia.

If this sounds fantastic, the simple fact remains that in the next thirty-five years the world must make room for an additional one billion Chinese. By the year 2000 the whole of Oceania will still contain less than thirty million while India will have an additional six to seven hundred million to feed. Every means, including migration, and advice in responsible parenthood, should be attempted. But at present there is silence on the possibility of migration as a partial solution.

The present dog-in-the-manger policy of the Western nations is unfortunately a witness to their sense of racial monopoly and indifference to the implications of world economic democracy, despite their democratic creed politically. It denotes a glaring blindness to the logic of historical and demographic development, and may, as well, offer a partial explanation of the lack of gratitude shown by poor countries for what aid is given them.

The Inadequacy of Catholic Social Teaching

It is showing no disrespect for the late Pope John XXIII to suggest that certain aspects of *Mater et magistra* and *Pacem in Terris* require further development. For example, though a good deal is made of the need for greater powers for the United Nations, there does seem to be a clear recognition that solutions to the problems of poverty in the midst of plenty should be based on social justice, rather than a mere extension of charity or voluntary international cooperation.

On some matters, such as agriculture, *Mater et magistra* described rather detailed remedies. Nearly ten of the encyclical's seventy-five pages are devoted to recommendations regarding public policy, taxation, capital at suitable interest rates, social insurance, price protection and so forth. However, on the problems of international justice, nowhere does the encyclical develop principles in any applied manner. The reference to the population problem is very general except for a four-page treatment of the errors of birth control. *Pacem in Terris* leaves the problem in much the same way. Nor does Catholic reaction to the documents, give the impression that they have been understood as appeals on the basis of social justice rather than that of benevolent paternalism. Though wonderful in other respects, in this sense they fail to measure up to the extent and urgency of the problem of world social justice.

Though the papacy says little today about immigration in connection with population problems, there was a period, roughly between 1939 and 1954, when it made repeated and pointed demands that nations become more open to immigrants. Migration was put forward as a natural right of man, subject to the world common good. Pius XII spoke of the cruelty of those who closed doors to migrants, adding that no reason of state or pretext of collective advantage could justify the denial of this fundamental right. He addressed appeals and quasi-reprimands to Canada, the U. S., Australia, Argentina and Brazil. Apostolic Delegates, as in Canada, were mobilized for the cause, and the Apostolic Constitution of 1952, *Exsul Familia,* summarized the teaching and made further appeals.

One can only speculate on the relative silence since 1955. Is it that the theory has changed? Or that other solutions have been found? Certainly the problems remain. But perhaps the success of the European Common Market has made them less acute for European countries, not to mention Italy in particular. The central authority of the Church has hardly ever raised the problems of anti-Asian legislation. It has made occasional reference to the needs of emigration for Japan, but has said or done very little in connection with the overall problem.

The Constitution on the Church in the Modern World refers briefly (in art. 69) to the problem of inequality among nations but does not deal with it in any adequate manner. While this is a most urgent world problem, there is only a passing reference to it in this document, and hardly any at all in the other fifteen constitutions, decrees and declarations of Vatican II.

Two Ideologies

The underdeveloped lands do not want to choose between mere political freedom, upheld by the West, and the Marxist promise of world economic democracy. This is all the more reason why the Church's failure to develop sufficiently clearly the theory of world economic relations in terms of justice is so crucial. It is also the paradox Christians in the East must live with: regarded by Easterners as too Western because we value what they call "this sham of mere political democracy," and by Westerners as not understanding them because we see the case made by Asians for world economic democracy.

The Church cannot for much longer continue to overlook the problems. What, for example, would Catholic social thinkers say if a few million Chinese were to walk into some underinhabited parts of "White Australia"? Would they regard it as an exercise of "the natural right of God's children to God's earth," or would they summon the "people of God" to a new nuclear crusade against the diabolical forces of atheistic communism? These are not abstract questions when even now over 500,000 Americans and Australians have gone forth to meet the Chinese in Vietnam "to make the world safe for political democracy." The

Church's ability for dialogue with China may, in a sense, become more and more a touchstone of her sincerity and sense of justice. As things stand now, Marxists and many non-Christian Easterners do not distinguish the spiritual concerns of the Church and the interests of the Western powers.

Although very important developments in theology have occurred during the past two decades, it is worthwhile noting that almost all of them originated in countries that are part of the affluent society. This is, of course, to the credit of these countries, but it may be less than ideal for the rest of the world. As scholastics used to say, nothing is in the intellect that has not been first in the senses; one cannot love without knowing. Infallibility does not compensate for lack of contact or openness of spirit. Between the seventeenth and nineteenth centuries Catholicism lost the workers because of value blindness to their yearnings for justice—yearnings which Marx was the first to appreciate, however much we may disagree with his analysis and solutions.

If Christians fail to realize the utter frustration being generated in countries like China and non-Communist Asia, as well as, to some extent, Africa and Latin America, the outlook for humanity and the Church is very bleak. The Church's silence may even be suicidal. The world is harsh in its judgment on the silence of the "Deputy," and the world is not less Christlike for it.

If Christians would at least dissociate themselves from this situation of glaring international injustice, the Church's credentials would be in better shape. But this does not solve the problems themselves. In any case, though I hope I am wrong, realistically I do not see any substantial signs of a change of heart deep enough and a commitment serious enough to have an impact.

THE CHRISTIAN IN THE SEARCH FOR WORLD ORDER AND PEACE

HELMUT GOLLWITZER

The Problem of World Peace

The most profound change in world politics today, in comparison with earlier periods in the history of mankind, would seem to consist in the fact that the traditional function of war, as a political method, has changed. Because of the development of armaments, war is no longer a calculable means to an end; it is no longer a means the precise object of which is discernible. This is an extraordinary innovation. We are living in a time of transition, during which humanity must get used to this situation and work out the consequences of it. To live in a time of transition means, in the first place, that, while modern war can no longer be relied upon as a political method and constitutes a risk we can no longer take, there still remains the possibility of traditional warfare, whether between countries that so far have no modern weapons, or as civil war, or between countries or groups of countries which are equipped with modern weapons, but which deliberately fight a limited war. Countries that are equipped with modern weapons cling to the hope that it may still be possible to adopt this third course so that they may not be forced to choose between capitulation and suicide (uncalculable atomic war) whenever armed conflict occurs. They retain conventional weapons and armies in order that they may have a choice of some other weapon before the last step is taken and in order to be able to meet on a conventional plane those countries that have atomic weapons. There is little likelihood of a conventional war between the great atomic powers; and there is even less likelihood that, if such a war did break out, anyone would succeed in keeping it under control and in preventing it from developing into a nuclear war; that is, from changing from a war to achieve an object into a war of annihilation as an end in itself.

Second, a time of transition means that military armaments still serve their traditional purpose of deterrence. But they can no longer serve as a means of waging war to a particular end, because the end is no longer calculable. A deterrent is a threat to use force. Between the atomic powers today, it threatens a use of force that is no longer calculable, but suicidal. Whereas previously the warning conveyed by the threat was "Do not drive me to the use of force!" today it is "Do not drive me to madness!" The deterrent works because the seriousness of the threat is uncertain and because there is a possibility, not clearly defined, that if too great a demand is made upon him and appears to affect his existence, the enemy may prefer madness and the risk of suicide to capitulation. Only if the atomic equilibrium were upset and one of the two great powers should feel secure from retaliation because of the superiority of the weapons it had developed could nuclear armaments again serve the second purpose, and the power that started the war would not need to fear an incalculably deadly reaction.

A time of transition is characterized, in the third place, by the existence of a large number of sovereign states, with all their complexities of foreign policies and conflicts. In fact, however, the sovereignty of many small states is limited first and foremost by their continued inability to compete in armaments and by the treaties that some of them have made for their protection with one or other of the atomic powers. Despite the dictates of common sense, and despite the fact that the future of all mankind is endangered, the egoism inherent in the sovereign state drives governments to overcome these limitations of sovereignty and to engage in conflicts with other states by the traditional methods of war and of the threat of war. As a result, because of their military superiority, and because of their interest in avoiding an atomic war, the two great atomic powers are forced to assume the role of world police and to seek to prevent the outbreak of armed conflicts between smaller states. They fulfill this role only imperfectly first, because their mutual competition causes them to take sides in conflicts of foreign policy between smaller states with which they are closely connected and to supply them with arms, thus keeping the conflicts virulent instead of ending them (for instance, the conflict between Israel and the Arab states); and second, because in view of their disunity and the danger of a nuclear war, they cannot exert the pressure of an ultimatum, threatening to make war on the smaller states unless they stop using force to settle disputes with neighboring states.

Hitherto, war has been the *ultima ratio* of politics—a means of order. It could serve to defend as well as to change the existing order.

In a time of transition, this way of keeping order has become too risky. Yet, as long as there are reasons to have recourse to war, the temptation to resort to it remains. The danger of atomic warfare, which everybody fears, has not so far proved a sufficient incentive for states to remove the causes of war with the energy that common sense demands.

It is true that the existence of atomic weapons today has a peace-preserving significance. The great powers have gone to war in the past for far more trifling reasons than exist in our day. The incalculability and the horror of an atomic war effectively strengthen the interest of the atomic powers in preserving peace and preventing war. But the peace maintained in this manner is extremely unstable. A one-sided lead in armaments, the unthinking and irresponsible action of any one government, outbreaks of extremism on the part of governments or nations, could lead any day to a sudden change from a supposed peace, guaranteed by atomic weapons, to the most terrible catastrophe, involving the whole of mankind, as a result of these same atomic weapons. If the atomic deterrent is reckoned to be needful today, it must, at the same time, be recognized that it is *even more* needful to find ways of replacing it as a guarantee of peace by a better one. The retention of atomic weapons cannot be justified, as was the case with armaments in the past, by the eventuality of an outbreak of war. Atomic weapons can be justified morally and politically only as a passing phase until the atomic deterrent gives way to a better guarantee of peace.

Accordingly, the aim must be workable international regulations, from which no state can withdraw, and which will also bring further technical developments under international or supranational control. It is imperative that steps be taken toward achieving this aim before further developments overwhelm us. One of the greatest dangers for the future of mankind is the superiority of particular interests that is still prevalent today, together with the delusion that we can afford this superiority under the protection of the balance of atomic power.

The Christian Attitude Toward War in a Nuclear Age

In a time of transition, the traditional Christian attitude toward war has to be re-examined. There are still situations in which it is possible to apply the war ethic of the major Churches and to maintain that "conventional wars" can still take place and that the military deterrent can serve its purpose. Yet such situations continue to exist only provisionally. Just as, in the past, the Christian attitude toward war has been concerned not only with the *threat* of force but with the *use* of force, so today it cannot be confined to thinking about the problem of a balanced atomic deterrent, but it must also take a definite stand in the event of an atomic war.

The Church must speak out clearly against atomic war. In doing so, it will only delude and deceive itself if it underestimates the difficulties in which it thus places statesmen. Atomic war can no longer be a means of enforcing justice, as a *bellum justum* [just war] was in the past. It can no longer be a means of defense or of restoring a legal position. The Church must not cloud this clear issue but must pierce the smoke screen that politicians and the armed forces are always inclined to set up in a time of transition. This *No* to atomic war has not been arbitrarily arrived at by the Church but is a command given to it by God. Therefore, the Church must first of all carry out its commission and tell the politicians what God's command says to all: that atomic warfare lies outside the limits of those forceful methods by which we may protect our goods and our rights. God's law is not against all use of force; but whoever has recourse to atomic warfare will have God against him. Only after such plain speaking can the Church proceed to take part in deliberations about the way in which this is to be translated into political practice; that is, what policy is adopted when God's *No* is not ignored and when that policy takes its bearing from him in a world in which atomic weapons have become a decisive and irrevocable factor. If its *No* is not to look like arrogance or self-righteousness or fanaticism, and if its ethic is not to be one of abstract principles removed from reality and "governed by sentiment" instead of a concrete "responsibility ethic" (Max Weber), the Church must take part with all seriousness in these deliberations.

The Church must oppose all the sharpening of antitheses that is characteristic of the Cold War. It must steer clear of them and must not identify itself, because of its own interests with one of the parties in the Cold War.

The major Churches must take more seriously than they have in the past the ethos and the arguments of Christian pacifist groups and must make use of the experience of these groups and see that it bears fruit. Because atomic war can no longer be used as an *ultima ratio* for the preservation of justice through force, the major Churches are coming closer to the position always held by the historic peace Churches—that war cannot serve justice.

The major Churches must firmly withstand the temptation to continue transmitting without reflection the traditional war ethic or even to reinstate it because it still appears to be suitable in some circumstances. Rather, they must recognize the theoretical and practical problems of this ethic and think out these questions anew. They must intercede in all countries for the legal protection of conscientious objectors, and they must recognize conscientious objection among their own members as a legitimate form of Christian obedience.

All Churches must take a decisive stand for the maintenance of peace and the achievement of a stable, peaceful order. They must demand that even justifiable interests and aims be sacrificed for this purpose. They can do this not only in the statements of Church leaders but by urging this attitude on their members and congregations as God's command and therefore the duty of the Christian in our time. Disarmament, peace settlements, the sacrifice of national interests to the cause of peace, the renunciation of war, the termination of the Cold War, the understanding of national as well as Cold War disputes—all these must deeply penetrate the consciousness of our congregations. Otherwise, it is no longer possible to be a true Christian in our time. The Christian Church must be the pioneer of efforts for peace in every place and in every country. It must impress this conviction especially upon those of its members who are active in politics and must ask them specifically how far their political words and deeds conform to it. If we apply this standard to our congregations today and to the actions of Christian politicians (or of those who call themselves Christians), it becomes clear how far removed we still are from it.

We do not know how much time we still have. We must not delude ourselves and others about security. . . . Since the irrationality of those who wield power has been proved in history, the outbreak of a catastrophic nuclear war in our generation is more probable than not. The timid efforts to relax tension during the last few years have not really altered this fact.

The East-West Conflict

If atomic war is the worst enemy of mankind today, the maintenance of peace and the achievement of a stable and peaceful order become more important than the victory of one ideology or the other. This thesis has important implications.

For the Church, it means first a completely different recognition of nonviolence as a means of achieving justice, on the lines followed by Gandhi and Martin Luther King. Since the time of Augustine and Constantine, the Church has looked mainly to force as a means of maintaining justice in a world in which evil is a reality and has understood nonviolence only as an abdication of justice. At a time when war can no longer serve this purpose, the Church has an urgent need to remember that justice can also be protected by nonviolence, in the form of passive resistance. It is not merely a question of refusing to use force; it is a question of active willingness to suffer in connection with nonviolent demonstrations that seek, by putting pressure on rulers responsible for injustice, to bring about a restoration of justice. In a sense then, nonviolence is also a weapon; but it is one that (in accordance with the Christian faith) is more appropriate to Christians than is the use of force. For the opponent is not treated as an enemy; the aim is rather to win him over by shaming him into right action. Those who adopt this course fear that the use of force will only increase evil and hatred, and so they put their faith in the power of love. The war ethic of the major Churches has hitherto been far too subservient to the superstition about force and has accepted the view that justice without force is lost. Minority groups, on the other hand, such as the Jews and Negroes in the United States, and religious minorities, have had less temptation to resort to force and know more about the power of suffering and of love. Now the whole Church must learn from them. It must embrace the cause of nonviolence; it must oppose the still-prevalent belief that justice cannot be achieved without force. It must oppose the view, in the struggle between the West and the communist powers, that armaments are the sole salvation and that the victory of the other side is the worst possible evil.

The antithesis between East and West becomes relative when one realizes that atomic war is the greatest external evil that threatens mankind today. But this realization must not, in any way, result in the surrender of one side to the other. It will still be possible to defend one side against the other by the military deterrent (and, in any event, there is no hope of diverting the nations from this course). But the aim will no longer be victory—the elimination of the opposing power; it will be coexistence, and a coexistence that permits communication. Although we are still a long way from this position, it is still, with atomic war threatening us like the sword of Damocles, the only possible one to adopt.

In the conflict between East and West, Christians and Christian Churches have widely supported the West and have furthered western concerns. This has been taken for granted with a certain naïvete based on the antagonism to religion that is inherent in Marxist communism. It is worthwhile to speculate whether the Churches would have reacted so definitely against communism if communism had remained neutral toward religion or had even supported the Churches. The opposition of certain systems of government to the demands of Christian ethics and to the Christian view of man has not hitherto prevented the Churches from condoning such systems. As long as they themselves were not oppressed but privileged, the Churches have, to a large extent, ignored slavery, the exploitation and pauperization of the masses, the suppression of free expression of opinion, the education of youth to hate, the arbitrariness of police methods (which include torture), prostitution and the degradation of man. All these things, if practiced by communism, are universally denounced in Christian sermons and in the Christian press of the West. A particularly striking example of this in our century is the different attitudes shown by the Roman Catholic Church (and reflected also in most other ecclesiastical publicity) toward the Batista regime and the Castro regime in Cuba. That communism, wherever it has been established, in spite of having done much harm, has also removed a great deal of evil that previously existed (the poverty of the masses, serfdom, the creating of enmity between the nations, the degrading position of women in the East, open prostitution) goes for nothing in the eyes of the average Church member. The same could be said of the improvements that have resulted from the abandonment of Stalinism in communist countries—they have hardly been acknowledged by Christians in the West, let alone thought of as the answer to prayer for the people in the East. The sincerity of the Communists in their open rejection of religion is, from the political viewpoint, their folly. It prevents communism from winning the allegiance of the religiously tied masses and from making full use, for its own benefit, of the historic corruptibility of the Churches.

The recognition of this corruptibility is both alarming and significant in respect to the Christian attitude toward communism. There are other reasons, besides its fixation on atheism, why we must, as Christians, object to communist doctrine. The communist superstition about force, about the end justifying any means; the communist ideal of the complete collectivization of man; the communist failure to recognize human dignity and the rights of the individual; the claims of the Communist party to a monopoly of knowledge of absolute truth and of uncontrolled authority not subject to any higher justice—all these are characteristics of communism that make it impossible for the Christian to be a Communist, as long as communism is as it is, and they also oblige a Christian to disagree with it. But our disagreement is untrustworthy as long as we tolerate feudalistic, fascist or similar regimes (which are characterized by the same terror, the same deprivation of human rights, the same hallowing of any means in order to retain power), and as long as we stand alongside them and even support them, for no other reason than that these regimes outwardly support the Churches and have not developed an antireligious doctrine. The Christian Church's criticism of capitalism has never had the same force and sharpness as its criticism of communism. Thus, the Church comes under heavy suspicion that its criticism is only an expression of egoistical ecclesiastical interest, and that it takes its principles of social ethics seriously only when the Church itself is injured by a regime. Only when the Church overcomes its moral corruption (which is the result of its alliance with the powers of state and of society) and opposes the misdeeds of its friends as sharply as those of its enemies can its criticism of communism carry weight with Communists. Only then can that criticism make a selfless contribution to the improvement of communism and to its liberation from erroneous ideas.

Is it, then, possible for communism to change? There was (and still is) a panicky view of communism, which the philosopher Karl Jaspers expressed in his book *The Atom Bomb and the Future of Mankind.* Here Jaspers advocates the thesis that modern totalitarianism, unlike former despotisms, if not removed in time, produces an irreversible distortion of human nature. From the standpoint of the dignity of man, this would mean that life was no longer worth living. Yet, according to Jaspers, the point is not whether mankind should live at all, but that it should live lives worthy of human beings. Therefore, if a decision must be made, it is more fitting to sacrifice the whole of mankind (through an atomic war) than to let it fall under communist totalitarianism without this final act of resistance. Such a viewpoint ascribes to communism monstrosities as great as the achievements in which communism prides itself. This view is just as godless, just as atheistic, as communism itself. Unfortunately, even Christians have adopted this apocalyptic vision without asking how it is related to the

Christian belief in God's lordship over history and to God's gracious covenant with mankind in Jesus Christ.

One may ask in the abstract the question that is raised in novels such as George Orwell's *1984,* whether it is possible for human power to transform humanity into a race of termites and thus to dehumanize it. The experiences of our time, even under the regimes of Hitler and Stalin, give us no grounds to answer this question in the affirmative. However terribly human power can dehumanize the individual and groups of human beings, it has not succeeded so far in dehumanizing whole nations. Although the means of power in the future will be much greater than in the past, and therefore the danger to humanity (as well as the opportunities) will correspondingly increase, the developments of the last decade give us no right to see communism as the only source of these dangers. Rather, this decade has already shown that communism is a world historical phenomenon in a totally different sense from that of the organized criminality of national socialism. Communism is capable of change and looks to the future. It is in no greater measure than any other movement the subject of history; it is equally the object of historical development and of pressure from the traditions of the nations it rules, with their needs and their desire for liberty. For good or ill, these nations have invested their work and their lives in communism, and they work at it in order to make it more bearable or useful for themselves. It does not occur to them that the seizure of power by the Communists may be the twilight of history, as Jaspers implied. On the contrary, they hope—and we must hope with them—that their life will continue, and that even under communism they may achieve a decent way of life.

Christians who live in communist countries also take part in this effort to achieve a decent way of life. We would suggest that, as they engage in this task, they—as well as Christians elsewhere in the world—should bear the following point in mind.

1. The right social contribution of Christians is always and everywhere directed toward the humanizing of society, toward the establishment of freedom and equality before the law for the members of society, toward the maintenance and the improvement of the law and toward the formation of areas of freedom in which the individual can act responsibly. In a society based on law and justice, Christians will realize that they are responsible for the maintenance of justice and freedom, of obligation and of the limitation of power. In a totalitarian society,

they will realize that they are responsible for achieving these good things; that is, for gradually breaking down totalitarianism.

2. Communism could lose its totalitarian character. The possibilities for such a development are inherent in its doctrine, but, more particularly, the pressure of historical events could bring this about.

3. Whether communism will always retain its hostile attitude toward religion no one can say. It is conceivable that many factors, including the existence and collaboration of a live Christendom in its midst, could cause the withdrawal, or at least the total decay, of that attitude.

4. In terms of human dignity, the communist countries today are certainly not to be depicted black and the other countries white. Christians must not support such black and white distinctions, which could incite the nations to atomic war. They are as slanderous as the picture of conditions in the capitalist world adduced in communist propaganda.

5. The problems of the last third of the twentieth century will trouble the communist countries as much as the noncommunist countries. Presumably, they will bring about profound changes in everything that today comes under the heading "communism" or "capitalism." To overcome these problems, both communist and noncommunist countries have positive and negative presuppositions, though of a different kind. Krushchev called upon his deputies to learn from the Capitalists. There is equal reason for the West to observe communist developments carefully and to ask, what can we learn from the Communists?

6. Today there is no longer a single, uniform type of communism, as Lenin and Stalin visualized it. It is likely that, in the future, there will be a series of very different types of communism, including some whose philosophy of life will be far less committed than that of the Soviet Communists. This is already so in Cuba and in Latin American communism generally. Thus, a crucial barrier, which has prevented Christians from participating in communist revolutionary movements, will fall. There is much to be said for the view that, unless there is a revolutionary upheaval, it will be impossible to bring about radical reforms in Latin America. The last and, presumably, final breakdown of Kennedy's Alliance for Progress will raise again and more urgently the question of Christian participation in communist revolutionary movements. There is need for a careful and profound theological examination of this whole question.

The political as well as the economic interests of the great powers (particularly those of the United States in Latin America) are affected by these revolutionary movements. The Church must not be a party to "mythologizing" the discussion, but must help to "demythologize" it, by making it clear that this is not a question of choosing between communist tyranny and freedom consonant with human dignity, or between ungodliness and Christianity. Rather, it is a question of conflicting power interests and, at the same time, a battle to ensure the possibility of existence for the impoverished masses. If conservative forces do not achieve the necessary reforms, that is no doubt deplorable; but it is not a matter for condemnation if reforms are achieved in a revolutionary manner, as in Cuba and China. In such circumstances, the Christian task is to cooperate in order that the transitory despotic phase may be alleviated and shortened.

In any event, none of the objects of this controversy is worth an atomic war. The competition between communist and noncommunist efforts to solve the social problems of our time must take place in friendly coexistence. This peaceful coexistence is thus a nonwarlike state of combat; and the outcome will depend on which solutions prove best. Its motto must be: Whoever wins in peacetime, let him win. Christians will await the outcome with neither a panicky fear (in the event of a communist victory) nor a messianic hope (if victory should go to the West); for whoever wins, we shall not be out of the wood. Much will remain for Christians to do. And, presumably, there will be no victor, but new situations that cannot at present be foreseen.

In respect to the East-West conflict, the Churches must help their members during this phase of world history to take an unbiased view of developments. Panicky fear of a victory for the opposite side leads to biased thinking, which sees only the crimes of the other side and is blind to those of its own, and which even declares everything to be good and just that furthers the interests of its own side. By such an attitude, Christians betray the freedom given to them in the gospel, and the commission that God has given to each in his political camp. Because of communist hostility to religion, Christians in the West identify themselves more easily with the measures of their governments than do those in the East. For instance, most Christians in the West violently condemned the Soviet oppression of the Hungarian people in October, 1956, and attributed its inhumanity solely to communist views. Yet they remain blind to—or justify with arguments that are equally applicable to the Soviet measures—the brutality with which Portuguese colonialism reacted to the insurrection in its African colonies, the aggressive behavior of the United States against little Cuba (behavior that was also contrary to international law), and the intervention of the United States, motivated solely by power politics in the Vietnamese Civil War, against the will of the majority of the suffering people there. Only when we Christians seize the privilege, which the gospel has given us, of a frank and just viewpoint and a candid word of criticism of our own side, will we truly serve our own countries.

WAR AND HUMAN LIFE

AMERICAN CATHOLIC HIERACHY

We share the deep concern of thoughtful people in our times, a concern voiced by the Vatican Council, that "the whole human family has reached an hour of supreme crisis." The crisis can ultimately offer great promise for a more abundant human life, but at the moment it portends grave threats to all life. The threats to life depend on urgent and difficult decisions concerning war and peace. In considering these we share the conviction of Vatican Council II that the horror and perversity of technological warfare "compel us to undertake an evaluation of war with an entirely new attitude."

This compelling obligation is the greater in our case since we are citizens of a nation in many ways the most powerful in the world. The responsibility of moral leadership is the greater in the local Church of a nation whose arsenals contain the greatest nuclear potential for both the harm that we would wish to impede or the help it is our obligation to encourage. We are acutely aware that our moral posture and comportment in this hour of supreme crisis will be assessed by the judgment of history and of God.

We renew the affirmation by the Council that "the loftier strivings and aspirations of the human race are in harmony with the message of the Gospel." We speak as witnesses to that Gospel, aware that the issues of war and peace test the relevancy of its message for our generation, particularly in terms of the service of life and its dignity. We seek to speak in the spirit of that Gospel message, which is at heart a doctrine of nonviolence rather than violence, of peace understood as Jesus proclaimed.

We call upon American Catholics to evaluate war with that "entirely new attitude" for which the Council appealed and which may rightly be expected of all who, calling themselves Christians, proclaim their identity with the Prince of Peace.

Of one mind with the Council, we condemn without qualification wars of aggression, however their true character may sometimes be veiled. Whatever case there may have seemed to exist in other times for wars fought for the domination of another nation, such a case can no longer be imagined given the circumstances of modern warfare, the heightened sense of international mutuality and the increasingly available humane means to the realization of that mutuality.

The Second Vatican Council, in a solemn declaration, endorsed "the condemnation of total warfare issued by recent popes" and stated: "Every act of war directed to the indiscriminate destruction of whole cities or vast areas with their inhabitants is a crime against God and man which merits firm and unequivocal condemnation."

The Council explicitly condemned the use of weapons of mass destruction, but sustained from condemning the possession of such weapons to deter "possible enemy attack." Though not passing direct judgment on this strategy of deterrence, the Council did declare that "men should be convinced that the arms race in which so many countries are engaged is not a safe way to preserve a steady peace. Nor is the so-called 'balance' resulting from this race a pure and authentic peace. Rather than being eliminated thereby, the causes of war threaten to grow gradually stronger. . . . Therefore it must be said again: the arms race is an utterly treacherous trap for humanity, and one which ensnares the poor to an intolerable degree.

The council did not call for unilateral disarmament; Christian morality is not lacking in realism. But it did call for reciprocal or collective disarmament "proceeding at an equal pace according to agreement, and backed up by authentic and workable safeguards." There are hopeful signs that such a formula may be strengthened by the Partial Test Ban Treaty and that the commitment under the Non-Proliferation Treaty to proceed to a negotiation of balanced reduction of nuclear weapons—at the same time extending the use of nuclear power for peaceful development of the needy nations under adequate inspection safeguard—may provide a positive, sane pattern for the future.

Meanwhile, it is greatly to be desired that such prospects not be dashed by irrational resolves to keep ahead in "assured destruction" capability.

Nevertheless, the nuclear race goes on. The latest act in the continuing nuclear arms race is no doubt the US decision to build a "thin" antiballistic missile system to defend against possible nuclear attack by another world power.

In themselves, such antiballistic missiles are purely defensive, designed to limit the damage to the United States from nuclear attack. Nevertheless, by upsetting the present strategic balance, the so-called balance of terror, there is grave danger that a United States ABM system will incite other nations to increase their offensive nuclear forces with the seeming excuse of a need to restore the balance.

We seriously question whether the present policy of maintaining nuclear superiority is meaningful for security. There is no advantage to be gained by nuclear superiority, however it is computed, when each side is admittedy capable of inflicting overwhelming damage on the other, even after being attacked first. Such effective parity has been operative for some years. Any effort to achieve superiority only leads to ever-higher levels of armaments as it forces the side with the lesser capabilities to seek to maintain its superiority. In the wake of this action-reaction phenomenon comes a decrease in both stability and security.

We cannot but question the depth of the commitment to peace of people of religious background who no longer pray for peace. But those who only pray for peace, leaving to others the arduous work for peace, the dialogue for peace, have a defective theology concerning the relation between human action and the accomplishment of that will of God in which is our peace. So, too, those who, neglectful of the part of prayer, rely only on their own power, or on the pooling of merely human resources of intelligence, energy and even good will, forget the wisdom of Scripture: "If the Lord does not build the house, in vain the masons toil; if the Lord does not guard the city, in vain the sentries watch."

The Council Fathers recognized that not even ending the nuclear arms race, which itself cannot be accomplished without the full cooperation of the international community, would ensure the permanent removal of the awesome threat of modern war. Nor would disarmament alone, even assuming it to be complete and across the board, remove the causes of war. "This goal undoubtedly requires the establishment of some universal public authority acknowledged as such by all, and endowed with effective power to safeguard, on the behalf of all, security, regard for justice and respect for rights."

Since war remains a melancholy fact of life today, we believe the United States not only should insist on adherence to and the application by all nations of existing international conventions or treaties on the laws of war, such as the revised Geneva Convention relative to the treatment of prisoners of war, but should take the lead in seeking to update them. Certain forms of warfare, new and old, should be outlawed, and practices in dealing with civilian populations, prisoners of war and refugees are always in need of review and reform.

A Catholic position of opposition to compulsory peacetime military service, first formulated on the level of the Holy See by Pope Benedict XV, has had for its premise the fact that such service has been a contributing cause of the breeding of actual wars, a part of the "great armaments" and "armed peace" security concept, and, in the words of Cardinal Gasparri in a letter to Lloyd George, the cause of such great evils for more than a century that the cure of these evils can only be found in the suppression of this system. In the spirit of this position, we welcome the voices lifted up among our political leaders which ask for a total review of the draft system and the establishment of voluntary military service in a professional army with democratic safeguards and for clear purposes of adequate defense. Our call for the end of any draft system at home which, in practice, amounts at times to compulsory peacetime military service, is in direct line with previous resolutions of the hierarchy of the United States on compulsory military training.

We earnestly appeal to our own government and to all governments to give the elimination of the present international "war system" a priority consistent with the damaging effect of massive armament programs on all the objectives of the good society to which enlightened governments give priorities: education, public health, a true sense of security, prosperity, maximum liberty, the flourishing of the humane arts and sciences, in a word the service of life itself.

Meanwhile there are moral lessons to be learned from our involvement in Vietnam that will apply to future cases. One might be that military power and technology do not suffice, even with the strongest resolve, to restore order or accomplish peace. As a rule internal political conflicts are too complicated to be solved by the external application of force and technology.

Another might be the realization that some evils existing in the world, evils such as undernutrition, economic frustration, social stagnation and political injustices, may be more readily attacked and corrected through non-military means, than by military efforts to counteract the subversive forces bent on their exploitation.

It is not surprising that those who are most critical, even intemperate, in their discussions of war as an instrument of national policy or as a ready means to the settling even of wrongs, are among the young; the burden of killing and dying falls principally on them.

The enthusiasm of many young people for new programs of service to fellow humans in need may be proof that some traditional forms of patriotism are in process of being supplemented by a new spirit of dedication to humanity and to the moral prestige of one's own nation. This new spirit must be taken seriously; it may not always match the heroism of the missionaries and the full measure of the life of faith, but it is not contradictory to these and may open up new forms of Christian apostolate.

If war is ever to be outlawed, and replaced by more humane and enlightened institutions to regulate conflicts among nations, institutions rooted in the notion of universal common good, it will be because the citizens of this and other nations have rejected the tenets of exaggerated nationalism and insisted on principles of nonviolent political and civic action in both the domestic and international spheres.

The present laws of this country, however, provide only for those whose reasons of conscience are grounded in a total rejection of the use of military force. This form of conscientious objection deserves the legal provision made for it, but we consider that the time has come to urge that similar consideration be given those whose reasons of conscience are more personal and specific.

The doctrine and defense of life require a renewed spirituality in the Church. Such a spirituality will reaffirm the sacred character of married love through which life is begun, the dignity of the family within which love brings life to maturity, and the blessed vision of peace in which life is shared by men and nations in a world community of love.

In her defense of human life the Church in our day makes her own, as did Moses, the words by which God Himself reduces our perplexities to a clear, inescapable choice: "I call heaven and earth to witness against you this day, that I have set before you life and death ... therefore, choose life that you and your descendants may live. . . ."

THE CHRISTIAN,
VIOLENCE AND SOCIAL CHANGE

JOSEPH C. HOUGH, JR.

Karl Menninger may or may not be correct when he asserts that the American style of living is less violent than it was one hundred years ago, but there can be little doubt about his concession that violence is more conspicuous in America today than it ever was before.[1]

There are at least six types of violence that are all a part of the nation's preoccupation with the subject. The most obvious example, of course, is the involvement of the nation in the war in Viet Nam. There is also the continued concern with the violent crime. For the last decade the index of violent crimes in the nation has been spiraling out of control, and there is a constant hue and cry for governmental authorities to do something about it. Third, there is what has been referred to as "systemic," "structural," or "figurative" violence. Into this category are lumped all the effects of unjust social systems upon those who are at the bottom of the social scale. This has been especially a concern of non-white groups whose position in American Society has been determined by a systematic discrimination and the creation of inferior life chances in a segregated society.[2] A fourth category of violence that is of concern to the nation might be labeled civil disturbance. This is usually a response to structural violence that involves burning, looting, and some attacks on persons. However, as has been demonstrated by the analysis in the Kerner report, this type of violence is seldom a planned strategy. As we shall see later, it may be used strategically, but does not begin with any type of conspiritorial action.

Civil disturbance often results in an over-reaction by the police agencies, a fifth type of violence. Police violence occurs when more force is employed than is necessary to contain a civil disorder, or when excessive force is used as an "example" to others who might be contemplating some kind of disruption.

Finally, there is a revolutionary violence. This is distinguished from a civil disturbance in that it is planned as strategy for social change, and the violent acts are calculated to effect a certain response from the established forces. This distinction between revolutionary violence and civil disorder is often very difficult to make, but it is a distinction that must be clearly made. As we have said earlier, there is no evidence that the violent disorders in our cities were planned as revolutionary strategy although they may have been interpreted as such.[3] In contrast, much of the disruption that is now taking place on college campuses is strategically planned with more or less clear goals in mind, among which is dissolution of the whole American system in which the university forms only a small part.

All of these types of violence are interrelated. For example, the Kerner report, in page after page of analysis, documents the fact that systematic deprivation and discrimination in our segregated society were the real causes of the disorders which have occurred in the American cities. Furthermore, this failure of the nation to deal with the problems which minorities face, together with the relentless pursuit of an expensive and militaristic foreign policy in Southeast Asia are two of the important causes for the disillusionment with our system that is so much a part of the violent disorders on the campus.

In between the system and the dissentors stand the police. Given the extent of provocation, they have often acted in a very restrained manner. On other occasions they have struck out with a viciousness like that in Chicago in 1968, like that in Alabama in the early 1960's, or in any of the major cities where disruptions occurred during 1966-67. It is, indeed, alarming that the Kerner report lists police brutality as a major Negro grievance against the American system. This means that those who are to administer and enforce the law in the ghettos are seen as the enemy, and this is a very dangerous situation. As long as the nation postpones the urgent matters of renewal of life in the ghettos and other domestic problems of poverty and injustice, the police will increasingly find themselves in an alien land within the communities where the minorities sub-cultures exist.

This is becoming no less true of certain segments of university students as well. The coalition between militant blacks and sympathetic whites, who have their own separate goals as well, is challenging the system in the heart of its prized institution, the university. Here again the police are called upon to intervene, and as they do, they are cast in the role of the enemy to be attacked rather than the upholders of law and order.[4] This sub-cultural alienation in the nation places the police in the most complex and dangerous position. They will increasingly be called upon by some segments of the society to react with vigor and force. That they can respond to this type of urging is no longer a matter of doubt since the debacle at Chicago. On the other hand, they will be continually cautioned against the use of excessive force and be urged to exercise restraint. This kind of confusion cannot help but add to the frustration of police work and may well increase the possibility of instantaneous police over-reaction in the future.[5]

This extraordinarily explosive picture of violence in the nation poses for the contemporary Christian one of the most complex and urgent ethical issues of our time. Hence, in the pages that follow, I make no pretense of having done an exhaustive treatment of the subject. What I shall try to do is to draw a preliminary sketch of some of the ethical considerations that might be employed as a Christian engages himself in the very difficult task of decision-making about violence as a strategy for social change.

There is a sense, then, in which Christians are open to the charge that they are guilty in participation of violence through their own apathy during the struggle for justice. But even more serious than that, we are open to the charge that we have, through our institutional structures, been a party to the creation of the very structural violence that is being so strongly protested by minority groups today. Taking this charge seriously, and attempting to change church institutions as well as other social institutions of which we are a part, remain at the top of the Christian's ethical agenda.

At the outset, I want to make it clear that from my perspective, the chief problem for the Church is its continued acquiescence in the perpetration of structural violences upon relatively powerless people. I have already argued elsewhere at length that the primary task for the Church in contemporary America is to produce a political translation of the message of the Gospel.[6] By this I do not mean that the Church as an institution should necessarily engage in party politics, but rather that we shift our attention from a hermeneutics that gives us an historical view of faith to one that gives us faith with a grip on history. Today, after years of transition from literalism and fundamentalism to Freud, Bultmann, and others, the Church still stands in a society dominated and determined by political action with an essentially a-political view of the Christian life. This is why in America, the nation with the largest percentage of church membership and attendance in the world, the churches still drag behind other institutions in our society even in ridding themselves of segregation and discriminatory practices. When one takes careful account of all the sociological factors and historical factors in the position of the Church on the major social issues that are facing our nation today, there is still the overwhelming fact that most of the popular theology as understood by the average church member in America today is simply a form of individualistic pietism or a psychological counterpart which is no less a-political and ineffective as an agency in social change.[7]

It is precisely this very deep concern for participation in the struggle for justice, together with disillusionment with the traditional means of achieving justice, that has led some Christians to consider the possibility of revolutionary violence as an ethical alternative. Strangely enough, even the now famous apostle of the democratic system, Reinhold Niebuhr, suggested that violence as a strategy for social change might be permissible if its ends were adjudged good. In his earlier writing, Niebuhr argued that certain moralists were ". . . wrong in their assumption that violence is intrinsically immoral," especially when it came to intergroup relations. "It is not self-evident that violence always thwarts the ends by which it is justified." What is more, Niebuhr continued, ". . . the immediate consequences of violence cannot be differentiated as sharply from those of non-violence as is sometimes supposed."[8] This kind of argument has been given fresh impetus recently by the publication in the United States of Frantz Fanon's *The Wretched of the Earth*.[9]

Fanon's writing focuses particularly upon the role of violence in the wars of independence by colonial people, and at the outset, he argues that colonialism itself is a brutal and violent form of dehumanization that has been visited upon native people.

> The violence which has ruled over the ordering of the colonial world, . . .
> has ceaselessly drummed the rhythm for the destruction of native social
> forms and broken up without reserve the systems of reference of economy,
> the custom of dress and external life.[10]

Revolutionary violence, argues Fanon, is but the response of the colonized people to the structural or systematic violence visited upon them for the sake of liberation.

In addition to the concrete possibility of freedom, violence is also seen as the source of a new creativity and unity among oppressed people. It serves to wrench them out of fear-inspired apathy and mobilize them for the struggle toward true nationhood.

> Violence alone, violence committed by the people, violence organized and educated by its leaders, makes it possible for the masses to understand social truths and gives the key to them. Without that struggle, without that knowledge of the practice of action, there is nothing but a fancy-dress parade and the blare of trumpets.[11]

On the individual level, Fanon argues that violence is a "cleansing force." It establishes manhood and self-respect, both of which are necessary for full humanity.[12] In fact, one might summarize all of Fanon's ethical justification of violence in terms of humanization. There is a new sense of selfhood, a new possibility of sharing, and a new evidence of mutual respect. In short, the motivation of revolutionary violence is liberation of the oppressed, and its goal is a new universal humanity.[13]

It is not too difficult to see the romanticism of such writing about revolutionary violence. The world still waits for the new humanity to appear in Fanon's Algeria, and there is no encouraging evidence that revolution is a one-way ticket to paradise even for the victors. Very often the bloody confusion results in nothing but a series of coups and counter coups, with the resulting oppression and open-ended anarchic situation like that in Colombia.[14] Even in relatively stable situations, the revolutions seem to need periodic orgies of violence that never come to an end. For example, the upheavals in Communist China instigated by the "Red Guard Movement" were a purification or cleansing movement according to official propaganda, but as far as can be determined they simply sowed further seeds of discord and extended the toll of the violence in China.

But one cannot simply dismiss Fanon as a romantic and let it go at that. His writings highlight a very serious ethical dilemma. It becomes very clear in the writings of this revolutionary that the ethical choice for a person who exists in contemporary social order lies not in violence as over against non-violence but in the choice of the degree to which, and the method by which, he shall exercise violence.

This choice is made even more difficult when we see that even within democratic societies the use of violence and the threat of violence have certain *necessary* functions. For example, Lewis Coser has argued that violence has three social functions in any society: (1) the manifest function of achievement, (2) the latent function of danger signal, and (3) the latent function of catalyst.[15]

Violence functions as achievement, particularly among underdogs, because it is the most direct form of action and is also accessible. It is, therefore, an attractive alternative road to the achievement of status or power to those who have either limited or no access to the normal channels of achievement and the exercise of power in a society. Commenting upon the study of juvenile gangs by Cloward and Ohlin, Coser writes: "Here the vaunted equal opportunity, which had been experienced as a sham and a lure everywhere else, turns out to be effective. In the wilderness of cities, just as in the wilderness of the frontier, . . . the successful exercise of violence is a road to achievement.[16] Coser goes on to note that revolutionary violence can be understood in much the same way. It offers the alienated and oppressed an opening to manhood and a positive identity that has been closed to them by their confinement within the operating social system. In addition to all of this, it gives the alienated man a cause which he can believe in and with which he can readily identify.[17]

It is, therefore, no accident that in the United States two groups who have the least number of openings to the normal channels of political power and achievement, young black ghetto youths and white middle class students still dependent upon parental support, are the locus of much of the current agitation for the use of violence as a strategy for social change in the United States.

But violence does not merely function in terms of the social and psychological need of the participants. It may well be the clearest and the most effective sign that there are serious problems within a social system that must be corrected. It is, of course, true that the problems can be identified by methods short of violent demonstrations, but experience in America has shown clearly that all the appeals of moralists and all the warnings of social scientists do not serve to pinpoint the malfunctioning of the system to the general public nearly so well as one violent disorder.[18]

This means also that violence may well serve as a catalyst for social change. It is no secret to anyone that more attention has been given to the problems of blacks in the cities of this nation since the Watts riot of 1965 than had ever been the case before. With the intensification of the disturbances through the summers of 1966 and 1967, national efforts to find solutions to the issues identified by the

Kerner Commission have increased phenomenally. This is not to say that the changes are fast enough to satisfy any of those who suffer. It is to say, however, that much effort is being put forth in the black and white community, both in the public and private sectors, to bring about the kind of changes that would at least begin to attack the problems that have been identified as the causes of the violent uprisings in the nation. And furthermore, it is to argue that this flurry of activity is directly related to occurrence of the violent uprisings which served as catalytic agents.

According to H. L. Nieburg, some violence and the threat of violence are part of the necessary process of democratic political life.[19] They are necessary in order to "... instill dynamism into the structure and growth of the law, the settlement of disputes, the process of accommodating interest." For this reason, a democratic state does not try to gain absolute control over the use of violence. In contrast to a totalitarian state, "... the democratic state permits potential violence, to have a social effect with only a token demonstration, thus fostering greater opportunities for peaceful, political and social change." Nieburg is very much aware of the fact that domestic violence may be explosive and may create utter anarchy and chaos, but he is nonetheless convinced that any attempt to suppress all violence on behalf of specific interest groups will lead to a totalitarian like rigidity, which is even more likely to be torn asunder by internal explosions.[20]

It should be noted, however, that Nieburg is referring to the "rational" use of violence in his remarks. Violence that is a necessary part of the process of social change is not random or spontaneous violence, but is a "... demonstration of the will and capability of action, establishing a measure of credibility of future threats." Rational violence does not aim to exhaust itself in actual violence at all. It is simply part of the process of bargaining that supports the threat of violence. Similarly, the "rational" use of the threat of violence is not to provoke violence on the part of one's supporters or of one's opponents. Rather it is a tool one uses to strengthen his bargaining position in the process of the accommodation of interest in the larger society.[21]

In light of these qualifications, therefore, it is important to realize most violence may be used rationally by someone who interprets that violence in terms of his own interest and who is able to convince his opponent of the credibility of his interpretation.

It is also possible for persons interested in preventing any kind of social change to use violence as an excuse for greater repression. This is especially true when any show of violence is immediately labeled as a plot to begin a revolutionary overthrow of the American government. Hopefully, the violence that has occurred in this country has not yet produced widespread sentiments of this sort. However, this reaction is always lurking just beneath the surface when the escalation of violence begins to approach the limits of tolerance which the social system can endure and still remain a viable system.

All of this discussion of the function of violence in social change must be seen in the context of some very important conditions. For one thing any state must be ordered by some system of law. The boundary line of human civilization is lawful existence. However, law does not merely form the boundaries. As Nieburg points out, it also gives an advantage to some within the social system over against others. It is of prime importance, therefore, who has the privilege of writing the laws in any state whether that state be totalitarian or democratic.[22] Here there is a difference between the totalitarian and democratic state which is very crucial. The democratic state makes two provisions that help modify the permanent power of the original law-makers. On the one hand, it allows for the formation of private groups to contest the role of law-making, and on the other hand, it puts severe restraints upon the arbitrary use of police power. In America we know these as the electoral process and the system of judicial protections largely contained in the Bill of Rights. While these function more or less imperfectly in various periods of history, they do make it highly unlikely that the system will ever become so rigid as to justify a complete revolution, and they make it just as unlikely that police terror under the name of law and order or something less respectable, can be pursued arbitrarily with impunity for any length of time. Paradoxically, this very restraint and openness increase the immediate risk of violence within the system during times of social crisis, while at the same time serving to lower the risk of the nation-wide "blood-bath" so confidently predicted by revolutionaries today.

By way of summary then, it seems that no society can exist without some form of violence or the threat of violence. This is easily seen when one recalls the various types of violence listed earlier in this essay. Therefore, the Christian's ethical situation is not nearly so clear as proponents of non-violent methods of social change might assume. On the one hand, non-violence may be participation in structural or systematic violence with a vengeance. On the other hand, the extent to which non-violent methodologies are dependent upon the tacit support to force has not been sufficiently acknowledged. For example, one can only speculate what might have been the accomplishments of the non-violent campaign of Martin Luther King in the southern part of the United States without the protective cover of the threat of federal intervention which was made credible on several occasions by the actual deployment of federal force. It might well have been the case that the actions of Bull Connor would have escalated and multiplied to the extent that the whole movement would have been destroyed. In any case, the campaign of Martin Luther King was strongly supported by the threat of violence implicit in federal power, and hence is not to be seen as an alternative to the use of violence in social change.

The reasons why Christians have traditionally chosen to participate in some forms of violence as over against others is not difficult to understand. Ordinarily, structural violence does not require the direct involvement of the person who is engaged in perpetrating that violence upon a powerless people. Hence it is an action that can be done inadvertently and with a degree of innocence over a period of time. Furthermore, participation in non-violent demonstrations may bring to bear the violent force of other agencies but this kind of participation does not involve the Christian himself in direct and overt violent action against the person of another. Because of the prohibitions against killing, together with the centrality of love for the other person in the teachings of the Church, participation in direct and overt violent action against persons has never been an easy option for Christians. For example, in response to the knotty problems surrounding the problem of military service, the Church has, for the most part, adopted the pattern of the classical Just War doctrine.[23] Even this doctrine, however, under the strict prohibitions against killing, has been qualified by succeeding generations of Christians.

The spirit of Christian thinking on this Just War doctrine is most adequately represented in the thought of St. Augustine. Augustine is clearly troubled by the thought of any Christian participation in warfare. Under the pressures of a world of sin, Augustine reluctantly concludes that it is permissible for a Christian to participate in warfare, but only under the strictest limitations. Even then, the spirit of his participation must be that of mournful penitence for his action.[24]

Much more difficult for the Church than the problem of war between nations has been the problem of violent revolution and internal disturbance, the problem we are facing in America today. No doctrine of "just" revolution has ever been developed that would clearly lay down the conditions under which Christian participation in revolutionary violence would be morally justifiable.[25]

Recently, however, under the pressure of revolutionary changes throughout the world, the Church shows some sign of wrestling with revolutionary violence as a possibility for the Christian.

During 1966 and 1967 three major Christian conferences seemed to have reached a consensus on several principles concerning Christian participation in revolutionary violence. (1) The Christian may participate in revolutionary violence which is a response to an intolerable social repression. (2) Christian participation in violence should be a last resort strategy employed only after all other means of social change have proved futile. (3) Christian participation in revolutionary violence must seek a more just social order and not merely the destruction of one's opponent. (4) Any Christian participation in overt violence against other persons must be cognizant of the enormous risk entailed in his action. This means that involvement in revolutionary violence, like Christian participation in war, must always be done in a "mournful mood" and in the hope of greater justice and peace.[26]

These principles are, of course, very abstract, and can only serve as a beginning point for Christian reflection about participation in revolutionary violence. As a whole, however, they do serve to warn the Christian of two dangers inherent in a revolutionary situation. On the one hand, we are reminded again that non-action may be a most violent kind of action, and non-violent action most often presupposed some threat of violence if it is to be effective. There is, therefore, *no absolute* distinction between non-action, non-violent action, and revolutionary action.

On the other hand, however, these principles are really a subtle warning against Christian participation in direct violent action. They are a *clear* warning against romanticising about revolutions, a warning coming from some who have experienced the reality of revolution rather than its rhetoric. The tendency to interpret every revolutionary upheaval as divine intervention in the affairs of men is, to say the least, not unknown among American Christians. This is an especially tempting stance to those who are deeply incensed over social injustice and yet have little or no access to power; for violence is the most direct form of power offering a quick and satisfying demonstration to the participants themselves that indeed something can be done. For the powerless, then, violence in itself may be a first line of strategy, but the principles articulated here serve notice that it is almost impossible to view as morally permissible any Christian participation in a strategy that has as its first line of action direct violence.

Therefore, there is a danger in America today that both black and white Christians under fire from revolutionaries will be pushed to strategies they find unacceptable in order to maintain rapport with the groups with whom they strongly identify. Such is often the case for Christians working among true revolutionaries who, as we have already seen, often view an act of violence as the final seal of commitment to the revolutionary cause. In this case, the principles arising from the current Christian discussions about violent revolutionary action warn strongly against too easy acquiescence in the demands of revolutionary allies that Christians personally participate in direct violent action.

Between the extremes of a strategy of direct violent action as a first response and the non-strategy of acquiescence in violence, there is a wilderness of possibilities for Christian involvement which require highly contextual Christian ethical decisions. The only guideline inherent in the preceding reflection about the American situation is the general admonition to the Christian to begin with some direct form of action that will not necessarily produce direct violent encounter. Yet, in the face of pressing needs for social change, the Christian should not hesitate to protest, picket, disrupt or confront, even at the risk of violence, provided the action has some "rational" goal in view that includes something more than mere destruction and romantic dreams.

With this reflection in mind we are, of course, still removed from the most concrete cases for Christian decision-making. But in the final analysis that is appropriate. For personal decision-making that partakes of freedom and responsibility are the very stuff of a dynamic and purposive Christian life. Such a life requires the constant articulation of moral principles as a basis for reflection, but the daily decisions by which it is constituted are the private province of the conscience of the individual Christian who assesses his own situation and with courage dares to decide.

1. Karl A. Menninger, "Violence is not Increasing: We're Just More Aware of It," **Los Angeles Times**, November 24, 1968, Section G, pp. 1ff.

2. That concern is expressed well by Reverend Archie Rich, a black minister in Detroit, in an article published recently by **Concern**. (Archie L. Rich, "The Black Revolt," **Concern**, Vol. 9, No. 16, pp. 17-18). It is not only deprivation, however, that lies behind the structural violence in our cities. Recent studies lend strong evidence to the conclusion that it is a gap between what we have and what we hope for or aspire to, i.e., subjectively **felt** deprivation that is one of the main causes of the frustration that lies behind civil disorders. (Leonard, Berkowitz, "The Study of Urban Violence: Some Implications of Laboratory Studies of Frustration and Aggression," **American Behavioral Scientist**, Vol. 2, No. 4 March/April, 1968, p. 15. See also Don R. Bowen, Elinor R. Bowen, Sheldon R. Gawiser, and Louis H. Masotti, "Deprivation, Mobility, and Orientation Toward Protest of the Urban Poor," **American Behavioral Scientist, Op. Cit.,** pp. 20-23.)

3. Cf. **Report of the National Advisory Commission on Civil Disorders,** New York: Bantam Books, Inc., 1968; Daniel Walker, ed., **Rights in Conflict,** New York: The New American Library, Inc., 1968, p. 110 (No. 3). But see also, Allen D. Grimshaw, "Three Views of Urban Violence: Civil Disturbance, Racial Revolt, Class Assault," **American Behavioral Scientist**, Vol. 2, No. 4, March/April, 1968, pp. 2ff.

4. Crane Brinton argues that this isolation and discrediting of the police **is** one of the important stages of any revolution. (Crane Brinton, **The Anatomy of Revolution,** New York: Vintage Books, 1957.)

5. This places an enormous amount of importance on the study of police techniques and the training of police forces. Burton Levy, a long time student of police problems believes that the entire police system, including police ideology needs overhauling. (Burton Levy, "Cops in the Ghetto: A Problem of the Police System," **American Behavioral Scientist**, Vol. 2, No. 4, March/April, 1968, pp. 31ff. James Q. Wilson tries to draw some helpful distinctions in police styles, pointing out some of the effects and implications of a "legalistic" style as over against a "watchful" style. (James Q. Wilson, **Varieties of Police Behavior,** Cambridge: Harvard Univ. Press, 1968.) Much more of this kind of study is needed if the nation is to cope with the burgeoning police problems.

6. See my **Black Power and White Protestants,** New York: Oxford University Press, 1968, pp. 129ff.

7. **Ibid.,** pp. 170ff.

8. Reinhold Niebuhr, **Moral Man and Immoral Society,** New York: Charles Scribners' Sons, 1932, (Rev. Ed., 1960), pp. 170-172.

9. Frantz Fanon, **The Wretched of the Earth,** Trans. Constance Farrington, New York: Grove Press, 1968 edition, first published in France by Francois Maspero, 1961.

10. Fanon, **Op. Cit.,** p. 40.

11. **Ibid.,** p. 147.

12. **Ibid.,** p. 94.

13. **Ibid.,** pp. 308-310, 316.

14. See Roger C. Williamson, "Toward a Theory of Political Violence: The Case of Rural Colombia," **The Western Political Quarterly**, Vol. 18, No. 1, March 1965, pp. 35-44.

15. Lewis A. Coser, "Some Social Functions of Violence." **The Annals of the**

American Academy of Political and Social Science, Vol. 364, March 1966, pp. 8-18.

16. Ibid., p. 10, referring to Richard A. Cloward and Lloyd E. Ohlin, **Delinquency and Opportunity**, Glencoe, Ill.: The Free Press, 1960.

17. Ibid., pp. 11, 12.

18. Ibid., p. 12.

19. H. L. Nieburg, "The Threat of Violence and Social Change," **American Political Science Review**, Vol. 56, No. 4, December, 1962, p. 865.

20. Ibid.

21. Ibid., p. 867.

22. Ibid., p. 868.

23. Of course, there is a strong pacifist strain in Christianity too. Many Christians have refused to participate in warfare at all. On the other hand, Christians have also adopted the position of the "Holy War" or crusade. Both of these positions however, are departures from the mainstream of the historical positions of the church. Cf. Roland Bainton, **Christian Attitudes Toward War and Peace**, New York: Abingdon Press, 1960.

24. Bainton, **Op. Cit.** and Paul Ramsey, **The Just War**, New York: Scribners, 1969.

25. An attempt was made by the Theological Commission of the Christian Peace Conference at Prague in 1966 to formulate a "just revolution" theory. But the results are too abstract to be very useful. ("The Just Revolution," **Cross Currents**, Vol. 18, No. 1, Winter, 1968, p. 68.)

26. The 1966 Report of the Theological Commission of the Prague Peace Conference is contained in "The Just Revolution," in **Cross Currents, Op. Cit.,** pp. 67ff. This is a reference to paragraph 10. See also **World Conference on Church and Society, Official Report,** Geneva: World Council of Churches, 1967, p. 115 and "The Role of Violence in Social Change," (the report of Section II, Group 5) Joint Issue of **Social Action**, Vol. 24, No. 6, and **Social Progress**, Vol. 58, No. 3, January/February, 1968, pp. 37-43.

LETTER TO THE WEATHERMEN

DANIEL BERRIGAN, S.J.

Dear Brothers and Sisters,

This is Dan Berrigan speaking. I want to say what a very deep sense of gratitude I have that the chance has come to speak to you across the underground. It's a great moment when I can rejoice in the fact that we can at last start setting up a dialogue that I hope will be a continuing thing through the smoke signals, all with a view to enlarging the circle of those who realize that the times demand not that we narrow our method of communication but that we actually enlarge it if anything new or anything better is going to emerge. I'm talking out of a set of rough notes and my idea was that I could not only discuss these ideas with you but possibly publish them.

The cold war alliance between politics, labor, and the military finds many Americans at the right end of the cornucopia. What has not yet risen in them is the question of whose blood is paying for all this, what families elsewhere are being blasted, what separation and agony and death are the other side of that coin of the realm—the connections are very hard to make, and very few come on them, and many can hardly imagine that all being right with America means that very much must go wrong elsewhere. How do we get such a message across to others? It seems to me that that is one way of putting the very substance of our task. Trying to keep connections, or to create new ones. It's a most difficult job, and in hours of depression it seems all but impossible to speak to Americans across the military and diplomatic and economic idiocies—and yet I think we have to carry our reflection further and realize that the difficulty of our task is the other side of the judgment Americans are constantly making about us. This determination to keep talking with all who seek a rightful place in the world or all who have not yet awakened to it, I think, is the revolution, and the United States perversely and negatively knows it, and this is why we are in trouble. And this is why we accept trouble and ostracism and the fear of jail and of death, as the normal conditions under which decent men are called upon to function today.

Undoubtedly the FBI comes after people like me with guns because deeper than their personal chagrin and their corporate machismo, which is a kind of debased esprit de corps since they always get their man, there was that threat that the Panthers and the Vietnamese had learned so well as a reality. The threat is a very simple one because we are making connections, political connections, religious and moral connections, connections with prisoners and Cubans and Vietnamese, and these connections are forbidden under policies which J. Edgar Hoover is greatly skilled both in enacting and in enforcing. They know by now what we are about, they know we are serious. And they are serious about us. Just as with a mortal fear for the last five years they have known what the Vietamese are about and the Brazilians and the Angloese and the Guatemalans. We are guilty of making connections, or urging others to explore new ways of getting connected, of getting married, of educating children, of sharing goods and skills, of being religious, of being human, of resisting. I am speaking for prisoners and exiles and that true silent, deathly silent majority which is that of the dead and the unavenged as well as the unborn, and I am guilty again of making connections with you.

The mythology of fear that surrounds you is exactly what the society demands, as it demands more and more mythology, more and more unreality to live by. But it also offers a very special opportunity to break this myth that flourishes on silence and ignorance and has you stereotyped as mindless, indifferent to human life and death, determined to raise hell at any hour or place. We have to deal with this as we go along; but from where, from what sort of mentalities, what views of one another and ourselves? Not from an opposite window of insanity or useless rage, but with a new kind of anger which is both useful in communicating and imaginative and slow-burning to fuel the long haul which is the definition of our whole lives.

I'm trying to say that when people look about them for lives to run and when hopeless people look for hope, the gift we can offer others is so simple a thing as hope. As they said about Che, as they say about Jesus, some people, even to this day, he gave us hope. So that my hope is that you see your lives in somewhat this way, which is to say I hope your lives are about something more than sabotage. I'm certain they are. I hope the sabotage question is tactful and peripheral. I hope indeed that you are remaining uneasy about its meaning and usefulness and that you realize that the burning down of properties, whether

Catonsville or in the case of Chase Manhattan or anywhere else, by no means guarantees a change of consciousness, the risk remaining always very great that sabotage will change people for the worse and harden them against further change.

I hope you see your lives as Che saw his, that is to say mainly as teachers of the people, conscious as we must be of the vast range of human life that still awaits liberation and education and consciousness. If I'm learning anything it is that nearly everyone is in need of this and therfore in need of us, whether or not they realize it. I think of all those we so easily dismiss and whose rage against us is an index of the blank pages of their lives, those to whom no meaning or value has ever been attached by politicians or generals or churches or universities or indeed anyone, those whose sons fight the wars, those whose wages are drained away paying for the wars, those who are constantly mortgaged and indebted to the consumer system, and those closer to ourselves, among fellow students who are still enchanted by careerism and selfishness, those who are unaware that the human future must be created out of suffering and loss.

How shall we speak to our people, to the people everywhere? We must never refuse, in spite of their refusal of us, to call them our brothers, I must say to you as simply as I know how, if the people are not the main issue, there is simply no main issue and you and I are fooling ourselves also, and the American fear and dread of change has only transferred itself to a new setting.

This, I think, is where a sensible, humane movement operates on several levels at once if it is to get anywhere. So it is saying communication yes, organizing yes, community yes, sabotage yes—as a tool. That is the conviction that took us where we went. And it took us beyond to this night. We reasoned that the effect of our act could not be to impede the war or much less to stop the war in its tracks. God help us, if that had been our intention, we were certainly fools before the fact and doubly fools after it, for in fact the war went on. And still we undertook sabotage long before any of you. It might be worthwhile just very quickly reflecting on some reasons why. We were trying first of all to say something about the pernicious effect of certain properties on the lives of those who guarded them or died in consequence of them. And we were determined to talk to as many people as possible and as long as possible afterward, to interpret and to write, and through our conduct, through the appeal, through questioning ourselves again and again, finding out where we were, where we were going, where people might follow.

My hope is that affection and compassion and non-violence are now common resources once more and that we can proceed on that assumption, the assumption that the quality of life within our communities is exactly what we have to offer. I think a mistake in SDS's past was to kick out any evidence of that as being weakening or reactionary or counter-productive. The mark of inhuman treatment of humans is a mark that also hovers over us. It is the mark of a beast, whether its insignia is the military or the movement.

No principle is worth the sacrifice of a single human being. That's a very hard statement. At various stages of the movement some have acted as if almost the opposite were true, in that we get purer and purer. More and more people have been kicked out for less and less reason. At one period of the past, way back, the result of such thinking was another of the religious wars, or wars of extinction. At another time it was Hitler; he wanted a ton of purity too. Still another is still with us in the war against the Panthers and the Vietnamese. I think I'm in the underground because I want part of none of these, whatever name they go by, whatever rhetoric they justify themselves with.

When madness is the acceptable public state of mind, we're all in danger, all in danger, for madness is not so much a phenomenon as an infection in the air. And I submit that we all breathe the infection and the movement has at times been sickened by it too.

It has to do with the disposition of human conflict by forms of violence. In or out of the military, in or out of the movement, it seems to me that we had best call things by their name, and the name of this thing, it seems to me, is the death game, no matter where it appears. And as for myself, I would as soon be under the heel of former masters as under the heel of new ones.

Some of your actions are going to involve inciting and conflict and trashing, and these actions are very difficult for thoughtful people. But I came upon a rule of thumb somewhere which might be of some help to us: do only that which one cannot not do. Maybe it isn't very helpful, and of course it's going to be applied differently by the Joint Chiefs of Staff and the underground group of sane men and women. In the former hypocritical expressions of sympathy will always be sown along the path of the latest rampage. Such grief is like that of a mortician in a year of plague. But I think our realization is that a movement has historic meaning only insofar as it puts its gain to the side dictated by human dignity and the protection of life, even of the lives most unworthy of such respect. A revolution is interesting insofar as it avoids like the plague, the plague it promised to heal. Ultimately if we want to define the plague as death, and I think that's a good definition, the healing will neither put people to death nor fill the prisons nor inhibit freedoms nor brainwash nor torture its enemies nor be mendacious nor exploit anyone, whether women or children or blacks or the poor. It will have a certain respect for the power of the truth, which created the revolution in the first place.

We may take it, I think as a simple rule of thumb that the revolution will be no better and no more truthful and no more populist and no more attractive than those who brought it into being. Which is to say we are not killers, as America would stigmatize us, and indeed as America perversely longs for us to be. We are something far different, we are teachers of the people who have come on a new vision of things. We struggle to embody that vision day after day, to make it a reality among those we live with so that the people are literally disarmed by knowing us, so that their fear of change, their dread of life is exorcised, and their dread of human differences is slowly expunged.

Instead of thinking of the underground as temporary or exotic or abnormal, perhaps we are being called upon to start thinking of its implication as an entirely self-sufficient, mobile, internal revival community, so that the underground may be the definition of our future. What does it mean literally to have nowhere to go in America or to be kicked out of America? It must mean to us—let us go somewhere in America, let us stay here and play here and love here and build here, and in this way join not only those who like us are recently kicked out also, but those who have never been inside at all, the blacks and the Indians and Puerto Ricans and Chicanos, whose consciousness has gone far under the rock.

Next, we are to strive to become such men and women as may, in a new world, be non-violent. If there's any definition to the new man, the man of the future, it seems to me that we do violence unwillingly, bar exception, as instrument, knowing that destruction of property is only a means and keeping the end as vivid and urgent and as alive to us as are the means so that the means are judged in every instance by their relation to the ends. I have a great fear of American violence, not only out there in the military and the diplomacy; in economics, in industry and advertising, but also in here, in me, up close, among us.

On the other hand, I must say, I have very little fear from firsthand experience, of the violence of the Vietcong or Panthers (I hesitate to use the word violence), for their acts come from the proximate threat of extinction, from being invariably put on the line of self-defense, but that's not true of us and our history. We can simply say from outside the culture of these others, no matter what admiration or fraternity we feel, we are unlike them, we have other demons to battle.

But the history of the movement, in the last years, it seems to me, shows how constantly and easily we are seduced by violence, not only as to method but as to end in itself. With very little politics, very little ethics, very little direction, and only a minimum moral sense, if any at all, it might lead one to conclude in despair: the movement is debased beyond recognition, I can't be a part of it. Far from giving birth to the new man, it has only proliferated the armed, bellicose, and inflated spirit of the army, the plantation, the corporation, the diplomat.

Yet it seems to me good, in public, as well as in our own house, to turn the question of violence back on the true creators and purveyors of it, working as we do from a very different ethos and for very different ends. I remember being on a television program recently and having the whole thing thrown at me, and saying—look, ask the question in the seats of power, don't ask it of me, don't ask me why I broke the law, go ask Nixon why he breaks the law constantly, ask the Justice Department, ask the racists. Obviously, but for Johnson and Nixon and their fetching ways, Catonsville would never have taken place and you and I would not be here today, just as but for the same people SDS would never have grown into the Weathermen or the Weathermen have gone underground. In a decent society, normally functioning for its people, all of us would be doing the things that decent men do for one another. That we are forbidden so to act, forced to meet so secretly and with so few, is a tragedy we must live with. We have been forbidden a future by the forms of power, which include death as the ordinary social method, by having rejected the future they drafted us into and having refused, on the other hand, to be kicked out of America, either by aping their methods, or leaving the country.

The question now is what can we create. I feel at your side across the miles, and I hope that sometime, sometime in this mad world, in this mad time, it will be possible for us to sit down face to face, brother to brother, sister to sister, and find that our hopes and our sweat, and the hopes and sweat and death and tears and blood of our brothers throughout the world, have brought to birth that for which we began.

Thank you and shalom.

LETTER TO FATHER BERRIGAN

ROSEMARY RUETHER

I think you are one of the few people in this land at this time who senses the ultimate proportions of our present evil, so I hope you will try to understand when I say that if you had asked me to help you napalm draft records I would have turned you down. This may not be any news to you, but since I have a feeling that in your present state of mind you tend to think that all who are not with you are against you and against "God" as well, I would like to spell out the reasons for my dissent.

It might be easy to say I agree with your vision, but not with your tactics, and that is part of it. Even more is a kind of sectarian ethos that emerges in this kind of action, and excommunicates the rest of mankind. I am suspicious of devil theories when they are applied too unequivocally, and the New Left way of talking about the "power structure" is a new kind of devil theory which rivals the old hang up on the "body" and could get us into just as much trouble.

Like Niebuhr, I tend to believe that imperfect justice practically conceived and carried out does more to advance the Kingdom than perfect love that gets everyone killed (or thrown in jail). If I thought that things were really equivalent to the reign of Nazism under Hitler, I would join the Resistance, but I would resist the way they resisted them. They didn't engage in symbolic action and walk into the arms of the police like lambs to the slaughter. There were enough lambs being slaughtered already. They went underground, engaged in serious sabotage, saw to it that they didn't get arrested if possible and lived to resist another day. Maybe you don't think things are that serious. Bonhoeffer was willing to plot to assassinate Hitler. Are you? Maybe you think there is some hope for turning the government around rather than unequivocally trying to overthrow it. So you engage in symbolic action for the purpose of conversion. The only trouble is that your symbols don't seem to be very effective in gaining converts. On the contrary, they alienate those who already are converted. Those most passionately committed to the cause have a hard time justifying them. That would seem to be a dubious kind of symbol. If these acts are intended as serious sabotage, then they don't do enough harm to be worth it. If they are intended as eloquent symbols, they don't speak well enough to get across the message.

I hate to subject poetry to logic chopping, but don't these questions have to be asked? Can the community test the spirits of the prophets? If we haven't come to the point where the assassination of the "leader" is justified, then where are we? If it is not overthrow, then it is some effort to change the system from within. If so, then wouldn't some massive action effectively designed to do that be more to the point than these gestures which only annoy the giant without really getting to him in any way?

Perhaps what it really comes down to is that you don't believe change is possible, either by revolution or by progressive change. The alternative then becomes apocalypse, the counsel of despair, jockeying for a place at the right hand of the crucified, as you put it. Maybe my problem is that I really don't believe that anyone has ever been redeemed in that way. I am looking for ways to seriously put vision and practical action together, and this is just where you are not speaking to me.

THE PROPHETS AND THE PROTESTORS

NICHOLAS PIEDISCALZI

Most of us over thirty have difficulty understanding the dramatic non-violent (but sometimes violent) protests of some of the young people in our society. Young persons dressed as clowns or flower children, or wearing gas masks, or shouting obscenities, or taking control of a university building and destroying records and property, or burning or pouring ox blood on Selective Service records—these activities fill most of us with disgust, confusion and anger. We find it practically impossible to fathom why protestors cannot express their criticisms and dissent through rational and legal means. Moreover, we find it easy to condemn the protestors as deranged, blind or evil, or as dupes of an insidious, well-organized conspiracy against our society. We call for law and order without a mention of justice, and we miss the point of the demonstrations by failing to see their religious and prophetic dimensions.

This article will develop a model derived from a study of the Hebrew prophets which will enable us to deal constructively and creatively with protestors. We shall begin with a description of some of the acts of the Hebrew prophets which seemed weird, violent and incomprehensible to the people of their days just as the activities of many of our young protestors and reformers appear to us. Then we shall interpret these prophetic activities in the light of the studies of the Old Testament scholar, Gerhard von Rad. Finally, we shall attempt to draw some conclusions for our day from the works of the Hebrew prophets and von Rad.

The prophets to whom we shall refer lived in times of actual or threatening cataclysmic wars, social upheaval and grave social injustices. They felt that their generation neither saw nor accepted responsibility for their part in the destructive events. They decided—or more accurately felt commanded by God—to perform dramatic, shocking acts which would serve as a judgment upon the people's blindness and move them to participate in creating a world free of these evils.

The prophet Isaiah, for example, was commanded by God to walk naked and barefoot for three years among his people. The purpose of this shocking activity was to show that the Assyrians would force the Egyptians and Ethiopians into exile as punishment for their evil ways (Is 20:1-5). Moreover, Isaiah's walking naked and barefoot among his people caused a reaction: the people asked themselves, if this is what will happen to our allies, who will save us? (Is 20:6)

The prophet Jeremiah felt commanded by God to buy a linen waistcloth, to wear and not wash it. After wearing the waistcloth for a period of time, he felt commanded by God to remove it and hid it in the cleft of a rock along the banks of a river. Finally, many days after burying the waistcloth he felt called by God to reclaim it from the cleft of the rock only to discover that it was spoiled and no longer good for anything. The purpose of this activity was to show the people of Judah and Jerusalem how God would spoil them for their great pride, apostasy and social injustice (Jer 13:1-11).

In Jeremiah 19:1-13 we find another dramatic act recorded. Jeremiah broke a potter's earthen flask before some of the elders of the people and senior priests. This act symbolized the destruction which would come to Judah and Jerusalem for their grave social injustices.

The prophet Ezekiel also performed several dramatic, shocking acts. Here we shall summarize only one of them from Ezekiel 12:1-7. In the sight of his fellow citizens Ezekiel dug through the city wall and went out through it carrying the baggage of an exiled person. This act was to show what was to happen to the people of Judah for their refusal to correct the gross evils in their society.

The prophets Elijah and Elisha not only carried out symbolic acts of protest but also initiated a revolutionary plot to depose a king and appoint a new one. This plot was not merely a political move but also a prophetic and religious activity. The prophets believed they were acting as instruments of God in cleansing their society of an unfaithful and unjust order and inaugurating a new religious and just one.

Gerhard von Rad points out that the Hebrew prophets used two modes of communication, *viz.*, the spoken word and the symbolic act.[1] The symbolic act was not merely a dramatic reinforcement of the prophets' words but also a powerful force through which God spoke to his people, judged them and offered them an opportunity for creating a new life. God's speaking—a symbolic act in itself—was viewed not only as a verbal expression but as a disruptive and creative activity.

Here it is important to note that the prophets' acts were not miraculous in nature but rather dramatic and shocking. He who possessed the sensitivity and courage necessary to be honest about the world about him was able to enter a new situation filled with the power to create a new society.

Of course, the prophets did not expect everyone to respond positively to their dramatic acts. They realized that many would not understand their actions, and that the full meaning of their behavior and of their new situation would not soon be understood. Moreover, they realized that their activities could very well polarize their people and lead to greater sufferings, divisions and destruction. But, for them, this polarization was a part of God's judgment and renewal. They believed that they and their small groups of followers were in step with history and would serve as the initiators of a new day; hence Isaiah's emphasis upon the role of the remnant in his society.

While the prophets saw the destruction of an old, oppressive social order as the prelude to a new day, they did not hold that violent destruction was inevitable or necessary, if men heeded the call for repentance and change. Men were free to reform themselves and their societies and thereby avoid violent destruction.

Because the new day was to be so dramatically different, the prophets felt compelled to live an entirely new way of life—"even . . . to the extent that a call meant relinguishing normal social life and all the social and economic securities which this offered, and changing over instead to a condition where a man had nothing to depend upon . . . [save his] dependence upon Jahweh. . . ."[2]

In summary, the prophets lived in times of actual or threatening cataclysmic wars, social upheaval and grave social injustices. Because the vast majority of the prophets' fellow citizens accepted no responsibility for the destructive events which were threatening or engulfing them, the prophets used dramatic acts to reveal to their contemporaries the seriousness of their situation and to show them how they could participate in the creation of a new era through repentance and reformation.

To state that we live in a similar situation is to state the obvious. However, most of us would not agree that many of the protestors of our day are fulfilling a religious and prophetic function. But I contend that they are. What then are the prophetic dimensions of the protest?

The most obvious prophetic aspect of the protest is the use of dramatic, shocking techniques to pronounce a moral judgment upon gross evils in our society. Of course, not all dramatic and shocking protests *per se* are prophetic or genuine moral judgments. Despite this fact, we must not permit their dramatic and shocking nature to blind us to many of their genuine prophetic and moral dimensions. Like the Hebrew prophets who resorted to dramatic and symbolic protest out of a sense of desparation, many of our activists have turned to dramatic and shocking protest as a last resort measure. They believe that our society is on the brink of destruction and that our leaders and the vast number of citizens in our country who elect them do not realize how serious our situation is and that they, like the Hebrew people of old, do not see that they are responsible for the highly explosive and potentially destructive situation which confronts us. Some of the more responsible and respected leaders in our society concur with this judgment. The former Secretary of Health, Education and Welfare, John Gardner, said recently, "We know our lakes are dying, our rivers growing filthier daily, our atmosphere increasingly polluted. We are aware of racial tensions that could tear the nation apart. We understand that oppressive poverty in the midst of affluence is intolerable. We see that our cities are sliding toward disaster. . . . But we are seized by a kind of paralysis of the will. It is like a waking nightmare."[3]

Furthermore, our protestors cry out against a meaningless and unjust war in Viet-Nam and an inordinately large military budget—both of which are destroying our moral fibre and consuming funds which we desparately need to solve some of our vexing domestic problems. Long before the National Advisory Commission on Civil Disorders concluded that our internal threats are far greater than our external ones, activists were trying to make this point. It is here in their protest against grave injustices and in their call for dramatic social change that the protestors are very much like the Hebrew prophets.

There are other gross injustices against which our protestors are symbolically acting out moral judgments. Paul Goodman in his penetrating article, "The New Reformation,"[4] reveals how a large number of our youthful activists are crying out against the ways in which we are making the human being more and more useless. In the name of science, technology, maximum industrial production and nationalism we sacrifice human individuality, sensitivity and initiative.[5] Moreover, we ignore the genuine and legitimate rights and needs of many minority groups in our society which when taken collectively form a majority. For example, at an increasingly early age we label older people obsolete and send them off to inhuman apartment dwellings or Disneyland-like retirement villages. We keep more and more young people out of the social, political and economic realms of our society until an increasing later age by demanding that they work for meaningless academic degrees. We treat as ungrateful and evil agitators minority groups which voice legitimate complaints and demand more just and humane treatment. Finally, as we move toward the shorter work week, we project dehumanizing leisure-time programs for the labor force rather than laying the foundations for new communities in which all individuals—including laborers—feel needed and valuable for the successful continuance of the society. I view the dramatic protests of some of our youth against these injustices to be as religious and prophetic as those performed centuries ago by the Hebrew prophets.

Also, our youth protestors—like the Hebrew prophets—have a vision of a new day dawning and feel compelled to live an entirely new way of life even to the extent of giving up all of the normal socio-economic securities afforded them. It is in this context that I interpret as prophetic and religious their rejection of the socio-economic benefits which our society offers them and their "bizzare" modes of dress and the attempt by some of them to experiment with communal living.

Finally, like the Hebrew prophets some of our young people are beginning to predict the eventual destruction of our society if we do not cure our blindness and carry out our much needed reforms. While we may not like to hear this prediction we should not reject it summarily and thereby miss its prophetic dimension. Rather, we should listen to it as a shocking and dramatic protest which has the capacity to bring us to our senses and quicken new forms of social responsibility. For if we repent and reform our society, then there will be no need for it to be destroyed. However, if we do not reform it then we shall bring destruction upon ourselves, and the new day which we resist by not reforming will be upon us.

Outright condemnations of dramatic and shocking protest carried out by the youth of our day are futile. In the words of Paul Goodman, "it is improper for us elders to keep saying, as we do, that their activity is 'counterproductive.' It's our business to do something more productive."[6] I contend that we can do something more productive by viewing the current protest in the light of Hebrew prophecy, discovering the genuine prophetic call for justice and reform contained in the protest of our day, and finding ways of correcting the grave social problems which threaten to destroy us.

1. See **Old Testament Theology**, Vol. II, translated by D.M.G. Stalker, New York: Harper and Row 1965, pp. 3-125.

2. **Ibid.**, p. 58.

3. As quoted by Tom Wicker in **The New York Times**, Sunday, December 28, 1969, Section E, p. 9.

4. **The New York Times Magazine**, September 14, 1969, Part I, pp. 33 **passim.** (This section of this article is derived from Paul Goodman's analysis.)

5. Cf. Erik H. Erikson, **Daedalus, Winter,** 1970, p. 160: "Even the most affluent and progressive systems seem to thrive at the expense of individual values: [sic] Their costliness may become apparent in the restriction of spontaneity in the midst of a system extolling individual freedom; in the standardization of information in the midst of a universal communications industry; and worse, in new and numbing denials in the midst of universal enlightenment.

6. **The New York Times Magazine,** September 14, 1969, Part I, p. 145.

THE UNIVERSITY COMMUNITY
IN AN OPEN SOCIETY

EDGAR Z. FRIEDENBERG

The central function of higher education in America has always been vocational. Harvard was founded to train clergymen; and as the society has become more a mass, open society, its dependence on the university system for vocational training and placement has, of course, become far greater and more complex. It is well understood that the university serves society by selecting and training a wide range and enormous number of technicians who, granting its present mode of organization, are essential. The university is the instrument of the continuous talent search by which an industrial democracy assures itself that it is not systematically ignoring lower—status social groups as a potential talent-source, thereby denying them access to opportunity and itself the value of their contribution.

In a mass, industrial democracy, no function could be more legitimate. Nor could any function be more heavily burdened by ideology. The furious controversy that has recently been aroused by Arthur Jensen's conclusion that there are significant innate differences of cognitive style between blacks and whites that, in this culture, operate to the disadvantage of blacks and these especially hamper them in school is, for example, totally ideological. . . .[1] Jensen's findings, if valid, certainly establish that blacks are less well adapted than whites to respond successfully to the demands of the dominant institutions of industrial democracy, especially its schools. They leave entirely open the question of whether this is a sign of inferiority, superiority, or neither. But they are nevertheless threatening because the conflict to which they point may be impossible to resolve for a society ideologically committed both to equality of opportunity and to popular sovereignty. Even if Jensen is right, there are two ways in which this resolution could be achieved, but both appear to be politically impossible for a mass democracy. One is to provide equal respect and rewards to people with the kinds of cognitive styles blacks—or poets, or hippies, or mystics, or police, or sexual deviants—possess. There are such people; and they are indeed different from one another and from the norm. This requires, in short, genuine pluralism: a great many small events, some competitive, in which different kinds of excellence could be demonstrated and rewarded.

The second way is for society to respond openly and generously to need, without requiring that the needy—which at different times and in different ways includes all of us—prove anything or win any race at all. Except, perhaps, in its Malthusian aspects, this is now technologically possible through the instrumentality of an enormously high technical level of productivity distributed through a high guaranteed annual income or a universal credit card—instead of a university degree. But our society lacks the political means to make any such commitment. The anxiety and *resentment* such proposals arouse among the bitter coalition of the self-made, the self-condemned, and the vast number of poor whose sole satisfaction seems to come from the prospect of others more impoverished still; of industrial leaders fearful that too few people would work unless compelled to by threat of humiliation and want, and union officials who fear that a general rise in the standard of living unrelated to membership in the labor force would deprive them of a *raison d'etre* make it impossible. . . . The major premise of our ideology of opportunity is that each should have an equal chance to succeed; but the minor premise is that only those who do succeed may be rewarded, and that refusal to compete should be punished or subjected to therapy as "dropping out."

The educational system has played a complex and delicate role in mediating among these competitive hostilities and ideological problems. It has, in effect, become a steeplechase in which comparatively few people fail utterly; but the hazards are so cunningly designed that many more fall somewhat behind and are cooled out. The more successful students have been precisely those whose cognitive skills and ideological positions have been most suited to the demands of middle and upper managerial positions in existing institutions; so that the school has served to rectify these qualities as characteristics of the worthiest members of society. But, in so doing, it has also established the educational system as the supervisor of legitimate people-racing in our society. It provides the anthrodrome; its staff are the judges and referees; it determines which events shall be accepted as part of the decathlon, which styles of competition are legitimate and which are cheating and hence grounds for disqualification and exclusion from subsequent competition.

Once one accepts in principle, then, that the university system is to be maintained as virtually the sole channel of mobility, the university must respond to demands for variation in the definition of achievement needed to recognize the way in which different social groups develop different styles and different merits; and if, in fact, they develop none, illusory merits will doubtless have to be ascribed to them. Society must recognize the claims to dignity and opportunity of all its constituent groups. If the university is to continue to stand astride the only legitimate highway to advancement, it must quit demanding tools in coins that only some travelers can acquire and calling this "maintaining standards." But the acceptance of more diverse modes of response nevertheless leads to conflict precisely with those groups which have forced themselves most recently and with greatest discontinuity to their earlier experience to make it on the more conventional terms already prevalent in the university system. No datum has more consistently recurred in current conflict within the university than the observation that the students who are least responsive to and most intolerant of the growing demands are whites whose parents never attended college; while those most sympathetic to and often so over-identified with the blacks as to court repudiation by them are higher-status white students who take college for granted, but are unable to tolerate its moral failures. To accede to the demands of blacks is not only to violate prejudices that many first-generation working-class students hold; it is also to change the rules of the game they have learned so laboriously and to discredit as irrelevant and morally fatuous or worse the instrument they have sought, at great sacrifice, for their deliverance.

This, I believe, is the major source of friction between the "jocks" and commuters, who still try to take the university system seriously on its own terms, and the higher-status white activists and blacks who denounce it. The Vietnam war has, of course, infinitely exacerbated this conflict, both because it has discredited the university system morally and, more directly, because the immediate vocational opportunities to which university education leads are so likely to be war-connected. These opportunities are, moreover, *more* likely to be war-connected for lower-status students than for higher; because these, differentially, tend to locate themselves in the technological rather than the humanistic curricula. . . . On the basis of this social model, I cannot but be convinced that black students, once they find themselves more at ease in what was never Zion, will join the jocks and repudiate their activist supporters, whose style they already seem to find grandiose and rather hysterical. Besieged college and university presidents on recent media presentations have seemed correspondingly less hostile to the blacks whose attacks on the university system, though often more aggressive than those of white activists, are also far more superficial. These men are trying, I believe, to convince black student leaders that the university system is still relevant to them, however strongly their more privileged white dissident colleagues may condemn it

A major function of the university has been to serve as a community in which many of its members have found intense and protracted satisfaction and have married or formed permanent friendships or taken lovers. This is why college and university life has become a pastoral legend in American folklore, and why alumni continue to attend class reunions in a nostalgic and futile effort to recapture briefly their student experience. Both the nostalgia and the futility have become cliches as aspects of such events. But nostalgia—grief for your own place, the guilt and loss of having uprooted yourself—is an emotion that a great many Americans would be better and more sensitive for having allowed themselves to feel, though it is more agonizing than any other experience that still leaves its victims with a future. . . . But people who have learned to respect this agony are less likely than others to set fire to peasant huts with their cigarette lighters, and this is a desirable form of self-restraint.

The futility, moreover, is ironical, because the university is still, for some of its students, the source of the kind of intense community alumni recall nostalgically; but alumni cannot recognize this because it is these students whose styles they find most repellent and who seem to them to be trying to destroy the university. So some may be; those who love their home would sooner burn it than see it defiled. But it is nevertheless precisely the militants who have found within the university fellows with a common vision of its purpose who care enough about it to risk beatings and imprisonment in the service of that vision and who are currently having the experience the alumni think they remember—not the jocks, at a time when the football hero has become anachronistic, and certainly not the commuters who would just as soon be in correspondence school if you could really make it there and the mail service were better. The more conservative alumni are more likely to be nostalgic than the liberals who, being dedicated to progress, will have gone on through several further stages of their life-cycle without much thought about their college days. But as conservatives they cannot recognize their deeper kinship with the radicals and hippies who make the university their home and not just a stopover on their career-line.

It must be granted that the fact that college life—as we used to think of it—should have become a basis for community is largely an unintended, and in some ways a paradoxical, development of American life. The educational system is designed to make schooling both a transient and a highly competitive experience, which is highly inimical to the development of a sense of community.... Schools generally speaking, are ill-designed to foster intimacy and a sense of identity among their members. The devices that are intentionally employed to foster school spirit destroy spontaneity and intimacy in the interests of an automatic *esprit de corps* which is anything but homelike.

But the unintended consequences outweigh the intended. College life, though growing continuously more competitive through the years as the educational system grows more universalistic, is still much less competitive than life outside the sanctuary. There is not the constant press for conspicuous consumption. The definition of the student role as impecunious and economically dependent is neither desirable nor just, and fosters the exploitation of students as sweated labor in under-graduate instruction. But it also provides the only enclave in American life in which poverty is not dishonorable and makes it far easier for people to accept one another for what they are, to establish coopera-tive living arrangements and open expression of feeling.... The uni-versities are now perceived by the general public as ghettos that are becoming useless because they no longer manage to protect the com-munity from the dangerous young aliens they contain. But this view, too, fosters a sense of identity and empathy among students as such—not strong enough to prevent them from being divided into warring factions by conflicting interests and values, but strong enough to leave them with a viable subgroup even when this happens. And, finally, the fact that our society withholds adult status till after the human sexual prime so that the peak of erotic intensity occurs during college years enhances students' impact on one another and the probability that something human and personal, if not necessarily agreeable, will develop. Sexuality in the young, though intensely competitive, resists the control of a competitive society, for the attributes that lead to erotic and economic success are different. . . . The conventional institutions of student life, as John Finley Scott has shown in his studies of the college sorority as a national marriage-brokerage system for conventional girls, function so as to rationalize students' erotic relationships and bring them into the university's total network of transactions.[2] But the fraternity and sorority system is declining and has largely been replaced by informal though enduring relationships; there are more liaisons and fewer conquests. This, too, adds to the confusion and hostility of the alumni who would never have claimed that a sexual relationship could be moral in itself, though marriage might make it legitimate and even obligatory.

There are clearly certain serious conflicts between the university's functions in providing economic opportunity in an egalitarian society and serving simultaneously as a base for community among the young. Competition itself poisons community; and young people for whom intimacy and communion are primary values deeply resent being forced to adopt standardized, competitive patterns of behavior by an impersonal grading system and examinations that are as objective and, hence, as unresponsive to their individualized qualities and feelings as they can be made. But this is what their peers who are using the university as an anthrodrome, and who are more concerned about the rewards to which academic success leads than with the quality of their college experience, need for their purposes. This, surely, is why the demand for ungraded curricula, experimental colleges, and the abolition of many forms of examination so neatly divides the activists and hippies from the more conventional and usually lower-status students who resist it.

But there are less direct but equally important reasons why the function of the university as a base of community interferes with its function as anthrodrome. As I have discussed more fully elsewhere, it is the community function of the university which most antagonizes the larger community outside.[3] Their hostility has several sources: a sense, more flattering than realistic, that student life is "privileged" and libertine compared to their own; the way in which the student-role is defined so that students—about the most sweated labor in America outside agriculture—are perceived as not working and as being supported by their parents or the welfare state. But most infuriating of all is merely the fact that a community exists. Below the level at which the corporate network can provide a sense of identity and of membership in a colleague group, most Americans today are bereft of intimacy and belong to very little that has meaning for them

This sense of being part of a meaningful coalition and bound by realities of feeling and genuine goals to its other members is, I believe, more coveted, and the source of more bitter conflict—inner and outer—in our society than any other treasure it might, but seldom does, afford. It is this, rather than sexual gratification, that remains the illicit satisfaction; though attacks on satisfying communities are usually directed against their putative licentiousness, which is often the only language in which their detractors can identify what they think they're missing. But the jealousy and sense of deprivation, and correspondingly the hostility, engendered are intense. . . . The conflict between the university as community and as anthrodrome is an absolutely real one, a conflict of interests as well as tastes; and it seems either fatuous or disingenuous, therefore, to deny that what advances the interest of one is likely to be costly to those of the other.

Meanwhile, constituencies of the university other than students are, of course, involved in the conflict. Generally speaking, the interests of the faculty and administration coincide with those of the anthrodrome and are opposed to those who would find community in the university. The university is indeed fundamentally involved in the industrial and governmental activities that its critics find most reprehensible and that even its supporters no longer defend. But these activities are not merely the stuff of which academic careers are made and the source of needed financial support. They also provide the upper stages of the anthrodrome itself. The more conventionally ambitious students need them as the next step in *their* careers. And an even more fundamental commitment to the anthrodrome has been made on what may be irreversible epistemological grounds. The very conception of what constitutes knowledge in every discipline; the prevailing empiricism that reduces research even in the humanities to objective and often quantitative terms; the official dominance of "value-free" social science that willingly sells itself to the highest bidder, though now with the hope that the arrangement may be handled with discretion—all these serve the needs of the anthrodrome and have a chilling administrator as the broker among the various interests that affect the university, whose professional responsibility actually *precludes* his attempting to exert any moral leadership among the university's various *liaisons dangereuses,* also serves the *anthrodrome;* as does the university's peculiar orientation to public relations, which leads it to court public support and hence public approval even under circumstances that would clearly favor instead a policy of coolly reminding the public that it, too, is dependent on the university as a major source of revenue and employment and that it might be well advised to avoid excessive harassment even of those it does not particularly like.

So far, I have made no reference to the official functions of the university on which it bases its formal claims to esteem and support: the creation and propagation of knowledge, or, as we now more frequently say, research and teaching. This omission is the more striking since these functions might be expected to support the community within the university and require its support in turn, rather than the anthrodrome. Both teaching and research are in essence, at their best, particularistic activities. No commitment to equality of opportunity can make a teacher as useful to the students he does not turn on as he is to those he does; no amount of ambition can help a student learn much of value from a teacher who has no interest in either students or what he is teaching. But the university has evolved a highly effective device to protect universalism under these conditions: rigid control of instruction through scheduling, credits, and the definition of the process as one involving abstract, symbolic communication rather than feeling, touch, or spontaneity. The effect of this is to keep instuction almost entirely in what the great psychoanalytic theorist Harry Stack Sullivan called "the syntactic mode" and so remote from the reality of sense-data and personal experience as to seem quite unreal. This makes academic freedom, defined as the freedom to teach whatever content one wishes provided the content remains turned-off, quite innocuous.

Liberalism's answer to this is familiar and compelling: Make it connect, find new ways to reach the disadvantaged and the merely uninterested and stimulate their interests. But education can only be planned and organized experience and must build on experience already had; it cannot be grafted onto a lifeless trunk or one which rejects it as incompatible with its development. Techniques for "reaching" or "motivating" students to learn something they do not care about initially seem to me most often devices for inducing them to abandon their own past for the sake of a deal with society that will pay off in the future. The anthrodrome is willing enough to do that—that is why it came to the university—but the process of helping it does not feel much like teaching. Nor would curriculum revision intended to adapt to its interests help very much, for students who come to higher education primarily to advance their careers quite often have no interests in either ideas or experience as such—and, indeed, sense that such interests would hamper their advancement in this society. What they want is a degree and the tricks of their trade.[4]

Under these conditions, then, both the significance of teaching as a university function and its potential contribution to the university community diminish, and too massive a claim for support should not be based on it. In the case of research, a quite different set of difficulties arises. There can be no question that our society, unless revolutionized, will continue to support and conduct the kind of research now done in our universities. Whether this is useful or leads to fundamental knowledge is irrelevant. Complex, literate societies usually maintain some costly and prestigious institution in which the kind of knowledge useful to their elites is codified, recorded, and interpreted. Such institutions take on a sacred character, and a threat to them is interpreted by the elite as a threat to the integrity of the society (which, from their point of view, it is).

If the United States is to continue its present course as a major power, it will continue to maintain knowledge factories whose product resembles that of the current multiversity. Such an institution will do what we call research, because in an open, technically advanced society empirical knowledge, which is the only kind useful for manipulating persons and objects in the environment, is the kind that becomes sacred. When an American speaks of "the advancement of knowledge" or "expanding the frontiers of learning," he almost always means the kind of learning that will enable him or his kind of people to control something or do something effective to somebody else: that is, science.

Scientific knowledge, in our society, is usually defined as morally neutral in itself; moral judgments may be made only about the uses to which knowledge is put, not about knowledge itself. This seems to me absurd. A moral judgment, though not a simple one, may be made about the *kind* of knowledge that makes it possible for me to think of a child as an object to be napalmed or of the manufacture of napalm as productive. It is not just our values nor our place in history that makes us not even wince at the idea that the *value* of our most gruesome armaments is included as part—and a very large part— of our gross national *product*. It is our epistemology as well—the character of what we regard as knowledge and respect as such—that has become an expression of our national character. This conception of knowledge also makes it possible for us to insist that people die later and in a somewhat different way than they would have otherwise, though so far no less frequently; and this, which we call modern medical science, is usually considered good. A complex moral judgment, then; but a moral judgment on the nature of science all the same.

It is clear that Western and especially American culture is locked into this empirical conception of knowledge, and equally clear that this favors the anthrodrome—those who enjoy doing and pushing more than feeling and being and reflecting on the process. The research function, then, is one more function of the university that favors them over the community-seekers. It is less clear, however, that the research function must be carried out within the same institution as the other functions of the university. This function, and this function alone, can dispense with the presence of young persons assigned the transitory and subordinate status of students. In many societies this separation is usual: The research institute has no teaching functions; the teaching institutions do not expect their staffs to make what we call contributions to knowledge—that is, to do research and publish it.

This separation, if it were real, would have a great deal to recommend it. Much research done in American universities is done there simply because this is cheaper and keeps it decentralized and out of sight. It is harder for a snoopy reporter to put the pieces togther if the answer to what happened to all those sheep lies concealed under the scanty ivy of the University of Utah rather than in the Dugway laboratory itself. Now that such functions have become an awkward source of controversy for the universities, a reverse process has set in, one in which universities divest themselves of formal institutional connection with the research institutes and laboratories to which they now assign their more macabre military contracts—a device which seems hardly sufficient to protect them from complicity and will probably not even save them embarrassment. For this separation is quite unreal and within the context of American life and values probably cannot be made real.

The problem is again epistemological; empirical research is only knowledge-function that has enough prestige, or is considered useful enough, to command genuine support in America. It is assumed, for example, that in a college devoted to teaching rather than research course-loads should be two or three times greater than in a university where the staff is expected to do research. But this assumption misses the whole point, which is that university teaching has come to be accepted as the kind of half-assed process it is because of the primacy of research; and to do it better means to do it entirely differently and probably in a much more leisurely, intimate and unstructured way.

The highest prestige *colleges* in the country ought to be free to do the best teaching, being relatively less impoverished and having better trained faculty than the more marginal institutions. But, in fact, they function as what Jencks and Riesman call university colleges: that is, they orient their teaching, their grading, and their curricula to the demands of graduate schools and pride themselves on the number of people they send on successfully to the doctorate, which ties them securely to present departmental organization, and precludes serious curricular experimentation which, again, would jeopardize the career interests of their faculty, the ambitions of their more striving students, and the college's prestige.[5]

All the major functions of the university which the society endorses and supports are opposed to its function of providing a home and a place of their own for young men and women in which they can develop a sense of personal commitment and a basis for moral judgment. These, indeed, infuriate our society, which prefers decorum to morality and success to either. They distress and frighten the universities' officials because they threaten the universities' sources of support. These officials avoid the moral issue when they can; those few who have attempted to respond to it with a measure of understanding and respect for their students have often been driven from their posts by outraged and punitive governing boards.

The American university system, like Dr. Frankenstein and Dr. Faustus, is in trouble not because it has failed, but because it has succeeded; and succeeded in undertakings to which it would not have committed itself had it not relinquished moral responsibility in favor of empirical mastery in the first place. If this is too harsh an indictment, it is so for one reason only: that it attributes too much autonomy to the university. University faculty, especially, are inclined to be taken in by their own traditional, but increasingly deceptive pretense that they run the place. In fact, universities are run as America is run: indirectly, by a power structure that depends on the ambitions of the faculty and the lust of its individual members to be close to sources of power to induce it to organize itself so as to do what is expected of it. Power within the university aligns itself to power outside it.

1. Arthur R. Jensen, "How Much Can We Boost IQ and Educational Achievement?" Harvard Educational Review, Vol. 39, No. 1 (Winter, 1969), pp. 1-123.

2. John Finley Scott, "The American College Sorority: Its Role in Class and Ethnic Edogamy," American Sociological Review, Vol. 30, No. 3 (June, 1965), pp. 514-27.

3. Edgar Z. Friedenberg, "The Campus Community and the Community," New American Review No. 6 (New American Library: New York, 1969), pp. 146-62.

4. By far the most vivid and insightful treatment of what such purveying to an aspiring urban proletariat does to the joy of teaching is to be found in Herbert Gold's sadly negelected essay on a crisis in his career as an instructor at Wayne State University a few years ago—a crisis whose illustrative significance has been greatly enhanced by subsequent events in Detroit: "A Dog in Brooklyn, A Girl in Detroit: A Life Among the Humanities," The Age of Happy Problems (Dial Press: New York, 1962).

5. Christopher Jencks and David Riesman, The Academic Revolution (Doubleday: Garden City, New York, 1968), pp. 20-27.

BLACK THEOLOGY AND SOCIAL ETHICS

ROBERT D. REECE

An analysis of Black Theology confirms the existence of inter-action between theological concepts, social conditions, and social ethics. This essay is an examination of this interaction in the writings of two significant pioneers in the growing Black Theology movement in America, Albert B. Cleage, Jr., pastor of the Shrine of the Black Madonna in Detroit, and James H. Cone, an associate professor at Union Theological Seminary in New York.

Cleage's ethical posture is evident in his fundamental claim that Jesus the Messiah was a black revolutionary leader, a Zealot, whose goal was the liberation of the Black Nation Israel from the domination of the white Roman Empire.[1] Cleage bases his assertion that Jesus was black on the assumption that all the inhabitants of Israel were black as a result of their mixture with numerous dark peoples of the ancient Near East, including amalgamation with people from Central Africa. He cites as further evidence the existence of numerous black madonnas in various parts of the world. What Cleage means by "black" is difficult to ascertain, for he intermingles the words "non-white," "dark," and "black" in his discussion, and he also makes occasional references to "Negroid" and "African" people. Clearly Cleage is saying that physical color was religiously and politically significant in Jesus' day and that Jesus was dark-skinned.

The mission of Jesus the Black Messiah was subverted, according to Cleage, when white gentiles usurped control of the movement. Cleage declares Paul to be the chief villain because he transformed Jesus' revolutionary goal into a quest for individual salvation. Nevertheless, the Black Messiah continues to work in every age, and today he is still calling the Black Nation to unite and throw off white domination. The belief that God and Jesus are black and that black people are God's chosen people, called to restore the Black Nation, means that blacks must fight oppression "by all means necessary," possibly even including guerrilla warfare.

To the extent that Cleage's thesis depends upon his historical assertions, his social ethic is questionable. That Jesus was Jewish is obvious,
and in the Middle East of the first century that would certainly have
meant "non-white." But if Cleage's ethic for Black Americans presupposes a Negroid Jesus, the argument is more dubious. More importantly, his assumption that color or race was a decisive social and
political characteristic in Jesus' day is probably an anachronistic reading
of ancient history in light of current problems. Likewise, it is certainly
debatable whether Jesus was an active revolutionary and a member of
the Zealot sect. S.G.F. Brandon has reopened that controversy, arguing
that the early Church, for apologetic reasons, glossed over the revolutionary aspects of Jesus' ministry; he likens Jesus to the Zealots, but
does not necessarily place him within the Zealot sect. Brandon's extensive work on the subject is impressive, but his thesis is not presently
widely accepted.[2]

James Cone articulates a more theologically sophisticated black
theology which circumvents Cleage's more extreme historical assertions.[3] Cone agrees with Cleage that Christian theology must be formulated in light of black experience. However, he contends that Jesus must
be interpreted not literally but theologically as being black. Cone finds
ample biblical evidence that God is a liberator. He delivered Israel
from Egyptian slavery and through the Hebrew prophets he continually
condemned injustice and championed the cause of the oppressed. Jesus,
whose ministry was located among the outcast and dispossessed of
Jewish society, continued and fulfilled God's liberating activity. He promised salvation and blessing to the poor and downtrodden. He condemned the religious and political elite for oppressing people. Jesus'
words recorded in Luke indicate his liberating mission.

> The Spirit of the Lord is upon me.
> because he has anointed me to preach the good news to the poor.
> He has sent me to proclaim release to the captives
> and recovering of sight to the blind,
> to set at liberty those who are oppressed,
> to proclaim the acceptable year of the Lord.   (Luke 4:18-19, RSV)

Cone interprets this liberation as deliverance from political, social,
and economic oppression.

However, Cone does not assert that Jesus was a Zealot. He simply
affirms that the import of Jesus' historical ministry was social liber-

ation. Furthermore, the work of the living Christ continues to be the liberation of the oppressed; and oppression in contemporary America can most readily be symbolized by "blackness." God did not choose to become incarnate in just any man. In Jesus he took the form of an oppressed Jew for the purpose of liberating oppressed Jews. Today Christ is to found in the black ghetto. "Thinking of Christ as non-black in the twentieth century is as theologically impossible as thinking of him as non-Jewish in the first century."[4]

Cone uses the term "black" in two senses. "Black" refers to a particular people who have long been oppressed in America because of their black skin. He also adopts the term "black" as an oppropriate "ontological" symbol for *all* oppression.

The broader definition of blackness appears more legitimate when the connotations of the term "black" are examined in the American social context. Many words have social roles built into them. The word "father" means more than "male parent"; it includes a social role and its accompanying responsibilities, illustrated by such a statement as "Dad was never really a father to me." Likewise, "black" and "white" are more than designations of color; they also indicate social roles. Sociologist Peter Berger observes that "being white" in the southern part of the United States has nothing to do with the color of one's skin, as the treatment of "very light-skinned Negroes" will show. "To be white" is not a biologically objective fact concerning skin pigmentation, but a "social fiction," the acceptance of a humanly constructed social role.[5] Those whose "Negro" ancestry is known are socially defined as black and see themselves as black, however white their skin may be. If skin color has been irrelevant in defining whiteness in America, it may also be irrelevant in defining blackness. Cone simply inverts the social myth of color. If blackness means an "inferior" social status rather than color, what better symbol could there be for oppression? Moreover, if the oppressed are those among whom God is found, then black is not only beautiful, but even holy. The term "white," as the polar opposite, becomes the symbol for the oppressor and hence for evil. Cone goes so far as to suggest that "whiteness" is the Antichrist, a theme reminiscent of the Black Muslim identification of the white man as a devil.

Since blackness and whiteness no longer designate simply skin color, it is not only possible but inevitable that every man chooses his own identity, whether he recognizes the choice or not. The decision is made, for example, in the selection of one's heroes. Those whose heroes are George Washington, Abraham Lincoln, and Richard Nixon are white, according to Cone. The other choice, to be black, means that "your heart, your soul, your mind, and your body are where the dispossessed are."[6] Knowing that the white man *can* become black should not be the occasion for an easy white conscience. The formation of black identity requires the radical repentance and conversion that the New Testament calls "being born again." Such regeneration is rare among whites.

Because the Black Power movement is the effort of the black man to affirm his humanity and to say a collective No! to white racism, Cone asserts that Black Power is not only compatible with Christianity; it *is* Christianity. Although not all Black Power exponents may be called Christian, at least, anyone who is genuinely Christian must be a Black Power advocate. The Church must become black, if it is to be the Church of Jesus Christ. The task of the black theologian, therefore, is to interpret God's revelation in terms of black experience, black history, and black culture, thereby liberating the black man's religious thought from the domination of "white" racist theology. Theology is racist, Cone says, when it endorses or tacitly accepts the premises of racism or even when it ignores the problem of oppression. Thus racism is evident in the assumption that God is "colorless." In a society in which race is of such fundamental social significance, God cannot be color blind; he must take sides. Even many of the white "theologians of revolution" are subject to Cone's attack, since they presume to speak for the black man rather than letting him speak for himself.[7]

Two dimensions of Cone's theology are particularly significant for social ethics. First is his view of Christian eschatology. He is convinced that Jesus' prophetic utterance, "The kingdom of God is at hand; repent, and believe in the gospel" (Mk 1:15, RSV), was distorted by white Christians when they accepted an eschatology of individual salvation and a future heavenly reward, thereby deflecting attention away from the alleviation of suffering and oppression in this life. Black theology now restores the true meaning of Jesus' words with a summons to participate in God's transformation of this world. The radical obedience that Jesus' eschatological teaching demanded can be translated today as the choice between black and white; there is no neutral ground. He who would be black must be committed even at the cost of "losing his life" for the sake of the gospel.

The second aspect of Cone's theology which is of utmost importance for social ethics is his treatment of Christian love. He insists that love cannot be defined abstractly nor its requirements be prescribed in general terms beforehand. The content of love can only be understood contextually; its demands are perceived only as one encounters a particular situation. The first demand of love upon the black man is self-love, self-affirmation. But what of love for the oppressor? Cone seems sympathetic to those who urge hatred of the oppressor, but he never endorses such a position. Love is the norm. But love is not passive forebearance; it actively seeks to meet the needs of the neighbor. Thus the oppressed must confront the oppressor and force him to cease his oppression. The oppressor needs this liberation, for no man who enslaves another is free. Moreover, since the goal of love is reconciliation, the black man must stand his ground, refusing to accept an inferior status, for genuine reconciliation can only occur between equals.

The goal of love is the recognition of the humanity of all men. But because love is not abstract, the means appropriate to eliminate oppression and affirm humanity cannot be dictated abstractly. The decision is situational and is in the hands of the oppressed. The loving action toward the white man is to "stop his oppression, by whatever means *I* think best."[8] Hence violence cannot be precluded. If it is objected that Jesus never advocated violence, Cone responds that we cannot base our decisions on what Jesus did in his time and situation, for to do so is to fall back into the kind of biblical literalism that liberal Protestant thought has long since abandoned.

A critical evaluation of black theology requires attention to several key questions. The first question concerns the nature of the liberating mission of Jesus. Cleage maintains that Jesus viewed love, unity, and sacrificial commitment within the Black Nation as the precondition for liberation from Rome, but he does not indicate what further strategy Jesus envisioned for throwing off the Roman yoke. Cone says even less about *how* the historical Jesus set about to liberate the oppressed. To demonstrate that Jesus was an overt and politically active revolutionary with a program for social change would require much more careful documentation than either writer even begins to provide. Moreover, their assumption that Jesus' eschatological expectations were historical rather than apocalyptic needs more defense than they offer, given the continuing debate among New Testament scholars concerning that key issue. The case of Cleage and perhaps even of Cone is built

270(Contemporary Religion And Social Responsibility

excessively and needlessly on an assertion of the overt revolutionary intention of Jesus. To discuss the revolutionary force of Jesus' teachings as *latent* rather than explicit might blunt the emotional impact and popular appeal of black theology within the black community, but it would probably be more accurate and no less potent theologically. Jesus may not have been a political revolutionary, but indirect and unintended revolutionary consequences result from taking his teachings seriously and acting them out in society. Even the politically conservative strategy of Paul is overlaid on a revolutionary doctrine that in Christ there is neither Jew nor Greek, slave nor free, a teaching that is social dynamite if people ever take it seriously. Peter Berger suggests that early Christianity was radically subversive, not because it advocated political rebellion against Rome, but because it challenged social assumptions at their very roots. The Roman authorities perceived this and with great political acumen fed the Christians to the lions.[9] This view of the latent revolutionary implications of the gospel is less dramatic than the view of Cleage and Cone, but it may prove more fruitful in the long run even for a black theology, because it is a more accurate interpretation of the New Testament sources.

The second question focuses on the relativity of all theological perspectives. Every theology must be related to some particular human experience. Therefore, one may appreciate the need for a theology arising from black experience. But should one not also be aware of the relativity of this perspective? Cone recognizes that black theology is not eternal, but he thinks that it is the best and perhaps the only valid Christian theology in America today. One can accept as theologically sound the idea that Jesus is *also* black. But the claim that he is *only* black risks absolutizing one particular perspective, a danger which black theologian Miles J. Jones expresses as the temptation to make an idol out of blackness.[10] Another black theologian, Major J. Jones, though sharing the conviction that a theology of black awareness is essential, is more sensitive than either Cleage or Cone to the limitations of an understanding of God that is less than the universal God of the Bible and a view of man that is less than fully human because it is not fully representative of the total human family. Such concepts may lead to a cult of black awareness that is devoid of true redemptive mission.[11] Cleage is more susceptible to this shortcoming than Cone, because he defines blackness more narrowly. But Cone's technique of exploiting the ambiguity of the word "black" leads him in the same direction.

Like many other Black Power leaders, he does not disregard other forms of oppression, but most of the time when he uses the term "black" he is designating that particular group of people with a Negro cultural heritage.

But even if the focus is clearly on the theology of "oppression" rather than "black" theology in the narrow sense, one must still ask whether the experience of oppression is *the* ultimate criterion for theology. Does not any theology which asserts that Christianity responds to only one human problem, be it anxiety, guilt, alienation, pride, or oppression, fail to do justice to the God of the Judeo-Christian tradition? Is economic, social, and political oppression the only human condition to which God speaks? Is Cone justified in claiming that Christian theology *only* arises from the oppressed community? Moreover, does not a theology of oppression, which is preoccupied with evil, run the risk of ignoring positive elements of human experience, such as joy, celebration, and gratitude?

We might further enquire whether Cone's analysis of American society is not simplistic. His writings can create a crisis of conscience for the white man who has some awareness that the plight of the Black American is at least partly the result of white decisions. But does he not overstate the case? Is not our social system too complex for a simple dichotomy that makes every man either an oppressor or one oppressed? Moreover, if Cone is perhaps too zealous in his condemnation of whites, is he not also too optimistic about the goodness of blacks? He maintains that few blacks have the desire to dominate or exploit nor do they have the power to do so. But are there not subtle ways in which even the relatively powerless can and do exploit and manipulate? Even if black supremacy is not a serious possibility for the immediate future, is there not still the danger of the sin of lust for power, which though less harmful socially may be no less destructive spiritually than the sin of pride of power? And is not the retaliatory dehumanization of whites, by treating them as non-existent, a danger about which blacks need to be warned? Are Cone and Cleage too reticent in acknowledging that God's judgment does not stop even at the boundaries of Black Power?

These questions indicate some reservations about the *excesses* of a one-sided, one-dimensional theology, even though one can appreciate the contribution of such an overstatement in bringing into focus a neglected perspective. Some further remarks about the *incompleteness* of the thought of Cone and Cleage with regard to social ethics need to be made. Clearly Cone's theology is ethically relevant; however, he writes as a theologian, not as an ethicist. He presents a new theological view of the black man and calls for a transformation of consciousness. The ethical importance of such a change of attitude is not to be minimized. But he does not make clear whether the new black man will perceive immediately what each occasion requires of him or whether the ethicist is still needed to suggest techniques of liberation most appropriate to various kinds of situations. Even if one cannot determine in advance what will be required in every instance, it is possible to say something about the technique of analyzing particular situations. There is some continuity to the demands of love, some consistency between what love has required and what it may require in the future. There is at least a *tendency* for love to be more compatible with some methods than with others. Even if violence is considered a possible requirement of love, it is *less* amenable to love than nonviolence. Therefore, it should be defined as a last resort, and some guidelines are needed to help discern when that point is reached. The moral virtuoso who perceives intuitively what a situation requires is rare; most people need to think more seriously in advance of decisions in order to be able to choose wisely when confronted with concrete choices; ethics is, in part, the discipline of such prior thought. Black theology, however valuable it may be as one dimension of the liberation movement, is truncated without ethical reflection concerning the implementation of the new black theological consciousness. Someone sharing Cone's and Cleage's perspective needs to write more explicitly and systematically the ethics portion of these black theologies.

Another problem needing more extensive treatment is the question of the extent to which one's ethical reflection and moral decisions are to be guided by pragmatic evaluation of what is possible. If the purpose of social ethics is to provide at least a sketchy road map to a better society, then the ethicist must seek not only what is theologically justifiable, but also what is strategically viable. Despite his more nationalistic fervor and his more rigid definition of blackness, Cleage seems more attuned than Cone to the ethical connection between means and ends and the need to calculate the possibility of success. Both men foresee the possibility of fighting and dying in the streets, but Cleage makes it quite clear that it is legitimate only if it promotes the cause of the Black Nation. Revolution is not *just* dying in the streets. More importantly, "we're *not* going to all die in the streets."[12] Survival of the group is primary. Cone seems less concerned than Cleage about "success" and "failure." Dying in the streets may be a form of self-authentication. Although Cone would vigorously deny it, he may even come close to subordinating the desire for social change to the idea of individual self-affirmation. The tension in his thought between the belief that change is desirable and possible and the commitment to die rather than to continue the way things are is evident in his statement, "We now believe that something can be done about this world, and we have resolved to die rather than deny the reality expressed in black self-determination."[13] Moreover, because Christ's resurrection has set the black man free from the fear of death, "it does not matter that white people have all the guns and that, militarily speaking, we have no chance of winning. *There comes a time when a people must protect their own and for black people, the time is now.*"[14] Whether Cone's writing will aid the cause of social change or will serve to dissipate the possibility of social transformation by engendering uncalculated acts of individual heroics, a new kind of individualistic eschatology, only time will tell.

What will be the future influence of Black Theology or any religious perspective in the American racial crisis? Even if the black liberation movement should leave traditional religion behind altogether, discussion of the religious dimension of that movement may still be necessary. Black historian Vincent Harding has traced some of the implicit religious themes and language of so-called "secular" Black Power leaders.[15] Even apart from his suggestion that these leaders are influenced, perhaps unconsciously, by traditional religious thinking, one can see a religious function in the Black Power movement itself, if one defines religion in terms of ultimate commitment around which life is organized. In this light "secular" Black Power as well as Black Theology may be viewed as a religious expression of a world-transforming sect, using the sociological definition of "sect." Its sectarian characteristics, particularly manifested in the deliberate cohesion of a group which is socially alienated and ethically zealous, are the foundation for a revolutionary community not unlike the revolutionary Anabaptists of the sixteenth century. Moreover, this "religion of Black Power" may yet find its greatest success by working through organized religion. The failure of many black radicals to win support from the black community, according to Cone, results from their inability to understand the religious character inherent in that community. In Cone's view, to speak meaningfully to the black community about liberation is impossible except from a Christian perspective. Some Black Panther leaders now seem to be recognizing the strategic importance of the black church and are urging militants to go back to church.

Black theology is, therefore, a challenge to both the secular black militant and the acquiescent black churchman to awaken to a new religious consciousness and to respond to the liberating activity of God. It could also become the source of a new perception of God and a renewed concern for social justice within white Christianity.

1. Albert B. Cleage, Jr., **The Black Messiah** (New York: Sheed and Ward, 1968).

2. S. G. F. Brandon, **Jesus and the Zealots** (New York: Charles Scribner's Sons, 1967).

3. See especially James H. Cone, **Black Theology and Black Power** (New York: The Seabury Press, 1969), **A Black Theology of Liberation** (Philadelphia: J. B. Lippincott Co., 1970), and "An Introduction to Black Theology," **Enquiry**, III (March-May, 1971), pp. 51-80.

4. Cone, **Black Theology and Black Power**, p. 69.

5. Peter Berger, **The Precarious Vision: A Sociologist Looks at Social Fictions and Christian Faith** (New York: Doubleday & Co., 1961), p. 196.

6. Cone, **Black Theology and Black Power**, p. 151.

7. For a critique of white theological ethicists from a black perspective, see Herbert O. Edwards, "Racism and Christian Ethics in America," **Katalagete Be Reconciled: Journal of the Committee of Southern Churchmen**, III (Winter, 1971), pp. 15-24.

8. Cone, **Enquiry**, III, p. 56. Italics mine.

9. Berger, **op. cit.**, p. 203.

10. Miles J. Jones, "Toward a Theology of Black Experience," **The Christian Century**, LXXXVII (September 16, 1970), p. 1090.

11. Major J. Jones, **Black Awareness: A Theology of Hope** (Nashville: Abingdon Press, 1971), pp. 116-117.

12. Cleage, **op. cit.**, p. 29.

13. Cone, **A Black Theology of Liberation**, p. 247.

14. **Ibid.**, p. 248. Italics in the original.

15. Vincent Harding, "The Religion of Black Power," **The Religious Situation: 1968**, ed. Donald R. Cutler (Boston: Beacon Press, 1968), pp. 3-38.

THE THREE GREAT HERESIES OF WELFARE

ALAN KEITH-LUCAS

It is always easier to look at heresies if we think of them as historical facts. The Arians, the Armenians, the Docetists, or the Manichees—we know or can find out quite easily what they believed, and how they distorted the gospel. It is harder to see heresy in ourselves. But sometimes if we look at the mistakes of others we can see our own. This is my reason for dipping now into the past—that we may see ourselves in it.

Heresies also occur when there is a difficult question to answer. And in the matter of the poor there are at least two difficult questions, closely interrelated, that every age has sought to answer in a somewhat different way.

The first is the cause of poverty. Is it God's action or man's? Has God ordained poverty, either individually—for the good or for the punishment of the individual—or for some wide purpose? Or is poverty the result of man's fallen state, either individually or collectively? The second question is how, and to what extent, the giver is responsible for the use made of the gift. To what extent should the provision of relief to the poor be an act of pure love, a treating one's neighbor as oneself, and to what extent should it be an attempt to reform him? To what extent is giving harmful to the character of the recipient? How much should his use of the gift be controlled?

These are still the central questions in the welfare field today. And still we are confused by them. Some of us think that we have the answer, but all too often we are, in fact, confused by one of the heresies, into which our Church or our culture has fallen along the way.

The very early Christians had no doubt at all. They felt an outpouring of love, which took the form of holding all things in common. But as the Christian community grew and became identified with society instead of remaining a little group within it, problems began to arise. Some of them are obvious even in the epistles. The major problem was the question of how one could judge rightly in giving relief. This we will take up later. But a very serious problem began to arise in the relationship between the giver and the recipient, and there are many traces of this heresy today.

The ancient Church, and indeed the Church as late as the nineteenth century, believed more strongly than we do in God's providence in social affairs. As a stanza, generally omitted today, of the hymn "All Things Bright and Beautiful" has it, "The rich man in his castle, the poor man at his gate; God put them in their places and ordered their estate." For a time the Church played with the theory that poverty was somehow holy. But the concept soon proved unworkable, if only because men were forced to recognize that many of the poor were far from holy or blessed.

Men therefore turned to the theory that the poor must be, in Chrysostom's term, designed by God to be "useful" to the rich in giving them a chance to get rid of their abundance and win treasure in heaven. Charity soon became the one certain way to salvation, perhaps to some extent because the former way, martyrdom, was no longer available. Cyprian describes charity as "needful for the weak"—for which he might be commended—but also as "glorious for the strong, assisted by which the Christian accomplishes spiritual grace, deserves well of Christ the judge, accounts God his debtor."

This was the great heresy of the medieval Church. It divorced charity and stewardship from any real love or justice. It did not die with the Reformation. An Anglican in the eighteenth century put it neatly: charity is a loan to God which he engages himself to repay.

Such bargaining with the Almighty may seem distasteful, but is it so very foreign from some of our practices today? What about the benefactor who patronizes the "poor little orphans" in a church home? Is his or her impulse really one of Christian love, or does the giving accrue more to the giver than to the recipient? What about the emotion of pity, which often means a sense of superiority? What about the all-too-frequent demand that the recipient be grateful or show due respect? How much demand for personal voluntary giving, and how much dissatisfaction with professionalism in modern welfare is not due to the feeling that giving should receive its reward?

But this heresy, great as it was, and persistent as it still is, was as nothing to that which arose over the question of the judgment that man should use in distributing alms. The problem arose early. As early as the second century we find discussions of "prudence" in almsgiving.

Evidently men and churches were making hasty judgments. Basil says that it takes great experience to distinguish between those who are really poor and those who beg only in order to collect money; other Fathers held that gifts to the undeserving were a lesser evil than overlooking the deserving—a point of view that could well be stressed today.

It was left to Chrysostom to put forward a wholly Christian point of view. His answer was that a personal judgment was impossible, both pragmatically and theologically. How could man, who was such a sinner, and who had been given so much that he did not deserve by God, judge another man's desert? To do so was not so much to prove the recipient unworthy of the giver's liberality as to prove the giver unworthy of God's. This understanding brought Chrysostom to positions that are startling like modern humanistic thought, but from the theological base. "The poor," he says, "have only one recommendation: their need. If he be the most perverse of all men, should he lack necessary food we ought to appease his hunger." He had a deep understanding of the temptations of the poor. Even, he says, if a man is practicing imposture, he is to be pitied in that he needed to do it. He would also have the citizens of Alexandria not confine their relief to their fellow townsmen because even to give relief to someone attracted to the city by its generosity was a tribute to it—a very different point of view from that of states which today maintain strict residence requirements for those to whom they will offer aid.

Chrysostom was no cloistered monk. He was Bishop of Alexandria, and dispensed its relief. He had recognized an essential Christian truth, but it could well be objected that his principles needed modification to be practical in this fallen world. This was very nearly done by Thomas Aquinas, who in his magnificent attempt to reconcile heaven and earth saw clearly that the only solution to the judgmentalism of man was the judgment of the law, which he considered to be a reflection, however imperfect, of God's will. Thomas, and Ambrose before him, insist that benevolence has to do with justice and not with charity. It may be that this was too radical a conclusion, threatening the picture of order that he was striving to create, for Thomas placed this justice in the realm of moral law and not as the subject of enforceable statute. It was left to the framers of the Social Security Acts of the world in the twentieth century to arrive by a different pathway at the concept of a legal right to subsistence under certain conditions of need. This is nominally the law in America today.

Thus there are sound theological reasons for the eschewing of personal judgment and the establishment in law of a "right to assistance" under certain conditions, and indeed medieval society at times approached this ideal. In Ypres and Bruges in the sixteenth century Juan de Vives established a system of collective responsibility for the needs of the poor that was remarkable for its justice and for its absence of condescension toward those in need.

The Reformation is sometimes blamed for sweeping all this away. But the fault lay not in the Reformation, not in the essential doctrines of Calvin and Luther, but in the use that was made of them to conform to the world. Calvin's belief in the unmerited love of God was just as strong as Chysostom's and his sense of duty was not far from Thomas' sense of justice.

Nevertheless, before long, and as certain doctrines were either emphasized or modified as in Puritan New England, the poor were reduced to an inferior class both socially and morally. In private charity personal judgments were allowed to flourish and might sometimes be favorable, but in the public sphere—and state programs were beginning to be established because of the fragmentation of the Church—the judgment was universally negative. So far from establishing any sort of "right to subsistence," the law was used mainly to punish those on relief. The poor became identified with those who were not elect. Human success and God's favor gradually became identified.

There have been many explanations of how this came about. Economic liberalism and an enhanced sense of the inviolability of personal property; a new emphasis on work as a primary Christian virtue, due perhaps to Luther's insistence on vocation or to the increasing demands of an industrial society; the uncertainty of "the saints" as to their own election, and therefore their search for outward signs, have all been given as reasons. So has the theory that the "saints" knew sin and thought that they could cure it, whereas, they admitted themselves helpless in the face of psychology or more complex economic trends. But the underlying answer is the same. Man was not really prepared to believe what the gospel taught him: that all men are genuinely sinners, that before God there is so little difference between the best and the worst of them, that God commands us not to judge but to respect and forgive our fellows, and that even in this imperfect world the purpose of law should be to enhance and not to restrict the right of life. Man could not believe that his worldly activities did not earn him "merit" in the sense of the right to judge and to control those who had not the same fortune. To him "original sin" was something that belonged to the other fellow, and "grace" was the perequisite of himself and those like him.

God, in fact, became identified with the interests of the successful, with the institution of private property, and with the civic virtues. He was no longer the Wholly Other, the Unknowable, before whom even the best of men merited damnation.

The result was that misfortune became almost as much of a sin as laziness or vice. The poor, good or bad, lazy or unfortunate, "deserving" or "undeserving," were treated as a class little, if any, better than criminals. Any kind of mercy or forgiveness for them was ruled out. As an English "expert" on the poor law, a churchman, said less than seventy years ago, "Kindness to an individual too often means cruelty to a class." The remedy was clearly to make the life of the poor person just as bleak, as gloomy, and as unpleasant as it was possible to do.

This meant in practice the workhouse test—the forcing of the poor out of their homes and into public institutions on the theory that only those who were really indigent would accept such degradation. It meant the loss of civil rights. As late as 1889 a farmer in Kansas lost the custody of his children solely on the grounds that he had accepted public relief as a result of a crippling drought. And it meant that the poor were deliberately allowed less to live on than the poorest laborer could possibly earn, so that the poor person might be spurred to greater efforts. Any possibility that it is love and not repression which overcomes evil—a lesson man might have learned from the cross—was forgotten in this relationship.

Along with this repression went the demand on the poor for a higher standard of morality than was required of the self-sufficient. Any deviation from the path of the strictest morality cost him his means of livelihood and he was expected to surrender all control of his normal business to the judgment of his superiors. How anyone ever expected him to regain his self-respect or to have the strength to assert his independence is indeed hard to see.

The picture in fact looks most unchristian. But doesn't much of this heresy still exist today? Don't many of us instinctively judge all public-assistance recipients by the few who seem to us unwilling to work? Don't many of us argue for more "control" of relief expenditures, for better "supervision" of the lives of those in need? Don't many of us demand a higher standard of morality among those on relief than we do of our fellows? How many of us are concerned that a man who asks for help retain his dignity in this crisis? How many of us deny to those on relief a minimum health and decency standard?

Let us look at several examples. The past few years have seen a resurgence, until the Federal Government intervened, of what are known as "suitable home" provisions in the program of Aid to Dependent Children. These laws in fact permit the state to force a child to starve or to be removed from his parents, not because the parents have been found guilty of neglect or the child is in need of protection by due process of law, but because the welfare department has made a judgement that the home does not meet its standards. The action is taken by withdrawing the grant. Is this not one law for those who have to ask for relief and another for those who do not? The most general grounds for this decision is a moral one. But how many "better class" homes are not equally immoral, and no one takes any action?

Again, let us look at the newspapers. How many articles does one see that deal sympathetically, with tolerance and understanding, with the plight of the family on relief, the struggle, even the shame? The great majority emphasize the few who cheat or misbehave.

How many people think about need, and how many more only about deterrence? How many have any idea what a public assistance grant will buy? How many know that their state grants less than a minimum health and decency budget and then expects recipients to be both healthy and decent? How many are much more concerned that relief may be "attractive" to people than disturbed at economic conditions that make it possible for such a miserable existence to be attractive to anyone? When a relief client buys some candy for his children, how many well-to-do people consider what it means never to have the slightest chance to give one's children anything not entirely utilitarian, and don't many blame him for poor management or deceit?

The same goes for our private giving. At Christmas many welfare agencies, public and private, ask for funds for Christmas dinners or presents for children. Most people respond, but with moral strings attached. Presents are to be given only to the children of "good" parents who will show appreciation. A "good" church family complained to our welfare department recently that their dinner went to children whose father was in jail. Who needs friendship most, the child whose father is in jail or the child whose father is at home? Whom did Christ come to save—the sinners or the good?

Indeed, the moralistic heresy is alive today. The Church becomes too easily the guardian of our cultural heritage. It rubs in the lessons that society teaches. It contributes nothing different, no new understanding of man.

There will be people who will protest that the Church has often, in its history, been the conscience of the people with regard to social injustice. This certainly seemed to be so at the time of the Evangelical Revival. In Great Britain, where it began, this was the time of the great humanitarian measures, the Reform Bill and the Factory Acts. It was also the beginning of the age of great philanthropies, of the founding of schools and colleges, orphanages, and other charities.

The reform movement was primarily religious. Two elements seem to have been important. One was the growing understanding that all men, being loved by God, had a worth that could not be denied. The other was the recognition that the rich were also sinful. Indeed much of the philanthropy was a kind of "fire insurance," a penitence for greed and for preoccupation with material gain. Wesley himself was much aware of this dilemma. He believed that religion would help a man prosper, that industry and frugality would inevitably bring riches, but he was also aware that possessions were a snare. His preferred solution was that a man should gain all that he could, save all that he could, but also give all that he could, and therefore "grow in grace" and "lay up treasure in heaven."

Yet the same Parliament that passed the Reform Bill of 1832 passed the Poor Law of 1834 that established workhouses and forced paupers to choose between starvation and the workhouse's deliberately contrived gloom, discomfort, and lack of hope. It was as if society was willing to consider the rights of those who contributed to the rich man's treasure, but denied them to people who were unproductive. Even the Evangelical churches were servants of our economy.

In welfare we have seen how Puritan thinking tended to pervert this doctrine into sin for the other fellow and grace for me and mine. The natural religious reaction to this trend was to stress man's natural goodness, the presence of God in every man. This emphasis was badly needed, as it sometimes is today. But to reject in its name recognition of man's shared sinfulness, of his common predicament, of the actual fallen state of the world, is to lose an important source of understanding

The great humanitarian movement of the nineteenth century was more or less based on this denial. It came in part, it is true, from the Methodists with their emphasis on God's indwelling grace, but also and much more strongly from the Quakers and the Unitarians, of whom a historian of welfare writes that they were not "hampered by belief in original sin."

This relieved the poor from the stricture of belonging to a sinful class and indeed provided a bridge between rich and poor that had not existed for several centuries. But because it in general approved the world as the better sort of people conceived it, Christian liberalism failed to see man's common responsibility for the conditions that breed poverty. It believed that what the poor man needed was not so much the means to live his own life, but the example and the guidance of the educated and the successful. And this in practice meant three principles that still color the Church's concept of what welfare ought to be. For paternalism is a very active heresy and is so much a part of the thinking of many people that it does not look like a heresy at all.

The three principles are "the personal touch," "guidance," and an ignoring of man's material needs in favor of counseling, exhortation, or as social workers sometimes express the same concepts today, "services" or "treatment." This is not to say that services, or even "treatment," may not often be needed. It is to say that they do not meet all the needs of a man. Men are not poor only because they lack education, guidance, or an ability to adjust to life. Man has an obligation, in simple justice or in atonement, to provide for others who have been denied the means to live a decent life. Jesus said, "Man does not live by bread alone," but he never denied the need for bread. In fact, he enjoined us to pray for it.

The finest expression of this kind of welfare was what became known as "friendly visiting" and sometimes as "Christian socialism" (which has nothing to do with Karl Marx). It sought to elevate the poor, but at its best also had ideals of friendship. Thomas Chalmers, a Scots Presbyterian minister who was one of its earliest exponents, was opposed to the workhouse as he saw it in England: "Their paupers are met by the same treatment as their criminals." He also had the grace to write, somewhat cautiously, that "by putting ourselves under the roof of a poor neighbor, we in a manner render him for the time our superior," an enormous concession for the early nineteenth century. It still would be so for many people today.

But love between equals cannot exist with a sense of superiority or a desire to reform. Chalmers, and all like him, are much too apt to fall into giving, not what a person needs, but what the giver thinks he ought to have. And generally this meant few comforts, a balanced diet, and a kindly mentor or father figure. There is something pharisaical about the follower of Chalmers of whom it was said that the poor "soon came to understand the man who was as liberal with his sympathy as he was chary with meat and coal tickets," and who said himself, "I am beginning seriously to believe that all bodily aid to the poor is a mistake."

Ambrose had said, several centuries earlier, that to give "without good will," without the interests of the recipient at heart, is harmful both to the giver and to the man who receives. The nineteenth century, however, turned Chalmers' paternalism into organized charity and parceled it out, in a cautious manner, in accordance with what its dispensers believed to be the "good" of the poor. Although their judgment was largely moral, they began to call to their aid the infant social sciences, and in doing so began the transition to another attempt to answer the Church's and society's problem about how to give wisely.

For let us be clear, objection to Chalmers' paternalism or to the Puritan's reprobation of the poor does not call on man to abdicate judgment. Christianity demands justice and love, not indulgence. If it should not be concerned with punishing him for his sins, nor arranging his life for him, neither is it called on to maintain the unfortunate in luxury or to remove normal responsibility from him. The problem is not to eliminate judgment, but to discover, in this fallen world, the way to make it most nearly in accord with a Christian view of man's relationship to his fellows.

There are three possible sources of judgment which the Church might consider. The first of these is the "judgment of the saint," or, in welfare, giving to people what the "best" people think they deserve. This is what the Puritans used and what Chalmers made more kindly, but still employed as his guiding principle. It is what many church people still want to use today. And this, despite its apparent connection with religious principles, is the least Christian of the three and was what Jesus meant, surely, when he told us not to judge lest we be judged ourselves. It is the assumption that we know enough about other people to pass moral judgment on them. This is seeing the mote in our neighbor's eye and ignoring the beam in our own. It is pre-empting

God's judgment and eating of the tree of knowledge of good and evil, contrary to his command.

The second might be called the "judgment of the scientist," or giving to people what it is thought they need. This allows a little less scope for the giver's predilections. It is the form of judgment most favored by today's society, and the one that the later nineteenth century began to call to its aid, but it too can lead to pride and to the assumption that judgment is a "right" exercised by those who know over those who do not. But judgment is not a "right." It is a regrettable necessity to be exercised with a due sense of humility. When it becomes more than this, it is unchristian.

The third is judgment by the law, or the giving to people that to which society holds they are entitled. Although law may be thought of as secular, and is often illogical and harsh, there is much to recommend it from the Christian point of view. It does not pretend to be anything but human. It knows itself to be an adjustment to an imperfect world. It is the least personal, and therefore in a way the most humble of all methods of judgment. The judge who tries to impose his personal will on others is restrained by the collective wisdom or foolishness of the last thousand years. And specifically it is rooted in the belief in equal rights, in the denial that wealth or position or superior knowledge or morality give to anyone the right to judge or to control his fellows. That it is sometimes abused in practice does not invalidate its attempt to arrive at common and humble judgment.

JUDAISM IN PURSUIT OF ECONOMIC JUSTICE

RICHARD G. HIRSCH

Wealth can be a blessing; it can also be a curse. Wealth can be a creative influence; it can also be a destructive force. The history of nations and the biographies of men attest to both. The attitude toward material possessions and the use to which they are put determine whether wealth is good or evil. A society can be judged by the way it treats its disadvantaged. The affluent society that tolerates poverty misuses and abuses its wealth.

Judaism has something to contribute to America. The contribution is not in offering pat solutions to complex problems, but in projecting a system of values directing man to serve God by serving his fellow man. These values, an integral part of Jewish life through the ages, evolved under varying social, economic and political conditions. Judaism does not advocate any economic or political ideology, but it is an advocate of a specific response to life's problems. It speaks to our day in the voice of the past, but in a language which is universal in time and place.

Wealth Belongs to God; Life is Sacred

"The earth is the Lord's and the fullness thereof; the world and they that dwell therein" (Ps 24:1). No man and no society are "self-made," declares Judaism. Both the resources of nature and the ingenuity of man are divinely bestowed. Every society builds upon the creativity of previous generations. The wealth of today is the fruition of the accumulated efforts of countless individuals. "Thine, O Lord, is the greatness and the power and the glory and the victory and the majesty, for all that is in heaven and earth is Thine; . . . Both riches and honor come of Thee" (I Chr 29:11, 12). Since wealth comes from God, it must be used to fulfill God's purposes. "Give unto Him what is His, for you and yours are His."[1]

Judaism rejects the concept of "survival of the fittest." Man is not engaged in a struggle for survival against his fellow man. Our sages formulated a philosophy which could be called "survival of the sustainers," succinctly expressed in the saying, "Not only does man sustain man, but all nature does so. The stars and the planets, and even the angels sustain each other."[2]

Human life is sacred, so sacred that each person is considered as important as the entire universe. When asked why God made only one man at Creation, instead of populating the earth immediately with many humans, our sages replied that God wanted to teach that, "If one destroys a single person, it is as if he had destroyed the entire world, and if one saves the life of a single person, it is as if he had preserved the entire world."[3]

These two emphases—all wealth comes from God; human life is sacred—became the foundation stones for Jewish treatment of the less privileged members of society. Biblical ethics are permeated with laws assuring protection of the poor. These laws relate largely to agriculture, having been developed in an agrarian society. The Bible prescribes that when a field is harvested, the corners are to be left uncut; the field is not to be gone over to pick up the produce which has been overlooked. The gleanings of orchard and vineyard are to be left untouched. All that remains is for the poor, the stranger, the fatherless, and the widow.[4]

Every seventh year was a Sabbatical year, during which the land was to lie fallow, and that which grew of itself belonged to all, "that the poor of thy people may eat" (Ex 23:11).[5] All debts were to be cancelled.[6] Every fiftieth year was a Jubilee year, during which all lands were to be returned to the families to whom they were originally allocated. The law of the fiftieth year was too complex to be observed and fell into disuse early in Jewish history, but the spirit behind the law was preserved. Our forefathers realized that an unrestricted pursuit of individual economic interest would result in massive concentrations of wealth for the few, and oppressive poverty for the many. They sanctioned competition, but they rejected "rugged individualism." The intent of the law was to restore the balance, to give those who had fallen an opportunity to lift themselves up again. Land was not the permanent possession of any man. "The land shall not be sold in perpetuity; for the land is Mine; for ye are strangers and settlers with Me" (Lv 25:23).

Jewish ethics sanction the institution of private property. "Let the property of thy fellow man be as dear to thee as thine own."[7] However, Jewish tradition never asserted that property rights take precedence over human rights—an assertion made by many in America today. Nor did Judaism accept the Puritan emphasis on the acquisition of property and worldly goods as a sign of virtue. On the contrary, for the Jew, human rights have priority over property rights. The tithe prescribed in biblical law was not a voluntary contribution, but an obligation imposed on all, in order that "the stranger and the fatherless and the widow shall come and shall eat and be satisfied" (Dt 14:29). Any man who was hungry could help himself to the produce in a field at any time, without asking permission of the owner, so long as he did not carry away food to be sold for his own profit.[8]

No man had absolute control over his own property. The person who cut down young trees in his garden was to be punished, because he had wasted that which did not belong to him."[9] The man who owned a well in a field had to make the water available to the inhabitants of a nearby community. Such requirements evolved out of the fundamental Jewish conviction that material possessions are gifts from God, to be used for the benefit of all men. Wealth, properly used, is a means of preserving and sanctifying life. Improperly used, it is a profanation of God and of the being created in His image.

Poverty Leads to Dehumanization

The poor man, as much the child of God as the rich man, has been disinherited from his Father's wealth. He has been deprived of his patrimony, of his share of the earth's bounty. Unlike some religions, Judaism does not encourage the ascetic life. Poverty is not the way to piety. Scarcity does not lead to sanctity. The search for holiness is not made easier by insufficiency of basic necessities. Without the necessary material goods of life man cannot attain the personal growth and satisfaction essential to human fulfillment. "All the days of the poor are evil" (Pr 15:15).

The common saying "Poverty is no disgrace" may offer consolation —to those who are well off. As a statement of morality, an ethical imperative, it would have much to commend it—"Poverty *should be* no disgrace." As a statement of fact, however, it is totally inaccurate. Poverty is a disgrace—for those who are poor. Poverty is destructive to the human personality. "The ruin of the poor is their poverty" (Pr 10:15).

Our sages taught that poverty was the worst catastrophe that could happen to a person. "If all afflictions in the world were assembled on one side of the scale and poverty on the other, poverty would outweigh them all."[10] The poor man is the lowliest of God's creatures, not only in the eyes of others, but in his own eyes as well.[11] "When a man needs his fellow men, his face changes color from embarrassment."[12]

Humiliation leads to dehumanization. The poor man is not a complete man. "Even his life is not a life," said one teacher.[13] The afflictions of poverty are so severe that Jewish tradition makes the seemingly radical statement that "the poor man is considered as a dead man."[14] Poverty is spiritual death. The poor man looks at life from another perspective. Like a space ship circling the moon, he sees only the dark side, while others may see only the bright side. As one sage declared, "The world is darkened for him who has to look forward to the table of others [for sustenance]."[15] The poor man's outlook is altered. "The sufferings of poverty cause a person to disregard his own sense [of right] and that of his Maker."[16]

The poor are different. The world asks, "Why are their values not like ours? Why are they so dirty or so sullen or so promiscuous or so indolent or so passive or so uncouth or so uneducated or so unambitious? Why are they not like the rest of us?" The Bible accurately states the consequences of difference: "All the brethren of the poor do hate him; how much more do his friends go far from him" (Pr 19:7).

Why are the poor different? Because they are poor. Because material circumstances shape human values. Judaism has never drawn a dichotomy between body and soul as other religions and systems of thought have done. Those who believe that the body is the repository of all evil and the soul of all good cannot see the dependent relationship between spirit and matter. But the Jew knows that a man's values are in great measure shaped by his life experiences. "Where there is no sustenance, there is no learning," declared a teacher of the first century.[17] Unless a person has the proper environment, learning cannot take place. To feed the mind, the body must also be fed. To nourish the spiritual life, the physical life must be nourished. A Chasidic rabbi of the 19th century expressed it well when he said, "Take care of your own soul and of another man's body, not of your body and of another man's soul."[18]

Poverty does not inevitably lead to ruination, just as wealth does not inevitably lead to well-being. But for the most part, the poor man in an affluent society lives in another world. Psychologically, it is a world of humiliation, a world which fails to see that a man cannot pull himself up by his own bootstraps if he has no boots and no straps. The world which callously calls upon the poor to disregard material circumstances, asks a man to be more than a man and makes him feel less than a man.

Not Charity, But Justice

To aid the poor is to "rehumanize" children of God. It is to restore rights which have been denied. The elimination of poverty is not an option, a voluntary decision benevolently made by an individual and a society. It is not charity as thought of in our day. The word "charity" originally derived from the Latin *caritas,* meaning "love," has come to have the connotation of contribution motivated by sentiment. In our day, a person gives charity not because he feels an obligation, but because he is moved by good will or social pressure. Charity is presumed to come from the goodness of the heart. In the Jewish concept of charity, the heart plays an indispensable role. But assistance to the poor is more than love. There is no word in the Hebrew vocabulary for "charity" in the modern sense. The word used is *Tzedakah,* which literally means "righteousness." *Tzedakah* is not an act of condescension from one person to another who is in a lower social and economic status. *Tzedakah* is the fulfillment of an obligation to a fellow-being with equal status before God. It is an act of justice to which the recipient is entitled by right, by virtue of being human.

Because God is a God of justice, the beings created in His image must treat each other with justice. Injustice to man is desecration of God. "Whosoever mocketh the poor blasphemeth his Maker" (Pr 17:5). On the other hand, "He that is gracious unto the poor lendeth unto the Lord" (Pr 19:17). Jewish tradition went so far as to state that "the poor man does more for the rich man than the rich man for the poor man."[19] The poor give the righteous an opportunity to perform good deeds, to sanctify the name of God.[20] Refusal to give charity is considered by Jewish tradition to be idolatry.[21]

Throughout the Bible, injustice is constantly identified as failure to relieve the plight of the poor:

> Cursed be he that perverteth the justice due to stranger, fatherless, and widow. (Dt 27:19)

Another frequently used Hebrew term for charity is *mitzvah,* which literally means "a divine commandment." Alleviating poverty is a *duty,* stemming not alone from a man's inner sense of love and justice. It is an obligation ordained by God. Our ancient commentators taught that Abraham was more righteous than Job. According to rabbinical tradition, when great suffering befell Job, he attempted to justify himself by saying, "Lord of the world, have I not fed the hungry and clothed the naked?" God conceded that Job had done much for the poor, but he had always waited until the poor came to him, whereas Abraham had gone out of his way to search out the poor. He not only brought them into his home and gave them better treatment than that to which they were accustomed, but he set up inns on the highway so that the poor and the wayfarer would have access to food and drink in time of need.[22] To fulfill a "divine commandment" is not to watch others struggle through the game of life, but to be an active participant to take initiative, to seek out those who require assistance, even if they do not request it. True charity is to "run after the poor."[23]

Self-Respect—Poverty's Antidote

Acts of charity are the means, but not the end. The end is to restore the image of the divine to every man. The essential ingredient is human dignity. The manner in which assistance is given is even more important than the assistance itself. The sensitivities of recipients are to be safeguarded at all times. "Better no giving at all than the giving that humiliates."[24] Every effort was made throughout Jewish history to dispense charity anonymously. "He who gives charity in secret is even greater than Moses."[25] In the Temple at Jerusalem, there was a "chamber of secrecy" where the pious placed their gifts and the poor drew for their needs—all in anonymity.[26] The same practice was observed until modern times. In every synagogue, a charity box with a sign "Matan Beseter" (an anonymous gift) was placed.

The Talmud recounts the lengths to which great scholars went in order to protect the self-respect of the poor. A rabbi and his wife, accustomed to giving alms while recipients were asleep, were surprised when one poor man awoke. In order not to offend him, they jumped into a still heated oven, risking serious burns.[27] Another rabbi would tie money in a scarf and when he was near a poor man, would fling the gift over his back, so that the poor man would not have to suffer the embarrassment of facing his benefactor.[28]

Tradition stressed human dignity in declaring that even greater than *Tzedakah* was "Gemilut Chasadim," or "acts of loving-kindness." "Loving-kindness" entails personal devoting, service, and empathy. "He who gives a coin to a poor man is rewarded with *six* blessings, but he who encourages him with kind words is rewarded with *eleven* blessings."[29] The Midrash interprets Isaiah 58:10: "If thou draw out thy soul to the hungry and satisfy the afflicted soul," to mean "If you have nothing to give a poor man, console him with kind words. Say to him, "My soul goes out to you, for I have nothing to give you." "Gemilut Chasadim" was considered superior to almsgiving in three ways: "No gift is needed for it but the giving of oneself; it may be done to the rich as well as to the poor; and it may be done not only to the living, but to the dead."[30]

In connection with funeral practices, an early custom had evolved to bring the deceased into the house of mourning in expensive caskets of silver and gold, whereas the poor were placed in wicker baskets made of willow. The Talmud decreed that everyone should be placed in wicker baskets "in order to give honor to the poor."[31] To this day, Jewish tradition frowns on lavish funeral practices, because "the grave levels all," and the primary emphasis of Jewish burial rituals is to ascribe equal worth to all men.

Jewish tradition wrestled with the problem of how to preserve the dignity of recipients of charity. People vary in their needs. Some have higher standards of living or higher values than others. If human dignity is the objective of charity, then will not some persons have to be given more than others—and wherein is the justification of such preferential treatment? The rabbis based much of their discussion on the commandment, "If there be among you a needy man . . . thou shalt surely open thy hand unto him, and shalt surely lend him *sufficient for his need in that which he wanteth*" (Dt 15:7,8). The phrase "that which he wanteth" was interpreted to mean that if a man did not have sufficient funds to marry, the community should assume responsibility for providing him with the means to support a wife.[32] The phrase "sufficient for his need" became the peg on which to hang the concept that a man was entitled to be sustained at a standard of living to which he had become accustomed. One Babylonian rabbi sent his son to give a contribution to a poor man on the eve of Yom Kippur. The boy returned to his father and complained that the poor man was not in need since the boy had seen him imbibing precious old wine. Over the protests of his son, the rabbi doubled his normal contribution, on the grounds that the gentle-

·man had been used to a better life than the rabbi had originally thought.[33] The Talmud recounts how the great scholar Hillel, learning of a man of high station who had become poor, gave the man a horse to ride, and when he could not find a servant to run before him as was the man's custom, Hillel himself ran before him for three miles.[34]

These incidents, similar to numerous others recounted in rabbinic literature, were undoubtedly exceptional, but they do serve to transmit the underlying spirit of Judaism. Throughout the Bible, the poor man is not called "poor," but "thy brother," to the donor. The poor man's needs are spiritual as well as material. Because the poor man lacks material blessings, he is likely to feel inferior. Therefore, treat him like a brother. Spare his feelings. Zealously guard his dignity. Respect from others is poverty's most helpful counterbalance. Self-respect is poverty's most effective antidote.

The Highest Degree of Charity

The verse from Deuteronomy quoted above also became the basis for a highly developed system of loans. "Thou shalt surely open thy hand . . . and shalt surely *lend* him." Throughout rabbinic literature, a loan is emphasized as the finest form of charity. "Greater is he who lends than he who gives, and greater still is he who lends, and with the loan, helps the poor man to help himself."[35] Almost a millennium after this was written, the medieval philosopher Maimonides defined the various types of charity and categorized them into his famous "eight degrees of charity," the highest of which is to enable a man to become self-supporting.[36] Until modern times, every Jewish community had a "Gemilut Chesed" society, whose primary purpose was to grant loans to the needy without interest or security.

Our tradition recognized that an outright gift, no matter how well-intentioned, still might instill feelings of inferiority in the receiver. However, a loan is a transaction between equals. Sometimes the loan was a delicate fiction. In those instances where a poor man is too proud to accept a gift, one should offer a loan, even though one might never expect to have the money returned, and then subsequently the loan could be considered as a gift.[37]

The rabbis dealt in a direct fashion with those who in our day would be called "freeloaders," the poor who exploit the system of welfare. They looked askance at beggars who went from door to door.

Instead, the rabbis favored the "silent sufferers." A man should exert every effort not to be dependent on others. "Skin the carcass of a dead beast in the market place, receive thy wages, and do not say, 'I am a great man, and it is beneath my dignity to do such work.' "[38] A person should esteem his independence more than his dignity, even more than his piety.[39] Nevertheless even though the rabbis maintained a severely critical attitude toward imposters, they were generally liberal in offering them assistance. They realized that even those who made false claims served some purpose. "Be good to imposters. Without them our stinginess would lack its chief excuse."[40] No man is beyond human concern. No man is beyond repentance and rehabilitation. The response to those who would eliminate or diminish welfare programs because of occasional abuse is to be found in the midrashic comment on a biblical verse:

> If your brother be waxen poor, you shall not suffer him to fall. He is like a load resting on a wall; one man can then hold it, and prevent it from falling, but if it has once fallen to the ground, five men cannot raise it up again. And even if you have strengthened him four or five times you must (if he needs it) strengthen him yet again.[41]

The task is never finished until "thy brother" is raised from a condition of dependence to the state of self-reliance and self-support.

The Organized Jewish Community

In the talmudic period, it became clear that the amelioration of poverty was too complex a task to be left to individuals or to privately organized charity groups. Personal charity alone was too haphazard and spasmodic. The Jewish community supplemented the obligations of private charity with an elaborate system of public welfare—the first in history. Jewish tradition has always been nurtured in and through the community. Hillel's famous "Do not separate thyself from the community" sets the pattern.[42] Even Jewish worship is a communal experience. Almost all the prayers, including those recited by an individual in private, are written in the plural. So it was only natural for the Jew to look upon poverty as the responsibility of the entire community. The existence of the poor was an indication of social inequity which had to be rectified by society itself. The system of social welfare became the means of restoring integrity to the community.

The practices and theories of Jewish philanthropy anticipated many of the most advanced concepts of modern social work and became the basis for the excellent programs and high standards of American Jewish welfare agencies. The organization of Jewish welfare evolved through the centuries, but the principles were established during the second century.[43]

Every Jewish community had two basic funds. The first was called *Kuppah,* or "box," and served the local poor only. The indigent were given funds to supply their needs for an entire week. The second fund was called *Tamchui,* or "bowl," and consisted of a daily distribution of food to both itinerants and residents. The administrators of the funds were selected from among the leaders of the community and were expected to be persons of the highest integrity. The *Kuppah* was administered by three trustees who acted as a *Beth Din,* or "court," to determine the merit of applicants and the amounts to be given. The fund was operated under the strictest regulations. Collections were never made by one person, but always by two, in order to avoid suspicion. The collectors were authorized to tax all members of the community according to their capacity to pay, and if necessary, to seize property until the assessed amount was forthcoming. All members of the community were expected to contribute, even those who were themselves recipients of charity—testimony to the principle that no man was free of responsibility for the welfare of all. "He who does not accept his part of the sufferings of the community will not share in the comfort it will receive."[44]

By the Middle Ages, community responsibility encompassed every aspect of life, as the community fulfilled obligations which its separate members were incapable of fulfilling. The Jewish community regulated prices so that the poor could purchase food and other basic commodities at cost. Wayfarers were issued tickets, good for meals and lodging at homes of members of the community who took turns in offering hospitality.[45] Both these practices anticipated "meal-tickets" and modern food-stamp plans. Jewish communities even established "rent control," directing that the poor be given housing at rates they could afford. In Lithuania, local trade barriers were relaxed for poor refugees. When poor young immigrants came from other places, the community would support them until they completed their education or learned a trade.

The organization of charity became so specialized that numerous societies were established in order to keep pace with all the needs.

Each of the following functions was assumed by a different society in behalf of the community at large: visiting the sick, burying the dead, furnishing dowries to poor girls, providing clothing, ransoming captives, supplying maternity needs, and providing special foods and ritual objects for holidays. A host of other miscellaneous societies were formed to cover every possible area of need. In addition, there were public inns for travellers, homes for the aged, orphanages, and free medical care. As early as the eleventh century, a *Hekdesh* or "hospital" was established by the Jewish community of Cologne—primarily for the poor. Many of the activities centered in and around the synagogue, which in some communities was the only building of a public character.

Caring for the poor became a matter of civic pride. Scholars were warned not to live in a community which did not have an adequate system of public welfare.[46] A community was judged by the extent to which it became the agent for guaranteeing just treatment to all its inhabitants.

Lessons For The "Great Society"

Our review of Jewish tradition has been brief, but sufficient to demonstrate that the message of Judaism is relevant to the issues of our day. Many of the most advanced programs of the American government were antedated by Jewish programs reaching as far back as biblical times. Jews developed unique forms of social welfare legislation which are equivalent to the "war on poverty," medical care for all, and, as will be seen subsequently, federal aid to education, protection of the rights of labor, and numerous other public welfare programs. It should be a source of gratification to Jews to see the government of the United States moving in a direction which is in consonance with the spirit of Judaism.

In a sense, American Jews provide "proof positive" that properly conducted community welfare programs are not deleterious for individuals or for a society. In part, at least, American Jews are products of the welfare-oriented civilization of Judaism. Yet, contrary to the admonitions of opponents of welfare programs, Jews have not developed the characteristics of dependency which are supposedly in store for such persons. To the contrary, as a group, Jews are known for their initiative, ambition, intellectual and cultural pursuits, and independence of thought and action. American Jews are living witness to a fundamental truth—the proper assumption of responsibility by a society expands the horizons of individuals, broadens the opportunity for service to fellow men, and stimulates the capacity for personal growth.

The concept of a "Great Society" is not new for Judaism. Every day Jews pray for a Messianic Era of brotherhood and peace for all men. In Judaism, there is no individual salvation. Salvation for the individual is inextricably dependent on salvation for the entire people, and salvation of the people is in turn dependent on the salvation of all mankind. Men live, work, create, and die in a community of fellow beings. Life's primary problem is not how to attain eternal life after death but how to bring eternity to earth. The focus is not the individual, but society. The perfection of mankind is the ultimate goal.

The nation which aspires to become the Great Society has not yet comprehended the full character of the task which it has set for itself. It would be inconsistent and immoral to shape massive programs for improving the quality of life for our own citizens, and to reduce our concern for the rest of mankind, as some persons have advocated. The poor of Asia are our poor also. The uneducated of Africa are our illiterates also. Unless our cause extends beyond America's borders, we shall never reach our goals for ourselves. The Great Society must strive for a Great Mankind.

The Talmud states, "There is no poverty in a place of wealth."[47] Where a society is really wealthy, it understands its purposes and allocates its resources in a manner which eliminates human want. "Who is wealthy?" asked one sage. "Everyone who has spiritual satisfaction in his wealth."[48] America will not be an affluent society or a Great Society until we have spiritual satisfaction, until we use our wealth to give all our brothers throughout the world an equal opportunity to "the fulness of the earth."

1. Abot 3.8.

2. Tikkune Zohar, 122, T. 43—quoted in Louis I. Newman's The Talmudic Anthology, Behrman House, 1945, p. 60.

3. Mishnah Sanhedrin 4.5.

4. Leviticus 19:9ff.; Deuteronomy 24:19ff.

5. See also Leviticus 25: 2-7.

6. Deuteronomy 15: 1,2.

7. Abot 2.17.

8. Deuteronomy 23: 25,26.

9. Sifre, Deuteronomy—cf. Essay by Jacob Z. Lauterbach, "The Ethics of the

Halakah" in **Rabbinic Essays,** Hebrew Union College Press, 1951.
  10. Exodus Rabba, Mishpatim 31, 14.
  11. Taanit 7; Leviticus Rabba 34, Midrash Proverbs 22.
  12. Berachot 6.
  13. Betza 32.
  14. Nedarim 64b.
  15. Betza 32.
  16. Erubin 41.
  17. Abot 3, 21.
  18. Sayings of the Kotzker, quoted in Lewis Browne, **The Wisdom of Israel,** Random House, 1945; p. 588.
  19. Ruth Raba 5, 9; also 19.
  20. Leviticus Rabba 34.
  21. Tosefta Peah 4.19.
  22. Aboth de Rabbi Nathan VII, 17a, b.
  23. Shabbat 104a.
  24. Hagigah 5a.
  25. Baba Batra 8.
  26. Shekalim V, 6.
  27. Ketubot 67b.
  28. Baba Batra 10b.
  29. Baba Batra 9b.
  30. Sukkah 49b.
  31. Taanit 27.
  32. Sifre Deuteronomy, Re'eh, 116.
  33. Ketubot 67b.
  34. Ibid.
  35. Shabbat 63a.
  36. Matnot Aniyim 10, 7.
  37. Ketubot 67b.
  38. Baba Batra 110a.
  39. Berachot 8a.
  40. Ketubot 68a.
  41. Sifra 109b.
  42. Abot 2.5.
  43. For background material on organized Jewish philanthropy, see: **Abraham** Cronbach, "Philanthropy in Rabbinical Literature" and "Jewish Philanthropic Institutions," in **Religion and Its Social-Setting,** The Social Press; Kaufmann Kohler, "Charity" in **Jewish Encyclopedia;** George Foot Moore, **Judaism,** Harvard University Press, vol. II, chap. 7; Israel Abrahams, **Jewish Life in the Middle Ages,** Jewish Publication Society, Chapters XIII and XIV.
  44. Taanit 11a.
  45. Jacob R. Marcus, **The Jew in the Medieval World,** Meridian Books, New York, 1960, Chapter 43.
  46. Sanhedrin 17b.
  47. Shabbat 102.
  48. Shabbat 25.

Excerpt From

THE URBAN CONDITION

POPE PAUL VI

There is a wide diversity among the situations in which Christians—willingly or unwillingly—find themselves according to regions, socio-political systems and cultures. In some places they are reduced to silence, regarded with suspicion and as it were kept on the fringe of society, enclosed without freedom in a totalitarian system. In other places they are a weak minority whose voice makes itself heard with difficulty. In some other nations, where the Church sees her place recognized, sometimes officially so, she too finds herself subjected to the repercussions of the crisis which is unsettling society; some of her members are tempted by radical and violent solutions from which they believe that they can expect a happier outcome. While some people, unaware of present injustices, strive to prolong the existing situation, others allow themselves to be beguiled by revolutionary ideologies which promise them, not without delusion, a definitely better world.

In the face of such widely varying situations it is difficult for us to utter a unified message and to put forward a solution which has universal validity. Such is not our ambition, nor is it our mission. It is up to the Christian communities to analyze with objectivity the situation on which is proper to their own country, to shed on it the light of the Gospel's unalterable words and to draw principles of reflection, norms of judgment and directives for action from the social teaching of the Church. It is up to these Christian communities, with the help of the Holy Spirit, in communion with the bishops who hold responsibility and in dialogue with other Christian brethren and all men of good will, to discern the options and commitments which are called for in order to bring about the social, political and economic changes seen in many cases to be urgently needed.

Urbanization

A major phenomenon draws our attention, as much in the industrialized countries as in those which are developing: urbanization.

After long centuries, agrarian civilization is weakening. Is sufficient attention being devoted to the arrangement and improvement of the life of the country people, whose inferior and at times miserable economic situation provokes the flight to the unhappy crowded conditions of the city outskirts, where neither employment nor housing awaits them?

This unceasing flight from the land, industrial growth, continual demographic expansion and the attraction of urban centers bring about concentrations of population, the extent of which is difficult to imagine, for people are already speaking in terms of a "megalopolis" grouping together tens of millions of persons. Of course there exist medium-sized towns, the dimension of which ensures a better balance in the population. While being able to offer employment to those that progress in agriculture makes available, they permit an adjustment of the human environment which better avoids the proletarianism and crowding of the great built-up areas.

The inordinate growth of these centers accompanies industrial expansion, without being identified with it. Based on technological research and the transformation of nature, industrialization constantly goes forward, giving proof of incessant creativity. While certain enterprises develop and are concentrated, others die or change their location. Thus new social problems are created: professional or regional unemployment, redeployment and mobility of persons, permanent adaptation of workers and disparity of conditions in the different branches of industry. Unlimited competition utilizing the modern means of publicity incessantly launches new products and tries to attract the consumer, while earlier industrial installations which are still capable of functioning become useless. While very large areas of the population are unable to satisfy their primary needs, superfluous needs are ingeniously created. It can thus rightly be asked if, in spite of all his conquests, man is not turning back against himself the results of his activity. Having rationally endeavored to control nature, is he not now becoming the slave of the objects which he makes?

Christians in the City

Is not the rise of an urban civilization which accompanies the advance of industrial civilization a true challenge to the wisdom of man, to his capacity for organization and to his farseeing imagination? Within industrial society urbanization upsets both the ways of life and the habitual structures of existence; the family, the neighborhood, and the very framework of the Christian community. Man is experiencing a new loneliness; it is not in the face of a hostile nature which it has taken him centuries to subdue, but in an anonymous crowd which surrounds him and in which he feels himself a stranger. Urbanization, undoubtedly an irreversible stage in the development of human societies, confronts man with difficult problems. How is he to master its growth, regulate its organization, and successfully accomplish its animation for the good of all?

In this disordered growth, new proletariats are born. They install themselves in the heart of the cities sometimes abandoned by the rich; they dwell on the outskirts—which become a belt of misery besieging in a still silent protest the luxury which blatantly cries out from centers of consumption and waste. Instead of favoring fraternal encounter and mutual aid, the city fosters discrimination and also indifference. It lends itself to new forms of exploitation and of domination whereby some people in speculating of the needs of others derive inadmissible profits. Behind the facades, much misery is hidden, unsuspected even by the closest neighbors; other forms of misery spread where human dignity founders: delinquency, criminality, abuse of drugs and eroticism.

It is in fact the weakest who are the victims of dehumanizing living conditions, degrading for conscience and harmful for the family institution. The promiscuity of working people's housing makes a minimum of intimacy impossible; young couples waiting in vain for a decent dwelling at a price they can afford are demoralized and their union can thereby even be endangered; youth escape from a home which is too confined and seek in the streets compensation and companionships which cannot be supervised. It is the grave duty of those responsible to strive to control this process and to give it direction.

There is an urgent need to make at the level of the street, of the neighborhood or of the great agglomerative dwellings the social fabric whereby man may be able to develop the needs of his personality. Centers of special interest and of culture must be created or developed at the community and parish levels with different forms of associations, recreational centers, and spiritual community gatherings where individuals can escape from isolation and form anew fraternal relationships.

To build up the city, the place where men and their expanded communities exist, to create new modes of neighborliness and relationships, to perceive an original application of social justice and to undertake responsibility for this collective future, which is foreseen as difficult, is a task in which Christians must share. To those who are heaped up in an urban promiscuity which becomes intolerable it is necessary to bring a message of hope. This can be done by brotherhood which is lived and by concrete justice. Let Christians, conscious of this new responsibility, not lose heart in view of the vast and faceless society; let them recall Jonah who traversed Nineveh, the great city, to proclaim therein the good news of God's mercy and was upheld in his weakness by the sole strength of the word of Almighty God. In the Bible, the city is in fact often the place of sin and pride—pride of man who feels secure enough to be able to build his life without God and even to affirm that he is powerful against God. But there is also the example of Jerusalem, the Holy City, the place where God is encountered, the promise of the city which comes from on high.

Youth

Urban life and industrial change bring strongly to light questions which until now were poorly grasped. What place, for example, in this world being brought to birth, should be given to youth? Everywhere dialogue is proving to be difficult between youth, with its aspirations, renewal and also insecurity for the future, and the adult generations. It is obvious to all that here we have a source of serious conflicts, division and opting out, even within the family; and a questioning of modes of authority, education for freedom and the handing on of values and beliefs, which strikes at the deep roots of society.

The Role of Women

Similarly, in many countries a charter for women which would put an end to an actual discrimination and would establish relationships of equality in rights and of respect for their dignity is the object of study and at times of lively demands. We do not have in mind that false equality which would deny the distinctions laid down by the Creator himself and which would be in contradiction with woman's proper role, which is of such capital importance, at the heart of the family as well as within society. Developments in legislation should on the contrary be directed to protecting her proper vocation and at the same time recognizing her independence as a person, and her equal rights to participate in cultural, economic, and social and political life.

Workers

As the Church solemnly reaffirmed in the recent Council, "the beginning, the subject and the goal of all social institutions is and must be the human person." Every man has the right to work, a chance to develop his qualities and his personality in the exercise of his profession, to equitable remuneration which will enable him and his family "to lead a worthy life on the material, social, cultural and spiritual level" and to assistance in case of need arising from sickness or age.

Although for the defense of these rights democratic societies accept today the principle of labor union rights, they are not always open to their exercise. The important role of union organizations must be admitted: their object is the representation of the various categories of workers, their lawful collaboration in the economic advance of society, and the development of the sense of their responsibility for the realization of the common good. Their activity, however, is not without its difficulties. Here and there the temptation can arise of profiting from a position of force to impose, particularly by strikes—the right to which as a final means of defence remains certainly recognized—conditions which are too burdensome for the overall economy and for the social body, or to desire to obtain in this way demands of a directly political nature. When it is a question of public services, required for the life of an entire nation, it is necessary to be able to assess the limit beyond which the harm caused to society becomes inadmissible.

Victims of Change

In short, progress has already been made in introducing, in the area of human relationships, greater justice and greater sharing of responsibilities. But in this immense field much remains to be done. Further, reflection, research and experimentation must be actively pursued, unless one is to be late in meeting the legitimate aspirations of the workers —aspirations which are being increasingly asserted according as their education, their consciousness which are being increasingly asserted as their education, their consciousness of their dignity and the strength of their dignity and the strength of their organizations increase.

Egoism and domination are permanent temptations for men. Likewise an ever finer discernment is needed, in order to strike at the roots of newly arising situations of injustice and to establish progressively a justice which will be less and less imperfect. In industrial change, which demands speedy and constant adaptation, those who will find themselves injured will be more numerous and at a greater disadvantage from the point of view of making their voices heard. The Church directs her attention to these new "poor"—the handicapped and the maladjusted, the old, different groups of those on the fringe of society, and so on—in order to recognize them, help them, defend their place and dignity in a society hardened by competition and the attraction of success.

THE JEW AND THE CITY

The father had taken his son for a drive. "There's where I was born, son." The boy saw a dilapidated house with swarms of colored children playing on the broken front steps. "Over there is the synagogue I used to go to with my grandfather." The boy saw a large dirty building over which had been placed a crude sign—"WAREHOUSE." "That's the Jewish center where I learned how to play basketball." The boy saw a ramshackle building with a cross attached to the roof and as they passed by heard the lusty sounds of a church choir.

The scene is not unique. It has been reenacted by almost every Jewish father and child in every large city in America. It is a sign of change in a changing scene. It is a manifestation, one among many, of the exploding, expanding, and excluding metropolis. It offers a motivation, one among many, which propels Jews to express concern for the city in which they live.

The Jewish Community

American Jews are predominantly city dwellers. Approximately one-half of America's five to six million Jews (an exact census has never been taken) live in the New York City metropolitan area and the overwhelming majority of the remainder reside in other major metropolitan areas. Within each city Jews tend to live in neighborhoods which have heavy concentrations of fellow Jews.

Every Jewish community develops numerous institutions and organizations. For the purpose of this discussion our chief concern is with those institutions which have physical facilities—the synagogues, the schools, the community centers, the hospitals, and the old age homes. These are the primary institutions in the Jewish community. They are symbols of the highest Jewish spiritual, cultural, and moral values and represent the fruits of years of community planning, organization and financial investment. When originally built these institutions are erected in well-established Jewish areas, but as neighborhoods change and Jews leave places of earlier residence, they are confronted with serious problems. The hospitals and old age homes, because of the nature of the service they provide, tend to be more stable. They can still cater to a Jewish clientele, even if no Jews reside in the immediate vicinity, though in the case of hospitals, location in a non-Jewish area necessarily involves serving a higher proportion of non-Jews and a correspondingly smaller proportion of Jews. However, the cultural and religious institutions can perpetuate their programs only if they are readily accessible to those who participate on a regular basis throughout the entire year. Is there a Jewish institution in America which in the last fifteen years has not undergone the agonizing reappraisal of determining whether "to stay or to leave"? If so, it is a rare and extremely privileged institution. Most Jewish communities have witnessed the tragic abandonment of buildings and programs which had not yet even reached their maturation.

The changing neighborhood affects not only institutions, but people as well. One of the by-products is prejudice, both in communities which Jews vacate and in communities which Jews enter. In many instances the Negro "invasion" takes place in a predominantly Jewish neighborhood. There are many reasons for this: the Jewish neighborhood itself is usually a result of an earlier Jewish "invasion" into an area which was already in process of deteriorating, and therefore is vulnerable to further decline; Jews tend to be more liberal in acceptance of Negro neighbors; Jews may object to the newcomers, but they will not initiate or condone violence against another minority. Unfortunately, by the very nature of the transition, many of the dwellings and businesses remain in the possession of the original inhabitants. The Negroes who are being exploited manifest their antagonisms against the landlords and shopowners, many of whom are Jews. Responsible Negro leaders, who are cognizant of the courageous stands by Jews in behalf of Negro rights and the benevolent acts of Jews in behalf of Negro education and security, are now expressing uneasiness lest the excellent relations between Jews and Negroes be dissipated by a rising anti-Semitism.

On the other hand, as Jews integrate more into the community at large, they assimilate some of the prejudices against the Negro. They fail to recognize that the Negro has developed a social consciousness, a capacity to organize his fight for civil rights by utilizing his vote and his purchasing power. The new status of Negroes frequently places them in competition with whites and the white competitor is as often as not the Jew. The ramifications of these new relationships require judicious study and discussion by both Negro and Jew, who have so often been united by common cause and common fate.

The Jewish influx into newer areas becomes the occasion for expression of prejudice by non-Jews. There are still some exclusive sections into which Jews cannot move, despite the decisions of the Supreme Court and lower courts. The handicaps of the Jew are minor indeed in comparison with the Negro, but they are sufficiently serious to warrant attention. Social discrimination, or the "five-o'clock shadow," affects not only the Jew's right to freedom of residence but also deprives the Jew of contacts necessary to advancement in the business and professional world.

The movement of the Jewish community to suburbia has consequences for the community as a whole. A city like Cleveland is "Judenrein," most of the Jews having fled to the suburban heights. What will happen to our central cities without the liberalizing, stabilizing, cultivating element of large Jewish populations? In most large cities Catholics already constitute preponderant majorities, while Protestants and Jews represent progressively weaker minorities. What will this mean in terms of interfaith and interracial relationships, church-state issues, and public education?

And what happens to Jewish values when Jews live in homogeneous self-ghettoized suburbs arranged according to social status and income? Already one can detect a diminution of the traditional Jewish passion for social justice, as Jews align and identify themselves with the top-dog rather than the underdog. Already one can sense that the distinctiveness and purposefulness of Jewish life are being submerged in the contemporary yearning for conformity and respectability. What happens to the Jewish concept of community, as countless organizations and synagogues scramble for membership and prestige in undignified, destructive, purposeless competition? What happens to the concept of democracy, when self-segregation raises barriers between Jews and their neighbors, depriving Jews of the contacts so necessary to integration and full participation in American life?

The Synagogue

The crisis of the city has taken its toll of the basic institution in Jewish life—the synagogue. Every congregation in the country has felt the impact of the changing scene. The extent of the impact is reflected in the fact that some of the older, well-established congregations have moved as many as five or six times, following their constituents in each stage of the journey from the core of the city outward. Few of these congregations remain in their original locations.

The restless mobility of the Jewish community adversely affects the internal character and program of the individual synagogue. The necessity of relocating or expanding facilities imposes tremendous financial obligations on the membership, with the consequences that more time, effort and money are invested in the property than in the program of the congregation. The sisterhood, men's club, and other auxiliary groups tend to assume fund-raising as their primary function. What rabbi has not complained that his congregants are so worn out from attending fund-raising and building committee meetings that they have neither the interest nor the energy to particiate in the worship and educational programs?

In order to keep pace with expanding buildings and budgets, congregations must attract more members. In large metropolitan centers like New York, Chicago and Los Angeles, the average congregation will have a ten to fifteen per cent turnover of membership every year. The mobility of population reflects a certain restlessness which is not conducive to developing loyalty to a specific congregation or a specific community. Both lay and spiritual leadership devote an inordinate amount of time to membership problems. One rabbi recently said, "It seems that I spend half my time trying to get members and the other half trying to keep them."

Constantly changing membership affects the congregation's capacity to integrate its members adequately into the lifestream of the synagogue. Protestant studies of city churches indicate that, whereas one-half of the membership of the average church joined within the last ten years, only one-fourth of the congregation's leadership comes from the newer members. Though no studies have been made of synagogues, the general impression is that a high percentage of the leadership comes from a small core of "ole-timers." The inequitable distribution of leadership responsibilities is a manifestation of serious integration problems which militate against the congregation's ability to serve the needs of all its members.

The proliferation of synagogues in suburban areas sometimes result in the establishment of ineffective congregations which will never be able to service their memberships properly. Instead of joining existing congregations, some groups organize with insufficient present or potential membership, with inadequate and inexperienced leadership and with low standards. In such cases, it is improbable that the congregation will ever be able to engage the professional staff or to offer the spiritual and educational program which Jews need in order to preserve their heritage.

All the problems referred to above interact on each other and produce a vicious circle. One of the means of dealing with these problems would be for the Jewish community to establish an over-all plan comparable to the community plans of metropolitan church groups. The plan would provide for the orderly expansion and development of all Jewish institutions and would be based on procedures accepted by the various religious movements and communal agencies. Given the present competitive state of the Jewish community, there is little likelihood of gaining the cooperation of all who should be concerned. The Union of American Hebrew Congregations should certainly consider such a plan within the Reform movement. However, even assuming its feasibility and workability, a synagogue comity plan would be ineffective, unless it were inextricably related to the broader and more basic problems of the city itself. In the final analysis, the fate of the synagogue will be determined by the fate of the community at large. The synagogue must therefore "seek the welfare" of the city.

How the Synagogue Can "Seek the Welfare" of The City

The import of this chapter may be expressed by paraphrasing a popular aphorism—*A synagogue is judged by the community it keeps.* What can the synagogue do? How can the synagogue "seek the welfare" of its community? Listed below are "Ten Commandments" which the synagogue, as an entity, or working through its Social Action Committee, can observe:

1. *Know and study the processes of planning and urban renewal.* City Planning Commissions and specialized citizen groups are devoting full-time efforts to urban renewal. They are anxious for the public to know what they are doing and will be eager to assist the synagogue in studying the problems of and the plans for the city. The Federal government and national organizations will also be most cooperative.

2. *Stimulate the formation of neighborhood citizen groups.* Representative citizen groups are essential in stimulating interest and in organizing the framework within which a community can help itself. If such

a group does not already exist, the synagogue can be instrumental in forming one. Every community contains many organizations whose purposes are in consonance with such a program.

3. *Participate responsibly in community groups.* The community requires the active and dedicated participation of its constituents. Some neighborhood associations assume purposes contrary to those contained in their constitutions and publicity releases. Some become a tool for prejudice and discrimination. The synagogue as the moral voice of the Jewish community must make its presence felt.

4. *Create a climate of opinion in the synagogue.* The apathy of congregants is the most difficult stumbling block. The synagogue must educate its own members and make them aware of the magnitude of the problem. It must undertake an intensive program to eliminate fears, misconceptions and prejudices. Individual members should be encouraged to serve on committees and organizations concerned with the problems.

5. *Create a climate of opinion in the community.* The synagogue as a vital community force should encourage cooperation between the various religious and cultural institutions. The synagogue can organize community-wide educational efforts to sensitize citizens and to lend moral support to public issues.

6. *Work for equal opportunity.* The synagogue should take stands in support of equal access to housing for all citizens. The stand must not always be in the form of a public resolution. Quiet pressure applied in the proper manner and at the proper place may have the desired effect. The synagogue need not stand alone. In every community there are groups which will help assume leadership.

7. *Support legislation.* All aspects of housing require legislative action at all levels of government—national, state, and local. The subject of legislation ranges from equal opportunity to housing codes and zoning ordinances. The synagogue should help to assure passage of appropriate legislation—sending letters and telegrams, contacting legislators, passing resolutions, and working with other community agencies.

8. *Maintain the property of the synagogue.* The synagogue should never forget that it is a key property owner in the community. The way it maintains its property will affect the attitudes of other institutions and of individual families.

9. *Encourage enforcement of housing codes and maintenance of*

property. Some churches have performed valiantly in this area by bringing pressure to bear on congregants, businessmen, police and government officials. They have engendered a pride in the commuity and a subsequent stabilization and upgrading of the neighborhood.

10. *Initiate and Pioneer.* The synagogue is the repository of values and traditions which are unique to Judaism—emphasis on education, purity and integrity of family life, respect for the aged. There is every reason to believe that the synagogue, motivated by the Jewish sense of justice and compassion, can initiate and pioneer in the development of new perspectives, new forms and new solutions. The synagogue can apply Judaism by applying itself to the problems.

The Task of the Synagogue—In Perspective

It is good for religious institutions to realize that they have a stake in the improvement of their communities. It is good for synagogues to participate in efforts to renew our cities. But Jews must be motivated by more than vested interests. Our actions must be in response to religious imperatives.

Many Americans cannot see why religion should concern itself with some of the problems herein discussed. They believe in morality, but confine its dimensions to personal relationships. They cannot comprehend the responsibility of the individual for society as a whole, nor the reciprocal responsibility of society for the individual. They fail to recognize the mutual dependence of human beings and their environment, and in so doing establish artificial dichotomies between the spiritual and the physical.

Here is where Judaism makes a vital contribution to America. Greek and oriental systems of thought draw sharp distinctions between the physical and the spiritual, portraying the body as evil and the soul as good. This world is the world of the body and is therefore only ephemeral. The real world is the world of the soul which a being enters only after death. In contrast to most religions, Judaism has always held that the physical and spiritual aspects of life are inseparable, and as the Midrash relates, body and soul are equally responsible for both good and evil. The fundamental emphasis of Judaism is on the events of this world. Man is not at the whim of circumstances beyond his control, as the Greeks depicted him. History is not a Major Bowes' wheel of fortune, "round and round she goes and where she stops, nobody knows." Judaism preaches that man has conrol of his fate and that history has a purpose.

The synagogue brings to the problems of the city the 3500-year-old perspective of Judaism. This is a perspective which does not permit society to isolate man's physical needs from his spiritual needs. Nor does Judaism permit us to salve our itchy consciences with the balm of worlds yet to come. The goal of mankind is the Messianic era, the attainment of a perfect society in this world. History teaches one fundamental lesson, the lesson originally learned in Egypt, but recounted again and again in man's struggle for perfection—the evil society inevitably perishes—God destroys the oppressor and redeems the enslaved. There is no such phenomenon as a Jewish hermit. No Jew can live apart from society. No Jew can "be at ease in Zion" so long as one human being is not at ease.

THE PERILOUS LINKS BETWEEN ECOLOGY AND POVERTY

NORMAN J. FARAMELLI

According to ecologists, we are threatened with extinction within fifty years if current pollution trends are allowed to continue. Despite some overstatements by a few "prophets of doom," an increasing number of reasonable people recognize that the ecological problem has reached a crisis state. All during 1970, leading magazines, newspapers, radio and T-V have announced that we are entering an "age of ecology." Although its popularity reached a zenith on Earth Day (April 22, 1970), ecology is still very much before the public. But despite the widespread rhetoric, the environmental problems are becoming more critical, as the summer smog along the East coast amply illustrated.

In theory, everyone wants a clean environment. But the real questions are: "How serious is the ecology problem in light of our other pressing needs?" and "who is going to pay for pollution control?" With regard to the latter, we must heed the cry of both the ecologist and the economist: Someone will pay for a clean environment. It is the belief of this writer that ecology is a profoundly serious matter, yet most of the solutions suggested for environmental quality will have, directly or indirectly, adverse effects on the poor and lower income groups. Hence, economic or distributive justice must become an active component in all ecology debates.

The Lord has entrusted man with the created order; he is to be a responsible steward of God's creation. Although the development of an environmental ethic is essential and long overdue, it should not overlook nor underpay the special role that man (particularly the poor and the oppressed) plays in the Judeo-Christian tradition. Now that an environmental ethic is being shaped, it is imperative that it be in harmony with concerns for economic justice.

As a prolegomenon to the central concerns of ecology and justice, we should first establish the seriousness of the so-called ecological crisis. For the problems of relating justice and ecology are real only if the environmental issues are truly significant. If environmental damage is not as bad as publicized, then we are suffering from grand delusions.

A Worsening Problem

One can recite a litany of woes concerning land, air, water and noise pollution:

Timber forests in the West are fast disappearing because we refuse to reuse paper. One of the wonders of creation, the Redwoods in California, is reducing in number. On the east Coast, the valuable salt marshes are being dredged and filled in by real estate and land developers, a move which is destroying some of our most productive land damaging chains of marine life. In Appalachia, strip mining has ravaged several states, and after the coal has been removed and the landscape destroyed, some states pass laws curbing strip mining. Add to these the cluttering of the countryside with billboards and junk. Each year in the U.S. we discard 26 billion bottles, 7 million automobiles, and 48 billion cans. It is no surprise that rubbish disposal is a mounting problem.

That same report noted that the U.S. emits 148 million tons of pollutants into the air each year, mostly from automobiles and power generators. The air pollution that used to be limited to central cities has now spread well beyond the suburbs. For example, the trees in the Sierra Nevada mountains, 100 miles from Los Angeles, are dying from air pollutants. The same holds true for other urban areas. Emphysema and other respiratory disorders are on the increase. Also, some studies have shown the links between air pollution and cancer growth.

Water pollution worsens each day. Lake Erie is undergoing a non-reversible biological decay, and many experts believe it might soon be a sewer. The Cuyahoga River in Cleveland, rich in contaminants, actually caught on fire, but it was not the first! In certain areas in the mid-West the "nitrogen run offs" from fertilizers are the principal causes of water pollution. The phosphates from detergents are creating magnificent algae blooms on our waterways which upset the ecological balance, and pesticides are poisoning our oceans. In addition, oil spills are polluting our oceans and beaches.

To this litany we can add the problems of noise pollution. Studies have shown that it influences arterial and neurological disorders. The noise near jet ports is already unbearable, yet the jets get bigger, faster and noisier.

If the items listed above represented the worse levels of pollution to which man will be subjected, we could all breath a sigh of relief. But conditions are getting worse, because current trends are being exacerbated. The effects of newly installed pollution control devices are more than offset by expanding the pollution base via increased production. For instance, Detroit has endowed us with 9 million new internal combustion engines per year and now anticipates that within ten years it will be manufacturing twelve to thirteen million automobiles per year. Power consumption is slated to double every ten years, which may lead to an enormous production of pollutants. Our President and others marvel at the U.S. Gross National Product, which will reach one trillion dollars in 1970 and will increase to one and five tenths trillion within ten years. If a substantial amount of this growth is in the material sector pollution will significantly increase. And, of course, all of these problems are made worse by rapid population increase. By the year 2000 the American population will increase from two hundred to three hundred million. Thus, one can see that the problems are serious, and necessitate a new ethic for the environment and a new look at our consumption of material resources.

The Two Revolutions

In the midst of the burgeoning interest for ecology, a few voices have warned that ecology is becoming a new cop-out, a way to refocus the enthusiasm of the young (especially college students) away from the war, urban problems, and poverty. One can rationalize that the young are frustrated over Vietnam, almost completely alienated from poverty and the ghettoes, so ecology buffs are now in vogue. In many ways, ecology is a logical successor to the middle-class concerns of conservation. But that explanation is too simplistic and misses entirely the seriousness of the ecological crisis.

The ecology rage must be understood in light of the two cultural, social, and political revolutions occurring in our society today. They can be termed the "pre-affluent" and "post-affluent" revolutions. The first is dominated by the poor and the black communties. Their primary focus is on social and economic justice as well as freedom and self-determination. The quest of the powerless and the alienated is primarily for human dignity and the restructuring of power relationships. Some in this revolution, however, want to move beyond "getting a fair piece of the pie" to new life styles where "soul" or spontaneity is an essential ingredient. But most want a redistribution of power—political, economic, and social. For the alienated youth in the "post-affluent" revolution, however, the emphasis is not on power, but on new life-styles. There is a flat rejection of the values of over-consumption, technical efficiency, and economic growth that has dominated American society. The ecology movement is closely linked with the "post-affluent" revolution. Only those who have been reared in affluent suburbs can rebel against over-consumption and the banality of materialism. It is no surprise that ecologists like Barry Commoner, Lamont Cole, Paul Ehrlich, and Eugene Odum receive their biggest ovations in jammed college auditoriums. The differences between the two movements were vividly expressed by a welfare rights organizer to a group of young ecology radicals. He said: "We will have some problems understanding one another for our welfare mothers want what you are rejecting."

Those who have been involved with urban and poverty problems have often distrusted the "ecology fad." On the other hand, most ecology enthusiasts, and especially the old-line conservationists who are becoming attuned to ecology, almost completely ignore the problems of the ghettoes and the poor. Ecology, for them, has more to do with saving a certain marine species than eradicating rats from infested ghetto apartments. To the ghetto resident, air pollution is clearly not at the top of his priority list. As one black community organizer in Chicago said recently: "The one thing I don't look forward to is living in a pollution-free, unjust and repressive society."

The anti-ecology sentiment among the poor, especially the blacks, is still prevalent. For example, one Black Panther leader in Roxbury said: "It is a sick society that can beat and murder black people on the streets, butcher thousands of children in Vietnam, spend billions in arms to destroy mankind, and then come to the conclusion that air pollution is America's number one problem."

Why do the poor distrust the ecology movement? First, a clean environment is not on their priority list, at least not in terms of air and water pollution. The poor are part of a different revolution; their focus is on justice. Also, the ecology groups have almost totally ignored the needs of the poor. Most of the images of environmental quality refer to improved life styles for suburban dwellers—cleaner air, more trees, better hiking, boating and swimming, etc. There is almost no emphasis on urban ecology.

Another reason the poor distust ecology is related to the priorities of the nation stated in President Nixon's 1970 State of the Union

Message. In a speech replete with many references to the environment, he said, "Restoring nature to its natural state is a cause beyond party and beyond factions." The President also noted that Americans have to make "some very hard decisions" on priorities, which meant "rejecting pending programs which would benefit some of the people when their net effect would result in price increases for all the people." In other words, urban spending, which benefits the white and black poor, is inflationary!

But will funds actually be diverted from poverty to ecology? As of now, the funds spent on either ecology or poverty are pitifully small. This year the federal government approved eight hundred million dollars for water pollution programs, although far more is needed. Expenditures on poverty are also grossly inadequate. To choose ecology instead of poverty, or vice versa, is to make a bad choice. We should not be asked to select between schools and homes for urban dwellers, on the one hand, and a clean environment on the other, while the ABM is expanded, the supersonic transport is developed, and Vietnam continues almost untouched by sanity. Despite the deceptive Defense Department cuts, new weapons systems are still top priority items on the national agenda and devour a substantial part of the federal budget. Today over sixty cents of every federal tax dollar is used to pay off past or current wars or to plan new ones. An apt metaphor to describe the competing concerns of ecology and poverty is two people arguing over the crumbs from a loaf of bread while others run away with the slices! From the standpoint of resources expended, the issue of "ecology as a cop-out on the poor" is largely academic since both ecology and poverty are being starved. Given the pittances that are now spent on ecology, the "war on pollution" proposed by the current administration will probably be as ineffective as the "war on poverty" was in dealing with the problems of the poor.

But let us suppose that ecology is taken seriously. Have we properly assessed the impact of the proposed remedies on low-income households? This is necessary from two standpoints: (a) someone has to pay for pollution control and the poor will be asked to pay disproportionately, and (b) some of the remedies proposed to halt pollution, such as curbing economic growth, will have severe repercussions on the poor.

Who Pays for Pollution Control?

The idea posed by Life magazine and others that "Ecology is

everybody's issue" is misleading. There is a widespread illusion that at last we have found a real national issue that is non-controversial, and thus, we act as if a clean environment can be obtained without cost. If, for example, the managers of a chemical or power plant install expensive pollution control equipment, they can do one of three things to cover expenditures: (1) raise the price of the product, (2) appeal for a government subsidy, or (3) reduce the corporate profits.

Capital expenditures in pollution control equipment is basically an investment in non-productive devices. Given our current accounting procedures, such a venture increases the cost of production. We have for years assumed that disposal of waste into the air or waterways is free! The ecological costs have seldom been calculated, let alone included in the costs of production. To do any of the three items will tend to slow down consumption and attack our cherished sacred cow—an increasing "standard of living." Raising the price of a product will surely reduce the amount that a family can buy. The price increase is tantamount to a sales tax—a regressive form of taxation that hurts the poor most severely when imposed on necessities. Each person will pay the same increased amount per item, but some can pay it easily and others cannot.

The federal subsidy also does not come free of charge because the taxpayer will ultimately pay it, even if by a progressive income tax. Any tax credits offered to industries for cleaner effluents are really another form of subsidy for pollution control. The third alternative—lowering the corporate profits—seems unlikely, given the power, prestige of, and lack of public controls over large corporations. If profits were somehow substantially reduced, however, industrial expansion would slow down. Of the three alternatives, the first seems to be the most likely. Yet increasing the price of the products will affect the poor most severely, unless we make special allowances or adopt new pricing mechanisms.

In order to have economic justice and ecological sanity we might have to revamp radically our pricing structure. For instance, we now pay less for additional units of electric power consumption, which means that the tenth electrical appliance is actually cheaper (per kilo-watt hour) to operate than the first. We are enticed into consuming increasing amounts of electric power that result in environmental contamination. In order to preserve a sound environment with economic justice, the basic units of power should be offered at the cheapest possible rates. Then a graduated price scale might be imposed on additional amounts so that the ninth appliance (a freezer?) will be more costly to operate than the first (a refrigerator?). The inversion of the rate structure would discourage profligate use of power.

Economic Growth and Environmental Destruction

But will not more technology solve the pollution problem? Our perennial faith in the "technical fix" to solve all of our pollution problems is being shattered. That notion naively assumes that no matter how badly the side effects of current technology destroy the environment, new technologies will appear that will fully ameliorate the damages. Just as the drug user becomes addicted to heroin, our society has become addicted to the technical fix. Technology, of course, can be useful in developing pollution control devices, but exclusive reliance on new technologies to extricate us from our follies has not and will not work repeatedly. We produce new problems faster than we solve old ones. In many instances initial steps that produced the pollution will have to be stopped. In fact, some times the technical fix creates problems that are more dangerous than the ones it tried to remedy. For example, the detergent used to free the ocean of the oil from the Torrey Canyon did more damage to marine life than the oil spilled!

There is a growing pool of data that shows that increased production will cause increased environmental contamination, even after the best pollution control devices are installed. Our current methods, for instance, extract raw materials from the earth and turn them into products that soon become obsolete. The disposal of these products often presents serious environmental problems. A classic case is that of bauxite ore which is extracted in Latin America and converted into billions of aluminum cans per year. Their disposal presents a fantastic problem since the cans do not decompose. Hence, many of our most secluded wildernesses are strewn with beer cans!

In order to conserve our natural resources a tax on extracting raw materials needs to be imposed as well as a tax on the disposal of the product. That is, the real cost of depleting natural resources and the cost of disposing of manufactured products should be included in the costs of production. Obviously, taxing the origin and the end of the production process would make recycling of products a more competitive operation. This would allow us to move to what the economist Kenneth Boulding has called, the "spaceship earth" society. Boulding believes that the U.S. is now wedded to a "cowboy" economy which knows no limits on natural resources and has no ecological constraints. A spaceship earth concept is one where the materials are recycled, just as occurs on space flights.

But a massive recycle industry cannot be developed without power consumption and environmental deterioration. Massive recycle industries would allow us to preserve natural resources and help solve the disposal problem, but the second law of thermodynamics cannot be reversed. Any power generating operation has some heat loss, and that is always a form of pollution! So increased recycling cannot be viewed as an unlimited process. Thus, some scientists are calling for a slowdown in economic growth.

Before proceeding, it should be first specified that not all economic growth results in pollution. Increased sales of pollution control equipment and gains in the "service" sector also increase the GNP. But growth in sectors that cause vast pollution should be restrained. Thus the issue is not growth or no growth, but what kind of growth.

Economic Growth and High Employment Levels

A cutback in material production, however, would have profound repercussions on the poor and lower income groups. Those who have doubts about this should observe the rising unemployment which is a result of our current attempt to "cool off" an inflationary economy. (Unemployment rates have already risen from 3.3% to over 5%.) Also, most industrialized nations finance their poverty programs via incremental economic growth or a growth dividend. More growth means more jobs for all (especially the poor and lower middle income groups) and more public funds available to finance welfare programs (i.e., without further tax increases.) We are addicted to the "trickle down theory," i.e., everyone must receive more if the poor are to receive more. That this theory has not been fully effective in ending poverty is irrelevant; it has worked in part. The poor may not have been helped appreciably by economic growth, but they certainly will suffer acutely if the growth rate declines. This paradox, which can lead to a host of questions about the structural injustices in our economic system, cannot be pursued at this juncture.

These effects on the poor and lower middle income families are most severe in an automated society. For years there has been a stalemate in the debate: "Does automation produce or reduce jobs?". The experts have argued on both sides of the issue. But from the maze of data some clear trends are discernible. During the Eisenhower years when economic growth was slow, unemployment rates soared (3% in 1953 to 5% in 1960). From 1962-68 (a period of economic growth) the unemployment rates dropped from 5.6% in 1962 to 3.5% in 1968. Such statistics led the "pro-automation" experts to say: "See! Automation produces more jobs, as long as economic growth is sustained." But if the ecological problems are as serious as many believe, then that provisional clause "as long as economic growth is sustained" radically alters the debate. For automation always increases productivity (i.e., units produced per man hour). If automation did not, it would be senseless to add new machinery. With a stagnant growth rate and increasing productivity, the logical result must be higher levels of unemployment as well as a shorter work week.

As our society becomes more industrialized, there is a shift from the "goods" to the "service" sector. As productivity increases (due to automation), more jobs will be available in the service sector. However, reliance on the service sector to take up all of the economic slack is another myth. With a slow industrial growth rate, the entire economy will slow down. Hence, the problems of unemployment that will result from the slowing down of economic growth, the necessity of an adequate guaranteed annual income for all, and the need for a redistribution of national income, must be included in all serious ecology debates.

The challenges should be clear to us. Although environmental problems are becoming critical, they must be interpreted in light of other problems and priorities. If the cost of pollution control is passed directly on to the consumer on all items, low-income families will be be affected disproportionately. If new technologies cannot solve the environmental crisis and a slowdown in material production is demanded, the low income families will again bear the brunt of it, as more and more of them will join the ranks of the unemployed. In the first instance, new pricing schemes are necessary in order to have ecological sanity and economic justice. In the latter case, we must either radically revamp our schemes for the distribution of national wealth and income or use ecology as a club over the heads of the poor and lower-middle income families. There are no other alternatives unless one decides that ecology is not a real problem. The mounting scientific evidence, however, stands as a staunch testimony against those who claim that ecology is a "faddish" and "overrated issue."

Global Ecology and Economic Justice: The Challenge to Social Ethics

The ethical implications of the above discussion are obvious—man must be a steward of God's creation at the same time he works for social and economic justice for all. We can sacrifice neither the God of Genesis nor the God of the prophets. We should realize, therefore, that the problems from the outset are not just national but global. As a result ecology and distributive justice have to be considered in an international context. Unfortunately, the wider global aspects of economic development of poor nations, the gap between the rich and poor nations, the ecological problems associated with full world-wide industrialization, cannot be explored in detail here.

One point, however, should be touched upon, i.e., disproportionate consumption of the earth's resources by Americans. The U.S., with 6% of the world's population, now uses roughly 40-60% of the non-renewable resources utilized each year. In order to sustain our increasing "standard of living," by 1980, with around 5% of the world's population, the U.S. will need roughly 55-70% of the non-renewable resources used each year. Can economic justice be a global reality if this trend continues? Is development of the third world precluded by our need for their raw materials? After all, non-renewable resources are finite, and took billions of years of evolution to reach their current state, and hence should be used sparingly and justly.

Therefore, the current American styles should be challenged. Concern for economic justice should lead an affluent American to say: "We must consume less, enjoy it more, and share our abundance with others at home and abroad." To some, that might sound naive, soft-headed, unrealistic and unpragmatic. Despite name calling, it may point to a central and essential ecological fact which is consonant with our theological and ethical heritage. In order to attain economic justice the gap between the rich and the poor should be closed. With modern technology skills, managerial skills and capital resources largely concentrated in the hands of industrialized nations, the rich-poor gap is widening. For example, from 1967 to 1969 the per capita income in the U.S. rose from $3,270. to $3,800., an increase of $530. Even discounting for inflation, that increase was about twice that of the entire annual per capita income in Guatemala which stagnated around $250. Some African and Asian nations are even poorer.

Many believe that it was the Judeo-Christian mandate that "man should have dominion" (Gen 1:26) over nature which led to the ecological crisis. Thus, a reformulation of a theology and ethic of nature is necessary. But this should not be done divorced from the notions of distributive justice especially in the economic realm. And the above statistics clearly point out the need.

A responsible environmental ethic would recognize man's finitude and his place in the cosmos. He has been selected to be a custodian of God's creation and to transform the natural order of human welfare. But he must appreciate the limits of technical transformation. The side-effects of all of his actions must be carefully calculated and appropriate plans made to offset their negative effects. He must further understand that even the positive aspects of his technical transformation affect various people differently. The costs and the benefits of each technical modification are not shared equally, so the question of who pays the costs and who receives the benefits is essential. A new environmental ethic would attempt to distribute the costs and benefits justly.

In order to manifest our ethical concerns, four things should be done simultaneously:

(1) We should direct citizens to see the root causes of the ecological crisis. The nation must move beyond the anti-pollution fad and deal with causes not symptoms. The myth that equates material prosperity with the "good life" has to be challenged.

(2) We should expose and oppose those who would use the current momentum of the ecology movement as the issue of the "silent majority," divorced from the needs of the poor. Rats, congested and dilapidated living spaces, and a repressive atmosphere are part of urban ecology. The rat infested apartment should not receive less ecological emphasis than bird sanctuaries!

(3) We should thoroughly investigate the allocation of the costs of pollution control. Often those who receive most of the benefits pay only a small portion of the costs, and vice versa. Passing the cost to the consumer might affect the poor unfairly.

(4) We should insure that the consequences of altering the economic growth rate become an integral part of all ecology discussions. A new distribution of income and wealth must be reckoned with.

Yet we should move beyond the immediate American situation to visions of global ecology. America offers false hopes to many poor nations that they, too, can imitate the American model of development. That model may be extremely difficult to reproduce and suicidal if it is reproduced. For instance, if the current global population (3 billion) consumed at current American levels the carbon dioxide and carbon monoxide levels would increase by a factor of 250 and sulfur dioxide by a factor of 200. The image of 7 billion people in 2000 consuming at even higher than American levels is horrendous even with extensive pollution control and recycling industries. There are limits to technology. Presently, America's over-consumption and over-pollution are made possible and sustained because of global injustice.

Can economic justice become a global reality as long as Americans are enamoured with an ever increasing "standard of living"? But if the entire world population were able to reach the consumption level of all Americans, would there be enough natural resources to sustain them? Would the resulting global pollution destroy the planetary life support systems? The answers to these questions depend on much scientific and technical data. But science and technology alone cannot provide the entire answer. Fundamentally, these are questions of human value and the human spirit. For example, the identity of increased "Standard of living" with psychic well-being and the "good life," so firmly established in the U.S. and industrialized nations, poses a spiritual as well as an economic problem. Theological and ethical reflection must link together ecology and distributive justice and move beyond national to global concerns.

In summary, we can say that the ecological crisis is grave, far more serious than the current publicity indicates. Much of the current debate still focuses on symptoms, not causes. There is still rampant the pious hope that new technologies will save us from the foibles and over-application of old technologies. New and more radical solutions are necessary. But the consequences of the solutions on all segments of society and the structural changes needed to offset the consequences must be dealt with. If economic justice for all is not an essential part of the debate, the ecology issue, despite its importance, will inadvertently be used as a club over the head of the poor and lower-middle income groups, which includes most of black America.

AN ECOLOGICAL ETHIC

IAN G. BARBOUR

The American Public is becoming aware of the devastation of our natural environment. We are poisoning our air and water with chemicals, fumes, sewage, detergents, pesticides, noise and heat. We dump 28 billion bottles and 48 billion cans each year. We have poured industrial wastes into Lake Erie until it can support no life except sludge worms and a mutant of carp which lives off the poisons. Such facts are widely known.

But I submit that this ecological concern will be short-lived and ineffectual unless it deals with the attitudes and values which have led to environmental deterioration. The basic disease is man's exploitative spirit which has prompted him to plunder the earth. If we treat a succession of symptoms—seeking technical remedies for one form of pollution after another—the task will be endless. Unless the disease is cured, it will simply break out in new forms as men find new ways to violate the web of life. The ecological crisis is a result of our attitudes toward nature on the one hand, and our attitude toward technology, on the other

Attitudes Toward Nature

Attitudes toward nature in Western civilization have been influenced historically by the doctrine of creation, which expressed the conviction that the world is orderly, dependable and intelligible. Biblical religion differed from most other ancient religions in holding that the world is neither divine nor demonic. If nature is created by God it is essentially good rather than evil or illusory. Judaism and early Christianity endorsed affirmative attitudes toward the world. If nature is orderly and good, man is free to understand and use it.

But the creation story also talks of man's dominion over the earth. One passage tells man to "be fruitful and multiply, fill the earth and subdue it, and have dominion over the fish of the sea and over the birds of the air and over every living thing." Psalm 8 says: "Thou hast given him dominion over the works of thy hands; thou hast put all things under his feet." Here is one of the roots of man's subjugation of nature. Man is portrayed over against nature rather than as an integral part of it. From such a passage one might almost conclude that nature exists only for man's use. A one-sided emphasis on this theme of dominion has contributed to Western man's exploitative attitude toward nature.

In the present ecological crisis, we could learn much from Eastern religions concerning respect for nature. Taoism, for example, has a sense of man's harmony and unity with nature. Buddhism encourages reverence for all living creatures and appreciation of the beauty of the natural world. But in the American context, I suspect, instead of turning to the East we might better examine the resources for new attitudes in our own culture. Moreover, if our religious tradition has a share of the blame for the crisis, it has a special responsibility for encouraging new attitudes.

Some of the needed correctives can be found by recovering biblical themes which have been neglected. The creation story, for example, speaks not only of dominion but also of responsibility, stewardship, and respect for nature. In the Old Testament, the land belongs ultimately to God ("The earth is the Lord's and the fullness thereof"); man is only the trustee. The created order is valued in itself, not simply as an instrument for man's purposes. The Sabbath is a day of rest for nature as well as for man; every seventh year, the sabbatical year, the fields are to lie fallow. Job was finally overwhelmed by the majesty and wonder of nature. Jesus considered the lilies of the field. God notices the sparrow's fall—even if the culprit is DDT. Think of St. Francis' deep love of the natural world, his sense of the dignity and equality of all creatures, his response to what he called his sister the earth—not mother earth, as in many ancient religions, and not earth as an object to be exploited, but sister earth.

Some of these themes can be recovered. But there are in recent religious thought several trends whose convergence might carry us considerably further toward an ecological theology which would support an ecological ethic. Let me mention three:

(1) A Theology of Nature. In orthodox and neoorthodox Christianity, nature is the unredeemed setting for man's redemption. In existentialism, nature is the impersonal stage for the drama of personal existence. But in process thought, nature is a single creative drama in which both God and man participate. In Whitehead and his Protestant

followers or Teilhard and his Catholic followers, there is an emphasis on the organic interdependence of all creatures. These philosophers speak of a continuing creation, portray an incomplete world still coming into being, emphasize divine immanence in an ongoing cosmic process. There are also scientists like Loren Eiseley, who confesses a sense of awe and reverent wonder as he confronts the mystery and beauty of living beings linked together across the immensities of time and space.

(2) Man's Unity with Nature. In place of the orthodox separation of man and nature and the existentialist retreat to inwardness, a new awareness is developing of man's interdependence with the whole web of life. This is, of course, partly a lesson learned from biology. The same four bases make up the DNA of all living things. Our genetic line goes back unbroken to the earliest organisms. We are, so to speak, thousandth cousins of an amoeba. We are kin to all creatures, sharing a common history, participating in a long and slow creative process. Man threatens to destroy in a few decades a fabric of life which has taken five billion years to come into being.

(3) Responsible Involvement in the World. Many recent writers have attacked the false dichotomy which sets the "secular" over against the "sacred." They insist that secular existence is precisely the sphere of our religious responsibility, that we are called to involvement in the world, even to celebration of the world, not to otherworldly renunciation. Now the theologians who have advocated a Christian secularity —Bonhoeffer, for example, or, in his own way, Harvey Cox—have been thinking mainly about involvement in the social order. But their idea must be extended to an ethic of responsibility for the whole interconnected order of which we are a part. We are called to responsibility in the community of life.

These three themes—a theology of nature, man's unity with nature, responsible involvement in this world—can be the basis of an ecological theology and an ecological ethic. They can help us recover a respect for the value of all living things, a sense of wonder and reverence for life. They can encourage loyalty to the wider community of life, so that we may learn to live with nature not as its master but as participants in it.

The Technological Mentality

Let me consider attitudes toward technology. Some students have opposed the environmental movement because they thought it would divert attention away from the urban ghetto. I would reply that pollution and urban blight are linked together as products of a technological society which is thing-oriented rather than person or life-oriented.

One symptom of this technological mentality is the frantic pursuit of comfort. Ours is an acquisitive society which awakens false desires through the deliberate creation of new cravings. A barrage of advertising stimulates our appetites as consumers, and engenders an insatiable drive toward greater and greater affluence. It promotes wasteful consumption and the production of luxury goods while basic needs around the world remain unmet. The U.S., with six per cent of the world's population, accounts for over half the world's annual consumption of raw materials. One American uses up resources faster than a hundred or more citizens of India. It would be simply impossible for the whole world to exploit its resources at the U.S. rate.

The technological mentality is also evident in our Vietnam policy. We have tried to use military technology to solve problems which are essentially social and political. When our policies did not succeed, we threw in more and more fire power; in one brief operation—the defense of the marine base at Khe Sahn—we used more tons of bombs than on Japan in the whole of World War II. A colonel's comment after a mission in the central highlands—"We had to destroy the town in order to liberate it"—describes the tragedy of Vietnam; we have wreaked ecological havoc on that tortured country. An estimated twenty per cent has been defoliated, and many areas will not recover for twenty-five years or more. We have been blind to the human consequences of the power we wield.

Another result of the technological mentality is the impoverishment of experience, the loss of man's imaginative and emotional life and the sensibilities expressed in poetry and art. Technological man is alienated from nature, treating it as an object to be used and manipulated. The calculating attitude of control and mastery militates also against the openness and receptivity which interpersonal relationships require. The I-Thou relation, as Buber calls it, requires availability, responsiveness, mutuality and personal involvement, in contrast to the I-It pattern of manipulation and detachment. The danger is that technological attitudes, which are necessary and valuable in their own domain, will so dominate life that important areas of human experience are jeopardized. The assumption that technological reason is omnicompetent leads to the truncation of man's capacity for response.

Biblical religion, I suggest, does witness to dimensions of human experience, which are not accessible to technical reason. It can uphold the dignity and value of the person against all attempts to manipulate or control him, and can defend individuality in a machine-dominated society. It can present a model of man as responsible self within a community of life, rather than as consumer or technician. It can cultivate and intensify human experience, richness of imagination and awareness of the sacred. It can provide a perspective for criticism of cultural values and reflection on the ends of human existence, a vision of a society in which technological progress is subordinated to man's true well-being. What is required here is a basic shift from thing-oriented culture to one which is person-oriented and, beyond that, life-oriented. The biblical message stands in judgment on a society of consumers dedicated to material comfort. We are called to a more authentic human existence, not to greater affluence.

The Redirection of Technology

I want to suggest, further, that both pollution and poverty are products of our failure to devise adequate social controls over technology. Concern for ecology need not compete with concern for social justice; they converge in demanding a fundamental redirection of technology. Let me spell this out:

First, the poor have benefited least from technology. Unemployment from automation hits the unskilled hardest. A freeway is seldom used by the ghetto residents whose houses are torn down to make room for it. The government subsidy of $5 billion for supersonic planes will mainly benefit the skilled workers in aerospace industries and the affluent who can afford to fly. Black Americans are special victims of pollution, since they usually cannot escape the dirt and noise of the ghetto. Both within our nation and between nations uncontrolled technology tends to widen the gap between the rich and the poor and to reinforce existing power structures. (For example, powerful lobbies from the auto and highway industries, insurance, oil and gas companies, etc., have worked to block public urban transit schemes.

Second, the "invisible hand" of the market place is inadequate to control technology. Classical laissez-faire economics assumed that if each person sought his own good, the law of supply and demand would regulate production and yield the social good. In the past, resources were bountiful, the detrimental social effects were tolerable, and private enterprise in the U.S. did engender productivity and higher standards of living—though not without great inequalities in the distribution of its benefits. Technology in particular became a major instrument of profit and power. The financial reward often went to the person who could find new ways to exploit natural resources quickly and cheaply. Today the social cost of that exploitation is intolerably high, and new forms of tax and incentive are needed so that the person who jeopardizes the general welfare is not rewarded. The influence of technological decisions is now so pervasive that such decisions cannot be left to the vagaries of the market place. We breathe or suffocate together.

Third, the social costs of technological innovations must be paid by their users. So far as possible, the price of an item should be determined by its total social cost and not simply by the immediate cost of production. The cost of resource conservation, pollution control and waste disposal should be carried by the producer and hence, ultimately, by the consumer. If soft drink manufacturers were assessed for the disposal of empty cans, they would try to minimize the total cost (production and disposal) and not just the cost of production. New methods of "social accounting" have been developed which allow at least some estimate of such costs.

National planning and control should go beyond the prevention of harmful consequences and foster the positive development of technology in socially desirable directions. Technology is the greatest single influence on the future, and it is indeed subject to social control; it appears as an autonomous force only because adequate mechanisms for its guidance have not been devised. The growth of particular technologies has been determined more by technical feasibility and economic profit than by social need. We have never had a coherent national policy for applied science. Instead we have had a mixture of laissez-faire with crash programs in response to a succession of crisis, from Sputnik to pollution.

In an important study entitled Technology: Processes of Assessment and Choice (House Committee on Science and Astronautics, 1969), a panel of the National Academy of Sciences has recommended new decision-making mechanisms through which the wider social consequences of a possible technological development could be taken into account in advance. The study emphasizes that so far the people most affected have had little voice in the early stages of decision-making, and that by the time deleterious effects are widespread, new industries and powerful vested interest (e.g., in particular types of detergent or pesticide) are strongly entrenched. It proposes technology assessment offices, with powers of recommendation only, placed close to the center of political power in existing agencies; specifically, (1) a new section of the Office of Science and Technology, which advises the President; (2) a new Joint Congressional Committee on Technology Assessment; and (3) a new division of the National Science Foundation, which would make grants for research on the social effects of new technologies.

I am myself inclined to think that technology can be controlled only by more powerful agencies with representation at the cabinet level —despite the dangers inherent in such centralized control. To avoid the problems that arise when the same agency is responsible both for promoting a new development and for protecting the public from its hazards (cf. the Atomic Energy Commission's dual role in nuclear power). I suggest the need for a department of science and technology and a separate department of environment. The latter would sponsor research and promote legislation on pollution-reduction, environmental preservation and consumer protection. It would include both natural and social scientists trained to study the effects of technological developments, in order to guide policy decision and suggest legislation for the regulatory powers needed. It would collect ecological data and establish enforceable environment standards. It would also conduct research on recycling procedures for reusing nonrenewal resources. We have to shift from a frontier mentality of using up and moving on, to a spaceship mentality of living on a fixed set of resources.

I do not mean to minimize the importance of individual action. There is a lot that you can do as an individual. You can use biodegradable detergents and returnable bottles, cut down on excessive consumption of goods, join community clean-up campaigns. But I have been suggesting that pollution must also be seen as part of the wider problem of the uses of technology—which is a question of national policy.

The Greatest Challenge

I have been suggesting, in sum, that technology must be redirected to abolish poverty, hunger and pollution, not to produce more luxury goods. Space and military technology are highly developed, but comparatively little effort has been given to the technology of urban housing, pollution abatement or population control. We have the technical ability and the organizational skills to achieve a world from which are banished man's ancient enemies, hunger and poverty, as well as the new enemy, pollution. To this redirection of technology the biblical tradition can bring a passion for social justice and equality, a prophetic concern for a more humane social order. That picture of our spinning globe from 100,000 miles in space shows the incredible richness and beauty of our earth, a blue and white gem, a garden of Eden among the barren planets. Let us commit ourselves to keeping it habitable. The greatest challenge of all is to prove that intelligent life can exist—on earth.

In the words of Deuteronomy: "I have set before you life and death. ... Therefore choose life."

PART IV

Who Speaks for the Churches?

Introduction

For many years the legislative assemblies, conferences and executive bodies of the major Protestant denominations and of Protestant ecumenical organizations like the World Council of Churches and the National Council of Churches of Christ in the United States of America have issued official statements on critical social problems. These organizational conferences and bodies frequently are accused of misrepresenting their constituencies by issuing statements which do not represent the opinions for all of their members—especially on social issues about which church members hold sharply opposing views. Many of these church members have questioned the right of these bodies to make such pronouncements. Paul Ramsey of Princeton University is among this group of critics. He charges that church bodies tend to follow one of two erroneous procedures when they issue statements on social problems. Either they make highly pious and abstract statements which are irrelevant or they go beyond their own competency by making policy-statements which are too specific. Neither approach is adequate or significant according to Ramsey and both are abrogations of the Church's responsibility for society. According to Ramsey, the Church's role is to sustain, criticize and reform the moral and socio-political ethos of the present world situation and not to make irrelevant or incompetent pronouncements.

In Roman Catholic circles—especially since Vatican II—several members of the Roman clergy and laity have voiced a similar criticism concerning the right of the Pope and Roman hierarchy to speak authoritatively on behalf of the whole Church or to dictate to the entire Church one policy on crucial moral, social, political and economic issues— especially on controversial issues on which all Roman Catholics do not hold the same opinion. What is at stake here is a rejection of the view that the Pope, bishops and hierarchy either individually or collectively constitute the absolute moral authority of the Church and are responsible solely for speaking on behalf of the Church to society and/or dictating to the members of the Church their moral position and their attitudes toward social problems. Those individuals who raise this criticism contend that the moral authority of the Church is vested not only in the Pope and hierarchy but the entire Church. According to the Catholic faith, magisterial authority in the Church belongs to the Pope and bishops and no "magisterial" authority in matters pertaining to doctrine or morals that contradicts theirs is to be recognized as Catholic.

In more conservative quarters of the Roman Catholic Church individuals like William F. Buckley, Jr. maintain that they are unjustly criticized and even maligned by the more liberal element in the Church for their conservative approach to society and its problems. They contend that Roman Catholic social theology neither prohibits nor precludes the possibility of adopting a conservative position toward moral, social, political and economic problems.

The readings in this section present Paul Ramsey's critique of Protestant ecumenical pronouncements on social problems and a critique of his position by John C. Bennett; a Roman Catholic statement on the roles of the Pope, hierarchy and laity in addressing the Roman Catholic Church to society and its problems; and William F. Buckley, Jr.'s defense of his right as a Roman Catholic to espouse and disseminate a conservative position concerning social problems.

THE ABSTRACTNESS
OF CONCRETE ADVICE

PAUL RAMSEY

It can be shown that a series of specific policy proposals issuing from an assemblage of churchmen is, for all the particularity of each, as abstract as a counsel of perfection issuing from the same source, so far as the real requirements of the sound formation of an actual national policy are concerned. For the Church to adopt the posture of giving concrete advice does not come any closer to shouldering the statesman's burden or illuminating his responsibilities for what must be done to hammer out the overall political policies of a nation (especially a nation that must have policies all over the world) than general directions to him concerning how he should shape events if he can. A series or a package of concretes is still a generality, I shall argue, until each is examined and corrected in the light of its effects on all other problems presently facing the nation anywhere in the world. No church council has ever assumed or ever can or should assume responsibility for this before it speaks to the world. Then the Church had better not undertake the semblance of being concretely political in its utterances.

The opening words of a report on the proceedings and findings of the Sixth World Order Study Conference meeting in St. Louis seem on first reading to be heavily laden with irony: "That 463 people from all sections of the nation could in a three-day meeting draw up and reach agreement on policy statements on all the major—and many of the minor—foreign policy issues affecting our country seems incredible. That, in addition, they listened attentively to eight addresses more or less pertinent to the sujects under discussion would tend to make this a minor miracle."[1] Those words were surely meant to call in question the worth of any such findings.

So it seems, until the correspondent's concluding remark that "the very fact that the delegates felt impelled to speak so forthrightly on a number of controversial issues is reassuring in a day when pressure to conform to Administration policy on foreign affairs is so strong."

This seems to say that in this instance, because it was contrary-minded, a church assemblage did something that was indirectly good for the political society no matter what was the substance of its many specific resolutions. But this faint commendation was not left on that ground. The final verdict upon the St. Louis conference, we are told, depends on how "zealously" these "goals" are pursued by the NCC's International Affairs Commission and its participating commissions.

In short, this conference represented only itself; it could not speak for the Church or for the Churches. It seemingly did very little to impose on itself by a self-denying ordinance the requirement that no more be said in addressing the urgent political problems of the present day than can be clearly be said on the basis of Christian truth and insights. Yet the conference spoke very particularly to the Churches and to the nation on a large number of very complex issues and problems. And now its findings are zealously to be made into precedental determinations of responsible Christian decisions and action in the political life of this nation. An individual Christian (no matter what his political persuasion) may well feel that there is something fundamentally wrong in this kind of address to him.

At the moment, however, we are concerned to ask: Is this the way (without speaking for the Church and without the self-limitation of saying only those "directions" that are clearly entailed in Christian truth and insights) to speak to the world, to magistrate, to the government?

Any assemblage can, of course, construct a number of historical predictions that have verisimilitude about the greater or lesser evil consequences that will come from the adoption of particular policies. There are always many such conjectures, supported by experts and by all sorts of facts to which to succumb when representing only oneself. If these "pictures of the world" are opposed to those held in government circles, they can be used in adopting a pose of being prophetic in criticism of present policy and in support of some alternate policy. In this way it is easy to attain prophecy and at the same time a feeling of being deeply involved and relevant. Yet this yields maximalist church pronouncements that are both jurisdictionally beyond the "competence" of churchmen as such and also as distant as any general principle could be from actual policy making.

Thus does the Church blur the distinction between itself and all other groups in the society which in any measure participate in the formation of public opinion; and it inordinately seeks to assume in the name of the Church (which cannot be detached from these findings by any denials that this was meant) decisions that belong in the realm of the state. Unless it can be made clear in what way Christian teaching can as such substantially and compellingly lead to these conclusions, then this is simply to put the engine of religious fervor behind a particular Partisan political point of view which would have as much or as little to recommend it if it had not emanated from a church council.

The shrewdest device yet for accomplishing this purpose is the reservation that the resolutions and the pronouncements on all sorts of subjects advising the statesman what he should do which issue from church councils (or from groups like the Clergy Concerned over Vietnam) in fact do not represent "the Church" (or Christian morality) but only the views of the churchmen who happen to be assembled. Thus a group of concerned Christians free themselves from having to weigh their words lest they falsely commit the Church and speak an inadequately Christian word to this age; and of course they are not in the position of the statesman who has to correct one policy by another and to bear the responsibility for any cost/benefits he may have left out of account. One can scarcely imagine a situation that to a greater extent invites irresponsible utterance, even while the participants feel they are being exceedingly responsible because they are talking in specifics and not in generalities. Precisely because, for historical and denominational reasons, councils convened by the NCC (National Council of Churches of Christ in the U.S.A.) and the WCC (World Council of Churches) cannot claim to speak for the Church, there is even greater need for every effort to be made that they say only what can be said in the name of Christian truth in every utterance addressed to the Church and to the world today.

The General Board of the NCC on December 3, 1965, did verbally refer its suggestions to the prudence of citizens and of statesmen and to the political process. "We, therefore recommend," it said, "that the U.S. in the interest of bringing peace and growing justice and freedom to the territories of Vietnam, should consider the following suggestions." But from that point on followed a number of specifics such as "request the UN to begin negotiations," "request the UN, further, as soon as possible to convene a peace conference regarding Vietnam," "with representatives from the National Liberation Front," without a shadow of a suggestion that nothing gives the General Board of the NCC the political wisdom to know whether this is an opportune moment or whether these are opportune things to do or not. At the same time, the injunctions that the bombing of North Vietnam cease for a sufficient period "with a simultaneous effort to induce the North Vietnam Government to stop sending military personnel and material into South Vietnam" shows that if you put together a couple of particulars you get a generality like "Let there be no war."

There were, of course, the necessary reservations about who was speaking. "Some believe. . . ." "Others believe. . . . Then came a welcomed sentence: "We hold that in the spectrum of their concern Christians can and do espouse one or the other of these views and still other views and should not have their integrity of conscience faulted because they do." The first of these views was that of those Christians who "believe that the military effort should continue and that unless the spread of communism by violent infiltration is checked by further military means, liberties of not only South Vietnam but of Southeast Asia are imperiled. In this view the war must go on until the military results bring the Viet Cong and the North Vietnamese to the conference table." It is hard to see how anyone holding that opinion, if it was represented on the board, could then have agreed with all of its particular policy statements. And certainly what was heard in the churches and by the world generally were these policy statements, and not that legitimate Christian position or the reservation that the NCC board does not speak for its member denominations or by its majority voice suppress points of view that are prominent in the churches.

Still, the Church speaking would be improved if this NCC example in stating divergent Christian political premises or conclusions about national policy were followed by other groups as well. Other official and unofficial groups of Christians and journals of Christian opinion, in voicing their opinions and protests to the rest of the Church and to the world, need to be equally candid in recognizing that there are equally valid contrary particular opinions held by other Christians who "should not have their integrity of conscience faulted because they do." Indeed, they need to have the same concern to include along with their own advice to statesmen such a clear statement of a contrary opinion. This would keep it ever evident (to ourselves and to others) that there is no way to speak for the Church, to be the Church speaking relevantly to political questions, and at the same time to address particular prudential recommendations to the leaders of the nations. This would keep clear the fact that prudential political advice comes into the public forum with no special credentials because it issues from Christians or from Christian religious bodies. It would also prevent the (inadvertent or purposeful) putting together of a consensus on these political questions where there is and should be none. Something is radically wrong when churchmen in council have enormous reservations and problems over who is speaking ("Some say. . . ." "Others say. . . .") and yet few reservations about addressing specific political advice to a multitude of the world's problems. The careful reporting of divergent Christian positions is good if these are general points of view relevant to action, or Christian outlooks upon public policy. But if the reported disagreement was over the specifics of policy decision, and then a vote is taken, what goes out to the world is a particular statement that will have the same actual or aspired influence upon public policy as if it had been unanimous, and as if it had been asserted to be the Christian thing to do.

On the other hand, a bag of specifics is still a generality in relation to actual policy. For ecumenical councils on Church and Society responsibility to proffer specific advice would require that the Church have the services of an entire state department. There would have to be officers permanently in charge of many, many separate "desks" whose responsibility would be to assess every proposed policy dealing with problems anywhere in the world and to urge the rejection or correction of these proposals in the light of repercussions upon the country or area each particular secretary should know more intimately than any other officer. And someone would have to resolve these interests, claims, and counterclaims into actual ventures of state. Otherwise, a recommendation like "Recognize China" or "Negotiate with the Viet Cong" is rather like the counsel "Do good" or "Feed the hungry."

At the level of the Central Committee of the World Council of Churches it is evident that ecumenical statements, so long as they remain specific and are not wholly irresponsible, are forced to rise above the real situation in which political leaders must live and decide and act. Pieces of particular advice are still offered (this for the sake of feeling concretely involved in the world's problems), but these must be a balanced set of particulars (for the sake of being responsible, and not partisan). It is sun-clear that this manner of the Church speaking puts together a package of specifics which amounts, when addressed to the statesman's actual world and his real options, to a counsel of perfection.

Thus the Central Committee of the WCC meeting in Geneva, February 16, 1966, adopted a resolution stating, among other things, (1) "that the United States and South Vietnam stop bombing of the North and North Vietnam stop military infiltration of the South" (this means there should be no war of subversion in Vietnam and no riposte to it needed); (2) that "arrangements be encouraged for negotiations between the Government of South Vietnam and the National Liberation Front in the hope that there may be found a negotiating authority representative of all South Vietnam" (this means there should be no civil war in South Vietnam; and if there were "a negotiating authority representative of all South Vietnam" none would be needed); (3) "that in order to relieve present international tension the United States review and modify its policy of "containment' of Communism, and Communist countries supporting 'wars of liberation' review and modify their policy" (this means, Let there be peace).

This is enough to show that balanced pairs of pieces of specific advice are no more than pious and irrelevant generalities issuing from a great distance above the problems facing the nations.

There is, however, a way, and (so far as I can see) only one way, to avoid this, while as churchmen still making particular political judgments. (This second way of remaining specific I in no sense endorse.) That would be to condemn forthrightly some concrete current practice or policy and then place beside this only a recommendation that statesmen search for an option on the optimistic premise that if present policy is so certainly censurable there must be an alternative that is presently practicable.

On one reading, this was the device used at the Geneva Conference in July, 1966, when one of the reports specifically condemned nuclear war in such an unqualified way that no conceivable use of any nuclears in any war (and consequently no deterrence of nuclear war) would be either possible or morally permissible for one moment after the unlikely event that the statesmen of the great powers took seriously this instruction. Then, among other things, this same report hedged the "realism" of its undiscriminating condemnation by calling for greater "imagination" on the part of "all the established powers" in this world. It condemned "lack of confidence" for bedeviling "the relations between the states of Europe," and addressed itself to the "real" problem of "how the supreme task to avoid nuclear war, can be carried out" by listing among the "measures" that "would help" a recommendation that the "mere balance of power" be changed "into a community with institutions for the prevention of escalation of conflict between the main powers."[2] Obviously, this measure is the same as the aspired goal and thus can help not at all in getting there. This is a direction of action, not a specific directive; and it is certainly a direction which churches and churchmen are competent to chart. But to condemn specifically and sweepingly while recommending alternatives in properly general terms is surely the way to succeed as prophets without really trying.

I want to give ... [an] additional illustration ... of this procedure of placing beside a condemnation of some particular policy not a balancing condemnation that is equally particular, but only a plea that there must be some other way.... The editorial in Christianity and Crisis, "We Protest the National Policy in Vietnam," March 7, 1966. ... [This] will show that particular political protests need not be forced to a distance above the actual problem (as in the case of well-balanced censures of both sides). Instead, when we stick with the ambiguities of politics and the undiminished crunch of political forces, our protests are required to take the form of rather excruciating assertions that present policy is wrong and pleas to the side in conflict that is most likely to be susceptible to moral exhortation. The balance between specific recommendations to both sides is undone; one alone is held firm with aknowledging that the practicability of this depended on simultaneous acceptance of the other also. The specific policy condemned or recommended is then coupled no longer with actions in the real political world that condition its practicability, but with pleas to be more imaginative or to venture more in milking from the ambiguities the always less grim alternatives that must somehow be there.

The statement of editorial policy in Christianity and Crisis, March 7, 1966 ... condemned in a very specific fashion without taking responsibility for the alternatives, or even for the conviction that there are any. It petered out into a comparison of "various possibilities with the present grim realities," without (of necessity) a sufficient penetration of any of these possibilities to see if they might not be grimmer. The editorial board's statement warranted this technique of censuring the real in the light of several ideals by the excuse that we should not look for "painless ways" out. The political question, however, is whether there is a way out, not a painless one; and any out that is less painful in facing all the grim realities. A statesman has to determine this; groups of Christians when speaking as such do not. It remains, however, open to them to condemn the present policy as worse than a number of possibilities not yet tested by reality, and to urge our statesmen to use their "moral imagination."

Here we come upon the generality that sustained in this protest its seeming realism and the seeming responsibility of its specific advice. It is easy to wax prophetic as long as one deals only in hypotheticals. A statesman, however, has to be beforehand while, amid the grim realities and the actions that come upon him, he posits a single course of action whose consequences he must take responsibility for saying will be less grim.

It required only twenty-four hours after taking the Vietnam conflict to the UN to display the fact that an opportune moment for this had not yet arrived. Yet proponents of this proposal, so long as it was only an untried specific possibility, could easily gain accolades for greater idealism or greater realism over our political leaders who on four separate occasions thought this through and judged it unrealistic. There ought to be better ways for churchmen to be the church speaking to the magistrate, and for them to help sustain the ethos out of which statesmanship may come. This leads in the direction away from specific utterances.

Was it in the other direction of constituting a "shadow" state department that Visser 't Hooft pointed when he acknowledged that the churches were not fully prepared for the new role many of them are assuming of giving specific recommendations to political leaders? To a greater use of churchmen who are political experts? To a better "methodology" for determining which specifics should specifically be said?

Was it in this same direction that the Geneva Conference on Church and Society pointed, when it stated that "real dialogue is needed" and that in the churches "an example of true community transcending the nations must be manifested"?[3] Does the older ecumenical movement hope to transcend the peoples among whom Christians are mingled in this world, not in the direction of clearer statement of Christian action-relevant perspectives upon the world's problems but in the direction of a universal view of concrete political policies for the world's statesmen? The latter seemed to be envisioned by the statement that to "make critical social and ethical judgments in a Christian perspective, the first essential is knowledge of the facts."[4] The worth of knowing the facts, of course, cannot be denied; but how are these fact-filled concrete universal judgments upon all the world's problems to be arrived at?

The call seemed to be for the Church to transcend the peoples of the world in the direction of a universal political community and not in the direction of some better form of universal ecclesiastical community in which churchmen exchange views and speak *ad extra* only on the basis of the Christian insights they should be exploring and deepening. The call was for "an exchange between nations of war and peace as an expression of love and our interdependent relationship";[5] and later we will see how specific was the American delegation's reason for wanting such exchanges: to help bring about a revision of this nation's Vietnam policy.

No one can question the need for many new means of ecumenical dialogue, if this has in view the deepening and broadening of ecumenical Christian political ethics. The Geneva Conference, however, had in view that such periodic consultations would keep developing situations "under constant review" and propose "suitable collective action"[6] The main body of this report recommended that the WCC be responsible for "the collection, critical evaluation, and dissemination of relevant facts to all the constituent churches" and that "the constituent churches should for their part collect clear information on situations of ecumenical importance for passing on to the appropriate department of the WCC."[7] Was this to the end that the ecumenical city increase its fact-filled competence in specific policy making? That would be a move in the direction of constituting at the world level a "shadow" state department believed to be competent to deal with the specific issues of international politics and economics.

This would be the reverse of the most urgent need at this hour. Certainly, the procedures of church councils sponsored by the older half of the modern ecumenical movement need to be radically improved so that sounder deliberations can be insured. But the aim of these procedures and deliberations should not be to improve the Church's speaking to the world its supposedly expert specific advice, but to make sure that in everything addressed to the churches and to the world today our church councils can better speak *for* the Church, for the whole of Christian truth, and every saving word but no more than can be said upon this basis. Even if these participating denominations, we need to know that so far as humanly possible in their deliberations and pronouncements they nevertheless are in a real sense trying to be the Church speaking.

We now have before us three possibilities, each in one way or another demonstrating how abstract can be the specific advice of the Church or from Christians as such to the world: (1) a well-balanced set of specific condemnations, rising above the ambiguities, "judging" both sides in some historic conflict or arbitrament of arms; (2) specific condemnation of one side only or mainly, coupled with the recommendation that political leadership imaginatively or creatively search for solutions that must be possible and are bound to be less grim than the present course of action; and (3) a possible final corruption of the social teachings of world Christianity if, on account of our captivity to the notion that the Church's address to the world must be in terms of specific recommendations and condemnations, we should yield to the dream of becoming a surrogate world political community, each where we are and in our various groupings particularly instructing one another and then telling the governments of the world how to bring about the solutions, the peace that passeth understanding.

This is enough to set anyone off in search of a way between irrelevant generalities and specific pronouncements.

None of the foregoing is intended to deny the importance of the transnational Christian community, which is more and more realized and realizable today, and which has always been a principal goal of the ecumenical movement. Nor should anyone deny that the worldwide Christian community can be of very real indirect aid to statesmen in the nation-state system. The unknown easily becomes the enemy, and channels of communication which are maintained despite national differences, even in wartime, have many political uses and general benefits. Indeed, variations (1) and (2) above—striking out the too particular recommendations or incriminations—would look remarkably like what I call direction giving. But the foregoing is intended to deny that the world church or ecumenical ethics should pour itself into the mold of particular policy formation. That mold needs to be broken.

1. Christianity and Crisis, November 15, 1965.
2. **World Conference on Church and Society: Official Report** (Geneva: World Council of Churches, 1967), Report of Section III: "Structures of International Cooperation—Living Together in Peace in a Pluralistic World Society," par. 95, with 44, 52, 94, and 97.
3. "Structures of International Cooperation: Living Together in Peace in a Pluralistic World Society." Report of Section III, par. 101.

4. **Ibid.**, par. 92. This statement is a prime example of how to be led away from the "first essentials" of Christian moral judgments.

5. **Ibid.**, par. 108.

6. **Ibid.**, par. 93.

7. **Ibid.**, par. 92.

A CRITIQUE OF PAUL RAMSEY

JOHN C. BENNETT

I agree with much that Professor Ramsey says about methodology. I think that the greater part of what church bodies say should be in the middle area where theology and social ethics overlap. The emphasis should be on what can be said with confidence from a Christian perspective. I am doubtful, however, about securing full agreement about theological foundations because we live in a highly pluralistic theological situation, pluralistic in terms of established traditions and also in terms of contemporary schools of thought. It is fortunate that in spite of this theological pluralism it is possible to agree over a wide spectrum on some of those theological and ethical issues that are most relevant to the Church's social responsibility.

The Risk in Speaking Specifically

I differ from Ramsey in believing that if this Christian perspective is emphasized in the light of the social realities, there should from time to time be more specific forms of teaching and action related to the concrete decisions of government. I value these less than the more basic teaching, but they are an inevitable overflow from it and a sign that the basic teaching is taken seriously.

If a Christian body never felt driven to relate its basic teaching to specific issues, this would be a sign that Christians were not very much concerned. Ramsey wants to wait until there is a position in the Church that is beyond significant debate, but this would involve a strong inhibition against speaking at all about specific decisions. I think that a sounder position in the long run is more likely to come from a process that would include the risk of error in speaking than from Ramsey's inhibition against speaking.

Often the Church's role will be to speak in criticism of the nation's actions, calling attention to the humanly destructive and self-defeating aspects of an existing policy, with some openness to diversity of judgments about alternative policies. At times a most fateful social decision will be tied to a "yes" or "no" about a particular act of legislation— the Civil Rights Law of 1964 and the partial test-ban treaty, for example. In such cases churches or their agencies may be justified in throwing their weight behind such a legislative decision. However, I regard this degree of specificity as exceptional.

I do not believe in "faulting" the consciences of dissenters, to use one of Ramsey's favorite words. All that is said by the Church or within the Church by its agencies should be said on pilgrimage with a realization that risks are involved, that many conditioning factors cause very sincere people to differ. In no sense should they feel unchurched. Nevertheless that does not make it unimportant for a council or a conference called by the Church to take such positions from time to time when pronouncements come out of processes that prevent snap judgments and unexamined partisanship.

Christians guided by a Christian perspective should think together about what this means for decision and action even though they must relate their Christian convictions to their best judgment about political and other considerations. Corporate thinking and speaking by Christians should not stop so short of concrete decisions that all that they say can be said only by them as individuals. Such thinking and speaking involves risks, but the Church should be a place of ferment where such risks are encouraged.

This picture of what the Church should be and do is different from Ramsey's. For one thing, much must be said explicitly to counterbalance what the Church communicates to the world by its institutional involvement in the status quo. Utterances that do not pass Ramsey's tests of what is fully within the province of the Church are not likely to be as false to the Christian perspective as the message continuously given by the fact that the Church lives so comfortably in the existing culture. They may also have the positive effect of helping to extricate the Church a little from its bondage to that culture.

When Should the Church Speak?

It is unfortunate that Ramsey directs his fire so much against a conference of the type held in Geneva, which speaks for itself on the understanding that what it says has no authority beyond its intrinsic merit. My interest is in the diversity of opportunities for witness of this kind in the hope that from them may come sound conclusions from a Christian perspective.

As Ramsey says of the role of experts in Geneva, experts differ, and it takes experts to choose experts. But there was a variety of experts with different biases and with different national backgrounds, and they were able to check each other. This was especially true of economists, and it is noticeable that Ramsey has little to say about the report on economic development to which they made their chief contribution, and which was a major center of interest at the conference.

I regard the war in Vietnam as another issue on which positions should be taken in the Church. However, I should leave open the choice between several alternatives to present policy and not insist on immediate withdrawal. I should not bring up many such issues for specific action, but from time to time one is forced upon us. Ramsey himself would speak out in the case of a particular episode such as the bombing of a city, (subject to his qualifications about the "double effect" of the bombing, which might keep him from saying anything very specific). I am concerned about the cumulative effect of the bombing of many villages, the saturation bombing with napalm of large areas of jungle because of the suspicion that they contain Vietcong, and I have never understood why these things worry Mr. Ramsey so little.

For a conference meeting in Geneva in 1966 to have been silent about the war in Vietnam would have given the world a false impression. Silence would have implied consent. What was said on Vietnam did not involve dogmatism about the way in which the fighting should be stopped, but its judgment that "the massive and growing American military presence and the long continued bombing of villages in the South and of targets a few miles from cities in the North cannot be justified" prodded the American "magistrates" to find such a way. It is those on the spot who must usually find the next steps, but they will not do so if they continue to believe that their present course is justifiable.

Correcting The Vision of Ramsey's Magistrates

To some extent magistrates limit themselves by their own propaganda. Take American policy with regard to Communist China. In recent years our policy-makers may have thought that they were imprisoned by a rigid public opinion about China, but it was a public opinion that they and their predecessors helped to create. The signs that public opinion on China is now more flexible are partly the result of the influence of American churches. But Ramsey seems opposed even to the very cautious statements made at NCC world order conferences on this subject.

Not only do Ramsey's magistrates seem to live in a political vacuum; they appear to be unaffected by the temptations that go with the American position of predominant power in the world today, and by our nation's tendency to identify its interests with the status quo. I know that Ramsey would not have had the Geneva Conference substitute his judgments for its own about immediate matters of US policy. His methodology would not allow that. On the other hand, why does he never say anything in criticism of the American stance in the world today?

I think that the basic theological and ethical teaching in the Church should encourage a critical attitude toward the following elements in the US stance: the hangover of capitalist ideology that causes us to drag our feet in relation to socialistic experiments abroad; our absolutistic, crusading anti-Communism in relation to Asia and Latin America; a counter-revolutionary bias that seems unwilling to allow nations in Asia and Latin America to have their own experiments with a revolution; a habit of over-stressing military solutions because we are competent in this field and have the hardware but do not understand the people in some other cultures enough to grasp the political aspect of their struggles; tendencies of a more idealistic sort that mask illusions, especially the tendency to assume that if we try hard enough we will compensate for all the evil that we do by producing a democratic or quasi-democratic solution. (There was apathetic eagerness about the recent elections in Vietnam because it was hoped that their results would give legitimacy to the Saigon Government and hence to our policy. All of this is most precarious.)

These are elements in a pervasive American ideology that greatly distort the vision of our magistrates. American churchmen who have had the Geneva experience need not take over any other country's ideology, but they may gain some freedom from our own. A succession of experiences of this type should enable the American churches to provide some corrective for the vision of the magistrates who now control our destinies.

If Ramsey would make room for this level of criticism, his book would be more convincing. As it is he gives the impression that there is no conflict between the Christian perspective and the American stance in the world. In contrast to this view the outcry from Geneva needed to be heard.

Ramsey and the Nuclear Question

Ramsey's own concentration on particular moral issues related to the actual conduct of war has caused him to present, as though it were a Christian position, a rather optimistic view about the limited nuclear war—limited either by the use of tactical weapons or by the selection of targets for strategic weapons. Abstractly both forms of limitation are possible, but surely they are not likely to continue for long if a nuclear war once starts. I think that a more tragic view of what is likely here would be closer to a Christian theological position, even if a particular prediction cannot be deduced from theology.

I welcome Ramsey's many careful discriminations about the conduct of war, but I think that he should give more emphasis to the danger that nuclear war may not be kept limited. He seems at times to be most concerned to have moral permission to use nuclear weapons in a limited way, but I suspect that all of this is not so different from the abstract and misleading forms of particularity that he finds in some of the Geneva statements.

I agree that we cannot leap out of the situation that involves the possession of nuclear weapons, but Ramsey makes this situation less difficult than it is because he has a residual nuclear optimism. It may be more important, therefore, for the Church to warn—as strongly as Geneva did—against all use of nuclear weapons than to emphasize the marginal possibility that they may be used within limits.

Despite what I have said, Professor Ramsey's book is good medicine for those who are too heedless in making pronouncements on specific matters of policy. His criticisms of much of the advice given to government is proper, especially the advice arrived at by way of compromise that puts contrasting specifics together and adds up to no more than the exhortation: "let there be peace." I could go very far with Ramsey about leaving the most specific judgments of policy to the magistrates— if he would have more to say to guide them in their presuppositions and to keep before them the human consequence of their judgments in the immediate past.

We may be able to get a fresh view of the problems discussed by Professor Ramsey if we admit that it is on rare occasions that anyone speaks *for* the Church. To be concerned with the dangers raised by Ramsey's title is a puristic preoccupation that may be quite sterile. What we should be concerned about is the encouragement of many corporate voices in the Church speaking to its members, to nations and governments.

In a similar way, let the Christian community to which the National and the World Councils of Churches are related encourage the opportunities for corporate voices to speak in the Church, to seek to do so from a Christian perspective, to counteract the message that is generally conveyed without words by the Church's inertia, to take risks in relating the Christian faith to concrete action.

HOPE AND TRUST IN
THE SOCIAL MISSION OF THE CHURCH

PAUL VI

The word which we all need is hope and trust. The Risen Lord repeats: "Take heart, it is I; have no fear." (Mk 6:50 RSV). "Let not your hearts be troubled; believe in God, believe also in me." (Jn 14:1 RSV). Christ is present in his Church; it continues the mission confided to her, indicating to the world that in him alone is peace, justice, and forgiveness.

This is the hope and trust that sustains us, founded on the word of Christ and the work that the Church, under his mandate, carries out in the world. We stress this because today, in the moment at which we are living, lack of trust in the Church is strong among a number of Christians, even priests and religious. This distrust sometimes even becomes a kind of aggressiveness, but more frequently it takes the form of disheartenment and disillusionment.

Negative Phenomena

For some this feeling comes from the fact that the ecclesial structure, which in their eyes represented a strongly coherent and organized whole, seems menaced in its unity. They are no doubt shaken by the criticism that has come to light in recent years, and by the daring character of certain initiatives that ignore tradition. They are upset by the abandonment of exterior witness or of forms of piety to which they were much attracted, so they tend to turn in on themselves and refuse to take part in the life and work of the Church. For others, lack of trust in the Church originated in their conviction that she is intermeshed with institutions that have outlived their time. In a secularized society, they think that the Church should give up most of her distinctive forms and even renounce the certainties she has achieved, in order to listen to the needs of the world. In the presence of the visible, institutional Church they feel a chill that leads them to become alienated from her, because they feel themselves sensitive to the profound changes that characterize our times—new cultural developments and scientific and technological possibilities.

These two opposing tendencies give rise to a state of uneasiness which we cannot and must not hide from ourselves. We find a false and abusive interpretation of the Council, which claims it to be a break with tradition, even in doctrine. It repudiates the pre-conciliar Church and gives itself license to conceive a "New Church," half reinvented, so to speak, from within—new in constitution, dogma, morals, and law.

The negative reactions we have mentioned seem to intend the dissolution of the teaching authority of the Church—either by an equivocating pluralism, conceived as a free interpretation of the doctrine of the Church and the unchallenged coexistence of opposing ideas, or by a subsidiarity which is intended to be autonomy.

In the Service of Justice and Truth

In the context of concerns internal to the Church, we cannot forget the difficulties and exigencies that the Church encounters in the exercise of her mission, which is not abstract and disembodied, but involved concretely in specific situations. In the first place, the Church has a problem of trust when she acts as a "prophet," which is not only when she announces truth and justice, but also when she deplores, denounces, and condemns transgressions or crimes against justice and truth.

In reality the Holy See is like a sentinal to whom the cries of the oppressed arise, the stifled groans of those who are not even free to cry out, the laments of those who feel that their rights have been attacked or abandoned in their needs.

But as in all times of deep divisions, men do not ask for the condemnation of all injustices, but only of those that have been committed by their opponents.

The Holy See is well aware of its duty to interpret the "moral conscience of humanity," not only regarding principles, but also regarding concrete realities. It would like to get to know even those things people would like to hide and so often succeed in hiding. But its responsibility demands that it not be content with news accounts that have not been fully verified, and that it seek the most complete and absolute objectivity. These are not always easy things to do. Our action proposes, within the limits of possibility, to come effectively to the aid of the suffering, calling for understanding and support. This calls for a rightful prudence and reserve in public witness, in order to give precedence to the attempt at serious and direct dialogue with those responsible for the situations being complained about, or in order to avoid provoking stronger reactions on top of the burden of those who await defense.

International Development

Among the most relevant activities are the contacts established at the levels of highest authority between two great nations, the United States of America and the People's Republic of China, recently admitted into the United Nations. An agreement has been signed in the Berlin situation, along with the ratification of the treaties among the German Federal Republic, the U.S.S.R., and Poland. This complex of acts concludes laborious negotiations, protracted for years, within a context of objective difficulties which, since the end of the last World War, had mutually provoked tensions that were sometimes quite grave.

But something new is coming to pass in the world. This is verified by the fact that there have been meetings which, until recently, could not even have been thought of.

It seems just as significant that while negotiations have begun among the nations having greater responsibility for balance in the world, other people have not remained inactive, as shown by several important international conferences. For instance, the Third Conference on Trade and Development (Santiago, Chile), and Stockholm Conference on Man and the Environment—these dealt with problems of prime importance for life and rapport among nations. It is affirming, in effect, when all peoples are given even greater possibilities for making their voices heard, when these discussions contribute to outlining a more united and coordinated vision of problems, and when this solidarity develops a more lively understanding of a kind of community, uniquely human.

Is it perhaps utopian in this context of lessened mistrust to hope that sincere and courageous solutions may finally be found for chronic conflicts, such as the wars in the Middle East and Vietnam? Vietnam— every day that peace is held back costs terrifying destruction that buries together in one tomb men and nature, fighting forces and unarmed populations, life and the hope of life. We hope and pray that this prospect will be confirmed by silencing arms, stopping the flow of blood, by conciliation and understanding, by reconstruction and healing.

Positive Aspects of Trust

We feel obliged, because of all this, to underline the affirmation currents that give wings to the action of the Church and her presence in the world today. For the Church is alive, active, and young!

Therefore, without questioning anyone's sincerity or failing to recognize the utility of serious and measured criticism on the part of competent and responsible men, we wish to mention the trust that the Church needs from all her sons. It is not based only on human viewpoints, but rather on the design of God. Confidence in the Church, and her trust in herself, are founded on the promises and charisms that accompany her; on the patrimony of truth transmitted by authentic tradition; on her constitutional and mystical structure. They are based on her capacity for restoring the broken unity of the Christian family, on the value and nobility of her pastoral work, and on her mission as a sign and instrument for all men, open as she is to the world of today and tomorrow.

The Church makes a continuous contribution by responding to the contemporary needs of the world. It is consoling to see what is offered in this regard by the bishops of the world, with the help of those agencies of which they avail themselves in their pastoral work. Social awareness and an operative charity are growing. There is a flowering of initiatives in catechetics, social action, care for the poor, spiritual help for workers, and the spread of Christianity by the comunications media. On its part, the Holy See tries to meet the world's demands with new and traditional initiatives. There is the silent and discrete action within organizations that unite peoples in a sincere effort for peace, collaboration, and progress, particularly in the field of social and economic advancement and culture.

Every day we must start anew. Since the [Vatican] Council, it is no longer a question of destroying or contesting, but of putting all to work improving, healing, planting, renewing, and constructing, the real feeling of unity, faith, worship, charity, obedience, and collaboration. The whole work of the Church comes from God, and must return to him. It cannot be realized without his grace. Structures can be transformed, but the Spirit must be infused into them. Tensions are inevitable, but communion in faith, rooted in a living tradition, and fidelity to the teaching of the magisterium always remain indispensible guarantees of unity, and are at the same time the only ways in which trust in the Church can be maintained and grow.

(From an address of Pope Paul to the College of Cardinals in June, 1972.)

A VERY PERSONAL ANSWER
TO MY CRITICS

WILLIAM F. BUCKLEY, JR.

I write as a Catholic, under my own name, in defense of myself and my views, and I bid them to listen who have in recent years, and with increasing intensity in recent months, spread the word about that I am either ignorant of the teachings of the Catholic Church, or disobedient to them. I address my critics publicly because they have made the effort by assaults upon me, to discredit the position of which I am a spokesman; and incidentally—let us be worldly—to rebuke other persons who hold to my views, and support me, but whom some of my critics would not find it seemly, or convincing, to excommunicate in direct address. "Buckley obviously has never read the papal encyclicals" comes out a lot more easily than the formulation (obviously in many people's minds): "Dear Your Eminence: Have you ever read Rerum Novarum?"

The issue I mean to raise goes beyond the question, "What is the Catholic community to think about my books, or about National Review?"—beyond the question, "What should be the attitude of the Catholic community toward the welfare state?" The issue is planted: what shall be the attitude of Catholics who feel one way about the welfare state toward other Catholics who feel differently? Has it been demonstrated, or if not quite that, is the demonstration crystallizing, that one set of Catholics is in virtue of their position on the welfare state, deficient in their allegiance to the moral authority of the Church? I cannot understand that anything less than that can be inferred from the nature of some of the criticisms by Catholics of my books.

For instance, Mr. Thomas P. Neill of St. Louis University writes blandly (The Sign, December, 1959), "Although he does not mention them by name, Mr. Buckley's generalizations also condemn much of the social program of the American bishops and the teachings of the last three popes, and the thought of almost every prominent Catholic thinker of the last half century."

In America (Oct. 17, 1959) Professor Francis E. McMahon of Notre Dame puts his finger on why I take so benighted a position. My "failure" is as easily explained as that I suffer from "a woefully inadequate grasp of theological and philosophical principles."

There are a few more of this effect here and there, though perhaps none quite so venturesome. Still, enough to encourage Father Kevin Lynch, C.S.P., to conclude in a book review in the Catholic World (November, 1959): "As has often been pointed out, Mr. Buckley's conservative economic stands place him in clear contradiction to Catholic moral teaching on social doctrine." And now Kevin Corrigan in "God and Man at National Review" (The Catholic World, January, 1961) writes that my position "is at grave variance with the social teachings of the Church."

It is widely assumed that my difficulty is ignorance—sheer, vulgar ignorance. As to this ignorance—have you noticed?—it is widely assumed that it is irremediable, i.e., that unless you read the encyclicals of Leo XIII and Pius XI while you were at college, you never, ever will. Eight years ago, Father Christopher E. Fullman, O.S.B., (The Catholic World, May, 1952) reviewing, or rather, interring, God and Man at Yale, concluded absolutely that I could not be aware of the existence of the relevant social encyclicals. He conceded that such an inference was extraordinary, in fact he used the word "incredible." "It is incredible to think that a young and brilliant graduate of a great University could be aware of this background of religio-economic thought." Eight years went by and Professor McMahon says, again in The Catholic World, November, 1959), "Perhaps the major defect in Yale's teaching was its neglect to provide men of the talent and religious background of Buckley with some understanding of the Church's doctrine on economic life. He had a right to that knowledge at Yale; he was deprived of it."

As one can see, the tendency of thought here is that unless you become acquainted with those encyclicals while at college, you never can again. I do not know that any other conclusion is possible. Presumably if you are publicly advised, after publishing a book, in 1951, that you are unaware of data indispensable to your thesis, you will, before writing a book in 1959 in which you reaffirm your thesis, consult those data—no?

To speak frankly, I detect in the language I have quoted a petty parochialism which is displeasing to the taste. To imply that because someone went to Yale he is therefore ignorant of the social encyclicals, and, moreover, that he is cast out into the world with a mind-set which makes it impossible for him ever to read those encyclicals, is to exercise a kind of sectarian snobbery.

Now let me say, publicly for the first time, that I first read Rerum Novarum and Q. Anno when I was a sophomore at Yale. Let me say further that I do not understand why any person of average intelligence could not read them, and read them searchingly, in a long evening. It is one thing to disarm your opponent by saying some such thing as: "You cannot understand what I mean because I have meditated upon the subject for thirty years"; or, "you cannot know what it is like because you didn't live through the Depression and see your little sister die of rickets." One cannot, in deference to such a critic, prepare oneself for one's next book by meditating thirty years or starving one's baby sister: but one can, very easily, if one has not already done so, read a couple of documents.

Let me go further. I have never affected an intimate knowledge of Catholic philosophical or social thought. But I am intimately associated with men who have probed very deeply into Catholic thought, and continue to do so; and who support the position of National Review. When someone like Professor McMahon, or Mr. Neill, speaks so apodictically about the inherent ignorance of my position in the light of Catholic social teaching, I find myself wondering whether for such prideful persons, Purgatory will not consist in a public examination of their knowledge by such learned Catholics as Garry Wills, Frederick Wilhelmsen, Colin Clark, Arnold Lunn, Stanley Parry, Colm Brogan, or Erik von Kuehnelt-Leddihn. I speak now of professionaly trained Catholics who write for National Review and are in sympathy with its position: not to speak of the thousands (yes, they number in the thousands) of conscientious Catholics who read National Review and are in total sympathy with its program. I speak not only of the laity, but of cardinals and bishops, and monsignori and priests, men who didn't go to Yale, and therefore had a chance to read Rerum Novarum and Quadragesimo Anno; and who have given evidence that they view the policies of National Review as the best secular expression of a Christian point of view on the problems of our time.

Assuming, as the gentlemen I have quoted are suggesting, that my views are counter to Catholic teaching, then so are the views of a formidable number of instructed and devout Catholics and again I say, including cardinals and bishops and monsignori and priests, who have declared themselves in unambiguous ways as supporters of the policies of National Review. To venture, then, as Father Lynch has done, to anathematize so very many human beings, is to take upon oneself a grave responsibility, one that should be assumed only after a detailed explication of one's charges.

What are these heretical, or unorthodox, or unenlightened views? Only two critics, Father Fullman and now Kevin Corrigan, have done me the courtesy to describe them. Father Fullman's objections I answered with great ease (The Catholic World, Aug. 1952); that is to say, I don't see that there was anything left over after our discussion that bore on his, or my, fidelity to Catholic thought—we were simply left disagreeing on matters of social policy. Mr. Corrigan says some very strange things, among the strangest that proof of my unorthodoxy lies in a statement I made in God and Man at Yale, namely: I am . . . committed to the classical doctrine that the optimum adjustments—private property, production for profit and by private ownership, and regulation by a free competitive economy—brings not only maximum prosperity, but also maximum freedom.

So? Who anathematized that position? No pope that I know of. For some reason Mr. Corrigan deduces that anyone who believes that must be a Benthamite, or a Spencerian; and that he has constructed a theology around the marketplace. I am neither a Utilitarian nor an Individualist (in Spencer's sense); and I have not founded a religion, nor found it in the least difficult to resist those who, admittedly, did. There are such people. But in this case we are talking about me, not them. Where have I implied that the situation cannot exist when the state, hearkening to an overriding human or social consideration, may not set aside the laws of the marketplace? The burden of showing that my belief in the wisdom of a free market has been transmuted into an inhuman and un-Christian dogma surely lies with the Savonarolas who are so concerned with my impurities. (The idea is, boys, you prove a heresy, then you burn him at the stake. . . .)

If I consider Situation "A" as not warranting state interference, whereas someone else considers that it does, the chances are we have not minted a theological difference. I am quite satisfied to abide by the doctrine of subsidiarity, approved by all the recent popes as the measuring rod: let no public agency take on a job a private agency can do, nor a larger political unit the job a smaller unit can do. I wish my critics would show equal respect for this article of papal wisdom.

It is only when social, political or economic institutions embody offensive ideas that they met with papal condemnation. When socialism was not merely an economic program, but a philosophy of man and history, it brought forth, e.g., from Leo XIII (Rerum Novarum), heated denunciations. Left-Catholics are never tired of stressing that the classical denunciations of socialism were denunciations of the philosophical, not the programmatic aspect of socialism (don't ask how they cope with Subsidiarity—they don't.) This distinction, which they are entitled to make, they make rather more regularly than the complementary distinction, namely, that the Popes' denunciation of individualism and liberalism (Rerum Novarum, Q. Anno, The Social Question in the New Order) is a denunciation of a perversion of free market economics, of the individualism generally associated with Herbert Spencer and (falsely) with William Graham Sumner, a virulent form of which is being pushed these days by Miss Ayn Rand (where has her individualism been attacked more forcefully than in National Review, pray tell?). Both Spencer and Miss Rand, carried away by the virtues of individual freedom, put human beings at the disposal of freedom, rather than freedom at the disposal of human beings. The Popes in short have denounced forms of government or economic systems which are intrinsically (eo ipso) immoral, and that is all they have done; and anyone who says they have done more—obviously went to Yale, and does not know what he is talking about.

Several Popes have attempted to isolate certain tendencies in political thought or economic organization which can lead to morally undesirable consequences. One must not (as Albert Jay Nock did) view the genus state as the natural enemy of the people. It is not merely a bureaucratic accretion which stands in the way of a pastoral fulfillment of our noble selves, as Rousseau and other mischievous dreamers (whose thought, ironically, encouraged the growth of totalist government) contended. But when we conservatives curse the state, we do not mean we would be without it altogether (where have I suggested otherwise?). The state is a divine institution. Without it we have anarchy, and the lawlessness of anarchy is counter to the natural law; so we abjure all political theories which view the state as inherently and necessarily evil. But it is the state which has been in history the principal instrument of abuse to the people, and so it is central to the conservatives' program to keep the state from accumulating any but the most necessary powers.

That position can hardly be offensive to the authors of the principle of subsidiarity!

One must not make the error of an "excessive exaltation of liberty" (The Social Question in the New Order), which can do to you what it did to Herbert Spencer and now has done to Ayn Rand. Such idolatry can have the grimly ironic consequences of leading to tyranny: at the hands of the state. Sometimes, in pursuit of freedom and free competition, the ruthless contender, in the words of Pius XI, attempts "to acquire control of the state, so that its resources and authority may be abused in the economic struggles; finally, there results a clash between States themselves. . . .You assuredly know, Venerable Brethren and beloved children, and you lament the ultimate consequences of this individualistic spirit in economic affairs. Free competition is dead (note, that according to the Pope this is lamentable); economic dictatorship has taken its place." What did the Holy Father say? "That too much freedom leads to no freedom." Such a statement is either self-contradictory (if viewed as theory), or very wise (if viewed as history). Obviously the latter was intended, though Liberals have cited it to justify big government. Obviously the maximization of freedom cannot result in the diminution of freedom: such a proposition is terminalogically chaotic. What Pius meant is that freedom ceases to be freedom when freedom includes the power to take over the government: for then freedom is inevitably contracted; then free competition is dead; and economic dictatorship takes over. That economic dictatorship, whose forms are discernible in the lineaments of New Frontierism, as in all other centripetalized visions of the good society, we conservatives have been resisting for a very long time. We dissent from the passion to federalize. To call us Subsidiarists, anti-Catholic, is about as convincing as calling the Popes anti-Catholic.

I concede there have been in history anti-Catholic popes. But I am prepared to defend the last Popes against the implied contumely of Catholic Liberalism.

List of Contributors

Rev. DR. PAUL ABRECHT is Executive Secretary in the Department of Church and Society of the World Council of Churches, Geneva.

The late MORRIS ADLER served a distinguished career as author and rabbi of a Conservative synagogue in Detroit, Michigan.

Rev. TISSA BALISURIYA, O.M.I. is rector of Aquinas University College in Colombo, Ceylon.

Dr. IAN G. BARBOUR is Chairman of the Department of Religion at Carleton Seminary in New York City. He is a minister of the United Church of Christ.

Rev. DANIEL BERRIGAN, S.J. is one of the leaders of the Catholic left.

Dr. NORBERT BROCKMAN, S.M. is associate professor of Political Science at the University of Dayton. He is presently on leave to study theology.

Mr. WILLIAM BUCKLEY, noted author and public figure, is editor of the National Review.

Rev. Dr. NORMAN J. FARAMELLI directs the Boston Industrial Mission and is lecturer at the Andover Newton Theological School.

Dr. EDGAR Z. FRIEDENBERG is professor of Education and Sociology at the State University of New York at Buffalo.

Dr. HELMUT GOLLWITZER is professor of Systematic Theology in the Faculty of Philosophy of the Free University of Berlin.

Rev. Dr. JAMES M. GUSTAFSON is professor of Religious Studies and Fellow of Ezra Stiles College at Yale University. He is a minister of the United Church of Christ.

Rabbi RICHARD G. HIRSCH is spiritual leader of a Reform synagogue in Detroit, Michigan. He was formerly director of the Religious Action Center of the Union of American Hebrew Congregations.

Dr. JOSEPH C. HOUGH, JR. is chairman of the Faculty of Religion of the Claremont Graduate School and also on the staff of the School of Theology there.

Dr. ALAN KEITH-LUCAS is Alumni Distinguished Professor of Social Work at the University of North Carolina.

Prof. J. M. LOCHMAN, a member of the Comenius Theological Faculty in Prague, Czechoslovakia, and recently Visiting Professor on the theological faculty of the University of Basel, Switzerland.

Rev. Dr. JOHANNES METZ is a member of the Catholic Theological Faculty of the Wilhelms University, Muenster, West Germany.

Dr. JURGEN MOLTMANN is a professor at the University of Tubingen, West Germany.

Rev. Dr. WALTER G. MUELDER of the United Methodist Church, is Dean of the Boston University School of Theology.

Dr. NICOS A. NISSIOTIS, a Greek Orthodox lay theologian, is Associate Director of the Ecumenical Institute, Chateau de Bossey, Switzerland.

Before being elected Pope in 1963, **PAUL VI** served many years in the Vatican Secretariat of State.

Dr. NICHOLAS PIEDISCALZI, a Unitarian, is Chairman of the Department of Religion at Wright State University in Dayton, Ohio.

Rev. RONALD PRESTON is Canon Residentiary of Manchester Cathedral (Church of England), and lecturer in Christian Ethics at the University of Manchester.

Rev. Dr. PAUL RAMSEY, a United Methodist minister, is Harrington Spear Paine Professor of Religion at Princeton University.

Rev. Dr. ROBERT D. REECE is a member of the Wright State University Department of Religion and a Southern Baptist clergyman.

Dr. ROSEMARY REUTHER, a prominent Roman Catholic theologian, is professor of Religion at Howard University, Washington, D. C.

Dr. LARRY SHINER is a member of the Religion Department at Cornell College, Mount Vernon, Iowa.

Rev. PAUL VERGHESE, a priest of the Syrian Orthodox Church, is Associate General Secretary of the World Council of Churches.